Jörn David

A Domain-Independent Framework for Intelligent Recommendations

Jörn David

A Domain-Independent Framework for Intelligent Recommendations

Design, Application and Evaluation of a Hybrid Machine Learning Framework using Case Studies within varied Domains

Südwestdeutscher Verlag für Hochschulschriften

Impressum/Imprint (nur für Deutschland/ only for Germany)
Bibliografische Information der Deutschen Nationalbibliothek: Die Deutsche Nationalbibliothek verzeichnet diese Publikation in der Deutschen Nationalbibliografie; detaillierte bibliografische Daten sind im Internet über http://dnb.d-nb.de abrufbar.

Alle in diesem Buch genannten Marken und Produktnamen unterliegen warenzeichen-, marken- oder patentrechtlichem Schutz bzw. sind Warenzeichen oder eingetragene Warenzeichen der jeweiligen Inhaber. Die Wiedergabe von Marken, Produktnamen, Gebrauchsnamen, Handelsnamen, Warenbezeichnungen u.s.w. in diesem Werk berechtigt auch ohne besondere Kennzeichnung nicht zu der Annahme, dass solche Namen im Sinne der Warenzeichen- und Markenschutzgesetzgebung als frei zu betrachten wären und daher von jedermann benutzt werden dürften.

Verlag: Südwestdeutscher Verlag für Hochschulschriften Aktiengesellschaft & Co. KG
Dudweiler Landstr. 99, 66123 Saarbrücken, Deutschland
Telefon +49 681 37 20 271-1, Telefax +49 681 37 20 271-0
Email: info@svh-verlag.de
Zugl.: München, TU, Diss., 2009

Herstellung in Deutschland:
Schaltungsdienst Lange o.H.G., Berlin
Books on Demand GmbH, Norderstedt
Reha GmbH, Saarbrücken
Amazon Distribution GmbH, Leipzig
ISBN: 978-3-8381-1375-3

Imprint (only for USA, GB)
Bibliographic information published by the Deutsche Nationalbibliothek: The Deutsche Nationalbibliothek lists this publication in the Deutsche Nationalbibliografie; detailed bibliographic data are available in the Internet at http://dnb.d-nb.de.

Any brand names and product names mentioned in this book are subject to trademark, brand or patent protection and are trademarks or registered trademarks of their respective holders. The use of brand names, product names, common names, trade names, product descriptions etc. even without a particular marking in this works is in no way to be construed to mean that such names may be regarded as unrestricted in respect of trademark and brand protection legislation and could thus be used by anyone.

Publisher: Südwestdeutscher Verlag für Hochschulschriften Aktiengesellschaft & Co. KG
Dudweiler Landstr. 99, 66123 Saarbrücken, Germany
Phone +49 681 37 20 271-1, Fax +49 681 37 20 271-0
Email: info@svh-verlag.de

Printed in the U.S.A.
Printed in the U.K. by (see last page)
ISBN: 978-3-8381-1375-3

Copyright © 2010 by the author and Südwestdeutscher Verlag für Hochschulschriften Aktiengesellschaft & Co. KG and licensors
All rights reserved. Saarbrücken 2010

Contents

Abstract	**9**
Zusammenfassung	**11**
Typographical Conventions	**13**

1 Introduction   **15**
   1.1 Contents 16
   1.2 Scope of the Dissertation 18

2 The Symbolic and the Connectionist Paradigm of AI   **21**
   2.1 The Symbol System Hypothesis and Formal Logics 23
   2.2 Connectionism and the Symbol Grounding Problem 27
   2.3 Applying Connectionist Models to Symbolic Domains 30
   2.4 Knowledge Representation and Knowledge-Based Disciplines . . . 33
   2.5 Principles of Machine Learning 38
   2.6 Existing Recommendation Concepts 43
      2.6.1 Intelligent Tutoring Systems 44
      2.6.2 Content-Based and Collaborative Filtering 45
      2.6.3 Case-Based Reasoning 46

3 Machine Learning Concepts and Fundamentals of SymboConn   **49**
   3.1 Framework Requirements 49
      3.1.1 Functional Requirements 50
         3.1.1.1 Learning By Example 50
         3.1.1.2 Generalization Capability 50
         3.1.1.3 Learning Types and Inheritance Hierarchies . . . 54
         3.1.1.4 Being Able to Incorporate Context 54
         3.1.1.5 Processing of Heterogeneous Knowledge 55
      3.1.2 Nonfunctional Requirements 56
   3.2 Knowledge Model of SymboConn 58
   3.3 Functional Model of SymboConn 64
   3.4 Framework Architecture 66

4 Machine Learning and the Framework Engine 75
4.1 Fundamentals of Neural Networks 75
    4.1.1 History of Neural Networks 76
    4.1.2 Feed-Forward Neural Networks 77
    4.1.3 Further Types of Neural Networks 78
4.2 Neural Networks between Computational Intelligence and Information Theory 81
4.3 Evaluation Criteria for the Framework's Machine Learning Engine . 89
4.4 The Modular Recurrent Neural Network 94
    4.4.1 Recurrent Dynamics 95
    4.4.2 Processing of Variable Node Sequences 97
    4.4.3 Modified Backpropagation Training Algorithm 98
        4.4.3.1 Forward Pass 100
        4.4.3.2 Backward Pass 101
    4.4.4 Experiment: Illustration of Intelligent Learning 106
4.5 Conclusion 110

5 Connectionist Learning of Symbolic Structures 113
5.1 Incorporating Domain Knowledge in Form of Rules 114
5.2 Type Representation and Type Hierarchies 121
5.3 Spread Spectrum Based Classification 125
    5.3.1 Encoding of Node Types Using Spread Spectrum 127
    5.3.2 Classification by Despreading 128
5.4 Rule Recognition Despite Heavy Noise 131
5.5 Holistic Learning of Structured Symbolic Contents 135
    5.5.1 Generating RAAM-Representations Using the MRNN . . . 139
    5.5.2 Hybrid Structure Transformation System 143
    5.5.3 Structure Transform Prediction 145
5.6 Conclusion 147

6 Application to Knowledge Engineering and Software Development 149
6.1 Classification of Software Development Artifacts 152
    6.1.1 Evaluation 153
        6.1.1.1 Activity Classification 155
        6.1.1.2 Status Classification 159
    6.1.2 Better Than Guessing? 161
6.2 Change Impact Analysis 162
    6.2.1 Change Impact Analysis on Graph-Structured Data 167
    6.2.2 Recommending Software Changes 170
6.3 Design Pattern Discovery 175
    6.3.1 Classification Based on Decision Trees 175
    6.3.2 Complex Types 181
    6.3.3 Symbolic Representation of Design Patterns 183
    6.3.4 Design Advice Upon Complex Design Patterns 184

		6.3.4.1	Recognition of the Template Pattern 190
		6.3.4.2	Recognition of the Observer Pattern 191
	6.3.5	Evaluation 193	
		6.3.5.1	Classification of Unknown System Models 193
		6.3.5.2	Transforming an Adapter Pattern into a Composite Pattern 194
		6.3.5.3	Generalization to Novel Complexity 199
	6.3.6	Advantages & Disadvantages of the Connectionist Approach 202	
6.4	Conclusion 204		

7 Navigation Recommendation   207
- 7.1 Required Data Mining Techniques 208
  - 7.1.1 Text Mining 208
  - 7.1.2 Association Rule Mining 210
- 7.2 Existing Recommendation Approaches 215
- 7.3 Knowledge Representation for Navigation Recommendation 218
- 7.4 Navigation Recommendation in SymboConn 221
  - 7.4.1 Adapting Principles from Content-Based and Collaborative Filtering 224
  - 7.4.2 Control Flow of Navigation Recommendation 226
- 7.5 Case Study: Web Navigation 228
- 7.6 Conclusion 235

8 Time Series Prediction   237
- 8.1 Stochastic Processes and Time Series 238
- 8.2 Covariance and Stationarity 241
- 8.3 Statistical Models for Time Series 243
  - 8.3.1 Moving Average Process (MA) 246
  - 8.3.2 Autoregressive Process (AR) 247
  - 8.3.3 ARMA Process 247
  - 8.3.4 Exponential Smoothing 248
- 8.4 Neural Networks Applied to Time Series Prediction 249
  - 8.4.1 MRNN Implementing Exponential Smoothing (ES) 252
  - 8.4.2 Connectionist Implementation of Autoregressive Processes . 253
- 8.5 Application to Business Forecasting 255
  - 8.5.1 Applied Time Series Analysis 255
  - 8.5.2 Quantitative Results 261
- 8.6 Conclusion 264

9 Conclusions   267
- 9.1 Contributions 268
- 9.2 Future Work 271
  - 9.2.1 Activity Classification Based on User Behavior 271
  - 9.2.2 Further Applications in Software Engineering 273

A	**Framework Extensions and Details**		**275**
	A.1 Future Implementation		275
		A.1.1 Decoupling of Domain-Specific Subsystems	275
		A.1.2 Extensions of the Framework Functionality	277
		A.1.2.1 Output-Input Refeeding for Navigation Sequences	277
		A.1.2.2 Combining Text and Association Rule Mining	278
	A.2 Technical Issues in Training the Framework Engine		279
		A.2.1 Limitations of Connectionist Learning	280
		A.2.2 Implicit Weighting of the Input Nodes	282
		A.2.3 Processing Arbitrarily Dimensioned Vector Sequences	283
		A.2.4 Principal Component Analysis	284

Acknowledgements   **287**

List of Figures   **289**

List of Tables   **297**

List of Algorithms   **299**

List of Abbreviations   **301**

Bibliography   **305**

Index   **329**

Abstract

Recommender systems assist the user in decision-making processes and automate information processing steps like the classification of artifacts. Intelligent recommendations help users to cope with the steadily growing information overload within the internet or when using information systems at their place of work, for instance. As an example, the recommendation techniques collaborative filtering and content-based filtering are mainly applied in the areas of e-Commerce and web navigation to recommend potentially relevant articles or websites. Recommender systems are either based on machine learning functions such as clustering, classification, and prediction or they are realized by symbolic methods like association rule mining, that is, by rule-based mechanisms in general. Rule-based methods often insufficiently support content-based knowledge representation and heterogeneous domain knowledge, so that available predictive information is not fully exploited. On the one hand, this shortcoming often negatively affects the recommendation accuracy and on the other hand it does not allow for computing recommendations for unseen contents by means of generalization.

The software engineering community has started to investigate the applicability of those methods from artificial intelligence in the areas of knowledge management and software development. An example of an heterogeneous software artifact is an Issue that may comprise a textual description, an ordinal priority attribute and a boolean status flag (isResolved). One possibility of representing domain objects is to use fuzzy set methods, especially when it comes to classification tasks under uncertainty. However, these methods do not provide a separate prediction functionality as required for time series prediction, for example. Finally, purely statistical methods such as the classical multivariate analysis (non-symbolic) mostly assume certain probability distributions of the variable of interest, which constrain the prediction model and may negatively affect the generalization capability and in turn also the prediction accuracy.

In this dissertation we propose a hybrid approach consisting of connectionist and symbolic methods, which combines the benefits of both methodologies and in addition offers a high generalization capability, flexibility, and robustness. The hybrid approach is especially suited for domains such as knowledge management and software engineering, since software development processes are based on incomplete and continuously changing information.

Our approach is first discussed from a theoretical perspective, where the particularities of both research areas, the symbolic on the one hand and the connectionist on the other hand, are analyzed. This is followed by a description of the functional requirements for a generic and domain-independent machine learning framework. From these requirements, we conclude that for the computation of intelligent recommendations, machine learning by numerical algorithms as used in artificial neural networks is preferable over symbolic algorithms. However, non-symbolic methods must be enriched with the capability of processing structured and symbolic knowledge to be useful for a generic framework. The newly developed machine learning framework called SYMBOCONN also supports symbolic knowledge, but is still based on a connectionist and thus numerical learning algorithm.

To represent knowledge from these different domains, the SYMBOCONN framework uses a generic graph-based knowledge model that represents both content and structure. Due to its generic learning capability, which is based on an abstract data structure in form of node sequences, SYMBOCONN is independent from concrete application domains. The core of the framework is a new variant of recurrent neural networks which we call *Modular Recurrent Neural Network* (MRNN). An MRNN operates like a dynamic system by explicitly modeling a logical timeline, which enables the systematic processing of structured knowledge. In order to enhance the exploitation of textual contents in the aforementioned domains, the MRNN is combined with *Latent Semantic Indexing* (LSI), which optimizes the text representation and enables content-based classification and prediction in the case of unstructured textual contents as well.

The framework was applied to datasets from real-life projects as well as to benchmarking datasets from several sources. In particular, we demonstrate its applicability by case studies in the areas of navigation recommendation, design pattern discovery, change impact analysis, and time series prediction. Within the scope of an industrial case study on time series prediction, the MRNN achieved a forecast accuracy about 10% higher than that provided by traditional statistical methods.

Zusammenfassung

Empfehlungssysteme unterstützen den Benutzer bei der Entscheidungsfindung und automatisieren Wissensverarbeitungsschritte wie die Klassifikation von Artefakten. Die von diesen Systemen generierten *intelligenten Empfehlungen* sollen den Benutzer auf kontextsensitive Weise führen und somit die *Informationsüberladung* gezielt reduzieren, mit der die Benutzer im Internet oder bei der Verwendung von Informationssystemen immer stärker konfrontiert werden.

Beispiele für solche Empfehlungsmechanismen sind *kollaboratives Filtern* sowie *inhaltsbasiertes Filtern*, die ursprünglich für die Bereiche e-Commerce und Web-Navigation konzipiert wurden. Empfehlungssysteme werden entweder durch Methoden des maschinellen Lernens wie Clustering, Klassifikation und Prognose oder durch symbolische Methoden wie dem *Mining* von Assoziationsregeln bzw. durch regelbasierte Mechanismen im Allgemeinen realisiert. Regelbasierte Methoden unterstützen inhaltsbasierte Wissensrepräsentationen und heterogenes Domänenwissen oft nur mangelhaft, so dass potentiell nützliche und prädiktive Informationen nicht für die zu generierenden Empfehlungen verwendet werden können. Dies wirkt sich zum einen negativ auf die Empfehlungsgenauigkeit aus und zum anderen können neue Inhalte dann nicht durch *Generalisierung* klassifiziert oder prognostiziert werden.

Die Softwaretechnik hat damit begonnen, die Nutzbarkeit von Methoden der künstlichen Intelligenz für das Wissensmanagement sowie für den Bereich der Softwareentwicklung zu untersuchen. Ein Beispiel für ein domänenspezifisches Objekt aus dem Bereich der Softwaretechnik ist eine *offene Fragestellung* (Issue), die z.B. eine textuelle Beschreibung, ein ordinales Prioritätsattribut und einen booleschen Statusindikator (z.B. istGelöst) enthält. Eine Möglichkeit der nicht-symbolischen Repräsentation von Domänenobjekten stellen Fuzzy-Set Methoden dar, die allerdings hauptsächlich für die Klassifikation unter Unschärfe geeignet sind und nicht für Prognoseaufgaben wie Zeitreihenfortschreibung. Nicht-symbolische, statistische Methoden hingegen nehmen für die numerische Prognose meist bestimmte Wahrscheinlichkeitsverteilungen der zu prognostizierenden Variablen als gegeben an, was sich wiederum einschränkend auf das Prognosemodell und damit negativ auf dessen Generalisierungfähigkeit auswirken kann.

Deswegen schlagen wir in dieser Arbeit einen hybriden Ansatz vor, bestehend aus konnektionistischen und symbolischen Methoden, der die Vorteile beider Methoden vereint und darüber hinaus hohe Generalisierungsfähigkeit, Flexibilität und Robustheit besitzt. Der hybride Ansatz ist besonders für den Bereich der Softwaretechnik geeignet, da Softwareentwicklung im Allgemeinen auf unvollständiger und sich ständig ändernder Information basiert.

Zunächst wird der hybride Ansatzes vom theoretischen Standpunkt aus diskutiert, wobei die Besonderheiten beider Forschungszweige, die der symbolischen Methoden einerseits und die der konnektionistischen Methoden andererseits, eingehend betrachtet werden. Anschliessend folgt die Formulierung der Anforderungen an ein möglichst generisches und domänenunabhängiges Rahmenwerk für maschinelles Lernen.

Aus den ermittelten Anforderungen schliessen wir, dass zur Erzeugung von intelligenten Empfehlungen statistische Algorithmen, wie sie z.B. in neuronalen Netzwerken verwendet werden, den rein symbolischen Algorithmen vorzuziehen sind. Allerdings müssen die eingesetzten nicht-symbolischen Methoden die Fähigkeit besitzen, strukturiertes und symbolisches Wissen zu verarbeiten, um für ein generisches Rahmenwerk geeignet zu sein.

Das neuentwickelte Rahmenwerk für maschinelles Lernen namens SYMBOCONN kann auch symbolisches Wissen verarbeiten, basiert jedoch auf einem konnektionistischen Lernalgorithmus. Das SYMBOCONN Rahmenwerk benutzt ein generisches graph-basiertes Wissensmodell, das sowohl Inhalt als auch Struktur abbildet, um Domänenwissen in unterschiedlichen Formen sowie in unterschiedlichem Detailgrad zu repräsentieren. Die generische Lernfähigkeit des Rahmenwerks wird durch die zugrundeliegende abstrakte Datenstruktur in Form von Knotensequenzen ermöglicht, so dass SYMBOCONN weitgehend unabhängig von konkreten Anwendungsdomänen ist.

Der Kern des Rahmenwerks ist eine neuartige Variante eines rekurrenten neuronalen Netzes, die wir als *Modulares Rekurrentes Neuronales Netzwerk* (MRNN) bezeichnen. Ein MRNN arbeitet wie ein dynamisches System, indem es mittels einer expliziten Zustandsschicht eine logische Zeitlinie bereitstellt, die die systematische Verarbeitung von strukturiertem Wissen ermöglicht. Um die Unterstützung von textuellen Inhalten in den vorgenannten Domänen zu verbessern, wird das MRNN mit Latenter Semantischer Indizierung (LSI) kombiniert, die die Textrepräsentation durch Redundanzbeseitigung optimiert und eine inhaltsbasierte Klassifikation und Prognose auch im Fall von Inhalten in Form von unstrukturiertem Text ermöglicht.

Das Rahmenwerk wurde auf Datensätze aus realen Projekten sowie auf Benchmark-Datensätze angewandt, die aus verschiedensten Domänen stammen. Insbesondere demonstrieren wir dessen Anwendbarkeit durch Fallstudien in den Bereichen Navigationsempfehlung, Entwurfsmuster-Erkennung, Analyse von Änderungsauswirkungen sowie Zeitreihenprognose. In einer industriebezogenen Fallstudie erreichte das MRNN eine um ca. 10% höhere Prognosegüte als traditionelle statistische Methoden.

Typographical Conventions Throughout this dissertation we use the following conventions:

- Citations are given in a comprehensive form (e.g. [ABC08]), indicating the first three authors (e.g. **A**lpha, **B**eta, **C**aesar) of an article by capital letters followed by the year of publication (2008). If a "+" appears in the citation, then more than three authors have contributed (e.g. [ABM+00]). In case of a single author, the first letter of his last name is written in capitals, followed by two further lower case letters (e.g. [Cal03]).

- Related work is given in form of *inline citations* wherever needed, instead of reporting existing research in a monolithic block at the beginning or end of a chapter.

- We use the *Unified Modeling Language* (UML) for the illustration of concepts and for modeling of software components. UML diagrams are also employed to clarify concepts from machine learning and knowledge discovery. All UML diagrams were drawn with the CASE tool ENTERPRISE ARCHITECT 6.0.

- Typewriter style is used for classes and objects in software models.

- Algorithms are given in pseudo-code and are printed in boxes, using the LATEX packages *algpseudocode* and *algorithm*.

- Technical terms are written in *italics* when they appear the first time.

- Important concepts are emphasized using **bold font**.

- Upper capitals are used for product names, such as APACHE LUCENE.

Chapter 1

Introduction

Intelligent recommendation assists the user with decision-making processes in order to cope with *information overload* and to focus on relevant entities. In this dissertation, intelligent recommendation is understood in the broad sense. Any system that learns from history data to produce non-trivial and potentially useful recommendations is considered as an intelligent recommendation system. An intelligent recommendation is computed based on empirical data, either given in symbolic or numerical form, and generalizes the given facts. Such a recommendation includes a prior learning process that enables the generalization in the first place and thus goes beyond simple table-lookups.

Intelligent recommendation can be realized by machine learning methods, if empirical values or experiences gathered from past user or system behavior is available. This dissertation uses methods from artificial intelligence, especially machine learning, in order to support knowledge-driven processes. Knowledge workers [SS05, ABM+00] need to be provided with rich, context-sensitive and proactive support to solve knowledge-intensive tasks and to cope with the information overload [Tof70]. The problem of information overload can be defined as an oversupply of pieces of information regarding a certain problem, which hampers or prevents the user from making proper decisions. This issue is increased by a low signal-to-noise ratio [LM06] as well as by incomplete and inconsistent information. The information overload can be mitigated by helping the user to retrieve preferred information first. The developed recommendation system provides decision support for arbitrary knowledge-based domains and combines aspects of content-based and collaborative recommendation.

Recommendation techniques such as collaborative filtering are mainly applied in the areas of e-Commerce and web navigation [RV97, SKKR01, GNP05, HZC05, XZZ05]. Many of these recommendation systems are realized by symbolic and rule-based methods such as association rule mining or semantic web technologies such as description logic. Usually heterogeneous application data represented by categorical, metric or textual attributes cannot be integrated into these symbolic machine learning algorithms. Their low ability to deal with fuzzy or incomplete information and the resulting lack of recommendation robustness constitutes a main criticism. Due to these deficiencies of symbolic methods, we propose the use of a hybrid approach consisting of connectionist and symbolic methods that unifies different machine learning functions and knowledge representations. Classification and prediction are supported in a content-based and structure-sensitive way.

We will show that a more sophisticated recommendation functionality can be achieved by exploiting both content and structure of the underlying knowledge base. So far, there are hardly any connectionist systems that provide recommendation functionality. As reported by Nasraoui et al. [NP04], by combining aspects of content-based and collaborative filtering, the connectionist approach is able to achieve a higher recommendation accuracy than most of the mentioned traditional methods.

1.1 Contents

This dissertation is organized as follows. In the first part (chapter 1 to 5) we describe the machine learning concepts that are used throughout this dissertation and that are prototypically realized in the framework.

Chapter 2, *The Symbolic and the Connectionist Paradigm*, gives a theoretical overview over the symbolic and connectionist paradigms, in particular their foundations and their ways of knowledge representation. The basic principles of symbolic systems are introduced by means of Newell and Simon's well-known *Physical Symbol System Hypothesis* [NS76], which is contrasted with the connectionist approach. We also give a short overview of machine learning and its most important aspects.

In Chapter 3, *Machine Learning Concepts and Fundamentals of SymboConn*, we describe the requirements and a functional model of the machine learning engine that is able to deal with symbolic or structured knowledge such as graphs of software artifacts. Furthermore, we report on the state-of-art in intelligent recommendation including the used knowledge representation and provided functionality. Based on these findings, we define the abstract knowledge model as well as the functional model and the system design of an architecture for a machine learning framework together with its application domains.

In Chapter 4, *Connectionist Machine Learning*, the core algorithms for training the Modular Recurrent Neural Network (MRNN) are formalized. Furthermore, the general capability of the technique to accomplish the machine learning tasks *classification* and *prediction* is measured and evaluated by domain-independent test scenarios[1].

In Chapter 5, *Connectionist Learning of Symbolic Contents*, we describe how the machine learning engine of SYMBOCONN is applied to structured contents. We make those contents machine learnable by employing the theory of formal languages according to the Chomsky hierarchy. Therefore a grammatical representa-

---
[1]The particular aspects of the developed machine learning functionality are validated in each chapter.

tion of rule-based domain knowledge is given, which is then incorporated into the framework engine. In particular, we apply the rule-based representation to software design pattern that are recognized within UML class diagrams presented to the machine learning engine.

Chapters 6 to 8 focus on the application of the hybrid machine learning approach to knowledge-driven problems. The SYMBOCONN framework is applied to the domains *knowledge engineering* and *software development, navigation recommendation*, as well as *time series prediction*.

In Chapter 6, *Knowledge Engineering and Software Development*, we demonstrate the benefits of the SYMBOCONN framework in three areas of software engineering. First, we present an approach to the automatic classification of software development artifacts according to their activity and relevance, which is important for project management. Subsequently, we present two forms of change impact analysis implemented into SYMBOCONN: the first variant operates on a training set of change packages, the second variant uses a graph of software artifacts. Finally, we demonstrate the capability of the SYMBOCONN framework to process structural knowledge in form of design patterns.

In Chapter 7, *Navigation Recommendation*, the prediction functionality of the framework is applied to user navigations. At first, the basic data mining techniques required for a connectionist recommendation system are introduced. *Text mining* and *association rule mining* are described with a focus on the navigation recommendation domain. Actual navigations on knowledge graphs reflecting the browsing behavior and interests of users are captured and taken as training patterns for the MRNN. Cohesive nodes sequences are then learned by the MRNN in a supervised training process. As a result, yet unknown user navigations are supported by a recommendation of the subsequent nodes.

In Chapter 8, *Time Series Prediction*, the basic theory of time series is described and we then demonstrate that the MRNN machine learning engine contains two traditionally isolated regression methods, stemming from statistics, as special cases. The SYMBOCONN framework is applied to non-symbolic but real-valued time series, which are predicted depending on their past realizations. The application to time series prediction demonstrates the universality of the framework, since time series prediction is typically done by statistical methods. A case study on demand planning of a large telecommunication company is presented, which shows that the sales figures of product lines from telecommunication can be forecasted with higher accuracy than with statistical methods.

Chapter 9 summarizes the contributions of this dissertation and gives an outlook of future work such as user behavior-based activity classification.

Appendix A.1 describes our plans to extend and advance the SYMBOCONN[2] framework. Finally, several technical issues in training the framework engine can be found in appendix A.2.

---

[2]Not to be mistaken for *SYMCONA Hybrid Symbolic/Connectionist System for Word Sense Disambiguation*, which was a system in the field of *natural language processing (NLP)* [WMO97].

1.2 Scope of the Dissertation

Intelligent recommendation is an abstract concept for several machine learning functions like classification, clustering, and prediction. An intelligent recommendation engine is based on methods from data mining and makes use of context information for computing a recommendation proactively provided to the user. In this sense, intelligent recommendation systems are similar to search algorithms, since these systems help users to discover entities they might not have found by themselves. The difference to search algorithms is that no matching of single information pieces, for example the comparison of object values in the nodes of a search tree to determine the further search direction, is done.

The framework presented in this dissertation is different from systems that try to simulate human intelligence [Xia06] in terms of the *Turing test*. SYMBOCONN neither simulates human intelligence nor imitates human behavior, which is a goal of *strong artificial intelligence*. The framework uses neural networks as a fuzzy optimization method and thus belongs to the branch of *weak artificial intelligence*.

A unique feature of the developed framework is its applicability to almost arbitrary domains. Therefore it is particularly *not* an application, component, nor a coordination[3] framework, although there is a similarity to the type of *class frameworks*. These frameworks integrate classes and methods that provide support for a *broad application area* at a certain abstraction level. The notion of a *framework* does not mean that the development of new machine learning methods is facilitated, but that machine learning functions are already provided.

The framework is also different from an *Intelligent Tutoring System* (ITS), since it does not follow a predefined syllabus and does not provide a *pedagogical component*. Intelligent tutoring systems usually model a teacher-student relation, which is not supported. Intelligent tutoring systems also focus on the way of interaction with the user to enable human learning, which is not a goal of the work at hand.

This dissertation does not address the area of *e-Commerce* either, which focuses on the relationships between consumer and trader as well as between consumer and product. Recommendation systems are being used by an increasing number of e-Commerce portals to help consumers find products to purchase. An example is the use of computational intelligence for adaptive lesson presentation in a web-based learning environment, as presented by Papanikolaou et al. [PMG00].

Finally, the framework does not represent an *Agent-Based System*. Intelligent agents that autonomously act in a given environment in order to achieve user-defined goals are not considered. *Deliberative* agent architectures are based on principles of symbolic artificial intelligence and hold a symbolic representation of their environment, thus decisions are made by symbolic reasoning. Deliberative agents are those which base their actions on the predicted actions of other agents [SV97]. They contain an explicitly represented, symbolic model of the world, in which decisions on actions to be performed are made via logical reasoning, based on pattern matching and symbol manipulation. Although symbol structures should be processable by

---
[3]Device interaction, interoperability

the SYMBOCONN framework, reasoning is not performed symbolically, but statistically.

Chapter 2

The Symbolic and the Connectionist Paradigm of Artificial Intelligence

Research in artificial intelligence has always dealt with symbolic methods on the one hand and with connectionist methods on the other hand. Symbolic or rule-based information processing as accomplished by expert systems benefits from strict systematicity and high interpretability. Symbols are arbitrary because their shape is unrelated to their meaning[1], but they can be arranged in meaningful symbolic structures like grammar rules for natural or formal languages. According to Fodor, systematicity [NvG94, J.97, BN00, CBB+01, Aiz05] is the property that a system of representations has if each of the symbols it contains occurs with the same semantic value as a constituent of many different hosts [J.97]. To obtain a more formal definition, we adapted another formulation of systematicity – the *systematicity schema* – from van Gelder et al. [vGN94]:

For every system S, and any given representation t of type T, there is some set $M_{S,T}$ of "structurally related" representations such that S is capable of processing all and only the representations in $M_{S,T}$. More precisely, structurally related means that there is an equivalence relation $\sim := \{(s,t) : \exists f : T \to T, s \mapsto t\}$ tying together the representations in $M_{S,T}$. An example in natural language is being able to process[2] both the expression $s :=$ "brown triangle and black square" and $t :=$ "black triangle and brown square". In this example, the operation f is the commutation of adjectives.

Usually two types of systematicity are distinguished, systematicity of *representation* and systematicity of *inference*. If a system is not only able to represent a term $y := p u_1 \ldots u_n$, but can also represent the substituted term[3] $p u_1(x/t_1) \ldots u_n(x/t_n)$, $x \in FV(y)$, then it supports a systematic representation of symbolic knowledge.

From the perspective of inference, systematicity describes the capability of generating new symbolic facts from given ones. For example, a system lacks systematicity of inference, if it can infer P from the formula $F_1 := P \wedge Q \wedge R$, but cannot

---
[1]*A symbol is nothing without its creator, who provides the symbol with a meaning.* [Cal03]
[2]If the system S is a human, processing means understanding the given expression.
[3]The free variable x is substituted by the term t_i in each subterm u_i, $i = 1, \ldots, n$.

infer P from the sub-formula $F_2 := P \wedge Q$ [Din92]. Such a behavior is not systematic, since the truth value of formula F_1 is determined by the truth value of each sub-formula, P, Q and R. If $P \wedge Q \wedge R$ is true under the interpretation I, semantically denoted by $(P \wedge Q \wedge R)^I = \max\{P^I, Q^I, R^I\} = 1$, then also each of its components must be true, $P^I = Q^I = R^I = 1$. From the syntactical perspective, there is an inference rule called $\wedge$-elimination that allows to derive P both from $P \wedge Q$ and $P \wedge Q \wedge R$. In this example, the system does not provide this kind of systematicity, but might only have memorized one example $(P \wedge Q \wedge R) \vdash P$. Systematicity is clearly distinguishable from (syntactic) consistency $\forall A \in \mathcal{L}_{FOL} : \Gamma \vdash (A \wedge \neg A)$, which can be reduced to $\Gamma \vdash \neg\bot$, where $\mathcal{L}_{FOL}$ is the set of all first-order formulas and $\Gamma \subset \mathcal{L}_{FOL}$ is an arbitrary set of satisfiable formulas. In the given example, consistency only claims that the formula $(P \wedge Q) \wedge \neg(P \wedge Q)$ is not derivable from Γ. In contrast to systematicity, consistency does not imply the validity of the inference rule $\wedge$-elimination, which states that whenever formula $P \wedge Q$ is derivable, also P and Q are separately derivable: $\Gamma \vdash (P \wedge Q) \Rightarrow (\Gamma \vdash P) \,\&\, (\Gamma \vdash Q)$.

In the above-mentioned sense, every logical calculus that provides a deduction relation $\vdash$ is inherently systematic. As opposed to the symbolic paradigm, connectionist information processing does not provide an inherent systematicity. However, in chapter 2 and 3 we will show that the connectionist (subsymbolic) counterpart of systematicity of inference is the *generalization capability* [GLZ04, Ham01]. From our point of view, the main difference between both concepts is that systematicity of inference works deductively and generalization capability is meant inductively. Unfortunately, in literature both notions are used in many different and often inconsistent ways [Phi96, HH97, NS93, J.97].

Besides generalization, high flexibility and robustness in information processing are further advantages of the connectionist methods, which have been perceived as cardinal weaknesses of symbolic methods [JPSS99, CF]. Neither of these paradigms can sufficiently solve problems like recognizing recurring patterns, ignoring irrelevant information, using given knowledge to draw new conclusions, or being capable of building abstractions. The article *Artificial Intelligence: Technology with a Future* [BBK02] boils down the applicability of both methodologies to the following rule of thumb:

"If we have more knowledge than data, then "hard" operators are proper[4]. Alternatively, if we have more data than knowledge, then fuzzy or neural operators are more adequate."

Recently, the integration of connectionist and symbolic methods has been addressed by many researchers [DOP08, RdPWB06, Sed06, HBG05, HHS04]. One important aspect of the dichotomy of symbolism and connectionism [FGV01, Pow01, JPSS99] is that symbolic methods provide a deductive inference mechanism while the connectionist methods represent the inductive equivalent.

In predicate logic, there are two central deductive inference mechanisms, the *modus ponens* (mp) inference rule and the *deduction theorem*. The modus ponens is

---

[4] Here, the "hard" operators are symbolic inference rules that hold a discrete definition and value space.

a classical form of syllogism[5] that uses an inference rule for drawing a conclusion C from a premise B. The syntactical version of the deduction theorem $(\Gamma \cup \{B\} \vdash C)$ $\Rightarrow (\Gamma \vdash B \to C)$ states that an assumption B can always be eliminated by introducing an implication. If C is inferable from the existing set of formulas Γ together with B, then $B \to C$ can be deduced without the assumption. If furthermore B is inferable, denoted as $\Gamma \vdash B$, then C can be deduced by a single application of the modus ponens rule.

By contrast, neural networks learn from examples, which is an inherently inductive process. If B and C mostly occur together and C also appears without coexistence of B, then the network generates the rule $B \dot\to C$ – which must not be interpreted logically.

Combining aspects from the connectionist and symbolic paradigm is a main goal of this work. We argue that for intelligent recommendation, the combination of connectionist and symbolic aspects of artificial intelligence is superior to applying each of them individually. In the following sections, this claim is discussed by clarifying how systematicity – a widely accepted key requirement for intelligent behavior – is achieved by both paradigms.

2.1 The Symbol System Hypothesis and Formal Logics

The Physical Symbol System Hypothesis[6] was first postulated by Newell and Simon: it assumes that a comprehensive structure of symbols, which represents the "world knowledge", together with operations on these structures should enable machines to process data like humans: *"A physical symbol system has the necessary and sufficient means of general intelligent action."* [NS76]. This statement aims at *formal systems* – a more well-known notion for *physical symbol system* – and claims that the behavior of artificial systems should be goal-oriented, domain-independent, and therefore also adaptable. General intelligent behavior is still a visionary scenario, because artificial intelligence can so far be realized on a restricted and specific domain at best [Cal03]. In this dissertation, a domain represents the entirety of knowledge within an area of expertise as well as the typical activities in that area. Especially formal systems are only able to operate on restricted domains of knowledge with a restricted set of operations.

Furthermore their power and expressivity are restricted by the *Gödel Incompleteness Theorem*. In 1931, Kurt Gödel showed that every formal system which contains a theory of the natural numbers[7] is either contradictory or incomplete. A consequence of this theorem is that a formal system cannot be used for proving its own *consistency*[8].

---
[5]Syllogism is a deductive form of logical inference or a way of conclusion in natural language.
[6]*In "Computer Science as Empirical Inquiry: Symbols and Search"* [NS76].
[7]The *Peano Axioms* are such a theory, for example.
[8]Consistency means that no contradictory axioms or propositions exist in Γ, that is, $\Gamma \not\vdash \bot$.

Formal systems as formalized by mathematical logic are a strictly symbolic form of knowledge representation and processing that provide a calculus to verify the consistency of propositions and to infer new knowledge by mostly deductive inference rules. Knowledge is tightly bound to the *semantics* of logical formulas, which is a mapping from symbol names to objects of the *domain of discourse*[9]. A characteristic feature of logic is its strict distinction between *syntax* and *semantics*, that is, the syntactical terms and operations are completely independent from any content or meaning.

Predicate logic is a formal system that allows the generation of new propositions via inference rules such as the modus ponens or *unification*[10], which is a form of substitution of variables by *terms*. If a proposition A is syntactically deducible from the set of valid propositions Γ, formally $\Gamma \vdash A$, it belongs to the *deductive closure*[11] $\{A \in FOR_{\mathcal{L}(\Gamma)} : \Gamma \vdash A\}$ of Γ and is accepted as another valid proposition.

To substantiate the symbol system hypothesis and to formalize the principle of compositionality, a representative and well-known mathematical logic has to be defined.

Definition 2.1.1: First Order Logic (FOL), Predicate Logic
The *predicate logic* or *first order logic* is a formal system with the following components [Buc07]:

1. A set of basic **logical symbols** LS that consists of the following elements:

    (a) $\bot$ (falsum), $\neg$ (negation), $\wedge$ (conjunction), $\vee$ (disjunction), $\rightarrow$ (implication)

    (b) $\forall$ (all quantor), $\exists$ (existential quantor)

    (c) $\approx$ (equals)

2. A **formal language** $\mathcal{L}$, which is a set of symbols $p \in \mathcal{L}$, $\mathcal{L} \cap LS = \emptyset$.

3. An $\mathcal{L}$-**structure** $\mathcal{M}$ is a pair $\mathcal{M} = (\mathcal{D}, (p^{\mathcal{M}})_{p \in \mathcal{L}})$, where $\mathcal{D}$ is the *discourse domain* or the *universe* and $(p^{\mathcal{M}})_{p \in \mathcal{L}}$ is a family of the following form:

    (a) $p^{\mathcal{M}} \subset \mathcal{D}^n = \mathcal{D} \times \ldots \times \mathcal{D}$ is a *relation*, if $p = R$ is an n-ary **relational** symbol.

    (b) $p^{\mathcal{M}} : \mathcal{D}^n \rightarrow \mathcal{D}$ is a *function*, if $p = f$ is an n-ary **functional** symbol and $n \geq 1$.

    (c) $p^{\mathcal{M}} \in \mathcal{D}$ is an *object* from the discourse domain, if p is a **constant** ($n = 0$).

---

[9]The set of individuals that are being dealt with by quantified predicates P, $\forall x \in \mathcal{D} P(x)$.
[10]*Unification* is a syntactical concept based on the *substitution of free variables* in terms and is an important principal of logic programming. Logic programming languages like Prolog unify terms by instantiating their free variables, as shown by the following example. The terms $\phi = (x, y, f(a))$ and $\psi = (p, q, r)$ are unified to equivalent expressions $\sigma(\phi) \approx \sigma(\psi)$, when $x \approx p$, $y \approx q$ and $f(a) \approx r$ by the substitution σ.
[11]See definition 2.1.2.

Definition 2.1.2: FOL Syntax

The central syntactical concept of predicate logic are $\mathcal{L}$-**terms**, which are inductively defined as follows:

1. Each **variable** $v_1, v_2, \ldots$ is an $\mathcal{L}$-term.

2. If $t_1, t_2, \ldots, t_n$ are $\mathcal{L}$-terms, then also the *string* $ft_1t_2\ldots t_n$ is an $\mathcal{L}$-term, where f is an n-ary function symbol ($n \geq 1$).

3. For $n = 0$, $f \in \mathcal{L}$ is a function symbol of arity 0, which is a **constant** and thus also an $\mathcal{L}$-term.

Based on these $\mathcal{L}$-terms, the set $FOR_\mathcal{L}$ of **formulas** can be inductively defined:

- $Rt_1t_2\ldots t_n$, $\perp$ and $\approx t_1t_2$ are **prime formulas** (atomic), where R is an n-ary relational symbol and $t_1, t_2, \ldots, t_n$ are $\mathcal{L}$-terms.

- If A and B are formulas, then $\neg A$, $A \wedge B$, $A \vee B$ and $A \rightarrow B$ are also formulas.

- If A is a formula and x is a variable, then $\exists x A$ and $\forall x A$ are also formulas.

These definitions point out what is meant by compositionality in general and concatenative compositionality in particular.

The *semantics* of the predicate logic are imposed by an interpretation $\mathcal{I} = (\mathcal{M}, \eta)$, which consists of a structure $\mathcal{M}$ and a mapping $\eta : Var \rightarrow \mathcal{D}$ from the set of variables ($Var \cap \mathcal{L} = \emptyset$) to the objects of the discourse domain. An example of a logical expression is the implication $A \rightarrow B$, whose semantics can be described by a truth table as represented by table 2.1. The truth value of a complex formula is reduced to a combination of the truth values of its single components. Vice versa, the truth value of a complex expression is uniquely determined by the truth values of the sub-expressions and by the operators that combine them. We refer to this principle as *semantic compositionality*.

$(A \rightarrow B)^I$	$B^I=0$	$B^I=1$
$A^I=0$	1	1
$A^I=1$	0	1

Table 2.1: Exemplary truth function for the *logical implication* $A \rightarrow B$ for propositional and predicate logic (first order). A mapping $\eta : Var \rightarrow \mathcal{D}$ is an allocation of the variables $x, y, z, \ldots$ to the objects of the discourse domain $\mathcal{D}$. A boolean or *truth function* $W : FOR \rightarrow \{0, 1\}$ assigns a truth value "0" (*false*) or "1" (*true*) to a formula of the given language, for example $W_\neg(A^I, B^I) = \max\{1 - A^I, B^I\}$. A pair $I := (\mathcal{M}, \eta)$ is called a *model* for the formula, if the formula becomes true under that interpretation, $\mathcal{M} \models (A \rightarrow B)[\eta] \Leftrightarrow (A \rightarrow B)^I = 1$.

On the syntactical level, terms and formulas are nothing other than character strings, which are uniquely decomposable according to the following lemma.

Lemma 2.1.1: Unique Decomposability If $t_1, \ldots, t_m, u_1, \ldots, u_n$ are terms with the constraint $t_1 \ldots t_m = u_1 \ldots u_n$, then we have $t_i = u_i$ for $i = 1, \ldots, n$ and $m = n$.

Proof 2.1.1: The lemma of unique decomposability is proven by induction over the length n of the composed term $u_2 \ldots u_n$.
It is $t_1 = p\hat{t}_1 \ldots \hat{t}_k, u_1 = p\hat{u}_1 \ldots \hat{u}_k$ with arity #$(p) = k$. This means that the two shorter symbol sequences without the k-ary function symbol p are equal again: $\hat{t}_1 \ldots \hat{t}_k t_2 \ldots t_m = \hat{u}_1 \ldots \hat{u}_k u_2 \ldots u_n$. Using the induction hypothesis $t_2 \ldots t_m = u_2 \ldots u_n$, we conclude that $m = n$, $\hat{t}_j = \hat{u}_j$ for $j = 1, \ldots, k$ and $t_i = u_i$ for $i = 2, \ldots, n$.

Symbols and symbol structures are separated from their meaning and can be concatenated purely syntactically to compose symbolic expressions, which is a requirement for constructing general intelligent behavior according to the symbol system hypothesis. The lemma of unique decomposability 2.1.1 tells us that the symbol concatenation is unique and invertible.

The crux of this lemma is that concatenative compositionality of symbols is not needed to provide systematicity. Compositionality of symbols is a crucial claim of the symbol system hypothesis for general intelligent behavior. The hypothesis is hardly doubted in literature, but compositionality does not necessarily have to be discrete and concatenative. As a counter-example, we quote the distributed but systematic representations created by so-called *Recursive Autoassociative Memory* (RAAM) networks, which are elaborated upon in chapter 4 (section 5.5). These recurrent networks can be used for encoding concatenative symbol structures like the term $ft_1 t_2 \ldots t_n$ defined by Def. 2.1.2, where t_i, $i = 1, \ldots, n$ are subterms. The created internal[12] representation is neither a concatenation of subterms nor a direct mapping of subterms to units of the neural network. In fact, a distributed and non-compositional representation of the composite term is computed, which can be inverted to regain the constituents $f, t_1, t_2, \ldots, t_n$. We see that systematic processes can be conceived without using concatenative principles, which is in favor of connectionist methods and allows to realize the claim for (symbolic) systematicity of the symbol system hypothesis in a connectionist manner.

Another interpretation of the symbol system hypothesis focuses on the search aspect of intelligent behavior and is called *Heuristic Search Hypothesis* [NS76]. Heuristic search is a possible solution to decision and optimization problems like computing the shortest connection between two nodes in a graph, but also provides a way of defining intelligent behavior. The difference between uninformed and informed search in their constraining effect on the search space can be interpreted as the degree of intelligence of a system. The more intelligent a search system is, the lesser the actually scanned fraction of the search space and the bigger the part excluded from the search. There are about 35 possible moves and about 50 moves on

---

[12]The numeric knowledge representation created in the hidden units of a neural network is often called *internal representation*.

average per game and player, which results in a number of 35^{50+50} search tree nodes, of which normally only about 10^{40} nodes represent valid moves. Chess[13] computers for example successfully constrain the branching factor of the exponential move space to compute the next move. The degree of restriction depends on the search strategy implemented by a cost function, which defines the quality of individual moves and their expected impact for the chess player and the opponent (*Minimax-strategy*).

Many problems can be modeled as informed or uninformed search problems, including those that do not look like search problems. An algebraic transformation of an equation to isolate the variable of interest can be seen as a search tree of branching factor one, which is, in fact, a linear sequence of symbol (structure) manipulations. Each state of the equation from the original form to the target form[14] represents a symbol structure, which is an element of the search space consisting of correct and incorrect symbolic equations [NS76], with respect to a given algebraic problem. If the distribution of these symbolic problem solutions is completely random and there is no information criterion (cf. section 4.2) to order the solutions, then no intelligent problem solving is possible since all solutions have to be checked by trial and error. The degree of order of the solution space can be measured by the *entropy* [NS76], which is a measure from information theory described and classified in section 4.2. Any order or pattern of the symbol structures in the solution space can be used to conduct an informed search for the correct solution and thus facilitates intelligent behavior. This order or pattern can be induced by a similarity measure or a distance function upon the search space, which indicates similar and dissimilar problem solutions. In the context of intelligent recommendation, problem solutions are mainly produced by classification and prediction, which make extensive use of distance measurements upon the recommended entities.

2.2 Connectionism and the Symbol Grounding Problem

The main benefits of connectionist models are computational robustness, inherent context-representation and high generalization capabilities. In connectionism, knowledge is represented in a distributed way and new knowledge is generated by the cooperation of many interconnected units. Hybrid techniques composed both of symbolic and connectionist methods belong to the class of *Hybrid Intelligent Systems* (HIS) [AN00, VS07] and have recently enjoyed great popularity. Neural networks, fuzzy and probabilistic methods can be applied to problems that are hardly-understood but well-observed – such as the classification of diseases and molecules in bioinformatics using gene expression data [BDD03].

The connectionist paradigm[15] defines information processing as the result of

---
[13] A chess game can be solved by a form of *perfect search* that is totally informed.
[14] The variable of interest was successfully isolated.
[15] The connectionist paradigm is also called *subsymbolic paradigm*.

the interaction of many small and simple units (neurons). A connectionist system is an abstract model which interprets information numerically and which does not depend on the concrete implementation by a neural network, for example. Neural networks are universally applicable to every problem that can semantically be represented by a functional mapping $f : X \to Y$. Thus, they can also be trained to syntactically process symbolic expressions defined by propositional logics. Niklasson and Sharkey [NS93], for example, taught a neural network to apply the rules of de Morgan to atomic symbols P and Q:

$$\neg(P \vee Q) = \neg Q \wedge \neg P \quad (2.1)$$
$$\neg(P \wedge Q) = \neg Q \vee \neg P, \quad (2.2)$$

These rules were generalized by the connectionist system to transform expressions where P and Q are simple, non-atomic formulas for themselves. Niklasson's result indeed showed that structure can potentially be represented without symbols. Allen Newell, one of the founders of symbolic systems, also formulated a connecting thought: *"There must exist a neural (biological) level of organization that supports a symbol structure*[16]*."* [AP06]

This is exactly what is provided by neural networks, though of course not in a biological but in a computational sense. Neural networks as implementors of recommendation functionality are not biologically motivated in this work; however, analogies to biology were extensively given in the 1980s [GWW91] and biological models are still used as archetypes for artificial neural networks [Par02, NN001].

Knowledge Representation in Symbolism and Connectionism Any knowledge can be represented by symbols, but since symbols are arbitrary, they have to be *grounded* in the domain of discourse[17], which is the carrier of the cognitive processes to be performed. The concept of symbol grounding proposed by Harnad [Har43] (symbol grounding problem [TF05]) takes into account that symbols have to be anchored in the external world, that is grounding them in non-symbolic objects, in order to be useful for cognitive processes. This is not a trivial task at all, since it raises the question of how knowledge about specific objects or concepts should be packaged to be transferable and applicable in different contexts. Making knowledge transferable is crucial for general intelligent behavior of an artificial system. But if we want to package this knowledge, we face the second question: where is the boundary of knowledge about a specific subject such as *coffee*? Can we obtain a complete and exchangeable package of (logical) facts on a subject of interest [Cal03]? The so-called *Terminological Box (T-Box)* used in description logics [ST07, SSS91] or ontologies provides *concept definitions* and *concept axioms* to state facts on arbitrary subjects. Knowledge is specified in a conceptional form by a knowledge tokenization comparable to the syntax of predicate

---

[16]"The notion that intelligence requires the use and manipulation of symbols, and that humans are therefore symbol systems, has been very influential in artificial intelligence." [AP06].

[17]A subset of the real world and its objects.

logics presented in definition 2.1.1. The following example gives naive definitions and axioms on the real-world object *coffee* within its different contexts.

Coffee = CoffeeBeans ∧ HotWater
CupOfCoffee = Coffee ∧ ∃isFilledIn Cup
CanOfCoffee = Coffee ∧ ∃isFilledIn Can
Coffee ↔ Cafe ∧ ∃isFilledIn (Cup ∨ Can)
Cafe = Company ∧ ∃sells Coffee

Of course, this T-Box on coffee is not complete and even partially confusing, since a *Cafe* is a synonym for *Coffee*, if it is filled in a cup or a can. The last concept definition states that a *Cafe* is a company, but does not tell whether it might be filled in a bin or not.

The symbol grounding problem is often underestimated by representatives of the symbolic branch of artificial intelligence. In symbolism, the symbols are isolated in the form of context-free information units in order to use them as constituents of more complex structures that are uniquely decomposable according to lemma 2.1.1. Symbols are *"independent of their specific physical realizations"* and thus create an *"autonomous symbolic level"* [Har43] that works strictly systematically. Symbolic variables are grounded in the domain of interest by the variable allocation $\eta : Var \to \mathcal{D}$ defined in section 2.1. We see that there is an ambivalence between grounding of symbol systems and independence of syntax from semantics.

The symbol grounding problem could be solved by combining context-sensitive with context-independent knowledge representations. To understand the following connectionist approach, a basic knowledge of the composition of neural networks is required, which is presented in section 4.1.2. According to Sharkey et al. [SJ94], the *hidden unit activations* of a feed-forward neural network can be considered as context-sensitive representation, while the network weights serve as context-free representation. Instantiated with the example above, a more comprehensive definition of *coffee* like

Coffee = Beverage ∧ ∃madeBy (CoffeeBeans ∧ HotWater) ∧ ...

is learned and stored by the set of weights between the input units and the hidden units. For all possible contexts such as ∃*isFilledIn X* the same stimulating signal is sent along these input weights, which results in a context-free representation of coffee.

Symbol Manipulation Besides the question of knowledge representation and its systematicity, we have to consider the manipulation of symbol structures to construct an intelligent recommendation system, which is the systematicity of inference. An example is the application of the *distributive law* on a set of variables $Var = \{a, b, c, \ldots\}$. The mapping $a * (b + c) \mapsto a * b + a * c$ describes a structure transformation in the sense of the symbol system hypothesis using two binary function symbols $+, * \in \mathcal{L}$. A possible semantics could be realized by an interpretation based on the natural numbers, $I = (\mathcal{M}, \eta)$, $\eta : Var \to \mathbb{N}$, $\mathcal{M} = (\mathbb{N}, +_\mathbb{N}, *_\mathbb{N}, 0, 1)$

with the usual addition and multiplication. This interpretation already goes beyond the mere symbol manipulation and does not necessarily have to be addressed by a systematic symbol processing system. The systematicity of inference is a purely syntactical capability that can also be realized by connectionist models.

A hybrid solution to such a symbol manipulation can be built on the connectionist structure representations created by *Recursive Autoassociative Memory* (RAAM) networks. The distribution of the binary operators over the variables is determined by the distributive law, which can be implemented by an ensemble of RAAM and standard feed-forward neural networks as elaborated on in section 5.5. An alternative are so-called *Holographic Reduced Representations* (HRR) that also provide a distributed representation for structural knowledge by circular convolution and correlation of high-dimensional feature vectors [Pla03, Neu00].

Both connectionist models achieve a similar computational systematicity than direct symbol manipulations as done by formal systems. However, compared to the large-scale capabilities of symbolic structure manipulation like logical inference, their systematicity is still underdeveloped. From the connectionist perspective, a hybrid intelligent system means a connectionist model that behaves as symbol and structure processor and which develops an "understanding" of the composed knowledge tokens by symbol grounding. The symbols used are anchored in the distributed representations, which are robust against noise and uncertainty and can be learned from examples. Thus a central issue of this dissertation is the treatment of symbolic and structured knowledge such as graph-based data or productions of formal grammars by connectionist models.

2.3 Applying Connectionist Models to Typically Symbolic Domains

Wherever strict verification of computational results is dispensable and validation based on tests and empirical studies is sufficient, neural connectionist model can often achieve higher performance than symbolic techniques. We will empirically show that connectionist models are appropriate to especially process structured knowledge like trees and graphs. This is especially shown for the concrete practices navigation recommendation and change impact analysis in this dissertation, without loosing the capability to accomplish statistical tasks like time series prediction. Therefore the developed connectionist model must be sufficiently flexible to deal both with symbolic and non-symbolic knowledge.

The inherent problem of purely symbolic techniques like expert systems is their disembodied abstractness in interaction with the real world, that is, the employed symbols are not grounded in objects of the real world. Symbolic systems are often tailored to only one application and therefore inflexible with respect to other applications. They are confined to infer new facts by applying inference rules to the fact base from the respective application. Moreover, they are generally not designed to allow exceptions from the anticipated facts (left rule sides); this is required, however, for dealing with uncertain and incomplete information. Therefore symbolic systems are not adequate for *commonsense reasoning*[18] [Mue06] either, but rather connectionist systems are expected to gain those humanoid capabilities.

Rule-Based Systems versus Neural Networks Classification of objects can be accomplished by a fixed set of (discrete) decision criteria, which have to be defined by domain experts. For example, in the medical domain diagnosis rules are defined in order to classify the symptoms of a patient according to known diseases. If the specified criteria are not significant or misleading for the basic population of patients, the classification performance of the expert system will be insufficient or at least suboptimal. The following simplified rule illustrates symbolic reasoning used in expert systems.

If (fever AND (headache OR stomachache) AND
'difficulty in swallowing')
Then Scarlet Fever

By contrast, a neural network is able to learn the characteristics of each object group from a set of *training examples*. The deciding object attributes, such as the patient's symptoms, are taken into account and these attributes are implicitly and automatically weighted according to their significance for the classification task. Insignificant attributes that provide a low *information gain*[19] are low-weighted while significant attributes are assigned to higher weights. The classification approach by a conventional neural network is illustrated by figure 2.1. When the application

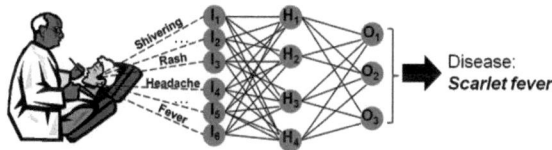

Figure 2.1: Connectionist disease classification by means of a feed-forward neural network that processes the diagnosed patient symptoms.

domain changes, the connectionist classifier can be incrementally retrained. Thus, the domain experts are freed from defining valid classification criteria that may even change rapidly, which leads to a reduced effort of maintaining the diagnosis system.

One example of a rule-based system in the context of the semantic web is the TEAM project [TEA09]. There, association rule mining is used to automatically discover behavior rules concerning the activities of software developers. The resulting rules are encoded in Semantic Web Rule Language (SWRL), which is a semantic web standard for defining domain specific rules. Thus, ontology-based

---

[18]Reasoning methods that exhibit the features of human thinking.
[19]See formula 4.6 in chapter 4.

rules are used to represent control knowledge and to dynamically fire the consequent parts of the rules when the incidence of their antecedents is sensed.

Going beyond rule-based systems, one possibility of integrating symbolism and connectionism is to equip logic with neural components and to realize logical inference by these augmented components [KA01]. Lamb et al. present the language of a *connectionist temporal logic of knowledge* (CTLK) together with a temporal algorithm that translates CTLK theories into ensembles of neural networks [DGL06]. The neural components provide fuzzy inference based on fuzzy premises that replace the strictly logical in the case of the modus ponens inference rule $\{\hat{B}, \hat{B} \to \hat{C}\} \vdash \hat{C}$, for example. The premise $B = \textit{fever} \land (\textit{headache} \lor \textit{stomachache})$ may be only partially fulfilled, denoted by $\hat{\cdot}$, which may cause a partially applicable consequence $\hat{C}$. Not only the constituents might be partially fulfilled, which is expressed by a fuzzy implication $\hat{\to}$ that corresponds to the *confidence* of an association rule elaborated on in section 7.1.2.

The second possibility to construct a hybrid system is to integrate symbolic capabilities into connectionist systems[20] [BGC98, AS97]. For example, a rule-based system incorporates prior domain knowledge as a set of *if-then* rules that can be learned by a neural network[21]. The great advantage of rule incorporation is that each constituent of a diagnosis rule $B_1, \ldots, B_n \to C_1, \ldots, C_m$ can be endowed with a content-based representation. The meaning of the domain objects can be encoded in the rules' *variables* by including their textual, categorical or metric content in the connectionist training process. This is similar to the variable allocation $\eta : Var \to \mathcal{D}$ of first order logic defined in section 2.1. Each further rule that is added by experts contributes to the similarity-based understanding of the domain, which allows the expert system to handle *gradual* rules of the form *the MORE x is A, the MORE y is B* [Amy03]. These are explicitly supported by a connectionist representation $\hat{B}_1, \ldots, \hat{B}_n \hat{\to} \hat{C}_1, \ldots, \hat{C}_m$ of rules, which also enables a gradual compliance of their left sides $B_1, \ldots, B_n$ that consist of several constituents.

Another study on connectionist models supporting symbolic rules was conducted by Prentzas et al., who proposed an explicit combination of neural networks and production rules called *neurules* [HP01]. Figure 2.2 shows a connectionist adaline unit that represents an *if-then* rule with a composite antecedent.

We follow the second approach of connectionist models with symbolic capabilities that are applied to practical problems.

---

[20]Ultsch and Korus [UK95] provide an overview about the integration of neural networks with knowledge-based systems.

[21]Also, the inverse process of extracting explicit rules from the trained neural network is possible in principle [ZJC03].

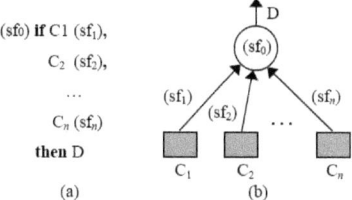

Figure 2.2: (a) Form of a neurule, (b) Corresponding adaline unit. Source: [HP01]

2.4 Knowledge Representation and Knowledge-Based Disciplines

Knowledge Management is the discipline of organizing knowledge into manageable pieces in order to solve knowledge-driven problems. Knowledge is systematically created, shared, and applied to achieve the goals of a company or an organization. Thereby, the knowledge base of an organization is exploited and manipulated by knowledge managers, and the contained information is enriched by imposing structure and annotations by means of metadata at authoring time or retrospectively. Knowledge managers significantly contribute to the success of the knowledge management process, for example, by determining what information is worth sharing across the organization.

The term *knowledge* is overloaded with several meanings. Software engineering knowledge is primarily represented in the form of system models like use-case specifications or system architectures. Graph-based notations similar to semantic networks are widely used to represent knowledge about a software system. For example, the *Unified Modeling Language* (UML) formulates aspects of software systems as abstract models that are highly structured and thus can be learned syntactically (grammar rules) and semantically (types). Furthermore, taxonomies are used to describe the type-relations between classes as *inheritance hierarchies*. Lately, ontology-based conceptualizations have emerged offering an alternative to specify software engineering knowledge [CRP06]. Compared to traditional software modeling, ontologies enable deductive reasoning over classes and their associations, for example, which are expressed as concept definitions and relations.

Knowledge Engineering addresses the building, maintaining and development of knowledge-based systems such as intranet portals of larger organizations. These systems are based on structured knowledge that has to be acquired and inserted into knowledge bases, depending on the intended functionalities operating on the knowledge. Thus, in contrast to knowledge management, the system development is the main focus in knowledge engineering. *Semantic Wikis* and standardized metadata added to web pages, as defined by the *Dublin Core* (DC) initiative, have emerged from knowledge engineering. The Dublin Core characterizes every document by a common set of 15 properties, which is widely used for annotating web pages. However, metadata approaches suffer from a lack of semantics and machine interpretability.

Knowledge Discovery in Databases (KDD) is an umbrella term for process consisting of a set of activities in the context of data mining. Starting with a database of potentially useful data, the KDD process comprises the activities *feature selection, data preprocessing, transformation, data mining*, and *evaluation/interpretation*. Knowledge is acquired from raw datasets in the form of patterns or regularities by aggregation, classification, clustering, correlation- and dependency-analysis, filtering, and others. As in statistics, the significance of these patterns provides information about their validity. High significance of an observation means low probability of being caused by coincidence. In general, KDD is defined as the process of the (semi-) automatic extraction of knowledge from large amounts of data [FPSS96], which is

- statistically valid (significant)
- yet unknown (not externalized)
- and potentially useful for specific applications.

The area of knowledge discovery comprises machine learning, statistics, and databases. Prominent methodologies such as text and web mining, clustering or ranking algorithms (*Google Page Rank*, cf. section 7.2) belong to the overlapping field of machine learning and statistics.

Knowledge Representation and Processing Techniques Knowledge representation means the specification of knowledge by formal or informal languages, to be usable by humans and especially by machines. The choice of an appropriate knowledge representation is the key to achieving intelligent behavior. Often, a heuristic search can be avoided or strongly pruned just by choosing the right knowledge representation. This section highlights the different possibilities of representing knowledge in a machine-processable and -learnable way in the disciplines software engineering, data mining, knowledge management, and logics. In each of these disciplines, the appropriate knowledge representation is the first step towards a problem solution.

Take the problem of correctly *parenthesized (arithmetical) expressions*, for example. We want to implement the convention that each opened parenthesis has to be closed again. Assume that we would like to create a well-defined[22] representation of the parenthesized expressions. One possibility is to specify the allowable constructs with a Chomsky 2-grammar. The context-free language $\mathcal{L} = \{(\ldots^n \ldots)^n \mid n \in \mathbb{N}\}$ can be used to specify the expressions in parentheses and the corresponding grammar productions could be of the following form, beginning with the start symbol

---

[22]Independent from a concrete representative.

CHAPTER 2. THE SYMBOLIC AND THE CONNECTIONIST PARADIGM OF AI 35

S:

$$A \Rightarrow B \mid A+B \qquad (2.3)$$
$$B \Rightarrow S \mid B \cdot S \qquad (2.4)$$
$$S \Rightarrow a_1 \mid a_2 \mid \ldots \mid a_k \mid (A) \qquad (2.5)$$

A simpler and more intuitive solution is to introduce a ternary tree-based knowledge structure like that depicted by the examples of figure 2.3. In this case, the parentheses are implicitly represented by the position or level of a node in the tree. For humans, a ternary tree is simpler and easier to understand than the grammar

Figure 2.3: Two concrete arithmetical expressions that require the correct insertion of parentheses. The use of parentheses can be omitted when leveraging an appropriate tree representation.

productions and still checks for the balancing constraint of opening and closing of parentheses.

There are several questions concerned with the representation of machine-processable knowledge, as for example whether a general purpose or a specific representation is required, or if the knowledge is represented in a *declarative* or a *procedural* way. Declarative knowledge is explicit and may be stated in the form of semantic nets, logics or declarative languages such as the resource description framework (RDF). An example of a declarative statement is a SQL[23] database query, which formalizes the result of the computation by operators on database tables and by attribute-value pairs, but does not specify the algorithm that actually computes the result. Procedural knowledge focuses on problem solving processes that determine *how* a certain result is computed or derived. New knowledge is the outcome of a knowledge manipulation process that can be given by *production rules* of formal grammars, for instance, which transform symbolic knowledge by sequential rule application. Thus, procedural knowledge representation is implicit and hidden in the work processes or algorithms (tacit).

Figure 2.4 gives an overview about the various forms of knowledge representation.

Taxonomies represent hierarchically ordered categories that do not provide additional relations between categories besides their hierarchical position.

---

[23] Structured Query Language.

Figure 2.4: Forms of knowledge representation together with their fields of application. Based on [Str03].

A **Thesaurus** extends the sub-concept-relation in taxonomies by a set of predefined relations such as *similar-to* or *synonym-for* between concepts, while instances are not supported.

An **Entity Relationship-Model** (ER) provides a formal description or conceptualization of a data model of the real world. Usually, a graphical notation consisting of entities, relationships, and attributes is used.

The **Unified Modeling Language** (UML) offers a spectrum of notations [BD04] to capture knowledge about three different aspects of a system:

- Describe system functionality from the user's point of view with use case diagrams.

- Describe system concepts and their relationships in different levels of abstraction with class, object and deployment diagrams.

- Interaction, activity and state diagrams can be used to represent the behavioral aspects of the system.

Uncertain knowledge can be modeled by **Fuzzy Sets**, which can be considered as an extension of multi-valued logics. Fuzzy elements are members of several sets to a certain degree, determined by a real-valued *membership function* m. A fuzzy set is a pair (A, m) where A is a set and $m : A \to [0, 1]$. For each $x \in A$, $m(x)$ represents the grade of membership of x. This allows for *fuzzy premises* that are the basis for drawing graded conclusions.

The **Topic Maps** standard [GM08] supports modeling of domain knowledge in the form of *associated* topics and facilitates structuring of existing knowledge. Concrete *occurrences* are linked to the identified topics and take the role of examples or instances; for example, as a set of web pages that address the same topic.

The most established formal **Logics** are propositional logics, description logics, first order logics, and higher order logics, which are distinguished by their

CHAPTER 2. THE SYMBOLIC AND THE CONNECTIONIST PARADIGM OF AI 37

underlying languages that determine their expressiveness (listed in ascending order). Logics with sufficient expressiveness, like description logics or first-order predicate logics, allow for reasoning both over instances and classes. In case of *description logics* (DL), for example, knowledge representation is twofold: the concepts are encapsulated in the *terminological box* and their instances are comprised by the *assertional box*. The *knowledge base* is the collection of concepts and assertions on instances (facts) like $(John, Paul)$: $hasFather$. ALC is the prototypical description logic, whose language is inductively defined by $F_{ALC} := \bot |\top| \neg F_{ALC} | F_{ALC} \sqcap F_{ALC} | F_{ALC} \sqcup F_{ALC} | F_{ALC} \sqsubseteq F_{ALC} | \exists R\, F_{ALC} | \forall R\, F_{ALC}$.

An **Ontology** represents a formal specification for domain-specific knowledge that allows for automatic reasoning over concepts as well as instances. Being the fundament for logical reasoners such as Racer or Pellet [CP08] differentiates ontologies from mere modeling languages like UML. Ontologies are a powerful formalism for structured knowledge, since they fulfill important requirements like richness, quality of information, dealing with incompleteness and ambiguity, varying level of formality, and applicability to existing environments. In terms of expressive power, description logics such as OWL DL used to specify ontologies are closer to first-order logics than languages used to model databases. For this reason, ontologies are said to be at the "semantic" level, whereas database schema are models of data at the "logical" or "physical" level [Gru08].

The chosen representation language should at least meet the following requirements to be useful for building an intelligent recommendation system.

- The language has to be concise to enable fast and manageable information processing. There is a trade-off between human-understandable and concise languages. The XML markup language, for example, provides a higher understandability at the cost of conciseness.

- The expressiveness of the language must be high enough to formulate all propositions that may appear in the domain of discourse[24]. The *Chomsky hierarchy* can be used to determine the expressiveness of a formal language [Sch01].

- In case of symbolic information processing by logics, for example, the representation language should be suitable for applying an *inference mechanism*, which derives new knowledge from valid facts. An example is the metalanguage of predicate logic, which defines functional and relational symbols of any arity (cf. definition 2.1.1). The fact base of the discourse domain is extended by inference, which can be realized by a *tableau calculus* as in the case of description logic [ST07].

As opposed to symbolic knowledge representation, connectionist representations work numerically. The internal representation of a connectionist model is able to capture the full information content of the respective domain objects with a low

---
[24]The objects across which the quantifiers of a formal theory may range.

degree of redundancy, which is important for the inductive generalization of the incorporated knowledge. Information can even be compressed by appropriate neural architectures, which will be shown in section 4.2 and 5.5.

2.5 Principles of Machine Learning

Knowledge-based systems, which operate on structured and unstructured data, should be automatically analyzed, mined, and finally generalized by machine learning algorithms. In this sense, machine learning algorithms can be considered as services for knowledge-based systems. Figure 2.5 shows an overview of these services. The ser-

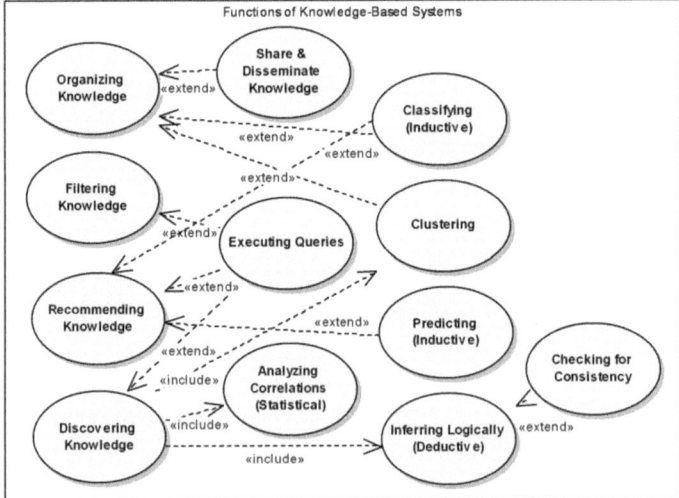

Figure 2.5: Use case diagram showing top-level services provided and used by knowledge-based systems.

vices Classifying, Clustering, Predicting, Inferring Logically, and Analyzing Correlations are classical tasks of machine learning, logic, and statistics, which extend the basic functionality of knowledge-based systems like Organizing, Filtering, and Sharing knowledge among a user group or an organization. In the following, we elaborate on those services that will be realized by the SYMBOCONN framework.

Machine learning systems learn from examples, that is, they discover regularities in given datasets and are able to deal with unknown data showing similar regularities. Thus, the examples – called the training set – are not only memorized, but the discovered regularities can be transferred onto unseen data. The *generalization* from these examples is an inherently inductive process.

From a mathematical perspective, learning means the optimization of an error or a fitness function, which is realized as *supervised, unsupervised* or *reinforcement learning*. Supervised learning assumes the existence of a virtual teacher who knows the target values to be approximated. By contrast, unsupervised learning does not require a specific learning target. Instead, characteristic groups of objects called *clusters* contained in the training set are autonomously determined based on a similarity measure or a *kernel function* $K(\vec{x}, \vec{y}) :=\, <h(\vec{x}), h(\vec{y})>$ on feature vectors $\vec{x}, \vec{y} \in \mathbb{R}^d$, where h is a non-linear mapping $\mathbb{R}^d \to \mathcal{H}$ into a usually higher-dimensional feature space $\mathcal{H}$. Kernels are scalar products on feature vectors representing domain objects, which can be computed efficiently even for high dimensional vectors [Bor07].

Reinforcement learning is similar to natural *conditioning* and is often employed in agent-based systems by means of a *reward function*. There are further learning types such as *transduction*, which is inference from specific training cases to specific test cases, or *meta learning*[25], that are not within the scope of this dissertation. Supervised and unsupervised learning are the foundation for the services *classification, clustering*, and *prediction*, shown in figure 2.5, which we define in the following[26].

Definition 2.5.1: Classification
Classification is a surjective mapping $\{o_1, \ldots, o_n\} =: \mathcal{D} \to \{C_1, \ldots, C_r\}$, $n >> r$, that assigns the objects $o_i \in \mathcal{D}$ to appropriate classes C_j, $j = 1, \ldots, r$, which are discrete. A classifier K realizes the mapping $K : \mathcal{D} \to C$ from objects to classes.

Definition 2.5.2: Clustering
Clustering is a mapping $\{o_1, \ldots, o_n\} =: \mathcal{D} \to CL \subset \mathcal{P}(\mathcal{D})$ from the domain to a partitioning $CL = \{S_1, S_2, \ldots, S_k\}$ of the domain consisting of not necessarily disjoint subsets S_i of domain objects. Clustering is based on *unsupervised learning*. In comparison to *classification*, the classes are not determined, but are discovered in a self-learning process. The goal is to minimize the sum of distances between objects within the same cluster for all objects in the domain. The *compactness* $TD(C)$ of a cluster C is computed by the sum of the distances between all cluster objects and its centroid μ_C. The Euclidean distance is often chosen as distance measure.

$$\mu_C := \frac{1}{k} \sum_{i=1}^{k} o_i, \quad o_i \in C, \ |C| = k$$

$$TD(C) := \sum_{i=1}^{k} d(o_i, \mu_C)^2 = \sum_{i=1}^{k} (\|o_i - \mu_C\|_2)^2$$

---

[25]Informally spoken, *meta learning* means learning to learn. An exemplary meta-algorithm is *AdaBoost*, which performs an iterative optimization upon a series of classifiers.
[26]We use the term *classification* for a mapping from objects to a finite number of groups. The value space of *prediction* may be innumerable like the set of real values $\mathbb{R}$.

The quality QC of a clustering consisting of several clusters $\{C_1, \ldots, C_r\}$ is given by

$$QC = \sum_{i=1}^{r} TD(C_i),$$

which sums up the degree of compactness $TD(C_i)$ of each cluster C_i. There are several different clustering types such as nearest neighbor clustering, density-based clustering or, more recently, Hough-based clustering[27] [ABD+08]. Density-based clustering applies a local cluster criterion: "Clusters are regarded as regions in the data space in which the objects are dense, and which are separated by regions of low object density (noise). These regions may have an arbitrary shape and the points inside a region may be arbitrarily distributed" [Kri00]. More formally, a data point is called *core object*, if it is situated in a dense region of the underlying feature space $|N_\epsilon(o)| \geq minPts$, $N_\epsilon(o) = \{p \in O : d(o,p) \leq \epsilon\}$ for a metrics d

Definition 2.5.3: Prediction
Prediction is a mapping $P : \mathcal{D}^m \to \mathcal{D}^n$, $m, n \in \mathbb{N}$ from history sequences to target sequences of domain objects $o := (f_1, \ldots, f_d)$ with feature values $f_i \in F_i$. The object features F_i that span the feature space $F_1 \times \ldots \times F_d$ are also allowed to be continuous $F_i = \mathbb{R}$, $i = 1, \ldots, d$, which is required for the prediction of numerical time series, for example.

Classification and prediction are closely related because classification can be interpreted as a subclass of prediction: to classify an object means to predict its class, which is a categorical or ordinal quantity. This relationship is shown in figure 2.6, which also illustrates other associations between functions on different types of knowledge and the responsible disciplines and research areas. Software engineering depends on knowledge engineering, since the creation of software systems requires a knowledge creation and management process. Especially during software development, knowledge management techniques are used, for example, to streamline the planned and unplanned communication of the project participants.

Inferring Logically Logics provide a further traditional formalism and calculus to represent and process knowledge symbolically. Based on the given syntax and logical calculus, different inference types are supported, while most of these are reducible to the consistency check $\Gamma \cup \{A\} \overset{?}{\vdash} \bot$ with respect to a given set of formulas Γ. The *subsumption check* tests whether a given concept B^{28} is subsumed by another concept C, formally denoted by $B \to C$, which can be done by assuming the opposite and checking for contradiction $\Gamma \cup \{B \land \neg C\} \overset{?}{\vdash} \bot$. *Realization* is the computation of all instance-concept relations in the domain, that is, for each instance its membership of one or several concepts (classes) is determined.

---
[27]A form of subspace clustering.
[28]B is the subordinate concept.

CHAPTER 2. THE SYMBOLIC AND THE CONNECTIONIST PARADIGM OF AI 41

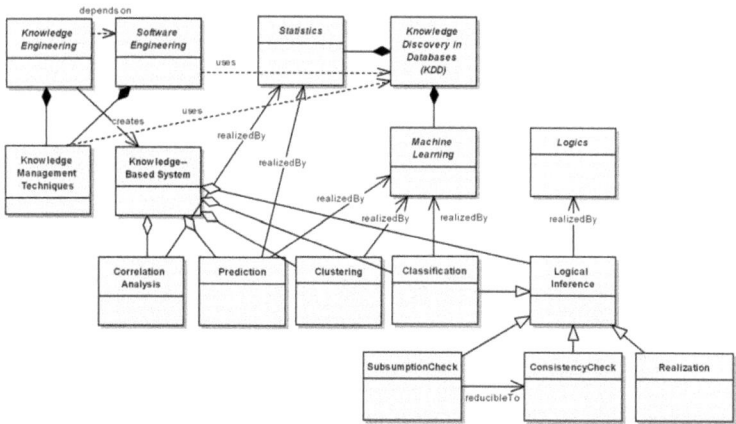

Figure 2.6: UML class diagram illustrating the associations and dependencies between functions of knowledge-based systems and the responsible disciplines relevant for this dissertation. Classification is both a concept of machine learning (inductive classification, non-symbolic) and of logic (deductive classification, symbolic), where the classification in logics is the computation of the subsumption graph that represents the concept taxonomy.

Correlation analysis is the pairwise computation of the correlation coefficient (cf. section 8.3, formula 8.13) based on the observations of the potentially relevant features. The aim is to discover functional dependencies between metrical or ordinal features, as for example, the impact of the marketing expenses on the disposal of a certain product, which are both time series.

Many activities from *knowledge management* such as *organizing* (clustering, aggregation) or *categorizing* (classification) demand for the introduced machine learning functions to add value to existing (information) services. Figure 2.7 provides an overview of machine learning and inference mechanisms, which are related to each other from the perspective of statistics (data, significance) and logics (symbols, inference rules). Ideally, these functions should be applicable to any kind of information – independent from the associated domain and especially independent from the form of its representation. Chapter 3 defines the requirements of SYMBOCONN, which assure that the provided machine learning functions are indeed this general.

In the following section, we focus on existing techniques that provide intelligent recommendation, which is an umbrella term for several inference and generalization methods as shown in figure 2.7. In particular, intelligent tutoring systems, content-based/collaborative filtering, and case-based reasoning are described. These recommendation concepts serve as the starting point for developing the SYMBOCONN machine learning framework.

42   CHAPTER 2. THE SYMBOLIC AND THE CONNECTIONIST PARADIGM OF AI

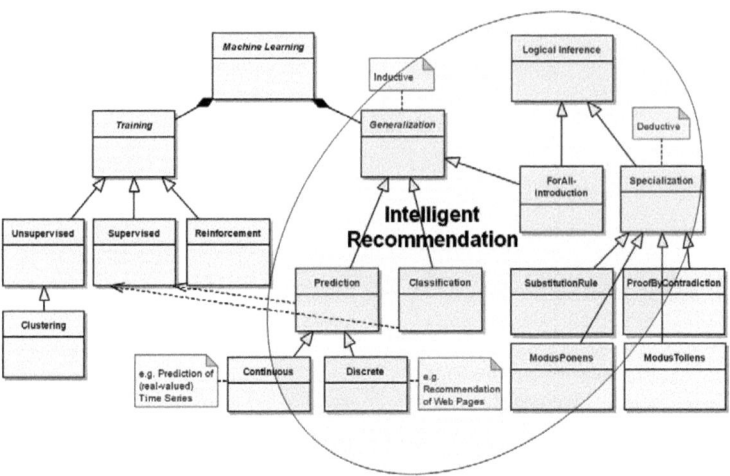

Figure 2.7: Machine learning, inference, and their interrelations expressed by *specification inheritance*. *Generalization* is an *inductive* form of knowledge generation and *specialization* is a *deductive* one. A *ForAllIntroduction* $A \to \forall x A$ works inductively and is bound to a variable condition $x \notin FV(A)$, where FV is the set of *free variables* of a term. The different inference rules *SubstitutionRule* $A[x_1/t_1, \ldots, x_n/t_n]$, $x_1, \ldots, x_n \notin FV(A)$, *ProofByContradiction* $\Gamma \cup \{\neg A\} \vdash \bot \Rightarrow \Gamma \vdash A$, *ModusPonens* $\{B, B \to C\} \vdash C$, and *ModusTollens* $\{A \to B, \neg B\} \vdash \neg A$ conclude from universal to individual formulas. The *ModusTollens* inference rule is also known as *Contraposition*. *Prediction* and *Classification* are generalizing machine learning functions that usually operate non-symbolically but numerically – as opposed to logics. *Intelligent Recommendation* is an abstract functionality that can be realized by different machine learning functions.

2.6 Existing Recommendation Concepts

There are many specific recommendation solutions tailored to a specific domain of recommendation. However, there are only a few standard methods offering intelligent recommendations, and these provide limited functionality or operate on a highly restricted domain. Their limitation either manifests itself in the types of supported recommendations or in the types of processable knowledge. Our focus is on domain-independent recommendation frameworks, which conceptually unify existing recommendation approaches.

Zan and his colleagues [HZC05] describe a domain-independent[29] recommendation framework based on *probabilistic relational models*, which are an extension of Bayesian networks. In this framework, links between products and consumers are modeled as conditional probabilities, and the complete probabilistic relational model is determined by the conditional probability distributions of all network nodes. Another example for intelligent recommendation is the work of Symeonidis et al., who developed an agent-based recommendation framework that focuses on Enterprise Resource Planning (ERP) systems [SCKM05]. This multi-agent framework is claimed to be reconfigurable, adaptive and cost efficient and works as a plugin on top of existing ERP software. The work of Chen et al. is even more specific, since it supports only obtaining IT certifications from a collection of approximately 200 to 400 computer-related certifications (e-Learning) [YWC02].

In the field of forecast applications, Moreno et al. proposed a computational hybrid system based on neural-fuzzy techniques and intelligent software agents [JMDO07]. Moreno uses neural networks to forecast temporal series describing the development of prices on the electricity market. For the prediction of a metric dependent variable called *contracting level* (variable to be predicted), a so-called *Fuzzy Inference System* developed by Moreno et al. combines the three independent input variables *price difference*, *risk disposition* and *financial capacity* defined by static formulas. However, the developed toolbox of neural networks, fuzzy-logic, and software agents does not represent a unified framework.

We see that isolated connectionist methods are again mainly applied to traditional fields such as time series prediction. As opposed to an ensemble of isolated machine learning methods, we propose a single recommendation engine that is capable of learning from arbitrary independent variables whose realizations are packed into sequences of multi-represented objects, as defined in section 3.2. No fault-prone and static calculation rule for risk or price variables should be used, as was done by Moreno, but the underlying classification or prediction function should be learned from the training samples.

Before focusing on the details of this engine and the associated framework called SYMBOCONN, we describe three state-of-the-art techniques that provide intelligent recommendations, namely *Intelligent Tutoring Systems*, *Content-Based*

---

[29]Zan et al. call their framework "unified", without clearly defining this term. In contrast, the related concept of *domain independence* is formulated as a nonfunctional requirement for the SYMBOCONN framework in section 3.1.2.

and *Collaborative Filtering*, as well as *Case-Based Reasoning*.

2.6.1 Intelligent Tutoring Systems

Intelligent Tutoring Systems (ITS) or intelligent teaching systems are an approach to apply artificial intelligence to education. An ITS is any computer system that provides customized instruction or feedback to students on a constraint knowledge domain without human assistance. These systems are capable of interpreting their subject area and use problem solving techniques tailored to the respective teaching domain [IAC06, Rot97]. An intelligent tutoring system normally consists of three modules, which are described briefly:

- *Expert/Domain Module*
  The expert module holds the content of the curriculum and the common sense knowledge. The expert module usually contains a comprehensive case database. Normally, the formally represented knowledge is linked to an inference engine that enables the system to draw conclusions and to generate feedback.

- *Tutor Module*
  The tutor module is the pedagogical component that communicates the expert knowledge to the student and makes use of several knowledge transfer strategies. This module is based on the archetype of a human tutor who takes corrective actions in case of discrepancies between expected and observed behavior of the student. Students learn from the intelligent tutoring system by solving posed problems, while being provided with help from the tutor module which also fulfills a pedagogical function. After submitting a solution for a certain task, the system performs a diagnosis based on the differences of the reference solution and that of the student one and gives individual feedback to the student.

- *Communication Module*
  This module implements the presentation layer of the system and is responsible for the interaction with the student. Furthermore, the students' inputs are converted to the knowledge representation used by the expert module and vice versa.

Intelligent tutoring systems focus on the interaction with the user and usually pursue a *teaching strategy*. There are *model-tracing tutor* systems, which continuously track students' progress and "keep(s) them within a specified tolerance of an acceptable solution path" [Fre00]. The SYMBOCONN framework also assists the user, but does not maintain a relationship between the user and the system. In fact, one of the design goals of SYMBOCONN is *domain independence*. We call an intelligent tutoring system domain independent if the knowledge encoded in the teaching model can be reused in different domains.

In general, three different types of knowledge are incorporated into an intelligent tutoring system:

- *Domain Knowledge*
  The domain model contains a description of the knowledge or behaviors that represent expertise in the subject to be taught. SYMBOCONN does not hold prior domain-specific knowledge but incorporates knowledge from empirical data, that is, from training examples.

- *Knowledge about the students and their behavior*
  An intelligent tutoring system creates profiles about the student including information about knowledge gaps and their individual problem solving strategies. SYMBOCONN also addresses this aspect in the form of user-dependent navigation or preference histories, but not in an explicit descriptive form as often given by profiles.

- *Knowledge about teaching strategies*
  Socratic, problem-based, task-based, or exploratory strategies are important types of teaching strategies. A socratic teaching strategy is a method that fosters insights of the student by clever questioning. Another example of a teaching strategy is to provide additional information on a false answer to a question or to pose an easier question. SYMBOCONN is not endowed with teaching strategies but with two different learning strategies, *supervised* and *unsupervised*, which determine whether machine learning is carried out with a virtual teacher or not.

Intelligent tutoring systems have been developed to substitute human instructors and thus to reduce the overall teaching costs of educational institutes. Their application has so far basically been limited to several United States high schools and military training for the U.S. Navy.

2.6.2 Content-Based and Collaborative Filtering

Content-based and collaborative filtering are two recommendation techniques which support exploration and retrieval of potentially relevant information or entities by personalized recommendations. For content-based filtering, recommendations are based on the user's profile captured from their past buying or navigation behavior and the focused objects. Items to be recommended are determined by a similarity computation between item properties and user preferences. For content-based filtering, no comparison of individual user preferences with those of other users (user groups) is done. Usually, the user profile is nothing but a collection of weighted keywords to describe the user's interests. These profiles are the result of statistical analyses, in the simplest case obtained by counting the number of item accesses.

In content-based filtering systems, content of known items is used to recommend new items to the users [PN02]. Collaborative filtering is designed to work even if no item content is available at all, which we call a *symbolic approach* in this dissertation.

Collaborative filtering is a *deductive* inference technique drawing conclusions for an individual user from a group of users. The captured preference patterns from a representative user group are instantiated and applied to a single user. Thereby, collaborative filtering systems also rely on user profiles and similarity-based profile matching, while sometimes also taking into account the user's social environment (*demographic filtering*). The underlying assumption of collaboration is that similar profiles of different users suggest similar buying or navigation behavior. The calculated prediction for single users also considers their individual behavior and is thus not merely an average of all user behaviors. The individual tailoring of recommendations for a single user conditioned by similar group interests is characteristic for collaborative filtering systems, such as the article recommendation mechanism used by Amazon [LSY03].

In both filtering techniques, user profiles are updated dynamically based on feedback information from the user, who agrees or disagrees with the provided recommendations. There are hybrid concepts that try to combine the benefits of both fundamental approaches. An example is the MARSYAS framework for music recommendation by Kamps and his colleagues [SK05]. They developed a hybrid system by first using collaborative methods to create clusters of songs and then using the features extracted from the song descriptions for a content-based – and thus more fine-grained – recommendation. Another technique is *demographic filtering* using demographic attributes such as gender, age or area code. This is based on the assumption that users' preferences are dependent on their provenance or parentage.

Different machine learning methods can be chosen to realize the recommendation techniques in particular. Recommendations can be computed by probabilistic methods like *Bayesian networks*, *association rule mining*, clustering (e.g. k-means) or *nearest neighbor* algorithms. An example for collaborative filtering is the item recommendation used by Amazon [LSY03], which assumes similar buying behavior within groups of customers. Content-based filtering systems adapt their recommendations to the users' characteristics, for example, their goals, tasks, and interests that are determined from observed behavior.

2.6.3 Case-Based Reasoning

Case-Based Reasoning (CBR) is another application of artificial intelligence whose main operating principle is *conclusion by analogy*. Case-based reasoning can be described with a sequential process model consisting of four phases:

1. *Retrieve*
   The most similar case compared to the posed problem is searched in the *case memory*, which is a database of solved problems. Thus a similarity measure has to be defined on the feature space representing the available cases.

2. *Reuse*

The most similar solution is taken as a first approximation of the solution to the new problem.

3. *Revise*
   The determined basic solution is adapted to the requirements of the new problem where applicable.

4. *Retain*
   Each solved case is stored in the case database for future requests, which automatically augments the experience and performance of the system.

An example of a case-based reasoning system is the *Experience Factory* [BCR], which gathers experience in a software project and generalizes the acquired knowledge in order to make it applicable to other software projects. This feature is also supported by the SYMBOCONN framework through its generalization capability. The experience factory likewise implements the retain-phase of case-based reasoning, which supports the project organization by managing the produced experience [BCR]. Gained experience is packaged for further reuse, comparable to the growing case memory or to retraining the SYMBOCONN engine with new domain information.

Case-based reasoning systems are usually employed for customer support, product consultancy, and e-Commerce. Similar to connectionist systems, a number of existing cases is collected and stored in the case memory to provide useful problem solutions. If the stored cases are not statistically significant, then failures of conclusion by analogy are the rule. Case-based reasoning systems rely on *anecdotal evidence*, which is a relatively weak form of inference, since no logical inference rules or statistical correlations are used to produce solutions.

Chapter 3

Machine Learning Concepts and Fundamentals of SymboConn

SYMBOCONN is a connectionist machine learning framework that supports learning from both symbolic and non-symbolic knowledge structures. Thereby, *new domains* and *new problems* can be addressed, which has heretofore not been possible by neural network based systems. This is possible because the machine learning engine does not distinguish between rule-based and empirical knowledge, but can incorporate knowledge that is heterogeneous both in content and structure.

In this chapter, the requirements, the knowledge model and the machine learning concepts of SYMBOCONN are defined independently from a concrete application domain. This is feasible due to the generic knowledge model based on abstract node sequences, and a flexible machine learning engine of the SYMBOCONN framework. Classification and prediction are realized by a sequence processing recurrent neural network which is the backbone of the framework. The framework also allows connectionist processing of symbolic knowledge.

3.1 Framework Requirements

A generic machine learning framework has to include *classification*, *clustering*, and *prediction* as defined in the last chapter. These functions can be used in a wide range of applications, from product positioning over document classification to sales prediction. Such a framework also requires a strong *learning capability* and *generalization capability*, two tightly coupled concepts. The connectionist approach to learning means trying to discover the correlations within the training data by numerical methods, in particular by neural training algorithms. Successful learning of the correlations between the features of the dataset is the crucial precondition for generalizing from the trained examples.

3.1.1 Functional Requirements

The functional requirements for SYMBOCONN are based on the machine learning concepts introduced in section 2.5. These are independent of the implementation, such that both symbolic and connectionist techniques can be employed to realize them.

Humans generally learn more efficiently and effectively when studying examples instead of abstract descriptions [Fle01]. Machine learning relies on this finding, which leads us to the first functional requirement *learning by example*. A second requirement is *generalization capability*, which is defined by a five-stage hierarchy. This hierarchy can be used to classify the generalization capability of any system that involves a learning and reasoning process. Additional functional requirements are *learning typed knowledge* and *context-sensitivity*. Finally, the SYMBOCONN framework must be capable of processing heterogeneous *contents* and *structures*, which is addressed by the functional requirement *processing of heterogeneous data*. In the following, we elaborate on each of these requirements.

3.1.1.1 Learning By Example

Learning by example is a form of *observational learning* [KSH08], which applies both to supervised and unsupervised machine learning. As mentioned in the beginning of this dissertation, if we have more data than knowledge, then learning by example is required. Learning by example is especially useful when no systematic domain knowledge, for example in the form of logical facts like $\Gamma \vdash A$ or rules like $\Gamma \vdash (A \rightarrow B)$, is available. Examples are instances of problem solutions. Instead of learning the underlying formation rule of parenthesized expressions, we can learn the composition of expressions in parentheses by studying a set of problem solutions $\{(a), (a(b)), (a(a(b(c)))), (((a))), \ldots\}$.

In a company setting, this might be the case when new business processes are introduced or information is acquired from new sources, which are structurally different. Thus, learning by example is essential for domain engineering, where new processes should be supported solely by observing their perceivable activities. Domain engineering [Bor03] means building a generic framework that can be employed for various applications in the same domain. It is a methodology that originally comes from *product line management* and consists of the phases domain analysis, domain design and domain implementation. During domain analysis, the commonalities and dependencies of the domain that hold across different applications in the domain are collected, which defines abstractions that can be used in the application. Subsequently, the domain design focuses on designing a generic system architecture [Bor03] that is extensible and application-independent.

3.1.1.2 Generalization Capability

Another requirement is the generalization capability, which is first considered from a symbolic perspective. The capability to generalize acquired knowledge is defined in terms of a hierarchy similar to the *Chomsky hierarchy* of formal language types. The generalization capability is categorized in a declarative way by formulating the expected system output as reference value for each hierarchy level. This hierarchy especially aims at generalizing symbolic knowledge structured in a systematic and compositional manner, e.g. by grammar productions. A similar issue is the use of abstractions when modeling a software system. The generalization capability allows us to find higher abstraction levels to suppress details and to manage complexity.

A machine learning system can be characterized by the generalization hierarchy initially defined by Niklasson and van Gelder [NvG94]. The definition of the hierarchy is based on *elements* as the smallest entities of the domain and consists of five levels described in the following.

We use the *distributive law*[1] from algebra to illustrate the different levels of symbolic generalization. This law applied to structures of increasing complexity that describe a term transformation in the form of the expression $input[term] \mapsto target[term]$. More formally, the terms consist of atomic elements or complex subterms that are combined by the binary operators "·" and "+". Thereby, the distributive law characterizes the distribution of these binary operators over the constituents of the underlying term. The distributive law is learned from examples over the alphabet $\Sigma = \{b, c, d, (,)\}$.

On the lowest level of the generalization hierarchy, called **Level 0** or **memorization**, no novel terms are presented and therefore no generalization takes place. Knowledge acquired by training can only be recalled, so every presented term appears in the training set. At this level the system simply works as a memory and does not provide intelligent capabilities – that is, the system is only able to reproduce the learned knowledge and its structure. If $b \cdot (c+d) \mapsto b \cdot c + b \cdot d$ was learned, then $b \cdot c + b \cdot d$ is computed when $b \cdot (c + d)$ is presented to a Level 0 learning system.

A **Level 1** learning system generalizes to **novel combinations** of elements in the comprising term, after having seen all existing elements in their syntactically allowed positions. The elements in the terms keep their previous syntactical positions, meaning that they have already been trained in the positions of the novel term, but not in the new combination with other elements. The following exemplary training set with four expressions clarifies the meaning of level 1 generalization.

Training set:

$$\begin{aligned} a \cdot (b + c) &\mapsto a \cdot b + a \cdot c \\ a \cdot (c + b) &\mapsto a \cdot c + a \cdot b \\ b \cdot (a + c) &\mapsto b \cdot a + b \cdot c \\ c \cdot (b + a) &\mapsto c \cdot b + c \cdot a \end{aligned}$$

---

[1]The *distributive law*, which is required for mathematical structures like *fields* or *vector spaces*, characterizes the distribution of the binary operators "·" and "+" over the elements of the underlying expression.

From this training set, a new combination of elements can be found: $N := b \cdot (c + a) \mapsto b \cdot c + b \cdot a$; this expression contains elements that have already appeared in the given position by themselves, but not in this specific combination with other elements.

When the term on the left side of the new expression N is presented, a Level 1 learning system is expected to generate the correct right side term. In other words, if this transformation is achieved, the machine learning system has a generalization capability of Level 1.

To reach **Level 2**, the system has to generalize to **novel positions** of elements in the terms, since not all syntactically allowed positions occur in the training set. The work of Hadley et al. [HH97] describes a connectionist system that can assign appropriate meaning representations to novel sentences, where nouns appear in new positions: "During training, two-thirds of all nouns are presented only in a single syntactic position (either as grammatical subject or object). Yet, during testing, the network correctly interprets thousands of sentences containing those nouns in novel positions."

To formalize this kind of generalization, elements associated by the operators "·" and "+" are again transformed according to the distributive law.

Training set:

$$b \cdot (c + d) \mapsto b \cdot c + b \cdot d$$
$$b \cdot (d + c) \mapsto b \cdot d + b \cdot c$$
$$c \cdot (b + d) \mapsto c \cdot b + c \cdot d$$

After providing this training set, the machine learning system is given the term $d \cdot (b + c)$, which is composed of the same elements, but at new positions. In fact, the symbol d has never appeared as first factor in the training set. If the correct target term $d \cdot b + d \cdot c$ is inferred, then this corresponds to a generalization capability of Level 2.

A **Level 3** machine learning system can transform terms whose elements have not been part of the training set. **Novel or unseen elements** are treated by generalization based on the known elements, for example, by similarity.

Training set:

$$A_1 := [\, b \cdot (c + d) \mapsto b \cdot c + b \cdot d \,]$$
$$A_2 := [\, c \cdot (b + d) \mapsto c \cdot b + c \cdot d \,]$$
$$A_3 := [\, d \cdot (b + c) \mapsto d \cdot b + d \cdot c \,]$$

If the system succeeds to correctly handle inputs like $a \cdot (b + c), a \cdot (c + d), \ldots$ over the extended alphabet $\hat{\Sigma} = \{a, b, c, d, (,), e, f, g, \ldots\} \supset \Sigma$, then the machine learning system exhibits a Level 3 generalization capability.

Level 4 generalization can abstract from compositional terms used in the training set towards **novel** and **higher complexity**, which is a very difficult task to accomplish for a machine learning system. From the perspective of logics, Level 4 allows to substitute the free variables by arbitrary *terms*, which hold their own structure. The challenging task for a Level 4 system is to correctly apply the distributive law to the input terms of the following structures of *higher complexity*. Given the inputs

$$(b+c) \cdot (c+d)$$
$$c \cdot ((b_1 \cdot b_2) + (d_1 \cdot d_2)),$$

the terms $(b+c) \cdot c + (b+c) \cdot d$ and $c \cdot (b_1 \cdot b_2) + c \cdot (d_1 \cdot d_2)$ can be inferred. Here the atomic elements b and d (terminal symbols) are substituted by complex subterms that are composed by the operations "·" or "+" over the same alphabet. Now the resulting terms of Level 3 can be presented to the system once more. Thus, the Level 4 machine learning system has reduced the term complexity by one level, which allows to employ an ensemble of systems of different levels concurrently.

A **Level 5** machine learning system combines the Level 3 and 4 capabilities so that a generalization to **novel elements in structures (terms) of higher complexity** is applied. This level is basically equal to Level 4, but new elements like "a" also may appear in the structures of higher complexity, disjoint from the elements in the training set.

The capability of generalizing to novel elements (Level 3) is essential for intelligent recommendation. This capability can be interpreted as a type generalization, which is important to obtain a higher systematicity of inference. Generalization capability is closely related to systematicity of inference described in chapter 2, since both concepts enable the generation of new knowledge facts from given ones. Based on the training set {*loves(Alex, Johanna), loves(Johanna, Alex), loves(Thomas, Monika), loves(Monika, Thomas), loves(Max, Barbara)*}, a weak systematic system[2] could derive *loves(Barbara, Max)* by generalization, for example. However, a system with higher generalization capability could generalize to *loves(Male, Female)* or *loves(Female, Male)*. This form of generalization was already achieved by Niklasson et al. [NvG94] by means of a RAAM[3] network (see also section 5.5) applied to expressions from propositional logics. A *Holographic Reduced Representations* (HRR) approach by Neumann [Neu00] was also able to provide Level 3 generalization capability.

In terms of logics, the placeholder variables b, c, d that occur in the transformation expressions A_i are its *free variables* $FV(A_1 \cup A_2 \cup A_3) = \{b, c, d\}$, since they are not bound by any logical quantor. Thus, free variables can be substituted by arbitrary variables, while the distributive transformation rule is still valid. This is exactly the degree of abstraction that should be achieved by the machine learning system at generalization Level 3. According to Neumann [Neu00], to achieve

---
[2] Example derived from [Cal03], p.217.
[3] *Recursive Auto-Associative Memory*.

Level 3 generalization, elements that fill the same roles in the structures should have similar representations. Representations of atomic symbols are usually constructed by *unary encoding*, which means that for n symbols each symbol is assigned to an n-dimensional unit vector that is orthogonal to all others ([NvG94]).

An even more fine-grained approach than terms of typeless symbols is to support taxonomical knowledge, which is arranged in a hierarchy of types.

3.1.1.3 Learning Types and Inheritance Hierarchies

The requirement *type learning* aims at categories among the data to be processed. Without types, the framework cannot meaningfully support taxonomical knowledge used in the analysis phase of software development or in ontology engineering. In the following, we extend the learning and generalization requirement to typed knowledge, where the types can either be predetermined in the form of fixed object categories, or are empirically discovered by clustering as defined in section 2.5.

In addition to learning of types or categories, the SYMBOCONN system must also be able to incorporate types that are classified by an *inheritance hierarchy*. That is, it must be able to recognize subtypes of more general types in terms of subsets $A_k \subset A_{k-1} \subset \ldots \subset A_0 \subseteq \mathcal{D}$ of the domain $\mathcal{D}$. In symbolic systems, for example, this simple form of specialization and generalization can be expressed by a logical implication $A_k \rightarrow A_{k-1}$, which means that if an object o is instance of a subclass A_k, $o \in A_k$, then it is also instance of the corresponding A_{k-1} superclass, $o \in A_{k-1}$. In description logics the notation $A_k \sqsubseteq A_{k-1}$ is common, which emphasizes the subset property.

3.1.1.4 Being Able to Incorporate Context (Context-Sensitivity)

The generalization hierarchy presented above was based on the transformation of symbolic phrases. From the perspective of symbol manipulation, the requirement of context-sensitivity means transforming or substituting input phrases dependent on the context. More formally, the context-sensitive rule $\alpha B \gamma \rightarrow \alpha \beta \gamma$ substitutes the variable B only in the context[4] of being enclosed by α and γ, which must be learnable by the machine learning engine.

From a more general point of view, context should sufficiently characterize the situation of a system by means of relevant and perceivable information. This information enables the dynamic adaption of the system to the new situation at run time. In case of systems that directly interact with the real world, environmental conditions such as temperature, air pressure or light conditions are often considered as context. A system is called context-sensitive if it supplies the user with different information or services depending on the respective context.

An example[5] for context-sensitivity represented in natural language is the following: assume a learner reads the sentence *"They ate rice with chopsticks"*. If

---
[4]$B \in V$, $\alpha, \beta, \gamma \in (V \cup \Sigma)^*$.
[5]Derived from [Cal03].

the learner has no idea what a chopstick is, he could assume *chopsticks* are either food or cutlery. The next sentence is *"The chopsticks together with the rest of the cutlery were placed in the dish washer"*. Now that the interpretation of *chopsticks* has changed, the learner can assume that these are a sort of cutlery. This conclusion was *inferred* from the *context* of the first sentence.

According to this example, a context can determine or clarify the meaning of an ambiguous concept. This fact also applies to software development, where the current working context of a developer reveals a lot of information about his task [HM03].

3.1.1.5 Processing of Heterogeneous Knowledge

Knowledge bases of different domains often represent knowledge in different ways. The resulting heterogeneity is characterized by domain objects of different types and by the heterogeneous topologies of different knowledge bases. Thus, the SYMBOCONN framework and especially its machine learning engine must also be able to process node sequences whose nodes carry different types of information. An example for heterogeneous knowledge is a tree with varying branching factor, which may describe a software design pattern. The tree is shown as a class diagram in figure 3.1.

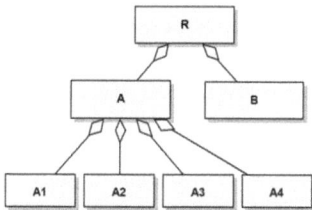

Figure 3.1: UML class diagram showing a tree-structure of three levels with varying branching factor. The aggregation that belongs to class A consists of four constituents $A1$ to $A4$, while the root class R comprises only two classes.

Processing of Arbitrary Node Sequences Conventional neural networks cannot process input or target sequences of varying size. Since the SYMBOCONN system provides classification and prediction for many different domains, it has to support variable node sequences $x_{t-k}, \ldots, x_t \mapsto y_{t+1}, \ldots, y_{t+m}$, $x_i, y_j \in V$ with arbitrary k and m. This property differentiates the SYMBOCONN engine from conventional neural networks with static topology. Moreover, handling of knowledge nodes with completely different information content must be supported, that is to process node representation vectors $\vec{x}_i = (x_{i_1}, \ldots, x_{d_i}) \in \mathbb{R}^{d_i}$ or $\vec{y}_j =$

$(y_{j_1}, \ldots, y_{d_j}) \in \mathbb{R}^{d_j}$ with arbitrary dimensionality $d_i \neq d_j$. This is necessary because domain objects of different types can be characterized by a different number of key-value pairs.

Integration of Previous Knowledge A persistent argument by critics of connectionism is that, in their opinion, including previous knowledge into connectionist models is not possible. Since this is indeed an important aspect of intelligent recommendation, the system must support the integration of previous knowledge in symbolic form. Domain knowledge which is given by logical or mathematical rules like the *distributive law* (cf. section 3.3) should be incorporated as previous knowledge. Domain-specific rules should be definable in the form of $Rule \equiv (Antecedent \Rightarrow Consequent)$ beforehand (cf. definition 3.2.3 of section 3.2). In the case of software development such a rule could be

HighPrioTask,SeriousErrorOccurs
$\Rightarrow$ WriteBugReport,InformChiefProgrammer

When the system observes a sequence of actions, the user's navigation history that matches the *antecedent* of a rule, its *consequent* part should automatically be fired. This part of the rule might, for example, correspond to a prescribed sequence of actions to be executed by the user as a counter measure, when an error was detected before.

3.1.2 Nonfunctional Requirements

Two nonfunctional requirements of the framework are extensibility and domain-independence. Extensibility is crucial for the support of domain engineering, which means building a generic process architecture that can be employed for various applications in the same domain. Domain-independence goes beyond domain engineering, since its goal is to provide machine learning capabilities for recurring problems such as classification of unseen entities across yet unknown domains. The nonfunctional qualities regarding execution and evolution of the SYMBOCONN framework either stem from the targeted application domains or are derived from existing recommendation systems.

Since domains with high-level security requirements are out of the scope of this dissertation, nonfunctional requirements like *reliability, availability, security* or *safety* are not discussed here.

Independence From Concrete Application Domains The developed framework must support all basic machine learning capabilities, which should be applicable to any kind of knowledge – independent of the form of its representation. Therefore, the machine learning system must be able to process generic and complex data structures such as sequences of graph nodes.

More than it is required of domain engineering, the SYMBOCONN framework has to support several domains, that is, it must comply with nonfunctional requirements coming from different domains as well as with different forms of knowledge representation that may even change over time. For example, prediction of navigations and prediction of time series are two completely different application areas. The first is often represented by unstructured and human-understandable text documents, while the second is a time-indexed and vector-valued series of numeric values[6]. Therefore, the SYMBOCONN framework uses service adapters, which map the relevant knowledge fragments onto node representations that can be composed to sequences and then processed by the machine learning engine.

Robustness and Fault Tolerance A system is robust if it continues to operate despite abnormalities in input, calculations, etc.. The SYMBOCONN framework must be robust, since a machine learning system that is trained by example is always confronted with empirical datasets consisting of possibly uncertain or inconsistent training examples. From the perspective of statistics, a statistical test is robust if it still performs well in case its assumptions are violated; for example, if the true data distribution (e.g. *exponential*) is different from the assumed one (e.g. *normal*). In terms of connectionist systems, high fault tolerance is often called *graceful degradation* [BA91]. For example, distorted, incomplete or erroneous input data must not cause a total failure of the inference capability.

Machine learning of software development activities requires an especially high degree of robustness and fault tolerance because software engineers produce error-afflicted or incomplete work products during the many phases of a software project. For example, the *analysis object model* of a system does not specify all attributes and operations required for the final implementation. Still, the machine learning system should be able to learn structures from these incomplete artifacts.

In fact, it should even be able to learn from inconsistent artifacts. For instance, design patterns are often used in a wrong way by beginners. When a class diagram is supposed to contain a directed association from class A to B, but the software developer draws an undirected association, the artifact is incomplete. If the association points from class B to A, then we have the case of an inconsistent artifact.

Response Time of Recommendation Finally, the system should offer ad-hoc recommendations, especially for navigation recommendation on artifacts such as text documents. The recommendation should be computed efficiently and displayed immediately to support interactivity with the user. Training of the system is not time-critical, because training activities can be scheduled offline.

---

[6]Realizations of time series are also stored as sequences of multi-represented objects (see section 3.2), because a time-indexed vector is structurally equal to a document representation vector.

3.2 Knowledge Model of SymboConn

The knowledge model of the SYMBOCONN framework considers both content and structure of the respective domain knowledge. To support heterogeneous domain knowledge, the content as well as the structure representation must be very flexible. Domain knowledge is stored in the form of different data types and may be unstructured, semi-structured or fully structured. Part of the core of the SYMBOCONN framework is a graph-based knowledge model, whose nodes represent the domain knowledge by means of multi-represented objects. We have chosen a graph of multi-represented nodes as knowledge model of the framework, because this is one of the most generic knowledge structures that can be implemented [BCER05]. Graphs with different types of nodes as well as links are commonly called *semantic graphs* [BCER05].

Abstract Knowledge Base The knowledge base of SYMBOCONN is defined as a graph $G = (V, E)$. Its nodes V stand for domain objects, that is V can be identified with the set of domain objects $\mathcal{D}$, and the edges E are directed or undirected associations between them, which may be labeled. There are different types of knowledge nodes with different kinds of content, depending on the represented domain object. Since the content of a knowledge node is freely composable, such a node can either provide a *rich representation*[7] [MG05, Kim02, MB00] of a domain object or a limited representation in the form of an atomic identifier, which can even be meaningless if no domain content is available. A rich representation consists of contents ranging from informal to formal characters [BSK05], as shown in figure 3.2. A generic graph node provides several basic attributes like *Name* and *Identifier*

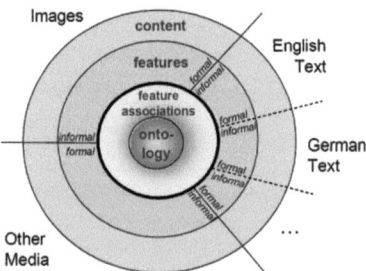

Figure 3.2: Layered model of a rich representation [BSK05], which can be based on an ontology defining the available features (attributes). In this model, associations between features are defined by the ontology and the declared features are filled with formal or informal contents illustrated by the outer model layers.

---

[7]"The collection of all these descriptors forms a rich representation of the object." [MG05]

as well as domain-specific attributes that store domain content. Nodes can be associated by *node sequences*, independent from their payload, which may differ from node to node.

Definition 3.2.1: Node Sequence
A node sequence is an ordered series of nodes $v_i \in V$ consisting of a *history* and *target* part $(v_1 v_2 \ldots v_k) \mapsto (v_{k+1} v_{k+2} \ldots v_{k+m})$. Such a sequence can be interpreted as a *word* over the alphabet of nodes V. Sequences of nodes are still meaningful even if when the single nodes do not contain any domain content. In this case, however, only their sequence structure is of interest.

An example of node sequences with multi-represented objects in the knowledge graph is depicted in figure 3.3.

Following the classification of knowledge representation methods in section 2.4, the SYMBOCONN knowledge model is a light-weight variant of a semantic network, since the relationships between the nodes do not have to be specified. When structure-sensitive applications such as change impact analysis [ZWDZ04, BA96, GR05] are treated, the link types are important and have to be included. When navigation recommendation is addressed, the links between different visited nodes are implicit or largely not available.

Nodes in the form of Multi-Represented Objects Data objects are becoming increasingly complex in data mining and machine learning applications [AKPS05]. *Multi-representation* is a concept to address the manifold contents carried by complex domain objects, that is a multi-represented object captures several aspects of a single domain object. This corresponds to the concept of aggregation in object-oriented modeling. The aspects are called *features* in the field of knowledge discovery, which is equivalent to *attribute* or *dimension*. An example is the encapsulation of all biometric features of a person like voice pattern, image and finger print, by a single multi-represented object.

Definition 3.2.2: Multi-Represented Object
Multi-represented (MR) objects take the role of nodes in the SYMBOCONN framework and are elements of a multi-dimensional feature space: $o = (f_1, \ldots, f_d) \in (F_1 \times \ldots \times F_d) =: F$, where F_i is a feature. Not all f_i need to be known, since modern machine learning algorithms are able to deal with incomplete data. Four feature types are supported:

- **Textual Feature.** Unstructured text that often appears in *description* attributes is supported in a content-based way by the framework. It is processed and learned based on a *vector space model* (see section 7.3) that is computed by counting keyterms per text unit.

- **Metric Feature.** By means of a mathematical metrics, distances can be computed upon metric feature values. This requires that the object features span a metric space equipped with a metrics $d : F \times F \to \mathbb{R}$, which fulfills the following conditions for $x, y, z \in F$:

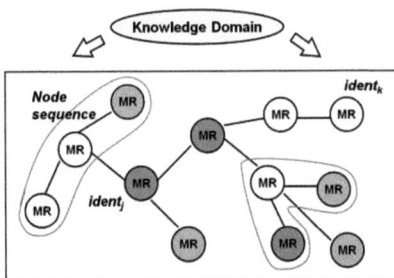

Figure 3.3: *Knowledge Graph* of *Multi-Represented* (MR) objects as introduced in definition 3.2.2. Multi-represented means that each object can be represented by a different set of features and their values, which is indicated by the different node shadings in the figure. Each node is identified by an unique label $ident_k$. Node sequences are ordered selections of nodes from the knowledge graph, thus they can be considered as subgraphs plus an order imposed by their identifiers.

1. $d(x, y) \geq 0$ (non-negativity)
2. $d(x, y) = 0 \Leftrightarrow x = y$
3. $d(x, y) = d(y, x)$ (symmetry)
4. $d(x, z) \leq d(x, y) + d(y, z)$ (triangle-inequality)

Condition 1. and 2. together guarantee the *positive definiteness* of the metrics.

- **Ordinal Feature**. The values of an ordinal feature F_i are ordered according to a total ordering, which means that any two elements from F are always comparable. Although it is not a strict order, a **partial order** $\preceq$ on a set F allows for comparing any two elements and $\preceq$ is characterized by the following conditions:

   1. $a \preceq a$, $\forall a \in F$ (reflexivity)
   2. $a \preceq b \land b \preceq c \rightarrow a \preceq c$, $\forall a, b, c \in F$ (transitivity)
   3. $a \preceq b \land b \preceq a \rightarrow a = b$, $\forall a, b \in F$ (anti-symmetry)

- **Categorical Feature**[8]. Since no order is given among categorical feature values, no metrics can be defined upon them. An example in programming languages are **enumeration** attributes which represent categorical features. The type **Boolean** is a two-valued subtype of the categorical feature type.

The usage of feature types to describe complex objects is illustrated in table 3.1. Each feature type requires its own treatment with respect to its possible value range

---
[8]Another denomination for these features is *Nominal*.

MR-Object Type	Feature₁[Type]	Feature₂[Type]	Feature₃[Type]	...
Requirement	Name[Txt]	Description[Txt]	...	
Issue	Name[Txt]	Description[Txt]	IsResolved[Bool.]	Prio[Ordinal]
KPI	Name[Txt]	Indicator[Metric]		
Picture	Name[Txt]	Caption[Txt]	Histogram[Metric[]]	
Web page	URL[Txt]	Head[Txt]	Body[Txt]	
⋮				

Table 3.1: Meta model showing the multi-representation of objects by different features. Each row defines the feature set of an object, which can have a different number of features, depending on the object type. The available feature types are: *Textual*, *Metric*, *Boolean* (a subtype of *Categorical*), *Ordinal* and *Categorical*.

and the appropriate data normalization to be applied during data preprocessing. Metric features require other scaling and encoding functions than textual features, and so the straight forward data normalization done by many statistical and data mining tools is not possible when dealing with features of fundamentally different types.

A concrete multi-represented object according to table 3.1 above would be an *issue* (*"DBIssue_0001"*, *"Solving the bug in the ODBC database connection"*, *false, 8*). Another example of a multi-represented object is a *Key Performance Indicator* (KPI) like ("Overall Equipment Effectiveness", 83%), which is often used in industry. In order to meet the requirements of the knowledge representation in the application domain, multi-represented objects can be represented as a container of attribute-value pairs. The configuration of the used feature set can even change within the same discourse domain, to represent, for example, informal documents about functional requirements on the one hand and a more formal use case on the other hand.

Multi-represented objects can be employed for all types of knowledge and all domains in the SYMBOCONN framework, since they provide a rich representation for application domain objects. In case of navigation recommendation, an example for a rich representation is the inclusion of the content of a web page, instead of reducing the page to its symbolic URL address as unique identifier. The approach of rich representations opens up more information that can be incorporated into the machine learning process.

Inconsistency and *redundancy* are the hazards that may occur due to contradicting or overlapping feature values of different features, which describe the same object. Inconsistency has to be avoided in particular to successfully perform any type of inference. Neural network and fuzzy-based approaches cope best with inconsistent information; thus, the framework has a connectionist engine.

A further issue addressed by the SYMBOCONN framework is *comparability* [AKPS05] among the different value ranges of different features. Two features that are both metric might apparently hold completely different value ranges, such as the *duration* of a development activity and the *probability* of a change in a use case. The implemented data scaling procedures individually scale each feature to the value range $[1, 0]$.

Definition 3.2.3: Content-Based Rule
A content-based (CB) rule, as opposed to a fuzzy or symbolic rule, is a rule of the form "IF A THEN C", where A and C are node sequences, that is, $A, C \in V^*$. What is special in this case is that the contained entities $v \in V$ are (multi-) represented by their content(s) stemming from the application domain – as opposed to purely symbolic rule constituents. Therefore, content-based rule is *hybrid*, defining both content and structure in a very generic way.

$$CBRule \equiv (Antecedent \Rightarrow Consequent)$$
$$Antecedent \Rightarrow V^*$$
$$Consequent \Rightarrow V^*$$

Content-based rules are a superclass of type-0 rules from the Chomsky hierarchy, since they have the same structure $\alpha \to \beta$, $\alpha, \beta \in Var^*$ and expressivity, but further include domain contents carried by their nodes.

Definition 3.2.4: Training pattern, Training set
A *training pattern* for the neural network consists of two node sequences and is represented as a generic pair $<input \mapsto target>$, where $input, target \in V^+$. This sequential structure holds for every application domain, since unordered node sets can be ordered by a fixed order convention to become node sequences. An input or target sequence must not be empty, but may consist of only one node, as in case of classification, where the respective class is represented by a single target node (class label). The *training set* is the totality of all training patterns.

Definition 3.2.5: Network Training
During *network training*, the specified *functional mapping* between the input and target sequence is established for each training pattern. Since training is a numerical optimization (cf. section 4.4.3), the deviation between the expected output and the current output is iteratively minimized. This minimization requires an appropriate *supervised training algorithm* both for classification and prediction. Supervised means that there are target sequences for each input sequence, which determine the expected output. Therefore, all node sequences have to consist of input and target subsequences, which make up the training set.

Definition 3.2.6: Sequence Prediction
Sequence prediction is a mapping $P : V^* \to V^*$ from history sequences to target sequences of nodes. Again, the nodes stand for arbitrary multi-represented objects. The represented object features F_i are also allowed to be continuous $F_i \in \mathbb{R}$, $i = 1, \ldots, d$ as in the case of traditional time series prediction.

Definition 3.2.7: Operative Application
When *operatively applying* the system, the training phase has already been accomplished and input sequences that did not participate in the training set are fed into the system in order to be classified or to induce a sequence prediction.

3.3 Functional Model of SymboConn

The SYMBOCONN framework provides the domain-independent functions Network Training, Classification, Clustering, and Prediction as depicted in figure 3.4.

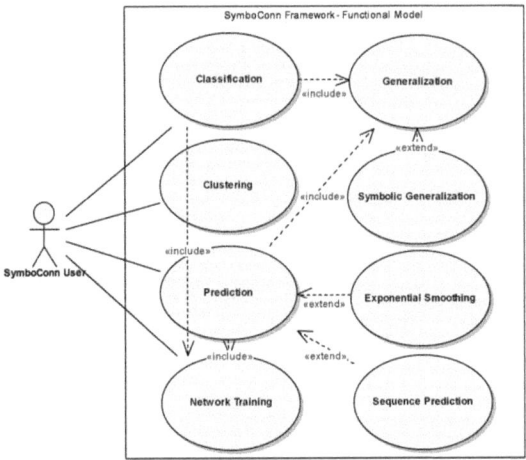

Figure 3.4: Use case diagram of the main functions offered to framework users such as experts in the respective application domain.

Classification as defined in Def. 2.5.1 assigns unknown objects to categories, after the classifier has been trained on labeled objects.

Clustering as defined in Def. 2.5.2 groups objects together that are similar according to a certain distance measure and is of minor interest for the recommendation framework. Clustering operates on the given data set only, without using a training set, since no further objects are produced or to be assessed.

Prediction (see Def. 2.5.3) and its variant Sequence Prediction (see Def. 3.2.6) enable the forecast of numerical variables (e.g. time seriesprediction) and the recommendation of a sequence of domain objects respectively. Viewed from the symbolic perspective, Classification and Prediction require a generalization capability of Level 3.

The use case Symbolic Generalization is an extension of the use case Generalization and was precisely described by the different symbolic transformations of an input structure to a target structure, which were assigned to the levels of the generalization hierarchy defined in section 3.1.1.2. To be useful for various application purposes, the classification and prediction functionality requires a high generalization capability, since objects that are not contained in the training set are to be classified and sequences of domain objects or numerical values are to be predicted. In analogy to the symbolic generalization hierarchy of section 3.1.1.2, at least Level 3 generalization is needed in this case.

Exponential Smoothing is a traditional statistical prediction technique, which is subsumed[9] by the SYMBOCONN machine learning engine.

Successful Network Training as defined in Def. 3.2.5 is the precondition for providing good Generalization, and therefore it is also required for Classification, Prediction, and their extensions.

Figure 3.5 shows the generic training phase and operative application of the framework as an activity diagram. The main activities during training are data preprocessing, setting up the training set, and executing the training algorithm. During the operative application, a sequence of input nodes is transformed to numerical input patterns, which are fed into the trained machine learning engine. Then, a sequence of output nodes that is of length one for classification and of arbitrary length for sequence prediction is generated. In case of Classification, only the class label is predicted, and in case of Prediction, the output represents the future development of a time series, for example, where the time index corresponds with the number of output nodes. The dynamical model divided into a training and an application phase

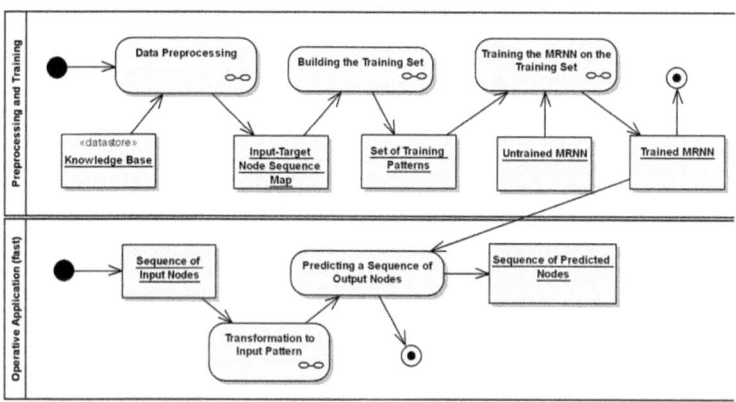

Figure 3.5: Activity diagram showing the training phase and the operative application defined by Def. 3.2.5 as upper and lower swimlane.

as shown in figure 3.5 covers the use cases Classification, Prediction and their extensions, which are typically expected from a machine learning system. Combined with the multi-represented knowledge nodes that can be composed to meaningful node sequences in the respective domain, a variety of possible applications arises.

---
[9] For the configuration of the SYMBOCONN engine to provide exponential smoothing, see section 8.3.4.

The degree of intelligence of a machine learning system is mainly characterized by its ability to generalize acquired knowledge. The use case Generalization addresses the abstract functional requirement *generalization capability*, which can be interpreted from a symbolic and a statistical point of view. In statistics, the term *generalization* is not very firmly established; instead, the corresponding concept of *extrapolation* is used for assessing a statistical process beyond its asserted scope. An example are countings of votes, where the in-advance estimation of the final election result is achieved by extrapolation of representative sample measurements. An extrapolation method for time series prediction is exponential smoothing shown as use case in figure 3.4, which is used when no formation rule or systematics such as a linear or periodic trend can be discovered in the time series. Exponential smoothing is elaborated on in chapter 8 (Time Series Prediction).

3.4 Framework Architecture

The SYMBOCONN framework is a knowledge-based system that supports knowledge acquisition and discovery activities in a specific target domain like navigation recommendation and software development. It is not a knowledge-based system in the traditional sense that aims at extending and querying knowledge bases. Instead, SYMBOCONN is a methodology for performing automatic knowledge acquisition without making domain knowledge explicit[10] – it is made applicable. Since software development is a knowledge acquisition activity, it is automatically supported by the framework.

The overall architecture of our approach is shown in figure 3.6. The framework layer contains the SYMBOCONN framework, which is the basis for the service layer. The service layer potentially provides several different domain-specific or domain-independent services, three of which are elaborated in this dissertation. These are Classification, Sequence Prediction, and Time Series Prediction. The specific services house several applications such as Navigation Recommendation or Stock Price Prediction, which are comprised by the application layer. Assessing the impact of artifact changes under consideration of their structural neighborhood within the knowledge graph is another application of the SYMBOCONN framework, called Change Impact Analysis.

The SYMBOCONN framework is divided into four major non-hierarchical subsystems called ConnectionistCore, KnowledgeConnector, Control, and FrontEnd that cover the core functionality, and one minor subsystem called Util. Figure 3.7 shows the system decomposition of the SYMBOCONN framework into these subsystems. The non-hierarchical decomposition of the framework was chosen to decouple the Machine Learning Engine from the knowledge representation and the control flow, which is strongly required to provide domain independence. The

---

[10]Domain knowledge could be elicited from a trained neural network by a reverse-engineering approach [ZJC03, MWM03, UK95]. Thereby, the incorporated knowledge is made explicit by a transformation into fuzzy rules.

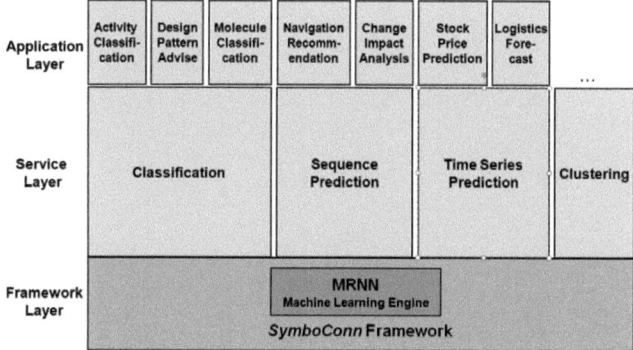

Figure 3.6: Three-layered application architecture of the SYMBOCONN framework with flexible MRNN Machine Learning Engine as foundation for different domains which in turn house several applications. Both the domain and the application layer are extensible.

framework architecture follows the *model-view-control* architectural pattern.

The model component of the framework is the ConnectionistCore subsystem that contains the Machine Learning Engine, which is again decomposed into three layers that consist of computational units called NeuronRecords. The utility subsystem Util provides preprocessing functionality like data scaling and data transformations, linear algebra computations (for example an implementation of the Principal Component Analysis) (PCA), and input/output functionality. The utility package also contains the database connectivity and basic reporting functions via graphical charts.

The Control subsystem in figure 3.7 is responsible for the global control flow of all provided functions shown in figure 3.4, such as training the currently chosen neural network or calling the prediction function on the trained network. The neural network is trained by a separate TrainingThread, which is executed concurrently with the main application. This thread is in turn controlled by the so-called TrainingAgent, another thread responsible for dynamically adjusting the training parameters like *learning rate* or *momentum*. Multithreading is necessary because training a neural network is an often tedious process that needs to be observed and controlled either manually or automatically by a software agent, whose role is taken by the TrainingAgent implementation in this case.

Observers like the standard graphical user interface can register at the MetaController in order to be notified about the most important events such as the training progress or the current system state. The most important framework functions can be accessed externally through a ControlInterface.

The ControlLogic subsystem is part of the Control subsystem and provides a *facade* to encapsulate all public services that are accessible from outside. The de-

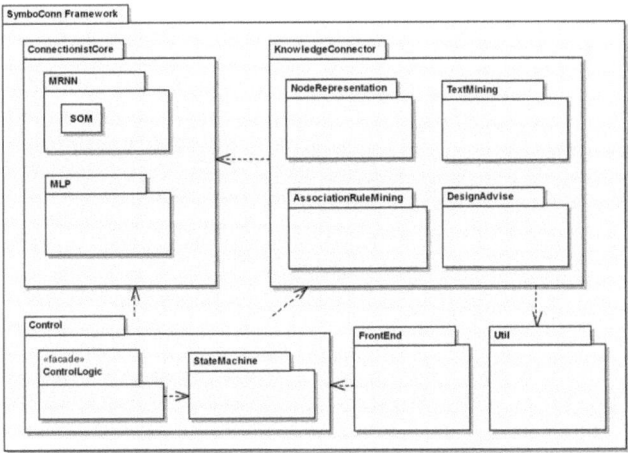

Figure 3.7: System decomposition of the SYMBOCONN framework as UML component diagram. The framework is decomposed into the four major subsystems ConnectionistCore, KnowledgeConnector, Control, and FrontEnd. Util is a minor subsystem responsible for database access and reporting.

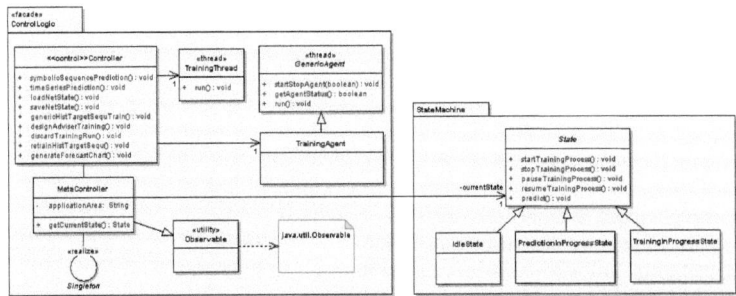

Figure 3.8: Control subsystem containing the ControlLogic subsystem, which is a facade for the services provided by Control, as well as the StateMachine subsystem.

tailed design of the ControlLogic is shown in figure 3.8. State transitions within the subsystem are based on a state machine that delegates function calls to the responsible components depending on the current state of the SYMBOCONN framework. This way, the same abstract function calls can result in different domain-dependent processes. For example, when the prediction functionality is called via the ControlLogic facade, the expected result depends on the concrete application of the target domain in terms of the application architecture in figure 3.6. In case of time series prediction, the final output is a sequence of numerical values, while for navigation recommendation, the output represents a sequence of recommended knowledge nodes such as documents. In any case, the predicted sequences consist of NodeRepresent objects.

The KnowledgeConnector subsystem in figure 3.7 connects the different domain-specific knowledge representations and controls the creation of numeric training patterns from abstract and domain-independent node sequences. Figure 3.9 shows a more detailed design. Encoding and decoding of symbolic data is delegated by

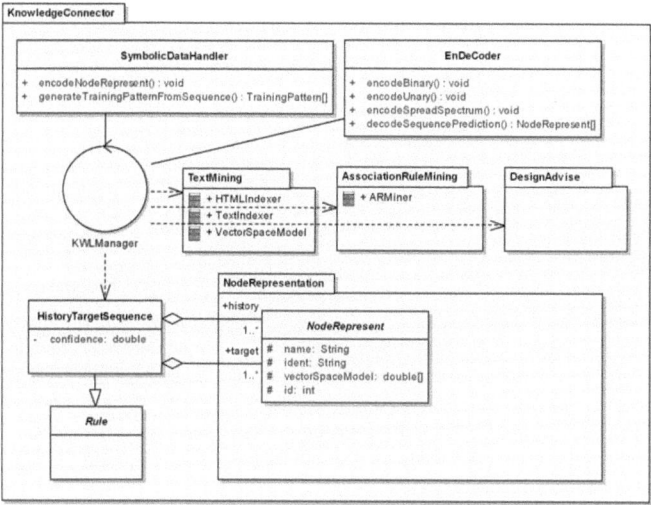

Figure 3.9: The KnowledgeConnector subsystem is crucial for the knowledge representation in SYMBOCONN, since it enables the processing of symbolic and non-symbolic information. Furthermore, it contains several supplemental subsystems for text mining, association rule mining, and design pattern advise.

the control object KWLBaseConnector to the realizing classes like EnDeCoder or SymbolicDataHandler. The KnowledgeConnector component principally enables the Machine Learning Engine to learn heterogeneous knowledge structures (sequences or trees) with their node contents. Furthermore, it contains the subpackages NodeRepresentation, TextMining, AssociationRuleMining, and DesignAdvise.

The subsystem NodeRepresentation in figure 3.9 provides the abstract representation of a knowledge node, which is a single constituent of a node sequence. The superclass NodeRepresent is the basic unit of information processed by the neural network. Each domain extends the abstract node definition by its specific knowledge representation. For instance, the service Navigation Recommendation requires a text unit representation, which holds the textual content of documents in a machine-processable form (DocumentRepresent). Implementation inheritance is used to integrate the domain-specific knowledge representations. MultiRepresentedObject is the abstraction of a multi-represented object as defined in section 3.2.

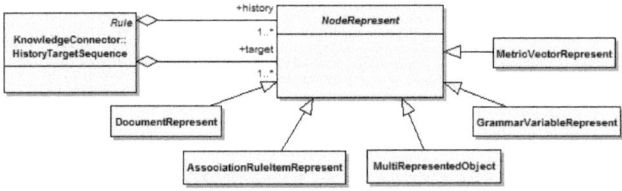

Figure 3.10: *NodeRepresentation* subsystem using implementation inheritance to integrate the domain-specific knowledge representation.

The subsystem TextMining provides a handle for processing knowledge nodes that contain unstructured text (cf. section 3.2), for example, a text document as part of a document base. The significance of a certain keyterm can be analyzed via different metrics from text mining like the *Term Frequency - Inverse Document Frequency* (TF-IDF). Related to mining of raw text, the subsystem AssociationRuleMining is responsible for discovering co-occurring keyterms in a text base. Thus, associated concepts lead to association rules, which potentially serve to link related documents in terms of their content.

The DesignAdvise subsystem shown in figure 3.7 is a supplemental and domain-specific package that defines several software design patterns in machine processable form; that is, patterns are transformed into typed grammar rules, which are considered in section 6.3. Additionally, the DesignAdvise subsystem is responsible for the rule-based recognition of design patterns in class diagrams that are represented in XMI language.

The KWLBaseManager control object offers functions that parse externally defined regular, context-free or context-sensitive rules to incorporate structured prior knowledge (class Rule). These are directly learned by the framework engine in the form $A_1 \ldots A_k \to B_1 \ldots B_n$, $A_i, B_j \in (\Sigma \cup V)$ as defined in section 3.2.

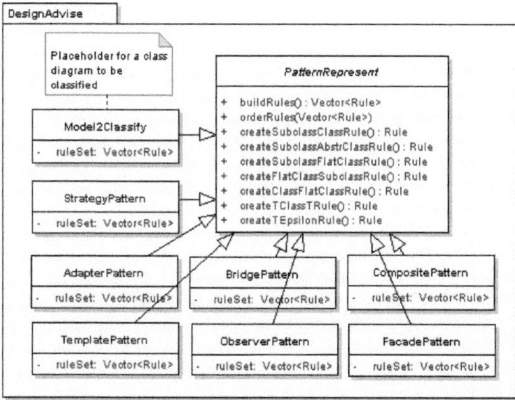

Figure 3.11: DesignAdvise subsystem that defines several software design patterns by a rule-based representation.

The ConnectionistCore subsystem, whose detailed design is shown in figure 3.12, provides the implementation of the framework engine and consists of two self-contained types of neural networks:

- The *Modular Recurrent Neural Network* (MRNN) as central class of the MRNN subsystem is the most modern and universal network in the SYMBOCONN framework, which resembles the behavior of a *dynamic system* as defined in section 4.4.1. The recurrent network is a composition of Neuron-Records that form the HiddenStateLayer, denoted by S in section 4.4.1. The HistoryTargetSequence of the KnowledgeConnector subsystem (see figure 3.7) is the central knowledge structure that is converted to a training pattern and finally processed by the MRNN.

The Self-Organizing Map (SOM) clusters objects into similar groups, which can be employed for learning and recognizing the type of user behavior, for example.

- The *Multilayer Perceptron* (MLP) is a standard feed-forward network with an arbitrary number of hidden layers. As predecessor of the MRNN, the MLP subsystem represents a separate implementation of a neural network that can be used as an alternative framework engine. It is trained by a conventional backpropagation algorithm (without backpropagation through time) and is composed of NeuronLayers which in turn are composed of Neurons. The MLP can be used both for classification and prediction tasks and might be easier to train on traditional applications, such as image recognition or time series prediction, than the MRNN.

MACHINE LEARNING CONCEPTS OF SYMBOCONN

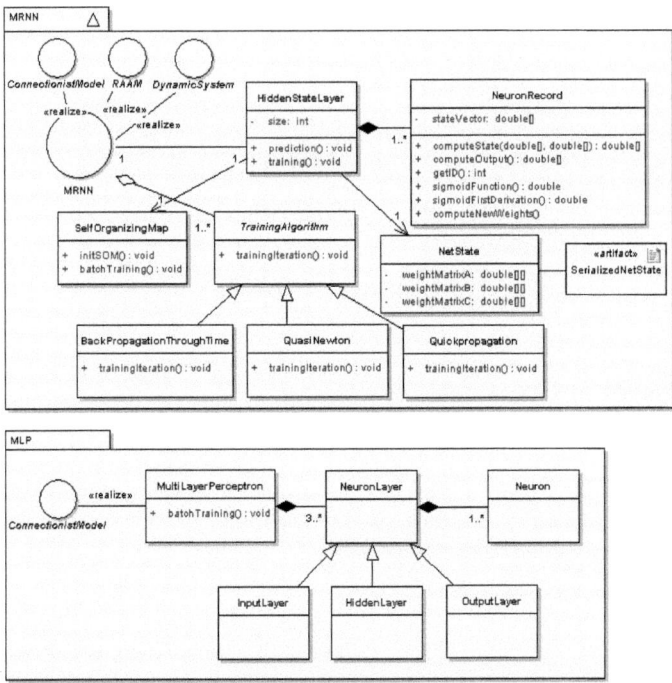

Figure 3.12: The ConnectionistCore subsystem contains all connectionist components offered by the SYMBOCONN framework layer.

Only a few implementations of advanced neural networks are freely available. Due to the complexity of implementation and application, there are mainly very simple neural network algorithms on the market for data mining and machine learning, like those of Microsoft [Mic05].

The FrontEnd subsystem basically offers supervision functionality for the semi-automatic training of the neural network engine. The training process can be intervened by the actor in real-time in order to adjust the learning rate, or to stop training when the model error starts to rise again, for example. The subsystem components are shown in figure 3.13. The MainGUI works as an observer of the control objects MetaController and Controller from the subsystems ControlLogic and Control following the observer pattern. Thus, the view is updated by notification each time a significant event occurs within the control objects.

MACHINE LEARNING CONCEPTS OF SYMBOCONN 73

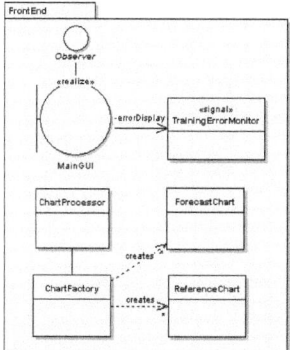

Figure 3.13: FrontEnd subsystem implementing the user front end that provides access to the learning and recommendation functionality.

SYMBOCONN uses four external Commercial-off-the-Shelf (COTS) components to realize text indexing, graphical output, XML processing, and persistence, namely APACHELUCENE, JFREECHART, JDOM, and MYSQL. Figure 3.14 shows the mapping of the COTS components to the existing subsystems of the framework.

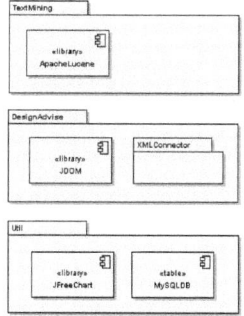

Figure 3.14: External COTS components are contained in the SYMBOCONN subsystems TextMining, DesignAdvise, and Util.

Chapter 4
Machine Learning and the Framework Engine

In the previous chapters, we have presented the motivation for a symbolic-connectionist machine learning framework and introduced its overall architecture.

In this chapter, we present the fundamentals of neural networks together with several typical network types. We then elaborate on the meaning of information theory to machine learning, which leads us to the rationale for employing a neural network as the machine learning engine of SYMBOCONN. Finally, we describe the structure of the newly developed machine learning engine and its training algorithm in detail.

Connectionist machine learning as a variant of machine learning in general is mainly characterized by its heuristic training algorithms and by learning from observations. A generic and intuitive definition of connectionist learning might be the following: learning takes place if the system is able to recognize *regularities* or *patterns* in a set of examples and to separate them from the *irregularities*. The regularities are either extracted in form of patterns, statistical or symbolic rules, or they are implicitly acquired by a connectionist system, which incorporates and directly applies them without being rendered explicit.

This chapter begins with a definition of connectionist models and gives an overview of typical neural networks. Subsequently, the meaning of the concepts (connectionist) *learning* and *information* is formatively described both from a practical and a theoretical perspective. Finally, the design and training algorithm of the MRNN framework engine are explained in detail.

4.1 Fundamentals of Neural Networks

Understanding the origin of artificial neural networks helps to understand modern connectionist models, which are much more powerful than the first neural structures developed by McCulloch and Pitt. Especially the training algorithms and the network topologies have made significant advances to overcome computational barriers, which earlier had prevented connectionist systems from solving nonlinear problems, for example.

4.1.1 History of Neural Networks

The research area of neural networks did not originally emanate from classical computer science or its predecessors. Artificial neural networks were inspired by the human brain and were mostly created by cognitive scientists and neurophysiologists to *simulate* the brain structure as well as to gain experience about human knowledge representation and processing. Neural networks go back to the year 1943, when McCulloch and Pitt developed the *McCulloch-Pitt-Cell* [MP43], the first neural network to realize a logical *NAND-gate*. This neuron model is a threshold-based unit that processes inhibitory and stimulating *binary* input signals $i_1, \ldots, i_n$ and $x_1, \ldots, x_n$. If the sum of all stimulating input signals $\sum_{i=1}^{n} x_i$ exceeds a given threshold, then the McCulloch-Pitt-Cell outputs a "1". This model is biologically motivated by the human brain, where the signal transition occurs at the synapses if the stimuli propagated from the dendrites are high enough.

In 1949, Donald Hebb formulated a hypothesis concerning the learning process in nervous systems, called the *Hebb learning rule*. A fundamental observation behind this rule was that connections between human neurocytes – a nerve cell of any kind – are strengthened when they are repeatedly activated. Hebb's finding was followed up by the early rise of connectionism in the years from about 1955 until 1969. The development of the first artificial neural networks and Hebb's findings resulted in the prominent *perceptron model* of Frank Rosenblatt in 1962.

Marvin Minsky and Seymour Papert showed in 1969 that one-layered perceptrons cannot model a logical XOR function, since the XOR-problem is not linearly separable. Thus, a whole class of nonlinear problems could not be solved at this time, which led to a general decline of the interest in connectionist systems. In the calm years from 1969 till 1985, several further connectionist models were developed, such as those of Kohonen (unsupervised training, Kohonen network) in 1972 and of *Hopfield* (auto-associative memory) in 1982.

When David E. Rumelhart, Geoffrey E. Hinton and Ronald J. Williams published their work on the *backpropagation algorithm* based on gradient descent to train neural networks with arbitrarily many layers in 1986 [RHW86], Minsky's XOR-problem from 1969 was finally solved. This milestone in connectionist research gave rise to a renaissance of research and application of neural networks that started in the middle of the 1980s and has not ceased until today. At the beginning of this era, Charles Rosenberg demonstrated the first neural network for *speech synthesis* called *NETtalk*, which was published in his paper *"Parallel Networks that Learn to Pronounce English Text"* in 1987 [SR87]. The developed three-layered feed-forward network was trained on a corpus of 20,000 English words together with their correct phonemes. The training process was captured on an audio file[1],

---
[1] *http://www.cnl.salk.edu/ParallelNetsPronounce/nettalk.mp3*

which reminds us of a small child learning to pronounce its first phrases.
Recent research focuses on recurrent neural networks and neuro-fuzzy systems. This has led to the emerging discipline of *computational intelligence*, which comprises all techniques that aim at creating intelligent behavior based on numerical methods.

4.1.2 Feed-Forward Neural Networks

Definition 4.1.1: Feed-Forward Neural Network
A neural network is a composition of atomic units – the *neurons*. Neurons are simple information processors, which possess a limited computation capability that is characterized by a rule like a weighted sum for combining the input signals and an activation rule for computing an output signal – usually by an activation function. These neurons are interconnected within a collective network, which is the carrier for the forward and backward signal propagation from the input layer through the hidden layer(s) to the target layer. The network topology defines which neurons are connected to each other, if there are recurrent connections, and how many neurons are contained in a layer.

This definition of connecting layers and neurons motivates the nomenclature *Connectionism* in contrast to *Symbolism*. A typical model of a feed-forward neural network is depicted in figure 4.1. An impressive feature of neural networks traces

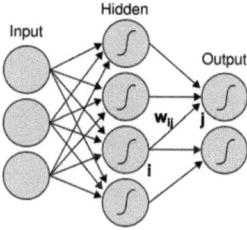

Figure 4.1: Example of a Multilayer Perceptron (MLP) with input, hidden, and output layer consisting of 3, 4, and 2 neurons. The feed-forward topology only allows a forward information flow through the network. The S-shaped pictogram symbolizes the sigmoid activation function in each neuron of the hidden and output layer. Neurons of different layers are connected by weights w_{ij}.

back to their connectionist structure. Although single network neurons have only a very limited computation capability, the neural network as an aggregation of many of those interconnected units is able to solve complex tasks.

In modern neural network architectures, the neurons play a subordinate role, since they do not have to be modeled explicitly. The connections between the neurons in the input and hidden layer of the network in figure 4.1 is now usually represented by a weight matrix $(W_{ij})_{i,j \in \mathbb{N}}$. An external input is fed into the input layer as a real-valued vector $\vec{x}$, which is propagated forward through the network weights.

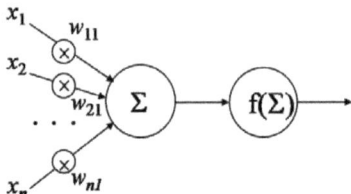

Figure 4.2: Dynamic model of the basic signal processing by a single neuron. Σ is the weighted sum of all input signals propagated through the weighted connections to a single neuron, f is a linear or nonlinear *activation function*, applied to this weighted sum ($f(\Sigma)$).

Definition 4.1.2: Network Activation, Activation Function
The *activation function* f of a neuron is applied to the weighted sum $\sum w_{ij} x_i$ of all incoming signals x_i in order to activate the neuron, which means to produce an *activation* or an activated state. The activation function may be linear or nonlinear, but for higher expressivity and computational power, f is often chosen to be nonlinear, for example $f(x) = \tanh(x)$ or as sigmoid function $f(x) = \frac{1}{1+\exp(-x)}$.

4.1.3 Further Types of Neural Networks

Artificial neural networks are computational models based on mostly numeric algorithms for training and application. Here, only the most important and well-known network types are mentioned in order to compare them with the proprietary *Modular Recurrent Neural Network* (MRNN) used as framework engine. The existing classes of neural networks technically vary in the activation functions, the training algorithms, the type of data to be processed, as well as in the network topology including the employed connectivity. Furthermore, they can be distinguished by their application purpose, which might be data compression, clustering, classification (with the variants pattern recognition and outlier detection), prediction, or simulation.

Feed-Forward Neural Network, Multilayer Perceptron   This network type was already discussed in the previous section.

Recursive Auto-Associative Memory (RAAM)   Another important type of neural network for structure processing is the *Recursive Auto-Associative Memory*, which is extensively elaborated upon in section 5.5.

Recurrent Neural Networks (RNN) Recurrent neural networks are a subclass of neural networks characterized by recurrent connections between their units [Gra08]. These typically form a directed cycle, while common feed-forward networks do not allow any cycles. The behavior of RNNs is usually modeled and analyzed by dynamical systems theory [MWH01, Str94].

The **Jordan network** [CSSM89] is one of the first recurrent networks. Recurrent networks are especially used to learn sequences, for example, when words of a formal language represented as sequences of symbols need to be processed. Thus, the signals are not only sent in forward direction but also fed back to the hidden or input layer by recurrent connections.

Simple Recurrent Networks (SRN), also called *Elman Networks*[2], feed the hidden activations back to the input layer. Thereby, the network contains a tempo-

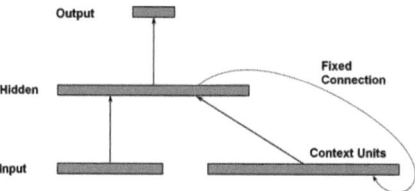

Figure 4.3: Schema of an Elman network with recurrent connections that feed the hidden activations back the input layer, which serves as context for the next external input (training example).

ral memory, which is required to learn context-free[3] grammars, for example. The network topology is illustrated by figure 4.3.

A **Hopfield network** is a recurrent and auto-associative connectionist model that works like a memory. There is no target pattern to be learned; only the input pattern is transformed into an internal representation, comparable to the one of RAAM networks. Trained patterns can be recalled even if they are incomplete or noisy. The Hopfield net is mainly characterized by its recurrent mode of operation. Given a certain fixed input pattern, the generated output pattern is repeatedly fed back as new input pattern until the network state converges. The state s_j of each

---

[2] According to their inventor *Jeffrey L. Elman*.
[3] The term *context* is overloaded here, since context in terms of the Chomsky hierarchy means even more than in the notion of *context units*. Context-sensitive grammars are far more difficult to learn.

network unit is updated by

$$net_j = \sum_{i=1}^{n} s_i w_{ij} \qquad (4.1)$$

$$s_j = \begin{cases} +1, & if\ net_j \geq 0 \\ -1, & if\ net_j < 0 \end{cases} \qquad (4.2)$$

Figure 4.4 shows a small exemplary Hopfield network. No conventional training

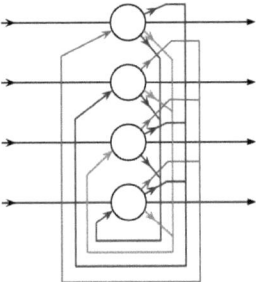

Figure 4.4: Hopfield network consisting of four fully interconnected units without reflexive connections. For each component of the input vector $\vec{x}$, illustrated by the horizontal arrows from left to right, there is a unit in the Hopfield network. (From Wikimedia Commons, Image copyright: GNU Free Documentation License)

takes place in Hopfield networks, since the weight matrix W required to store an input pattern is directly determined from the input vector $\vec{x}$:

$$W = \vec{x}^T \vec{x}$$

During operation, only one unit is updated at each adaption step, which operates on the single weight matrix W.

Self-Organizing Feature Maps (SOM) This type of a neural network is also known as *Kohonen network* and is typically used for data clustering. It serves for learning and internally representing a set of numeric feature vectors. The input data space is aggregated by a set of so-called *prototypes* that are representatives of different aspects of the training set [Cal03]. Thus, the main purpose of Kohonen networks is to cluster and bundle the input data (cluster analysis). This is done automatically by an unsupervised learning algorithm, which does not require a parameter specifying the number of supposed data groups in advance.

Radial Basis Function Networks (RBF) The class of Radial Basis Function networks can be used to solve the same problems as feed-forward networks trained by backpropagation. Like conventional feed-forward networks, they are especially capable of approximating any mathematical function.

$$net_j = \|\vec{x} - \vec{w}_j\|_p$$
$$= [\sum_{i=1}^{n}(x_i - w_{ij})^p]^{1/p}, \quad j = 1, \ldots, m \quad (4.3)$$

The radial basis functions reside in the hidden layer of the network and are applied to the network input (formula 4.4), which is computed by formula 4.3. Usually, the norm is chosen as Euclidean distance ($p = 2$) and the radial basis function is realized by a Gaussian function.

$$\phi(r) = \exp(-r \cdot net_j^2) \quad (4.4)$$

As opposed to the first mapping between input and hidden layer, the mapping from

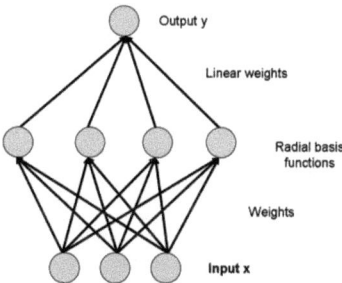

Figure 4.5: Exemplary topology of a Radial Basis Function network consisting of three layers.

the hidden to the output layer is linear. The different layers are shown in figure 4.5.

4.2 Neural Networks between Computational Intelligence and Information Theory

In order to determine a machine learning engine that best fulfills the requirements for a generic and domain-independent machine learning framework, this section touches upon several areas of expertise like *information theory* and *statistics* that are highly relevant for connectionist and symbolic machine learning.

Neural networks that use supervised or unsupervised training algorithms[4] belong to the field of machine learning employed by the field of computational intelligence. *Computational intelligence* is a recent subarea of artificial intelligence consisting of artificial neural networks, neuro-fuzzy systems, and evolutionary computing (e.g. genetic algorithms), which relies on optimization algorithms and fuzzy knowledge representation. Neuro-fuzzy-systems are hybrids of neural networks and fuzzy rules, which can be interpreted as a system of fuzzy rules generated by neural learning of training data. The main concepts of computational intelligence are learning (optimization), adaptation, and evolution.

Neural networks provide an algorithmic implementation of *adaptivity*, since they can adapt their behavior according to changes in the application domain, which become manifest in the training set. Furthermore, neural networks as *non-parametric models* do not follow any predetermined data distribution, as shall be explained in section 4.3. Thus, the adaption of the network weights is *emergent*, that is, induced by the respective environment. Evolution, which is not covered by SYMBOCONN, is a principle of genetic algorithms and is a generic term for mechanisms such as reproduction, mutation, recombination, and natural selection. Genetic algorithms are related to neural networks since they can be used to automatically determine a network topology that best fits the domain problem to be learned.

When building a connectionist model to solve a classification or prediction problem, the discipline of information theory is involved. This is due to the questions of knowledge representation[5] and input-output encoding, which both play important roles in the model building process. In section 4.2, the information content of the chosen representation is especially considered, which can be measured in *Shannon* indicating the minimal number of bits required to encode a message (detailed in section 4.2).

Figure 4.6 illustrates the functionalities and relationships of neural networks regarding computational intelligence, information theory, and machine learning in general. It is proven that neural networks with one hidden layer and nonlinear activation function (e.g. logistic function, *tanh*) are at least as powerful and expressive as a *Turing Machine* [SS92, AJ96]. Some argue that connectionism even enables a higher form of computability, due to its distributed knowledge representation that enables computational parallelism in the neurons [Bou97].

The further relationships of connectionist models to other topics shown in figure 4.6 are explained in the following.

Connectionist Models and Data Compression The process of machine learning can inherently be seen as compression; at the same time, machine learning provides the functionality of *data compression*. Any auto-associative network can accomplish data compression tasks with an arbitrary compression rate, which im-

---

[4]The class of *Reinforcement Learning* (RL) algorithms is possible as well, but is of minor importance for connectionist models. Reinforcement Learning is often used to teach autonomous agents to perform optimal actions.
[5]As described in section 2.4.

CHAPTER 4. MACHINE LEARNING AND THE FRAMEWORK ENGINE 83

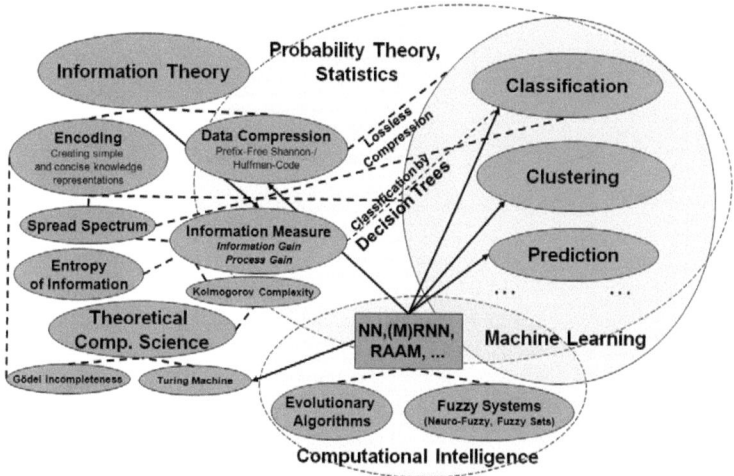

Figure 4.6: Machine learning, information theory, computational intelligence, and their interrelations. The solid line stands for a provided functionality, while the dotted line indicates a given dependency between different knowledge areas (in form or content). (M)RNN stands for *(Modular) Recurrent Neural Network* and RAAM means *Recursive Auto-Associative Memory*, which is a special neural network for processing of tree-structured data.

plies the degree of data loss. Figure 4.7 shows an appropriate connectionist setup for the compression of an arbitrary feature vector. A multi-layer perceptron (MLP)

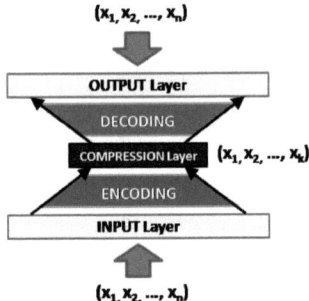

Figure 4.7: *Auto-associative network* that encodes and decodes a given feature vector $(x_1, x_2, \ldots, x_n)$. The compressed version $(x_1, x_2, \ldots, x_k)$, $k < n$, is pending at the hidden layer, which is called *compression layer* here.

with one hidden layer as well as identical input and output layer is able to compress numerical data by auto-association. The data compression is enforced by mapping the input vector onto a copy of itself at the output (target) layer, while using a lower dimensionality for the hidden (compression) layer. Associating a vector with a copy of itself is called auto-association; there is a whole class of auto-associative neural networks. The auto-associative mapping can be trained by a backpropagation algorithm as usual. After completion of the training process, the *activation* of the hidden layer makes up the compressed representation of the original input vector.

A special form of an auto-associative network that is able to represent and *compress structured data* is the *Recursive Auto-Associative Memory* (RAAM). RAAMs create a fixed-length representation of tree structures with arbitrary branching factors and thus perform (lossy) data compression (for further details see section 5.5).

Decision Trees *Decision trees* are a popular method to classify metric or categorical data. They achieve a comparatively high classification accuracy and the result is easier to interpret than in most other classification methods, but they tend to *overfitting* and require many training examples. In software engineering, decision trees have been used for software decision analysis and support [Tre07], for classifying incomplete software project data [TCL06], or for classifying the expected project risk [HLC06].

In terms of *classification* by decision trees, the *Information Gain* (IG) is a measure or information criterion indicating the pureness (*purity measure*) of a set of training objects concerning their membership with respect to the classes $C =$

$\{C_1, \ldots, C_r\}$. It is depicted as subtitle of the bubble *Information Measure* in figure 4.6 and can be computed by means of the entropy formally defined as follows.

Definition 4.2.1: Entropy and Information Gain

$$H(X) := -\sum_{i=1}^{n} \mathbb{P}(X = z_i) \cdot \log_2 \mathbb{P}(X = z_i)$$
$$= -\sum_{i=1}^{n} p_i \cdot \log_2 p_i \quad [\frac{bit}{symbol}]$$
(4.5)

$$IG(X) = H(Y) - H(Y|X)$$
$$= H(Y) - \sum_{x \in X} \mathbb{P}(x) \cdot H(Y|X = x)$$
(4.6)

The information gain $IG(X)$ is interpreted as the entropy reduction after the split

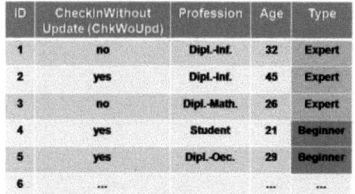
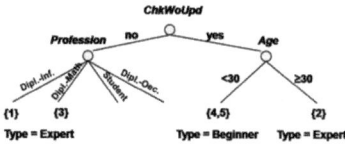

Figure 4.8: Exemplary data table and corresponding decision tree for the classification of software developers according to the types *beginner* and *expert*. The tree is not optimized and the value space of the attribute *Age* is arbitrarily partitioned by the threshold 30.

by the random variable X, which implies that the information gain is complementary to the entropy in some respects. $H(Y|X)$ is the conditional entropy after the split by a discrete attribute X, which takes m different values and thus partitions the training set into m subsets. Figure 4.8 gives an exemplary decision tree together with the underlying dataset.

An optimal decision tree does not come out of nothing – in general it takes exponential effort to determine an optimal decision tree according to a particular information criterion. A popular means for computing an optimal decision tree is the *C4.5 algorithm* [Qui93]. It is well-known that decision trees are susceptible to overfitting, which is the strong adaption to the training examples at the expense of the generalization performance. In section 6.3, both decision trees and the connectionist framework engine are employed to discover design patterns in class diagrams by classification.

From an information-theoretical perspective, machine learning can also be considered as *lossless compression*. This is because a compact description of a message or information leverages its systematics. The inherent systematics need to be understood and exploited to generate a shorter description than given by writing out the uncompressed information. This means that regularities within a message of length m enable a more concise encoding of length $m_c < m$. An example are words over the alphabet $\{0, 1\}$, like $\omega = 001001011101001111\ldots$, $|\omega| =: m$, which consist of arbitrary symbols at the first and second position but always contain a "1" at the third position, that is $\omega_{m \mod 3} = 1$. Such a regularity allows to encode the words by only $m_c = \frac{2}{3}m + c$ bits, where c is the constant number of bits to express the regularity *"Every third symbol is a "1""*, formally encoded by rule 4.7:

$$S \Rightarrow AB,$$
$$A \Rightarrow (0|1)^2 \qquad (4.7)$$
$$B \Rightarrow 1AB$$

By contrast, a random sequence with the probability distribution $\mathbb{P}(``0``) = \frac{1}{2} = \mathbb{P}(``1``)$ is not compressible, since the production rules do not hold in this case. Determining when to put a "1" requires representing each of the m symbols of the message.

Machine learning attempts to elicit the regularities of a training set and to exploit them. A totally random sequence of symbols cannot be learned in terms of generalization, but can only be memorized. Since such a sequence is completely *non-deterministic*, it holds the maximal entropy H_{max}. In case of words $\omega = 001001011101001111$ following rule 4.7, a neural network learns that every third symbol is a "1", while it is already sufficient that the majority of the training patterns conforms with the production rule.

Entropy of Information In chapter 2, the technical term *entropy* was introduced in the context of the symbol system hypothesis. By defining the entropy in the context of computational intelligence and machine learning, the relationship of symbol systems, information theory, and connectionist machine learning is conceptually established in this section.

Whenever the entropy of a natural or artificial space is high, then its degree of order is low, and thus the prospect of creating intelligent behavior by using informed search is low as well. Now, the antagonism between *learnability* and randomness is pointed out by defining the entropy from the original information theoretic and statistical perspective. Shannon [Sha48] defined the entropy as the information content carried by a discrete random variable X as a function[6] $X : \Omega \rightarrow Z$. The entropy $H(X)$ of the random variable can be considered as the mean information content of a symbol that stems from a fixed alphabet $Z = \{z_1, \ldots, z_n\}$.

---

[6]In probability theory Ω is the event space. A real-valued random variable ψ is a function $\psi : \Omega \rightarrow \mathbb{R}$.

The maximal entropy H_{max} is achieved when all symbols appear with the same probability $p_1 = \ldots = p_n = \frac{1}{n}$, meaning that they follow a *uniform distribution* of the underlying alphabet.

$$H^*(X) := \frac{H(X)}{H_{max}(X)} = -\sum_{i=1}^{n} p_i \cdot \frac{\log_2 p_i}{\log_2 n} \leq 1 \qquad (4.8)$$

$H^*(X)$ is the normalized variant of formula 4.5, which is computed by means of the maximal entropy $H_{max}(X)$. To compute the entropy of an information source X, which is formally represented by a random variable, the probability distribution over the alphabet Z must be known. $H(X)$ represents the *expected information content* of a symbol from the alphabet, which is the actual information content weighted by the frequency of its occurrence. If a single symbol with probability p_i actually appears, that is $X = z_i$, then it can be considered to be chosen from a hypothetical set of $\frac{1}{p_i}$ equally probable events. Thus, $\log_2(\frac{1}{p_i}) = -\log_2 p_i$ bits are required to distinguish between these possible events. The higher the probability of a symbol, the lower its corresponding information content.

The entropy H is used for the so-called *entropy encoding* and the required number of bits b to encode a word $\omega \in Z^*$ over the alphabet Z is calculated by means of formula 4.5. A word ω of length $|\omega| = m$ can be represented by $b = m \cdot H(X)$ bits approximately.

Definition 4.2.2: Kolmogorov Complexity
The Kolmogorov complexity (K-complexity) [Sch95] is an algorithmic complexity measure that is not computable but can only be approximated by an upper bound. The K-complexity can be interpreted as an inherent and absolute property of strings, which monotonically increases with the length $|\omega|$ of the string ω. $K(\omega)$ is the length (binary) of the shortest program p runnable on a universal Turing machine U, which outputs the string ω (writing ω on the band). The length of the program is measured by the number of bits needed to represent the program.

$$K(\omega) = \min_{p}\{|p| \,|\, U(p) = \omega\} \qquad (4.9)$$
$$K(\omega) \leq |\omega| + c \qquad (4.10)$$
$$\forall n \, \exists \omega : K(\omega) \geq n \qquad (4.11)$$

Formula 4.10 states that a program obviously does not have to be longer, except a constant, than the message to be encoded itself. Finally, formula 4.11 expresses the unboundedness of the K-complexity. The higher the randomness of a string ω, which results in lower periodicities and regularities, the harder it is to compress ω, and thus the higher is its Kolmogorov complexity $K(\omega)$. The K-complexity does not make any statements regarding the runtime complexity of the described program.

Both concepts from information theory, Shannon's entropy and the Kolmogorov complexity, measure the information content of a message represented as a string.

The entropy from Shannon quantifies the expected information content based on a probability distribution, while the K-complexity quantifies the actual information content of a given string by the length of a generating program.

Against this information-theoretical backdrop, the crucial question is whether a so-called *Minimum Description Language* (MDL) is appropriate for encoding information that is processed with a neural network. The MDL method encodes a message with the minimum number of bits b on average and therefore realizes the minimal entropy. Alternatively, there are further encoding methods such as *unary* or *binary encoding* that do not realize a minimal description of a given message, but show benefits in discriminating between different symbols of the alphabet Z. We will distinguish four different encoding schemas called

- *Unary Encoding*. The unary encoding approach assigns each symbol to be encoded to an orthogonal bit vector with a "1" at the ith component, $(0, 0, \ldots, 0, 1, 0, \ldots, 0)$.

- *Binary Encoding*. n symbols can be encoded by n vectors each consisting of $\lceil \log_2 n \rceil$ bits.

- *Entropy Encoding*. Encoding by a *Minimum Description Language* (MDL) such as *Huffmann Encoding* by prefix-free codes [Huf52].

- *Spread Spectrum Encoding*. A different information encoding that does not compress, but pumps up the given information, is called *spread spectrum encoding* and is typically used for multiplexing in signal transmission technology. The data spreading approach imposes artificial redundancy and requires a prior fundamental encoding such as unary or binary encoding. We have adapted the spread spectrum technique to improve the classification capabilities of the SYMBOCONN framework, but this mechanism can be integrated into many classification processes.

  The spread spectrum encoding does exactly the opposite of a minimum description language, since the binary representation of a piece of information is systematically blown up by well-defined redundancy. The information to encode is *spread* onto a multiple of its original length. This redundancy makes it less vulnerable to noise and transmission errors. The obtained *process gain* enables a higher classification accuracy, which is expressed as a relationship (solid line) between *information theory* and *classification* in figure 4.6. The detailed spread spectrum process is described in section 5.3.

- *ZIP Encoding*. On a higher abstraction level, ZIP encoding is an established lossless compression algorithm based on Huffman encoding and the LZ77 and LZ78 dictionary coders.

An illustration of these encoding variants is given by an exemplary look-up table 4.1. Regarding the network weights, we know that a *minimum description length* encoding is beneficial for the generalization capability of a neural network

CHAPTER 4. MACHINE LEARNING AND THE FRAMEWORK ENGINE   89

Term	Unary Encoding	Binary Encoding	Huffman Code	
"u"	(1,0,0,0,0)	(0,0,1)	(0,0)	
"v"	(0,1,0,0,0)	(0,1,0)	(0,1)	
"w"	(0,0,1,0,0)	(0,1,1)	(1,0,0)	
"x"	(0,0,0,1,0)	(1,0,0)	(1,0,1)	
"y"	(0,0,0,0,1)	(1,0,1)	(1,1)	
Term	Spread Spectrum Encoding		ZIP Encoding	...
"u"	(0,0,1,1,1,0)		(...)	
"v"	(0,1,0,1,0,1)		(...)	
"w"	(0,1,1,1,0,0)		(...)	
"x"	(1,0,0,0,1,1)		(...)	
"y"	(1,0,1,0,1,0)		(...)	

Table 4.1: Exemplary look-up table that contains different representations of symbols from an arbitrary alphabet. The Huffman encoding as a Minimum Description Language uses bit vectors of different lengths that reflect the frequencies of the symbols in their instantiation. The depicted spread spectrum codes were computed by an xor-operation of the binary codes with the spreading sequence $(0, 1)$ here.

[HvC93, HZ96]. For input information encoding on the other hand, less literature is available and less empirical facts are known. However, it is well-known that pattern recognition works better if the data holds low redundancy and consists of independent parts.

Since the primary goal of information encoding in this dissertation is not a maximal data compression but the creation of an optimal knowledge representation for neural information processing, the most compact representation does not have to be the best. Unary encoding is usually preferred with respect to binary encoding, due to the reduced error probability when distinguishing between different code words, which differ in less components if they are represented in unary form. In case of neural information processing, the neural network can specialize in the activation of only one output node. We will see that the output encoding plays an important role in neural information processing, as it directly effects the robustness and accuracy of the classification of domain objects represented by feature vectors, for example.

Having seen the classification of neural networks within the context of information theoretical, statistical and machine learning methods, we now analyze the advantages and disadvantages of a connectionist framework engine in detail.

4.3   Evaluation Criteria for the Framework's Machine Learning Engine

Combining the connectionist and symbolic paradigms is a main focus of this dissertation. Since neural networks are universally applicable to a high extent, all of the framework's machine learning tasks, namely clustering, classification, and prediction, can be realized by appropriate network types. Their universality is a strong argument for an inclusion in a generic machine learning framework. Furthermore, neural networks are able to *learn from examples* and can handle noisy, incomplete and uncertain information. Handling of imperfect information is required, for instance, when processing real (non-synthetic) time series, which are usually affected by inaccurate or missing measurements.

Parametric versus Non-Parametric In comparison to *parametric* statistical methods, connectionist models do not hypothesize a specific underlying probability model. The model that explains the observed data is only based on the observations, which means that no fixed type of probability distribution, like a normal or exponential distribution, is assumed in advance. From the statistical point of view, neural networks are just like *Bayes classifiers* in that they represent *non-parametric models* [Was07]. Under the assumption that a certain metric feature M realized by the observations in a given dataset is normally distributed, a parametric classification model can be built. If it is exponentially distributed, the generated prediction is likely to be misleading or at least distorted.

Of course, concrete neural network models are also determined by a set of parameters such as the network weights $w_{ij} \in \mathbb{R}$, but there are no prior parameters like the expected value μ or the variance σ^2 of a preconditioned normal distribution $\mathcal{N}(\mu, \sigma^2)$, for example. This means that neural networks support arbitrarily distributed observations by building a non-parametric and nonlinear model that best fits the observed data.

As mentioned, a Bayes classifier like *Naive Bayes*, which is a probabilistic method based on the Bayesian theorem, does not assume a fixed probability distribution, either. Unfortunately, the Naive Bayes classifier makes the restrictive assumption that the features M_i are stochastically independent. This means that on a probability space $(\Omega, \mathcal{B}^n = \mathcal{B}(\mathbb{R}^n), \mathbb{P})$, the joint probability of these features remaining in certain value ranges equals the product of the single probabilities, more formally:

$$\mathbb{P}(M_1 \in I_1 \wedge M_2 \in I_2 \wedge \ldots \wedge M_n \in I_n | C_j) = \prod_{i=1}^{n} \mathbb{P}(M_i \in I_i | C_j), \quad (4.12)$$

$I_i = [a_i, b_i] \in \mathcal{B}^1$, $a_i < b_i$, $a_i, b_i \in \mathbb{R}$, $j = 1, \ldots, r$, where C_j is the respective object class. The object classification is then obtained by applying the Bayesian theorem with the total probability in the denominator of equation 4.13:

$$\begin{aligned}\mathbb{P}(C_j | M_1 \in I_1 \wedge \ldots \wedge M_n \in I_n) &= \frac{\mathbb{P}(C_j)\, \mathbb{P}(M_1 \in I_1 \wedge \ldots \wedge M_n \in I_n | C_j)}{\mathbb{P}(M_1 \in I_1 \wedge \ldots \wedge M_n \in I_n)} \\ &= \frac{\mathbb{P}(C_j) \prod_{i=1}^{n} \mathbb{P}(M_i \in I_i | C_j)}{\sum_{j=1}^{r} \prod_{i=1}^{n} \mathbb{P}(M_i \in I_i | C_j)}.\end{aligned} \quad (4.13)$$

This is a disadvantage compared to neural network classifiers that are free from this assumption of independence.

In any case, this simplification does not imply a failure of the Bayesian classification in general. In many spam filters, the Naive Bayes technique works very well for recognizing junk emails. However, there are also cases that require to consider stochastic dependencies, for example in the field of change impact analysis. The change probabilities of software artifacts should be learnable and representable by the machine learning engine. Let $A_1 :=$ "Design goal *Use modal dialogues* is changed" and $A_2 :=$ "Sequence diagram *Notify actor about malfunction* is changed" with the prior probabilities $\mathbb{P}(A_1) = 0.05$, $\mathbb{P}(A_2) = 0.15$ and $\mathbb{P}(A_2|A_1) = \frac{\mathbb{P}(A_2 \cap A_1)}{\mathbb{P}(A_1)} = 0.45$, which means that A_2 is conditioned by A_1, $\mathbb{P}(A_2|A_1) \neq \mathbb{P}(A_2)$. A Naive Bayes classifier would not be capable of modeling these dependencies, which are critical for change impact analysis. Furthermore the SYMBOCONN framework must also be able to accomplish prediction tasks without employing a separate prediction engine, and so a bare classifier without prediction functionality is not sufficient.

Nonlinearity A further requirement that aims at the universality aspect of the framework is that most of the appearing domain-specific problems should be learnable, which means fitting the provided classification or prediction model to the respective problem should be feasible for a possibly large class of problems. Since neural networks can also model nonlinear problems such as the discrete *XOR-problem*, they displace methods that are restricted, for example, to a small class of linear problems.

In a geometric interpretation, there is no plane in $\mathbb{R}^3$ that contains the four points $\{(0,0,0), (0,1,1), (1,0,1), (1,1,0)\} \ni (x, y, z)$, as visualized by figure 4.9. This is equivalent to the classification problem with the two classes "0" and "1" and the class assignment $C_1 = \{(0,0), (1,1)\}$ and $C_2 = \{(0,1), (1,0)\}$. Only a nonlinear hypercurve like the depicted Gaussian curve is able to separate both classes properly.

Any classifier that is based on a linear discrimination function like a hyperplane[7] will fail to model the XOR-problem, which is clarified by figure 4.9. The first perceptron models that consisted of only one layer were not able to solve these problems, but modern neural networks with at least three layers trained by back-propagation are able to model those nonlinear functions.

Another method that can also be employed for trend estimation and prediction of time series is linear regression. It is a common misbelief that linear regression (see section 8.3) cannot model nonlinear problems. Linear regression means that the regression is nonlinear with respect to the *regression coefficients*, but **not** that the outcome of the regression function has to be linear. Consequently, the XOR-problem can be modeled by linear regression using a sinoidal transformation of the independent variables x and y (multivariate regression).

---

[7]For the purposes of this dissertation a hyperplane is defined as a $(d\text{-}1)$-dimensional subset of the standard vector space $(\mathbb{R}^d, +, \cdot)$, thus it is a generalization of a plane as a geometric object. It can be spanned by d-1 linear independent vectors $\vec{v} \in \mathbb{R}^d$.

92 CHAPTER 4. MACHINE LEARNING AND THE FRAMEWORK ENGINE

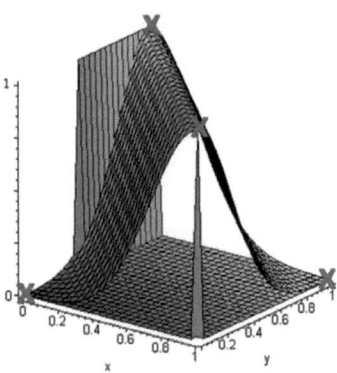

Figure 4.9: Three-dimensional illustration of the *XOR-problem*. The function values $f(x,y) \in [0,1]$ of the binary XOR-function are indicated by steep shoulders along the z-axis. The shifted nonlinear Gaussian hypercurve covers all four points $(0,0,0)$, $(0,1,1)$, $(1,0,1)$ and $(1,1,0)$. There is no plane – generated by a linear function – that covers these four points, thus non-linearity is required.

Another, more recent method is the *Support Vector Machine* originally used to model binary classification problems with two target classes. SVMs compute a so-called *maximum margin hyperplane* (MMH) that defines the class boundary with the highest possible discrimination between the two object classes. The MHH is determined by the support vectors only, which are a subset of the training data set that lies close to the class boundary. In general, SVMs achieve high classification accuracies comparable to neural classifiers.

Robustness Regarding Fuzzy and Incomplete Information A further criterion to be fulfilled by the employed machine learning algorithm is the ability to deal with fuzzy or incomplete information as described in section 3.1.2, because the framework especially focuses on knowledge and software engineering. The required *robustness* is, amongst others, enabled by fuzzy (numeric) knowledge representation and processing, which are intrinsic properties of connectionist models. There already exist techniques that rely on fuzzy logic to deal with vague knowledge. Xiaowei presented a multi-agent recommendation system that simulates human intelligence to provide recommendation to users [Xia06]. The recommendation system is based on fuzzy user profiles, fuzzy filtering and recommendation agents. Xiaowei claims that the results of a case study showed that it "is more convenient for users to find computer programs of their interest with the proposed recommendation system".

CHAPTER 4. MACHINE LEARNING AND THE FRAMEWORK ENGINE   93

Technique	Non-Linearity	Robustness	Classification	Prediction
Decision Tree	++	−	++	−
Linear Regression	+	+	+	++
Naive Bayes	−[8]	+	++	−
Neural Network	++	+++	+++	++
Support Vector Machine	++[9]	++	+++	+[10]

Technique	Interpretability	(Negative) Constraints
Decision Tree	+++	Exponential number of training examples
Linear Regression	+	Linear combination of regression coefficients
Naive Bayes	+	Features assumed to be independent
Neural Network	− −	Determination of the topology
Support Vector Machine	− −[11]	Determination of a kernel function

Table 4.2: Evaluation matrix comparing several fundamental techniques from machine learning and statistics. *Non-Linearity* means that domain problems can still be addressed, which are either nonlinearly separable in case of classification or are described by a nonlinear function in case of prediction. *Robustness* is a nonfunctional requirement from section 3.1.2 and is both required for classification and prediction. *Interpretability* is meant as the ability to expose and explain the results of classification or prediction, which is very high in case of decision trees, for instance. *Constraints* are restrictions in the application of the technique. The maximum rating is +++, the minimum is − − −.

In comparison to symbolic systems, neural networks still work properly even if a substantial part of their connectivity is malformed or destroyed. This fact was already observed by Rosenberg in his speech synthesis system *NETtalk* in 1987. After making random changes of varying size to the weights, the network was still able to accomplish the speech synthesis task: *"Random perturbations of the weights uniformly distributed on the interval $[-0.5, 0.5]$ had little effect on the performance of the network, and degradation was gradual with increasing damage."* [SR87]

The noise-robustness of the SYMBOCONN machine learning engine (MRNN) was elaborated on in [Dav08b] when it was applied to the classification of a dataset of molecules. In the presence of interfering noise up to a degree of 25.0%, a classification accuracy of 75.9% was achieved, which demonstrates the high robustness of the framework engine.

There are also symbolic techniques which are able to deal with incomplete symbolic information. Handling incomplete and changing rule-based knowledge means that the correctness of a drawn conclusion may vary over time or that it only remains true when its conditions (antecedent) are properly adjusted. *Non-monotonic reasoning* is a branch of computational logics that allows to revise conclusions that have been drawn based on uncertain propositions. This form of reasoning with uncertainty is enabled by non-monotonic logics based on rationality and plausibility rather than on truth and valid conclusions like in monotonic logics. Monotony is given when a formula A inferable from a theory T (a set of closed formulas), $T \vdash A$, stays inferable for all theories T' that include T, $T' \supseteq T$. By contrast, in non-monotonic logics, a new fact B added to the theory $T' = T \cup \{B\}$ may invalidate the set of hitherto inferable formulas. Therefore non-monotonic reasoning is also called *defeasible reasoning*, since conclusions or assumptions that have been made can be revised in light of new evidence. In this way, non-monotonic reasoning can deal with uncertain and changing symbolic knowledge and conclusions are drawn by non-monotonic inference rules. Nevertheless, non-monotonic logics as a deductive inference technique are not capable of learning by example, which disqualifies them with respect to the universality requirement.

Table 4.2 sums up the strengths and weaknesses of the discussed machine learning techniques. The advantages speak for using a generic neural network as framework engine in order to meet the identified framework requirements, in particular the universality requirement.

4.4 The Modular Recurrent Neural Network

The *Modular Recurrent Neural Network* (MRNN) serves as core engine for the SYMBOCONN framework, as shown by the framework architecture depicted in figure 3.6 in the previous chapter. Figure 4.10 illustrates the topology and the information flow of the three-layered recurrent neural network. An important characteristic

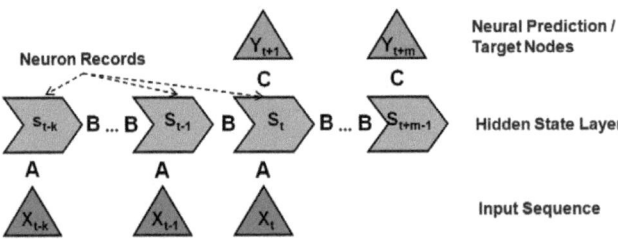

Figure 4.10: Schematic topology of the modular recurrent neural network MRNN used in SYMBOCONN. The arrows indicate the internal state transition $\vec{s}_t \rightarrow \vec{s}_{t+1}$ that takes place in the hidden layer. The forward propagation phase is from left to right. The triangle $\vec{x}_t$ is the external input vector at time t, $\vec{y}_{t+1}$ is the correspondingly predicted output vector. The letters A, B and C denote weight matrices. For classification as opposed to sequence prediction, only one output unit $\vec{y}_{t+1}$ is used.

of the recurrent network design is its inherent temporal memory. Due to the *temporally unfolded network topology* [NZ99], the MRNN can learn the *sequential structure* of a set of node sequences. Thus, the logical order of the nodes is explicitly modeled in the *hidden state layer* $\vec{s}_{t-k}, \ldots, \vec{s}_{t+m-1}$. Since there are no branches in the hidden layer, a linear discrete timeline $T = (t\text{-}k, t\text{-}k\text{+}1, \ldots, t, t+1, \ldots, t\text{+}m)$, $k, t, m \in \mathbb{N}$ is modeled, and thus the structural or temporal dimension of the input and output data is explicit, as opposed to *feed-forward* networks like the multilayer perceptron. This is necessary in order to represent and process time-indexed data such as time series for trend prediction or forecast. Moreover, the representation of structured information like software artifact graphs for the Design Pattern Adviser or Change Impact Analysis (see figure 3.6) require a sequential order of their constituents.

The block arrows depicted in figure 4.10 are called neuron records[12] and serve both as *hidden* and as *context units*, because $\vec{s}_{t-1}$ provides a context for the recursive computation of the subsequent hidden state $\vec{s}_t$. Thereby, one input vector $\vec{x}_t$ or output vector $\vec{y}_{t+1}$ corresponds to one node of the knowledge graph defined in section 3.2. The target sequence $\vec{y}_{t+1}, \ldots, \vec{y}_{t+m}$ (neural prediction) is computed based on the *history sequence* $\vec{x}_{t-k}, \ldots, \vec{x}_t$. The neuron records for $m > 0$ that result in the sequence of target nodes represent the autonomous part of the network, where external inputs x_i are no longer available. In this segment of the topology, the network is not triggered by external inputs anymore, but its internal state is propagated autonomously, resulting in a momentum.

The modular composition of the network can also be represented as a UML diagram, which is presented in figure 4.11.

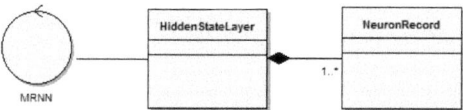

Figure 4.11: UML representation of the Modular Recurrent Neural Network (MRNN). Each hidden state $\vec{s}_t$ as shown in figure 4.10 is realized by a NeuronRecord. The number $k+m$ of NeuronRecords is determined by the length of the history sequence and the prediction horizon, which is the number of target nodes.

4.4.1 Recurrent Dynamics

The technical design of the MRNN is defined by the following recurrent model of forward propagation. A is a $\mathbb{R}^{h \times d_1}$, B is a $\mathbb{R}^{h \times h}$ and C is a $\mathbb{R}^{d_2 \times h}$ matrix. d_1 is the dimensionality of the input space X and d_2 is the dimensionality of the output space Y (feature spaces). $h = dim(\vec{s}_i)$, ($i = t\text{-}k, \ldots, t+m$) is the dimensionality of the (hidden) state layer S. h is independent from d_1 and d_2 and its concrete value is determined at runtime by stepwise reduction from an initial value, as long as the training process does not stagnate (and therefore sufficient network resources are still provided). The same three matrix instances A, B and C are reused in every neuron record of the network, which correspond to the constituents (indexed by

---

[12]NeuronRecords represent a virtual aggregation of conventional neurons, which are not explicit in the composition of the MRNN. A NeuronRecord is an abstraction of several neurons.

$t \in T$) of the training pattern.

$$\vec{s}_\tau = \begin{cases} f(B\vec{0} + A\vec{x}_\tau), & \tau = t - k \\ f(B\vec{s}_{\tau-1} + A\vec{x}_\tau), & t - k < \tau \leq t \\ f(B\vec{s}_{\tau-1}), & \tau > t \end{cases} \quad (4.14)$$

$$\vec{o}_{\tau+1} = f(C\vec{s}_\tau), \quad \forall \tau \in T \quad (4.15)$$

$$\vec{o}_{t+i} \xrightarrow{training} \vec{y}_{t+i}, \quad i = 1, \ldots, m \quad (4.16)$$

As introduced above, $\vec{s}_t \in S$ denotes the internal state at the discrete time step t. The state layer consists of all these states and is the backbone for learning *history-target sequences* as well as for predicting target nodes during the operative application. The crucial recurrent equation 4.14 combines an external input $\vec{x}_t$ with the previous state $\vec{s}_{t-1}$ to the subsequent state $\vec{s}_t$, which indirectly depends on all foregoing external inputs $\vec{x}_{t-k}, \ldots, \vec{x}_{t-1}$ and internal states $\vec{s}_{t-k}, \ldots, \vec{s}_{t-1}$. In case of supervised network training, the target symbols $\vec{y}_{t+1}, \ldots, \vec{y}_{t+m}$ are known, while in case of actual prediction, the output sequence $\vec{o}_{t+1}, \ldots, \vec{o}_{t+m}$ is computed solely based on the respective inputs (equation 4.15). Here, the activations function is chosen as sigmoid function $f(x) = \frac{1}{1+\exp(-x)}$, which provides an established nonlinear input transformation[13].

The mathematical concept of *dynamic systems* introduced in the following is useful to formalize the state transition behavior of recurrent neural networks like the MRNN.

Definition 4.4.1: Dynamic System
A *dynamic system* is a mathematical model for time-dependent processes. It can be formalized as a triple (S, T, Φ) with $\Phi : S \times T \to S$, where S is the *State-* or *Phase space* and $T = \mathbb{Z} = \{\ldots, -2, -1, 0, 1, 2, \ldots\}$ is a discrete *timeline*. The system always holds a current state $s_i \in S$ and takes an element $t \in T$ from the timeline to proceed to the next state $s_{i+1} \in S$ via the transition function Φ. Furthermore, Φ fulfills the following *semigroup* properties with the neutral element $0 \in T$, written in prefix-notation:

$$\Phi(s, 0) = s$$
$$\Phi(\Phi(s, t), u) = \Phi(s, t + u)$$

The first equation represents the group property as identity function in the first argument: the system state does not change after 0 time steps. The second equation is the semigroup-property that describes a state transition of $t + u$ time steps, which has the same effect as two separate transitions of time lags t and u. The intermediate state $s' := \Phi(s, t)$ is reached after the first t steps, a further transition of u steps leads to the final state $s'' := \Phi(s, t + u)$.

The MRNN as core engine of the framework implements a dynamic system $MRNN$:

---
[13] Alternatively other activation functions like $f = \tanh$ or radial basis functions can be used.

$S \times X \to S$, while, in general, few neural networks behave like dynamic systems [ADES02]. The class of feed-forward networks is not able to implement a dynamic system; this is mainly due to the lack of recurrent connections. But exactly this dynamic system property, which is realized by the recurrent state layer, enables *explicit systematicity* when processing structured knowledge. Structures such as grammar rules or navigation sequences are composed of single constituents that can be directly fed into the MRNN.

The MRNN is trained with a modified *Backpropagation Through Time* (BPTT) algorithm [Cal03] (p. 52 et sqq.) that is able to process variably dimensional vectors $\vec{x}_t$ and $\vec{y}_{t+m}$. There are no further external inputs after t, since the observed history sequence is exhausted. For $t+1$, $t+2$, ... the network propagates activations only through its hidden layer. The hidden temporal representation by the MRNN's state layer enables theoretically infinite long prediction sequences, since the MRNN possesses a *continuous internal state layer* [GSW05]. Thereby, the current state $(\vec{s}_t)_{t \in \mathbb{N}}$ is repeatedly propagated through the *state transition matrix* B, even when external inputs $\vec{x}_t$ are no longer available.

4.4.2 Processing of Variable Node Sequences

Training patterns of varying length are a challenge to connectionist models, as standard feed-forward networks with fixed topology cannot directly process input and target sequences of varying length. In general, the topology of a neural network determines the structure of the patterns that can be processed and vice versa. This means that a variably sized input pattern consisting of k single components $\vec{x}_1, \ldots, \vec{x}_k$ implies a network with k input records (or *neurons* in the terminology of standard networks). The network will be trained on this pattern structure, such that its topology is already *predetermined*. As a consequence, further patterns can only be processed if they hold the same structure.

The case is exactly converse with regard to the MRNN, since the heterogeneous training patterns determine the particular structure of the neural network. A non-static network topology allows to dynamically vary the size of the hidden state layer (the number of comprised neuron records) as shown by figure 4.10 in the previous section. When applied to navigation recommendation, for example, not only sequences of the trained length should be processable, but also variably long history sequences have to be exploited to predict the most likely target sequence. In order to process variably long node sequences of the form $(\vec{x}_{t-k}, \ldots, \vec{x}_t, \vec{y}_{t+1}, \ldots, \vec{y}_{t+m})_{k,m \in \mathbb{N}}$ as part of the same training set, the neural network has to adapt to the number of history and target nodes in a single sequence *at runtime*. During one training epoch[14], the network adapts at runtime to the individual structure of the respective node sequence with its history and target part. Depending on the current input pattern length, which corresponds to the length of the past user navigation for instance, the network adapts to the given length and propagates the input vectors

---

[14] A *training epoch* is a single training cycle through all patterns contained in the training set.

through the hidden layer.

Due to the modular design of the MRNN model, it is not only possible to treat variably long training sequences, but even to handle arbitrarily dimensioned input and target vectors (see appendix A.2.3).

4.4.3 Modified Backpropagation Training Algorithm

Different types of training algorithms like supervised, unsupervised, reinforcement, etc., as introduced in section 2.5, can be employed to train neural networks. For classification and prediction tasks, supervised training is used to determine a set of network weights that best models the domain-specific problem. The oldest and most simple learning principle for neural networks is *Hebb learning*, which was formulated by Donald Hebb in 1949 [Heb49].

$$\Delta w_{ij} = \eta \cdot o_j \cdot x_i \qquad (4.17)$$

As depicted in figure 4.12, the network weight w_{ij} between neuron i and j is adapted based on the learning rate η, the signal coming from neuron i, and the output o_j of neuron j, called *activation* $o_j = f(net_j)$. The underlying idea is that neurons which are often activated together (the neuron "fires") establish a stronger connection between them, expressed by the amount of the respective network weight[15]. Both the input signal x_i and the activation o_j contribute to the magnitude of the weight adaption.

A more modern and effective learning rule is the *Delta rule*, which is also known as *Widrow-Hoff rule*

$$\Delta w_{ij} = \eta \cdot \underbrace{(t_j - o_j)}_{\delta_j} \cdot f'(net_j) \cdot x_i, \qquad (4.18)$$

where f is the activation function as defined by Def. 4.1.2. The weight change is dependent on the error value δ_j, which is the backpropagated deviation between expected output and actual output. A high error leads to a bigger weight adaption in order to reduce the output deviation in the next forward propagation. In case of a linear activation function, the derivation factor $f'(net_j)$ in formula 4.18 can be omitted. Since the t_j, $j = 1, \ldots, n$ are the learning targets that serve as reference values, the delta rule is used by the class of supervised training algorithms.

The algorithm used in the SYMBOCONN framework for training the MRNN is a variant of the established *Backpropagation Through Time* (BPTT) [RHW86] algorithm and makes use of the Delta rule. It incorporates a few novel properties that enable the training of a modular RNN which operates on multi-dimensional data *at each time step* and is able to train the network despite missing inputs or targets at certain time steps. Furthermore, the whole forward pass of our algorithm is based on matrix operations, which are computationally more elegant and easier

---
[15]"what fires together, wires together".

CHAPTER 4. MACHINE LEARNING AND THE FRAMEWORK ENGINE   99

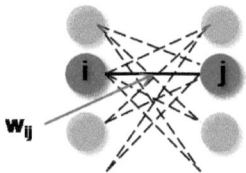

Figure 4.12: Two neurons i and j interacting via a direct connection, whose weight w_{ij} can be adjusted according to the Hebbian learning rule or the Delta rule.

to understand than multi-indices referring to single neurons. These and some minor properties advance the standard BPTT algorithm.

In fact, the SYMBOCONN framework allows for plugging in[16] several training algorithms as subclasses of the abstract class TrainingAlgorithm which is shown in figure 4.13. Typically, the algorithm implementation is shielded from the access of the client, which is the Controller from subsystem Control in this case. Three

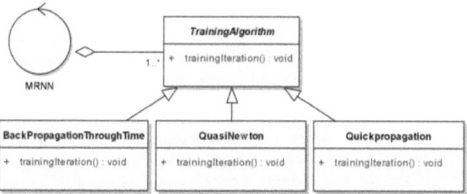

Figure 4.13: Generic plug-in architecture for training algorithms. QuasiNewton and QuickPropagation are alternative training algorithms that can be used to train the MRNN. They are more efficient in theory.

algorithms with different characteristics concerning memory and time efficiency are available in the SYMBOCONN framework, which all were adapted to the modular structure of the MRNN. Another training algorithm which was not implemented but could be used to train the MRNN is *Real-Time Recurrent Learning* (RTRL) [WZ89]. For all applications studied in this dissertation, the modified BPTT algorithm was employed, since the best results were achieved with this nonlinear and iterative optimization method.

Like many stochastic problems, network training is an *optimization problem* that is solved by a variant of the *Least Squares* (LS) method. This method minimizes the difference between the observed output $\vec{o}$ and the expected output $\vec{y}$ of a model

---

[16]This structure partially follows the *Strategy* design pattern, which is described in section 6.3.5.

function F, $\vec{o} = F(\vec{x})$. The *functional*[17] L to be minimized has the general form

$$L : F(\vec{x}) \mapsto \sum_{i=1}^{n}(y_i - F(x_i))^2 = \sum_{i=1}^{n}(y_i - o_i)^2 \qquad (4.19)$$

In comparison to the classical least square method, the model function F is realized by a neural network here, which makes the optimization process more complex because F is *nonlinear*.

Adapted to the case of a recurrent neural network that realizes this model function, the situation becomes even more complex, because the timeline T has to be considered as well, meaning that the optimization also depends on the time-dependent input[18] $x(\tau)$ and state $s(\tau)$ for all steps $\tau \in T$.

Independent of the length k of the history sequence or the length m of the target sequence, the weight matrices A, B and C are continuously adjusted[19] in the training process, because they are reused at each time step τ. This implies that there are exactly three matrix instances for the training of all variably long sequences, independent of the respective time step. As described by Hinton et al. [JH92], it is important to favor simpler network topologies with less weights to obtain a high generalization capability, which can be accomplished by weight sharing. Penalty terms that penalize the emergence of big weight values and foster weights close to zero are another way of reducing complexity.

4.4.3.1 Forward Pass

We now describe how the computation of the complete forward propagation is carried out. Firstly, we recall the network topology by figure 4.14, which serves as basis for the computation of the formulas 4.20 to 4.25.

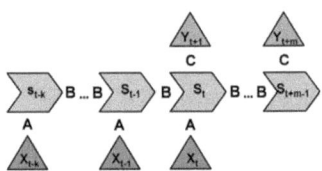

Figure 4.14: Copy of figure 4.10 recalling the three-layered structure of the MRNN. The block arrows indicate the internal state transition $\vec{s}_t \to \vec{s}_{t+1}$. $\vec{x}_t$ is the external input vector at time t, $\vec{y}_{t+1}$ is the correspondingly predicted output vector.

The parameters to optimize are the network weights $w_{ij}^M \in M \in \{A, B, C\}$

---

[17] L is called a *functional*, because it is a function that takes functions as arguments.
[18] Corresponding to the length of the processed node sequence.
[19] The continuous weight adaption is called *online* training, as opposed to a *batch* training mode.

of the three time-invariant weight matrices[20], whose horizontal and vertical dimensionalities $row(M)$, $col(M)$ are determined by the network topology.

$$net_j^{(B)}(\tau) = \begin{cases} \sum_{i=1}^{d_1} w_{ij}^{(A)} x_i(\tau), & \tau = t-k \\ \sum_{i=1}^{d_1} w_{ij}^{(A)} x_i(\tau) + \sum_{i=1}^{h} w_{ij}^{(B)} s_i(\tau-1), & t-k < \tau \le t \\ \sum_{i=1}^{h} w_{ij}^{(B)} s_i(\tau-1), & t+1 \le \tau \le t+m, \end{cases}$$
$$j = 1, \ldots, h \quad (4.20)$$

$$s_j(\tau) = f(net_j^{(B)}(\tau)), \quad j = 1, \ldots, h \quad (4.21)$$

$$net_j^{(C)}(\tau) = \sum_{i=1}^{h} w_{ij}^{(C)} s_i(\tau), j = 1, \ldots, d_2 \quad (4.22)$$

$$o_j(\tau) = f(net_j^{(C)}(\tau)), \quad j = 1, \ldots, d_2 \quad (4.23)$$

$$E_p(\tau) = \frac{1}{2} \sum_{j=1}^{d_2} (y_j(\tau) - o_j(\tau))^2 \quad (4.24)$$

$$E = \sum_{p \in TS} \sum_{\tau=t+1}^{t+m} E_p(\tau) \quad (4.25)$$

The formulas 4.20 to 4.25 describe the complete forward propagation computed by the MRNN, detailing the matrix notation used in formula 4.14. Furthermore, the time is explicitly denoted by the free variable τ. The j-th net input $net_j^{(B)}(\tau)$ of the hidden layer component indexed by τ is computed as a result of the external input and the previous state $s_j(\tau-1)$. For the first external input $\vec{x}_{t-k}$, there is no previous internal state yet, and after $\tau = t$, the forward propagation is solely computed as a continuation of the current internal state $s(\tau)$. Thereby, the global error function E on the whole training set TS is to be minimized, where $\vec{o}$ is the observed output and $\vec{y}$ is the target vector at a single time step $\tau \in T$. The local error function E_p is summed over all m target nodes of a single pattern p (see Def. 3.2.4 in chapter 3) and the factor $\frac{1}{2}$ is set in order to simplify the computation of the first derivative[21].

4.4.3.2 Backward Pass

The chain rule of differentiation is especially important for the computation of the single weight adjustments in each of the three network layers. Since the error or objective function $E := E_p(M) : \mathbb{R}^{a \cdot b} \to \mathbb{R}$, $a = row(M)$, $b = col(M)$ should be minimized, we are interested in its first derivative with respect to the network weights, $\nabla E = (\frac{\partial E}{\partial w_{11}}, \frac{\partial E}{\partial w_{12}}, \ldots, \frac{\partial E}{\partial w_{ab}})$, $w_{ij} \in M$.

---

[20] M is an upper index that indicates the concerned weight matrix $M \in \{A, B, C\}$.
[21] If $\frac{1}{2} E_p$ is minimized, then also E_p is minimized.

CHAPTER 4. MACHINE LEARNING AND THE FRAMEWORK ENGINE

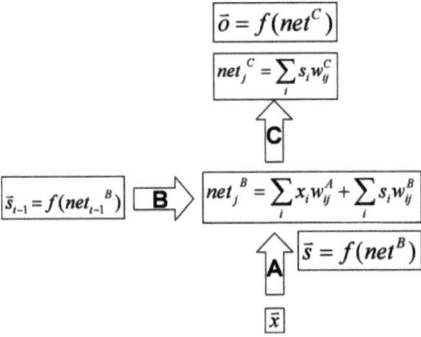

Figure 4.15: Assignment of the formulas to the schematic network topology for one time step of the forward propagation phase. The external input signal $\vec{x}$ at time t is fed in through the matrix A first, $f(x) = \frac{1}{1+\exp(-x)}$ is the used sigmoid activation function.

Definition 4.4.2: Chain Rule of Differentiation
The gradient of the error function E is computed as function of the weights.

$$\frac{\partial E}{\partial w_{ij}} = \frac{\partial E}{\partial o_j} \frac{\partial o_j}{\partial net_j} \frac{\partial net_j}{\partial w_{ij}} \qquad (4.26)$$

The chain rule is needed because E_p is no direct function of the weights w_{ij}, but the weights serve as input for two constituent functions, namely net and $\vec{o} = f(net)$. Since the activation function f is the logistic function, its first derivative simplifies to an easily computable term:

$$\begin{aligned}
\frac{\partial f}{\partial net_j^{(M)}} &= \frac{e^{-net_j^{(M)}}}{(1+e^{-net_j^{(M)}})^2} \\
&= \frac{1+e^{-net_j^{(M)}}}{(1+e^{-net_j^{(M)}})^2} - \frac{1}{(1+e^{-net_j^{(M)}})^2} \\
&= \frac{1}{(1+e^{-net_j^{(M)}})} \left(1 - \frac{1}{(1+e^{-net_j^{(M)}})}\right) \\
&= f(net_j^{(M)})(1 - f(net_j^{(M)})) \\
&= \begin{cases} s_j(1-s_j), & M = B, \quad j = 1, \ldots, h \\ o_j(1-o_j), & M = C, \quad j = 1, \ldots, d_2 \end{cases}
\end{aligned} \qquad (4.27)$$

The specialty of our training algorithm is the backpropagation of the gradient information through the whole network to the proper entries of all three matrices, while the size of the network is completely variable. Thereby, the nonlinear activation function f has to be passed in reverse direction, depicted in figure 4.16 and 4.17. The derivative of the local error function E_p to the weight matrix C is given

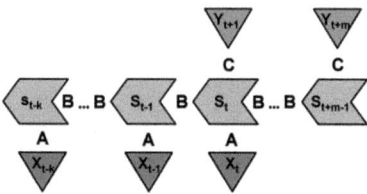

Figure 4.16: The depicted block arrows in reverse direction show the backward information propagation. A forward pass is followed by a backward pass during training, which is called *Backpropagation Through Time* (BPTT) characterized by the state transition $t \to t-1$.

by

$$\frac{\partial E_p}{\partial w_{ij}^{(C)}} \stackrel{4.24}{=} \underbrace{-(y_j - o_j)f'(net_j^{(C)})}_{\delta_j^{(C)}} s_i \qquad (4.28)$$

The error backpropagation starts at the output layer, where $\delta^{(C)}$ is sent back through the matrix C at first:

$$\delta_j^{(C)}(\tau) = (y_j(\tau) - o_j(\tau))f'(net_j^{(C)})(\tau), \quad j = 1, \ldots, d_2 \qquad (4.29)$$

$$\epsilon_j^{(C)}(\tau) = \sum_{k=1}^{d_2} \delta_k^{(C)}(\tau) w_{kj}^{(C)}, \quad j = 1, \ldots, h \qquad (4.30)$$

The error for a hidden record $\vec{s}_\tau$ is composed of both the external error $\delta^{(C)}(\tau)$ and the error $\delta^{(B)}(\tau+1)$ to be backpropagated from the subsequent[22] hidden record $\vec{s}_{\tau+1}$. Before the error of each component of the hidden layer can be computed, the external error $\delta^C(\tau)$ and the error of the subsequent state $\vec{s}_{\tau+1}$ have to be available. $\epsilon^{(M)}$ is the *internal error* after backpropagation of the external error $\delta^{(M)}$ through

---

[22]*Previous* in terms of backpropagation, *subsequent* in terms of forward propagation.

the respective matrix M as done in formula 4.30 and 4.31.

$$\epsilon_j^{(B)}(\tau) = \sum_{k=1}^{h} \delta_k^{(B)}(\tau+1) w_{kj}^{(B)}, \quad j = 1, \ldots, h \quad (4.31)$$

$$\delta_j^{(B)}(\tau) = \begin{cases} 0, & \tau = t+m \\ f'(net_j^{(B)}(\tau)) \, [\,\epsilon_j^{(B)}(\tau) + \epsilon_j^{(C)}(\tau)\,], & t \leq \tau < t+m \\ f'(net_j^{(B)}(\tau)) \, \epsilon_j^{(B)}(\tau), & \tau < t \end{cases} \quad (4.32)$$
$$j = 1, \ldots, h$$

Figure 4.17 clarifies the error flow through the network, depending on the respective matrix and on the time step t. For $\tau = t\text{-}k, t\text{-}k\text{+}1, \ldots, t\text{-}1$ there is no target

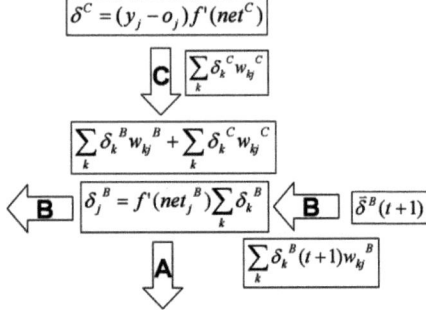

Figure 4.17: Assignment of the (error) gradient computation formulas to the schematic network topology for one time step. The reversed block arrows show the *backpropagation* of the output deviation $(y_j - o_j)$ from the expected output (target) through the weight matrices C and B. The first derivation of the activation function at the output layer is $f'(net_j^{(C)}) = o_j(1 - o_j)$.

available, thus the error $\delta_j^{(B)}(\tau)$ consists only of the backpropagated error $\epsilon_j^B(\tau)$ as expressed by the third case $\tau < t$ of formula 4.32. The error $\delta^{(B)}$ is computed under consideration of the sigmoid function f in each record of the hidden layer and will be required for adapting the weight matrices A and B later on. Similar to the direct computation of the external error $\delta^{(C)}$, the first derivative $f'(net_j^{(B)}) := \frac{\partial f}{\partial net_j^{(B)}}$ of f is needed here. The backpropagation principle of formula 4.31 and 4.32 is crucial to the whole backpropagation procedure which allows to distribute the external error across the activation functions and across arbitrarily many hidden layers (here we have only one, represented by the matrix B). The weighted sum $net^{(B)}(\tau)$ of the input vector $\vec{x}_\tau$ and the previous state vector $\vec{s}_{\tau-1}$ propagated through the matrix A and B, respectively, has to be stored during the forward propagation. Now it is

required for the computation of the gradient information $\delta_j^{(B)}$ in formula 4.32.
Due to the analytically unknown error function E defined by formula 4.25 and the nonlinear transformation in the network, it is not possible to give a solution to the optimization problem in a closed form. The network weights have to be approximated iteratively by *gradient descent*.

Weight Adaption Due to the different weight matrices A, B and C, a separate adaption has to be computed for each matrix. Time indices (τ) are omitted where they are equal for all participating terms. During the backpropagation procedure, the output matrix C is first adapted by means of the corresponding gradient $g_{ij}^{(C)}$:

$$\frac{\partial net_j^{(C)}}{\partial w_{ij}^{(C)}} \stackrel{4.22}{=} s_i$$

$$g_{ij}^{(C)} = \frac{\partial E_p}{\partial w_{ij}^{(C)}} \stackrel{4.26}{=} -(y_j - o_j) f'(net_j^{(C)}) \frac{\partial net_j^{(C)}}{\partial w_{ij}^{(C)}} \quad (4.33)$$

$$= -\delta_j^{(C)} s_i,$$

where $i = 1, \ldots, h$, $j = 1, \ldots, d_2$ and s_i takes the role of the external input in the delta rule 4.18. Normally, the gradient of a function $E : \mathbb{R}^n \to \mathbb{R}$ is a column vector with n entries; however, here the gradient has two indices corresponding to the weight matrix that determines the value of E_p. The gradient $\vec{g}^{(B)}(\tau)$ of the hidden layer is computed by

$$g_{ij}^{(B)}(\tau) = \frac{\partial E_p(\tau)}{\partial w_{ij}^{(B)}} \stackrel{4.26}{=} \frac{\partial E_p}{\partial o_j} \frac{\partial o_j}{\partial net_j^{(B)}} \frac{\partial net_j^{(B)}}{\partial w_{ij}^{(B)}}$$

$$= -\delta_j^B(\tau + 1) s_i(\tau), \quad i,j = 1, \ldots, h \quad (4.34)$$

Finally, the error $\delta^{(A)}$ for the input matrix A has to be computed based on the error of the hidden layer $\delta^{(B)}$ at the same time step τ:

$$\frac{\partial net_j^{(B)}}{\partial w_{ij}^{(A)}} \stackrel{4.20}{=} x_i, \quad i = 1, \ldots, d_1, \quad (4.35)$$

$$g_{ij}^{(A)} = \frac{\partial E_p}{\partial w_{ij}^{(A)}} \stackrel{4.26, 4.32}{=} -\delta_j^{(B)}(\tau) x_i, \quad j = 1, \ldots, h \quad (4.36)$$

The weights of all three matrices have to be adjusted contrarily to the gradient direction, since the minimum of the error function should be approached:

$$\Delta w_{ij}^{(M)} = -g_{ij}^{(M)} \quad (4.37)$$

$$\hat{w}_{ij}^{(M)} = w_{ij}^{(M)} + \eta \cdot \Delta w_{ij}^{(M)}, \quad \forall i,j, \forall M \in \{A, B, C\} \quad (4.38)$$

The magnitude of weight change is controlled by the learning rate $\eta \in [0, 1]$, resulting in the adapted weight $\hat{w}_{ij}^{(M)}$. All matrices are adapted immediately at each time step τ of the same training pattern p, which is called *online learning mode*. Depending on the learning rate, the error decreases monotonically or the training progress is interwoven by momentary hazards of increased training error E. Figure 4.18 shows the temporal development of the vector-valued training error with its single error components as colored curves.

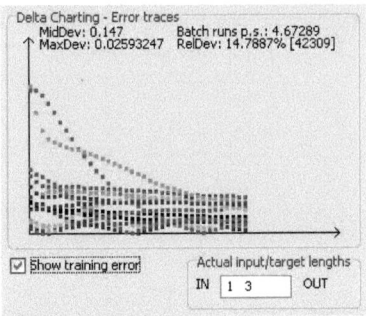

Figure 4.18: Visualization of the training process showing the temporal development of the vector-valued training error. The single error curves stand for the d_2-many different error components $[y_j(\tau) - o_j(\tau)], j = 1, \ldots, d_2, \tau > t$ in the output layer, averaged over τ.

4.4.4 Experiment: Illustration of Intelligent Learning

In this section, we demonstrate the learning capability of the SYMBOCONN machine learning engine (MRNN), especially its ability of learning to ignore insignificant information. We use a learning task with two degrees of difficulty to illustrate what connectionist learning means in practice.

The difficulty of connectionist machine learning tasks and the time required to learn them (training speed) are correlated. In general, their relationship is not proportional, but all practical evaluations of the MRNN done for this dissertation showed a strong dependence of both magnitudes. The harder the task, the more time is required for convergence of the current network output with respect to the expected output, which also applies to the learning tasks discussed below. Thus the different degrees of difficulty were also reflected in the training behavior.

The following scenario is derived from a classification aimed at a biological dataset, which was accomplished by the SYMBOCONN framework [Dav08b]. The connectionist classifier was applied to the publicly available MUSK2 classification benchmark - a pharmaceutical dataset of molecule data. These molecules can be considered as multi-represented objects as defined in section 3.2 and are to be divided into two distinct classes "0" and "1". The task is to identify the significant information contained in the training examples that determines whether a given molecule belongs to class "0" or "1". The class label indicates whether a molecule has the phenotypical *musk* property or whether it is non-musk[23]. These molecules, of which 39 are judged by human experts to be musks and the remaining 63 are judged to be non-musks, appear in 6,598 different conformations. In molecular biology or biochemistry a conformation is a structural arrangement which determines the molecule's shape by the kind of folding. The molecules are described by 166 attributes that are used to build a straight-forward feature vector representation:

$$\vec{x}_t = (\underbrace{x_1, \ldots, x_{162}}_{f1\ to\ f162}, \underbrace{x_{163}, \ldots, x_{166}}_{f163\ to\ f166}), \quad x_i \in \mathbb{R} \quad (4.39)$$

The attributes *f1* to *f162* are distances that are measured in hundredths of Angstroms, while the remaining attributes are categorical.

During the evaluation of this case study, we found an interesting characterization of connectionist learning and its self-learning capabilities. We conducted two learning tasks of different complexity that were both accomplished by the SYMBO-CONN engine without being taught where to "search" for the relevant information to classify the molecules.

The Easy Classification Task The training examples for the neural network consist of two input nodes and one target node, which represents the respective class membership. The input sequence is heterogeneous, since its first node directly carries the relevant class information encoded by two bits, while its second node represents the molecule information. Thus the first input node and the target node are identical. For example, the first input node states that the molecule is a musk and the second input node carries the feature values $(f_1 = 49, f_2 = 11, \ldots, f_{165} = -191, f_{166} = 42)$.

Only for this scenario, the system was implicitly told the correct class of the respective molecule by an additional input node. For the actual classification task performed in [Dav08b], the class label was obviously not fed in as input, but had to be predicted by the system. However, this experiment evaluates the capability of learning the significant information for correctly classifying molecules. The system is provided with both the class label and the feature values of the molecule. The corresponding training data is shown in figure 4.19. The classification task is easy since the class label that should be predicted by the network is fed in as an additional input besides the feature values of the respective molecule. Hence, the task degenerates to recognizing that the correct class information to be predicted is always contained in the first node of the input sequence, while ignoring the second

---

[23] *"Musk odor is a specific and clearly identifiable sensation, although the mechanisms underlying it are poorly understood. Musk odor is determined almost entirely by steric (i.e., "molecular shape") effects (Ohloff, 1986)."* [DJLLP94].

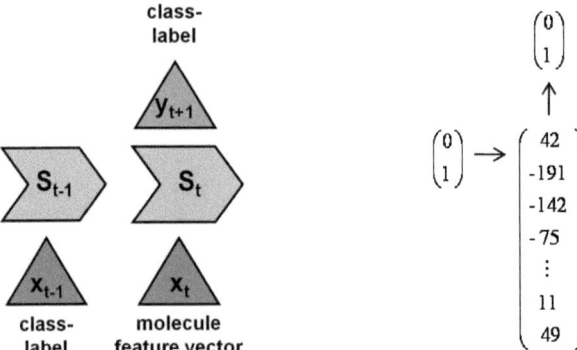

Figure 4.19: Training setup of the MRNN for the learning experiment (easy task) described in this paragraph. The network topology (see section 4.4) corresponds to the training examples that consist of two input nodes and one target node.

Figure 4.20: Corresponding to figure 4.19, the second input node is the vector representation of an exemplary molecule. Both the first input vector and the target vector carry the same information $(0, 1)$ – the class label of the current molecule.

node.

During the training phase, the MRNN indeed focused on the first input node that directly replicates the class information of the target node and completely ignored the second input node, which is the optimal problem solution. Since the first node explicitly states the class label of an object, while the feature values only indirectly and partially determine the object's class, the MRNN focused on the decisive piece of information. It has learned from the empirical data that the second information unit, which is even of 83-fold vector dimensionality ($166 = 83 \cdot 2$) compared to the first node, is completely irrelevant here and can thus be ignored for the determination of the object class. The non-trivial achievement of the neural network is that it autonomously identified the significance without being told which piece of information is decisive. On the contrary, the network was even biased with the superfluous high-dimensional second feature vector.

The Hard Classification Task In the second part of the learning experiment, the class information is not fed into the network as a separate input node, but is integrated into the molecule feature vector $\vec{f}$. This is achieved by *spreading* the object type (class) information onto the feature vector of the multi-represented object via the function spr (see also section 5.3). This xor-convolution of type and feature value information makes it difficult to extract the type information from the vector representation $\vec{d}$, since this requires high systematicity. Both class labels "0":= $\vec{c}_1 = (0, 1)$ and "1":= $\vec{c}_2 = (1, 0)$ are encoded by vectors of the same length, such that there is no possibility of differentiating between the classes upon distinct code lengths. For the harder learning task, an exemplary training pattern $input \mapsto target$ for the MRNN is of the following shape:

$$[\,\vec{d} := spr(\underbrace{binary(quantize(\vec{f}))}_{\vec{b}}, \vec{c}_i)\,] \quad \mapsto \quad \vec{c}_i \qquad (4.40)$$

$$spr((0,0,1,0),(1,0)) \stackrel{xor}{=} (1,1,0,1,0,0,1,0) \quad \mapsto \quad (1,0) \qquad (4.41)$$

After quantizing the numerical feature vectors (lossy transformation with quantization factor q) and converting the discretized result to binary vectors, these were spread with the class information $\vec{c}_1$ or $\vec{c}_2$ respectively. After each numeric feature value was quantized into a range of $q = 8$ ordinal features, these were binary encoded into $\log_2 8 = 3$ bits. For a numerical feature f_1 with the value range $[0, 50]$, the following mappings would be conducted, for example: $(f_1 = 5.5) \mapsto 0$, $(f_2 = 23.7) \mapsto 4$, $(f_3 = 49.5) \mapsto 7$, etc.

Finally, the obtained binary vector $\vec{b}$ was spread (convoluted) with the unique class information[24] $\vec{c}_i$. The dimensionality of the final vector $\vec{d}$ is calculated based on the original feature vector $\vec{f}$ as follows: $dim(\vec{d}) = (dim(\vec{f}) \cdot \log_2 q) \cdot dim(\vec{c})$. The useless information in form of the vector $\vec{b}$ can be interpreted as noise that is imposed on the class information in a systematic way. Figure 4.21 visualizes both the network topology and the vector representation.

After accomplishing the training phase, untrained molecules should again be classified. Therefore, these objects are assigned to the correct class label by spreading their feature vector with the respective type code vector, as done before for the training examples. They are now fed into the network and the classification accuracy is measured for all test samples. The MRNN successfully discovered the convoluted type information from the feature values. One hundred percent of the test objects were classified properly, even if the type information is *xored* in this systematic way (see spreading function) with the objects' feature values.

This finding may be quite astonishing to the reader, because the connectionist system achieves better results than learning the training examples by rote. *Rote learning* is a learning technique which avoids the understanding of a subject and instead focuses on memorization [CV08]. Doing better than learning by rote, that is providing a certain generalization capability, is commonly expected from connectionist systems and can be understood as intelligent behavior according to chapter 1. In the present learning scenario, the network is not told which information is reliable in determining the correct object class with a certainty of one hundred percent. Hence, the proper information selection was self-learned by the MRNN. This form of intelligent behavior even contradicts the usual notion of "garbage in – garbage out" [SJ00] to some extent, since the network not only picks the relevant vector components, but even recognizes the systematicity of the xor-operator when combining the useless transformed feature vector $\vec{b}$ with the decisive bit sequence $\vec{c}_i$,

---

[24]Encoded by a spreading code in terms of section 5.3.

110   CHAPTER 4. MACHINE LEARNING AND THE FRAMEWORK ENGINE

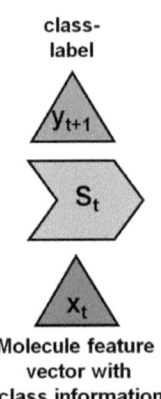

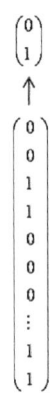

Figure 4.21: Training setup with single input node that carries both the feature values and the class information of the respective molecule.

Figure 4.22: Vector representation $\vec{x}_t := \vec{d}$ of molecule features that was discretized and digitized first and then xor-ed with the class information $\vec{y}_{t+1} = (0,1)$, resulting in a dimensionality of $dim(\vec{x}_t) = 2324$. The setup corresponds to figure 4.21.

$i = 1, 2$. Thus, it could be proposed that the connectionist system is smarter than required for usual supervised learning.

These two experimental tasks show that the connectionist model indeed possesses an "intelligent" learning capability as defined in the very beginning of this chapter: the system succeeds in recognizing regularities or patterns in a set of examples and separates them from the irregularities. In this case, the irregularities are given by the quantized and binary vector $\vec{b}$, resulting from the feature vector $\vec{f}$, which is not necessary for predicting the correct class label. This requires considerable systematicity from the connectionist system, which provides further evidence for the connectionist capability of systematic processing discussed in chapter 2.

4.5   Conclusion

In this chapter, we introduced neural networks as a connectionist machine learning method. We defined the basic architecture of a feed-forward network and we gave an overview of further network types. In a short excursion to information theory, we presented the role of information and its representation, which was classified by concepts such as the information entropy or the Kolmogorov complexity. Subsequently, we discussed the rationale for a connectionist framework engine and the benefits of neural networks and other machine learning techniques.

Furthermore, the design of the SYMBOCONN framework core, the *Modular Re-*

current Neural Network (MRNN) and its training algorithm were described, which represent the backbone of the connectionist learning capability. Finally, connectionist learning was illustrated from the practical point of view by a learning experiment based on the classification of molecule data. The goal of this experiment was to make the machine learning engine distinguish between significant and insignificant information in a self-learning process, which clearly showed the capabilities of connectionist machine learning.

Chapter 5

Connectionist Learning of Symbolic Structures

The SYMBOCONN framework described in chapter 3 must be able to process structured symbolic knowledge and thereby provide a degree of systematicity. Compositional structures that are composed of simple or complex entities can be described by formal grammars. In order to open up structured contents to connectionist models, we make these contents machine learnable by employing the theory of formal languages according to the *Chomsky hierarchy* [Sch01]. For this purpose, a transformation into a grammatical formulation is required.

In the first step of developing connectionist-symbolic capabilities, the context-free grammar productions are composed of symbolic constituents which do not contain actual domain content, such as textual or numerical attribute values.

In a second step, the context-free Chomsky grammars are extended by a *typing mechanism*, which overcomes the limitations of untyped grammars and enables to consider *simple* and *complex types*. Formal grammars are often untyped; for example, the Chomsky hierarchy defines grammar productions whose variables and terminal symbols are not assigned to certain categories (types). By contrast, categorical or typed grammars are often used in (computer) linguistics and natural language processing, where the constituents of the productions are assigned to categories such as noun, verb or adjective [Lam61, Wes00] (see also *syntactic structure tree, phrase structure grammar*). The grammar rules to be learned by the SYMBOCONN engine can be advanced to *content-based rules* as described in section 3.2. For this purpose, the atomic symbols are substituted by multi-represented objects that reflect actual domain contents in addition to the structure reflected by the grammar. The resulting *semantically rich complex structures* are learnable by the framework and are especially suitable to describe knowledge from the disciplines of software and knowledge engineering.

We introduce a *spread spectrum* encoding technique that improves the robustness of connectionist classification against noise – in the case of structured data as well, for example, in UML diagrams. At the end of this chapter, a connectionist technique is presented that enables to represent and transform non-flat but tree-shaped knowledge structures. By learning to holistically transform symbolic expressions according to the distributive law, we demonstrate a realization of the generalization hierarchy presented in section 3.1.1.2. Providing different levels of generalization is a major functional requirement of the SYMBOCONN framework. A specific topology and training configuration turns the MRNN into a *Recursive Auto-Associative Memory* (RAAM), a special neural network for holistic processing of recursively nested structures. That is, the SYMBOCONN framework supports RAAM networks as special configurations of the more generic MRNN. Its modular composition enables the reproduction of a RAAM network by presenting the training patterns in a prescribed order.

In software engineering, holistic processing is useful to represent tree-shaped knowledge such as class hierarchies or to incorporate – by machine learning – model transformations on tree- or graph-based structures such as class diagrams according to given design patterns.

5.1 Incorporating Domain Knowledge in Form of Rules

Symbolic knowledge is often represented in the form of logics or rules, while rules can be viewed as a special case of logics since they mainly correspond to a logical implication $A \rightarrow B$. Rule-based domain knowledge represents a pillar of knowledge-based disciplines and applications, which is comprehensible and traceable, at least on a smaller scale.

Rule-based systems, which are also referred to as knowledge-based systems, have been the standard approach to intelligent symbolic information processing, as demonstrated by Newell and Simon in their original work on "Human Problem Solving" [NS72]. An early system was MYCIN, which was based on a relatively simple inference engine with a knowledge base of less than 1,000 rules. It was augmented by a numerical uncertainty model [SB75]. Further prominent expert systems were XCON [BVO89, Svi90] and XSEL [MM89].

A significant problem of expert systems is that they must be constantly updated with new information. A further disadvantage of a rule-based approach to an intelligent system which can operate on different domains is that the knowledge is generally too broad and diverse to be represented completely. Thus, either the considered rule set is too narrow to cover all relevant domain problems or the rule set becomes large and, as a result, impossible to maintain. An even worse case presents itself when knowledge is not readily available or is difficult to elicit from humans due to cognitive or organizational limitations. If knowledge was successfully elicited, then the question of whether the conclusions given by the domain experts – the consequent part of a rule – are valid or how they can be validated, arises. So-called knowledge engineers, who conduct or support the knowledge extraction process and have to be kept available for updates of the rule-base, are required. Again, the maintenance of the corpus of rules, of which some are frequently and others less frequently used, represents a significant challenge.

For these and other reasons, the development and commercial application of expert systems came to a halt in the 1980s. But the field of rule-based systems has never declined [Dur96]. In fact, it experienced a revival in the form of the Semantic Web initiative, which advanced the symbolic approach to artificial intelligence. Still, rules are an important component of the symbolic knowledge-representation and reasoning process. For example, the *Semantic Web Rule Language* (SWRL) is a semantic web standard for defining domain-specific rules.

Due to the described importance of symbolic knowledge, the functionality of rule learning must be integrated into the SYMBOCONN framework. The framework must be able to incorporate domain knowledge in the form of rules. Often, a small set of rules is enough to train the neural network and to acquire a basic understanding of the domain. Based on this prior knowledge, the target domain is further discovered by learning from examples, that is, learning from empirical data and not from symbolic rules. This step represents a fuzzyfication, since the observational knowledge can partially contradict the learned rules. Finally, to close the process of knowledge acquisition, the hybrid rule-based and empirical knowledge will again be elicited from the machine learning engine. The inverse process of extracting rules from the trained neural network is possible in principle [ZJC03] and should be addressed by the SYMBOCONN framework in scope of future work. In the following, we will see that the MRNN machine learning engine facilitates the rule extraction process, since its topology corresponds to the structure of context-free or context-sensitive rules.

We introduce the use of formal grammars to explicitly specify structured knowledge in a formal and hence machine-learnable way. *Compositional structures* that are composed of simple and complex entities can be described by formal grammars. Thus, knowledge which is represented in *semantically rich complex structures*, as for example, the models in software development are, becomes learnable by the SYMBOCONN framework.

Definition 5.1.1: Context-Free Rule
Let Σ be the alphabet of *terminal symbols* (lowercase letters) and V the set of variables or *non-terminal symbols*, $V \cap \Sigma = \emptyset$ (capital letters). Context-free grammars consist of production rules of the form

$$A \to \alpha_1 \ldots \alpha_n, \quad A \in V, \alpha_i \in (\Sigma \cup V)^*. \tag{5.1}$$

Thereby, the left rule sides always consist of a single variable $A \in \mathcal{V}$, while the right sides may contain terminal symbols or variables $\alpha_i \in \Sigma \cup \mathcal{V}$.

Recurrent neural networks have already been applied to incorporate context-free grammars and shown to be capable of classifying or predicting words $\omega \in L$ of the generated language L. These words are sequences of terminal symbols of the underlying alphabet Σ. Different types of RNNs like Elman's *Simple Recurrent Network* (SRN) or *Jordan Nets* were utilized to classify words in terms of membership $\omega \in L$ or $\omega \notin L$ – the so-called *word problem* [Sch01] (cf. section 5.1). The

SYMBOCONN framework should be able to learn symbolic information schemas such as document grammars either by example or by directly learning the rule corpus. As an example, a structured document is depicted in figure 5.1, which is *valid* with respect to a certain context-free grammar. Thus, the document is an instance of the grammar. With regard to the implicit multiplicities for the elements <TR> and

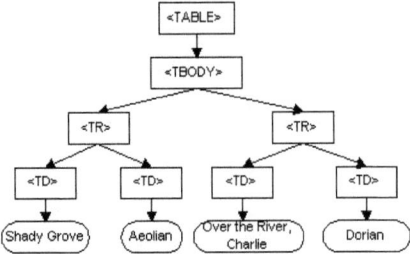

Figure 5.1: Graphical representation of an instance of the *HTML-Table* schema (grammar). Source: *http://www.w3.org/TR/DOM-Level-2-Core/introduction.html*.

<TD>, the exemplary table definition in figure 5.1 is an instance of the following grammar with additional auxiliary variables $V_i \in \mathcal{V}$, $i = 1, 2$:
$P := \{$

$$\begin{aligned}
<TABLE> &\Rightarrow <TBODY>, \\
<TBODY> &\Rightarrow V_1, \\
V_1 &\Rightarrow <TR> V_1, \\
V_1 &\Rightarrow \epsilon, \\
<TR> &\Rightarrow V_2, \\
V_2 &\Rightarrow <TD> V_2, \\
V_2 &\Rightarrow \epsilon, \\
<TD> &\Rightarrow \{ShadyGrove, Aeolian, OvertheRiver, Dorian\}
\end{aligned}$$

$\}$

Definition 5.1.2: Context-Sensitive Rule
The context-sensitive rule

$$\alpha B \gamma \to \alpha \beta \gamma, \quad B \in V, \; \alpha, \beta, \gamma \in (V \cup \Sigma)^* \tag{5.2}$$

substitutes the variable B only in the context of being enclosed by α and γ.

Even a context-sensitive rule can theoretically be recognized by neural networks with the appropriate learning algorithm. The expressiveness of context-sensitive grammars is high, which, in practice, makes it quite difficult to learn context-sensitive grammars. Consider the context-sensitive rule $\alpha B \gamma \rightarrow \alpha \beta \gamma$, which allows a mapping of B to β only in the context of α and γ. Despite its high expressiveness, such a rule is learnable by the MRNN, since the network possesses three layers, two of them being endowed with a nonlinear activation function. The appropriate topology for this task is shown in figure 5.2. The structure of the recurrent neural network adapts to the structure of the rule. In the case of multilayer perceptrons with feed-forward propagation, the data is usually fitted to the network topology, which is not feasible for rule-based knowledge.

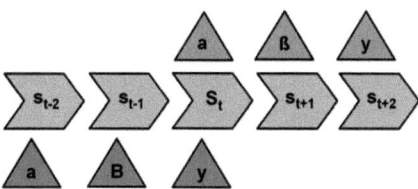

Figure 5.2: Topology of the SYMBOCONN machine learning engine for context-sensitive learning of the production $\alpha B \gamma \rightarrow \alpha \beta \gamma$. The variable B is substituted by the terminal symbol β only in the context of being enclosed by α and γ.

Learning context-free and context-sensitive expert rules is not a simple task for neural networks and not all network types are appropriate for this task. An actual example of domain knowledge which is represented and processed in the form of context-sensitive *If... Then...* rules is knowledge about *business processes*, which can be formalized by *decision tables* and *decision rules*. Many insurance companies and banks use this representation to describe the *conditions* and *actions* of their business processes.

Figure 5.3 shows an incomplete but consistent decision table as could be used to describe a business process in a bank.

Consistency is implicitly guaranteed by a connectionist realization, since nonfunctional mappings of conditions to actions cannot be learned by neural networks as explained by section A.2.1. The shown table is incomplete, since the rules for four combinations of conditions are missing. What happens if the credit line is exceeded, the payment behavior is not blameless, and the overdrawn amount is below EUR 500,-? That is, $Y \ N \ Y \mapsto ?$, since for this combination of conditions, there is no corresponding action in the decision table 5.3. Connectionist incorporation of business rules provides the chance to handle combinations of rule conditions that have not been given by the decision table, if the conditions and actions are represented in a content-based manner by means of *content-based rules* as defined in section 3.2. This is a generalization task of Level 1 or 2 according to the hierarchy of section 3.1.1.2, because either the realizations of the conditions appear in new combinations, or they occur in new syntactical positions. The example $Y \ N \ Y \mapsto ?$

Decision Table for *Cashing Checks*		Rules			
Conditions	Credit line exceeded?	Y	Y	Y	Y
	Payment behavior blameless?	Y	Y	N	-
	Exceedance < EUR 500,-?	Y	N	-	Y
Actions	Cash the check	X	X		X
	Don't cash the check			X	
	Present new conditions		X		

Figure 5.3: Exemplary and simplified decision table for the business process *cash check* of a bank. The table is incomplete, since not all $2^3 = 8$ combinations of the given binary conditions are defined as antecedent part of a rule. Legend: Y = *Yes*, N = *No*, - = *irrelevant*, X = *execute action*.

requires Level 1 generalization, since the realization 'N' of the second condition has already appeared at the second position, but not in this combination.

The generalization performance of the system could easily be measured by training the MRNN on incomplete decision tables, while the corresponding complete tables are available for testing. With a representative and comprehensive dataset, an acceptable generalization rate is likely to be achieved, since Level 1 or 2 generalization are significantly easier tasks than handling novel entities (Level 3).

Another technique for representing domain knowledge with rules is the Semantic Web Rule Language mentioned above. These rules are specified in XML syntax and can be integrated into the reasoning process based on description logic[1] and OWL-ontologies (Web Ontology Language), thus becoming executable. In general, content that is represented according to the XML standard can be indirectly learned by the framework, since it can automatically be transformed to a set of formal grammar rules. Normally this would imply an information loss, because element annotations like *XML attributes*[2] cannot be considered by the grammar. Its variables and terminal symbols only stand for XML elements, while the additional information given by the attributes is not representable by conventional grammar rules, since they only define the content structure. Again, the *content-based rules* introduced in section 3.2 provide a solution to this problem by integrating an arbitrary set of attribute values into the rule constituents using *multi-represented objects*.

In the next section, we address the recognition of rules that are relevant for the business rule scenario; for example, by means of the Reber grammar, which is often used to determine a system's capability of learning a context-free grammar.

---

[1] There are the description logic (DL) standards OWL Lite, OWL DL, and OWL Full [SWM04].
[2] *XML attributes* enable the consideration of numbered multiplicities, for example.

CHAPTER 5. CONNECTIONIST LEARNING OF SYMBOLIC STRUCTURES 119

Learning the Reber Grammar The *Reber grammar* G_{Reb} is a regular grammar defined by a set of productions that generate all words of the corresponding language $L(G_{Reb})$. These productions can be expressed by a deterministic *Finite State Machine* with anonymous or unnamed states in a complete way, which is shown in figure 5.4. The automaton is deterministic because there is no node that has an

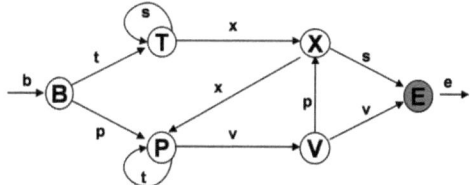

Figure 5.4: Deterministic finite state automaton for the *Reber grammar*. The determinism enforces that there is no transition a, which leads to different states z', z'': $\nexists a : z \stackrel{a}{\Rightarrow} z'$ & $z \stackrel{a}{\Rightarrow} z''$.

ambiguous transition via the same symbol to more than one node (state). The productions of the Reber grammar can be extracted from this automaton.
$P_{Reber} = \{$

$$b \Rightarrow t, T$$
$$b \Rightarrow p, P$$
$$T \Rightarrow s, T$$
$$T \Rightarrow s, X$$
$$X \Rightarrow x, P$$
$$X \Rightarrow s, E \quad\quad (5.3)$$
$$P \Rightarrow t, P$$
$$P \Rightarrow v, V$$
$$V \Rightarrow p, X$$
$$V \Rightarrow v, E$$
$$E \Rightarrow e$$

$\}$

Note that these rules are ambiguous and cannot be learned in the given form, since they represent a relation, but not a functional mapping, as stated in section A.2.1. For example, the start symbol b is either followed by the symbol t or p, which is deterministic in terms of the subsequent states T or P, but there are two possible transitions that leave state B. Regular or context-free grammars may contain several productions with the same left side, which contradicts the functional mapping realized by a recurrent neural network. In this case, the grammar is called *ambiguous.*

The Reber grammar can, however, be learned by example, which is presented in the following. Therefore, it is sufficient to train a recurrent neural network in the way that it behaves like a *Finite State Automaton* (FSA) (cf. [CF00]). An FSA as depicted in figure 5.4 can only generate or respectively accept the *regular languages* $\mathcal{L}_3$, according to the *Chomsky-hierarchy*. These are generated by the grammars of type three in this hierarchy, whose regular production rules are the least expressive ones, but are nevertheless sufficient to describe all relevant node sequences on the abstract knowledge base. Formal grammars are also useful for modeling user navigations on a graph. For instance, *loop detection* can be formalized as a special word classification problem: $\exists i \geq \kappa \in \mathbb{N}, \omega = pt^i v$. This repetition of the symbol t corresponds to a cycle at the node with a reflexive connection via t in figure 5.4.

While structured knowledge exists in many application domains, its building rules are not explicit. This form of tacit knowledge is often hidden in the form of individual expertise of domain experts; however, one can benefit from this procedural knowledge by incorporation from examples. The Reber automaton could be used to represent procedural knowledge[3], since its states could be mapped to states and activities of an activity diagram, and its transitions would correspond to the branching conditions, for example.

Assuming that a machine should be constructed which decides if a word is conform with the Reber grammar or not, and this machine succeeds with high probability, then learning by example is an adequate means which does not require information about the explicit grammar productions. Samples of Reber-conform and non-conform words are given in table 5.1. Now, the MRNN should decide whether these words stem from the Reber grammar or not, which is a binary classification task also known as the *word problem*.

Word	Length	Reber-conform
"btsxse"	6	yes
"btsssxse"	8	yes
"btsssxs"	7	no

Table 5.1: Words of different lengths generated by the Reber automaton depicted in figure 5.4.

Word Problem: Classifying Words w.r.t. Reber-Conformity The classification task was conducted especially to assess the learning and generalization power of the *Modular Recurrent Neural Network* (MRNN) in the SYMBOCONN framework. The network was trained on 1,000 words of average length 8.2 – split into 500 Reber-conform words and 500 arbitrary non-Reber-conform words. Then, 10,000 further test words were generated according to the *Reber Grammar* [CSSM89]. These were processed by the MRNN; 99.71% of the positive and negative samples

---
[3]Procedural knowledge is also called *control knowledge*.

of the Reber grammar, which had not been presented in training, were properly classified.

Completion of Partial Reber Sentences Differing from the decision whether words stem from a certain grammar or not, the *completion task* aims at reading a partial word and predicting the missing subsequent symbols in order to produce a complete word according to the given grammar. More formally, the completion task is to continue the symbol sequence $\check{\omega} = a_1 \ldots a_k$, $a_i \in \Sigma$, for a given partial word $\check{\omega}$, $\omega = \check{\omega}\hat{\omega}$, such that the predicted sequence of subsequent symbols $\hat{\omega} = a_{k+1} \ldots a_n$ is also conform with the rules of the grammar.

The results for the completion of 1,010 partial Reber words are presented in table 5.2, both for the immediate prediction and for the stepwise prediction technique. The average length of the input parts $\check{\omega}$ of these test words was $\frac{1}{n}\sum_{i=1}^{n}|\check{\omega}_i| = 5.75$. While the prediction accuracy could have been further improved, the goal of this

Prediction technique	Test set size	Properly continued [%]
Immediate	1,010	74.26
Stepwise	1,010	97.23

Table 5.2: Results of partial word completion according to the Reber grammar. Two different prediction techniques are distinguished and their performance is compared in terms of prediction accuracy. Compared to the *immediate* prediction, the *stepwise* mode refeeds the one-step output o_{t+1} as input x_t for the next one-step prediction. The hidden layer dimension was set to $h = 25$, the remaining training error was $E = 9.23\%$, since we did not remove all ambiguous training patterns (relational mapping).

test was to show that the MRNN is able to learn a grammar from only few examples and then works effectively on a comparatively large and unseen test set. Only 160 Reber-conform input-target pairs were trained, which was sufficient for properly continuing 982 words out of a test set of 1,010 words $\check{\omega}$ (97.23%) in *stepwise prediction mode*. Both prediction modes are further explained and illustrated in appendix A.1.2.1.

In addition to incorporating conventional grammar productions, the SYMBOCONN framework also supports typed grammars. Usually, formal grammars $G = (\mathcal{V}, \Sigma, P, S)$ are type free in the way that their variables $V \in \mathcal{V}$ and terminal symbols $\sigma \in \Sigma$ are not assigned to types that group them according to their similarities. This extension of symbolic knowledge representation, which should be learnable by the SYMBOCONN framework, is addressed in the next section.

5.2   Type Representation and Type Hierarchies

To the best of our knowledge, processing typed symbolic structures by means of connectionist models like recurrent neural networks is a novel contribution of this dissertation. The additional capability of type learning is built on top of the MRNN and opens up new perspectives in machine learning of symbolic constructs such as UML class diagrams, for example.

Knowledge nodes are assigned to types by a *typing function* $\mu : V \to C$, which is a mapping from the node space to the type or class space. The set $C = \{C_1, C_2, \ldots, C_r\}$ is composed of concrete types C_i that can be considered as classes of homogeneous instances. The node set V is partitioned into sets C_i, such that the union of all instances $\bigcup_i^r C_i = V$ is the definition space of μ. An example of a concrete type C_i is *text document* or *XML element* in terms of the *XML schema definition* (XMLS) [Fal04].

In order to deal with object types, the sequence-learning MRNN is extended by classification capabilities. Symbols or symbol structures are represented as nodes v_i or subgraphs (V', E'), $V' \subset V, E' \subset E$, respectively, and are learned as sequences of typed nodes with given types $\mu(v_i)$. Inference of new knowledge is conducted as classification of unknown and untyped objects or whole structures built of these objects (e.g. subgraphs such as class diagrams), where the expected output is the respective type label. In other words, when a yet unseen structure is presented to the neural network in the form of the left side of a grammar rule, the most likely type of that structure (*complex type*, cf. section 6.3.2) is classified[4] according to the given class labels $\{1, \ldots, r\}$.

Type Hierarchies Beyond the learning of flat types, the machine learning system should also support types that are arranged in an inheritance hierarchy. Therefore whole *inheritance* or *type hierarchies* are treated, which arrange the types to be learned in a subsumption relation. The system must be able to recognize subtypes of more general types in terms of subsets $A_k \subset A_{k-1} \subset \ldots \subset A_0 \subseteq D$ of the domain. The series $(A_k, A_{k-1}, \ldots, A_0)$ can be identified with the general type set $C = \{C_1, C_2, \ldots, C_r\}$, but C does not provide an order. Let $\leq_S$ on C be the *subtype relation*, where $C_j \leq_S C_i$ means that C_j is subtype of C_i.

The knowledge of discourse can also be considered from a set-theoretic point of view with $\mathcal{D}$ being the set of all domain objects. Types are mapped onto not necessarily disjoint sets C_i, $C_i \subseteq \mathcal{D}$, which are also called *concepts* or *classes* of the domain. The example in figure 5.5 shows the types $A_1, A_2, A_3, B \subset \mathcal{D}$ (cf. section 2.1), which are subtypes of the domain $\mathcal{D}$.

The given type taxonomy is realized by *prefix-based sub-typing*, which is a novel encoding schema for typed contents. Types are mapped to binary spreading codes of different lengths that are arranged in a code tree, which is isomorphic to the type taxonomy.

For connectionist learning of type hierarchies, the concept of *orthogonal spreading codes* is employed in a novel way. As described in section 5.3.1, spreading codes are used to spread the input vectors onto the shared state space.

---

[4]Compare *Maximum Likelihood Classifier*.

CHAPTER 5. CONNECTIONIST LEARNING OF SYMBOLIC STRUCTURES   123

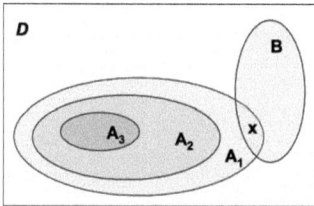

Figure 5.5: Set-theoretic interpretation of symbol types. The object $x \in V$, which is numerically represented by a vector $\vec{x}$, is an instance of the set A_1 as well as of the set B. Therefore, its type is a subtype of both super types A_1 and B ($A_1 \not\subset B$, $B \not\subset A_1$), which is called *multiple inheritance*.

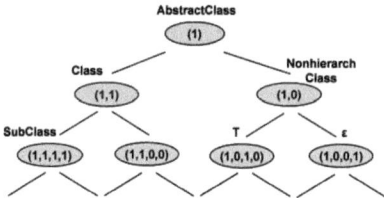

Figure 5.6: Prefix-based type taxonomy exemplarily labeled with generic classes (types) of an UML model, further discussed in section 6.3. The subordinate types *Class* and *NonhierarchClass* of level 2 determine the code prefix of all subsequent child nodes. Obviously, there remains a degree of freedom in assigning symbols to codes, since only the correct mapping of inheritance relations to cross-correlating codes has to be preserved.

Correlation properties For separation of different node types, which are each assigned to unique code sequences, it is necessary to consider the correlation properties of such codes.

Definition 5.2.1: Autocorrelation
Correlation of a bipolar sequence $\vec{c}$ of N elements with all phase shifts n of itself.

$$\Phi_{\vec{c},\vec{c}}(n) = \frac{1}{N}\sum_{m=1}^{N} c[m] \cdot c[m+n]$$

A spreading code $\vec{c}$ holds a *good autocorrelation* if its inner product $\Phi_{\vec{c},\vec{c}}(0)$ with itself is high and $\Phi_{\vec{c},\vec{c}}(n)$ is low for all shifts $n = 1\ldots N\text{-}1$ [Kü04].

Definition 5.2.2: Cross-correlation
Correlation of two sequences $\vec{c}$ and $\vec{d}$, while $\vec{d}$ is shifted N times.

$$\Phi_{\vec{c},\vec{d}}(n) = \frac{1}{N}\sum_{m=1}^{N} c[m] \cdot d[m+n],$$

$n = 0..N\text{-}1$, $c[i] \in \{-1, 1\}$. For good separation properties between different types C_i, C_j, the respective spreading codes $\vec{c}_i$ and $\vec{c}_j$ must possess a low cross-correlation value $\Phi_{\vec{c}_i,\vec{c}_j}(n)$ for all shifts $n = 1\ldots N\text{-}1$. If their cross-correlation is zero, then these codes are said to be *fully orthogonal*.

In signal transmission, good autocorrelation is essential for achieving synchronization between sender and receiver. Here, it is useful for recognizing the length of the employed spreading code in the decoding phase, since codes of different lengths are allowed for different types.

We use the *Orthogonal Variable Spreading Factor* (OVSF) method for creating type codes for the nodes from V. For separation of a high number of different object classes, these are assigned to unique OVSF codes, which hold appropriate correlation properties [Kü04] and can be generated recursively via a tree schema as shown in figure 5.7.

The inheritance hierarchy is mapped onto OVSF codes that show distinct cross-correlation properties among each other. The cross-correlation among OVSF codes of the same level is actually zero, $\Phi_{\vec{c}_i,\vec{c}_j}(n) = 0$, $i \neq j$, $i,j = 1,\ldots,7$, $n = 0,\ldots,N\text{-}1$, which makes them fully orthogonal. In contrast, codes of different levels on the same path from the root node hold non-zero cross-correlations and are thus appropriate for expressing the type-to-subtype relationships. A type A_i and all of its subtypes $A_j \subseteq A_i$ are represented by spreading codes $\vec{c}_i^T = (c_{i,1}, \ldots, c_{i,\lambda_i})$ and all $\vec{c}_j^T = (c_{i,1}, \ldots, c_{i,\lambda_i}, c_{j,(\lambda_i+1)}, \ldots, c_{j,(2\lambda_i)})$ always coincide in the first λ_i components; that is, all $\vec{c}_j$ have a *common prefix* that expresses their similarity. In other words, all code pairs (*parent,child*) in one branch from the root of the taxonomy hold a cross-correlation of $\frac{1}{2}$, while type codes of different branches but of the same length are *fully orthogonal*.

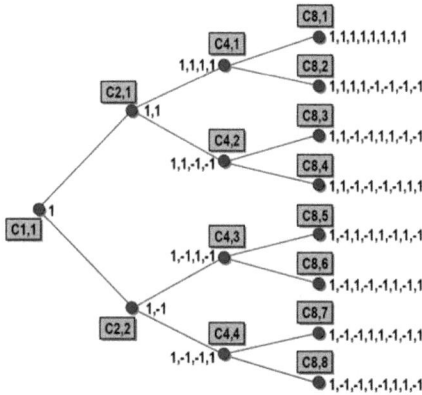

Figure 5.7: Recursive generation schema for OVSF codes in bipolar denotation [Kü04]. Codes that stand in a direct or indirect father-son relationship such as $C2, 1$, $C4, 2$ and $C8, 3$ can be mapped onto the type hierarchy of figure 5.6.

When processed with a neural network, codes with coincidences in λ_i components (prefix) lead to the same activations in the λ_i-dimensional subspace $\mathbb{R}^{\lambda_i} \subset S = \mathbb{R}^h$, $\lambda_i < h$ of the hidden state space S. Accordingly, symbolic data spread by these common-prefix codes also causes similar activations when propagated through the network. Thus, the prefix-based type encoding facilitates meaningful representation of nodes standing in an inheritance relation, which expresses the degree of compliance between the father and the child node.

In the following section, we introduce a novel classification mechanism based on the MRNN and on error-correcting output coding, which is robust against fuzzy or incompletely represented information. We develop this robust classification technique both to recognize fuzzy business rules and to classify incomplete software design patterns.

5.3 Spread Spectrum Based Classification

Many knowledge-driven and domain-specific problems such as speech and handwriting recognition, biometric identification, credit scoring, document classification, or design pattern recognition can be turned into statistical classification problems $O := \{o_1, \ldots, o_m\} \rightarrow \{C_1, \ldots, C_r\} =: C$ by partitioning the domain objects $o_i \in O$ into appropriate classes $C_j \in C$. A classification mechanism must be robust and capable of handling fuzzy, incomplete, and partially incorrect data, which may result from incomplete and inaccurate sensor measurements. Multi-represented objects should be reliably classified even when affected by high extents of noise. The field of knowledge discovery in databases already provides a variety of techniques for noise robust clustering in high-dimensional spaces and in their arbitrary subspaces, which are either based on similarity, density or subspace hyperplanes [ABD+08, ABK+07, YW04, CW99, FK96]. By contrast, noise robust classification is mainly found in speech recognition [RSS+07, XTDL06], but not as a general purpose application. However, there exists a need for noise robust classification methods. An example of this is learning and recognition of fuzzy business rules [Yag08] which is relevant to software development and knowledge management, in particular. In these areas, there are semi-formal or formal rules within the different development activities. For example, whenever a developer submits a new version of the program files in his local working directory to the repository, he must have accomplished an update operation before.

The central idea of the encoding and decoding algorithm presented in this section is to boost the classification accuracy and robustness by an approved and noise-resistant method from signal transmission (*spread spectrum*), which is adapted to the SYMBOCONN machine learning engine. Our technique transforms the output space into a higher dimensional space that eventually serves for the object classification. This idea was already employed in a similar way by *Error-Correcting Output Coding* (ECOC) [Gha00, Liu06]. Error-correcting codes have, for example, been used with decision trees and neural networks for classification tasks by Diettrich et al. [DK95]. Berger [Ber99] improved the classification of unstructured text using ECOC. The voting that is performed among the multiple classifiers in the case of ECOC corresponds to the despreading step of our new encoding technique, which also determines the class that matches best with the computed output signal. Compared to these error-correction approaches, we do not solve k-class supervised learning problems by training multiple 2-class classifiers. Instead, only one instance of the MRNN is trained upon the whole training set. The insertion of redundancy is similar to adding parity information for error recognition in binary sequences as done by *Cyclic Redundancy Check* (CRC) or *Hamming codes*. The strong benefit of our adaption of this technique is the achievable degree of discrimination between all existing classes $C_j, C_k, j \neq k$. As a consequence, the correct class $\mu(\vec{x}_t) = C_j$ can be determined with higher probability after the despreading process.

According to Diettrich et al., ECOC reduces both bias and variance of the used classification model. In contrast to the bias, the related concepts *noise* and *variance* represent unsystematic errors. A systematic error of a classifier is its deviation from the correct class label for all objects of the definition space, which – in the systematic case – is not random but follows a certain probability distribution.

For example, the residuals resulting from a least square optimization may still contain information, while noise as an unsystematic error does not. The variance of a classifier appears when classifying unseen instances from the test set with a certain misclassification rate. Similar to error-correcting output codes, the spread spectrum technique also reduces bias and variance of the classification model, which was underpinned by the higher generalization performance on benchmark datasets [Dav08b].

The spread spectrum technique [And97] stemming from mobile communication, spreads data over a wide bandwidth for transmission via the *air interface* [KFM+02]. The spread spectrum mechanism is characterized by a wideband transmission of signals[5], which is very robust against external interferences and noise. We exploit this mechanism for the precise discrimination between classes.

In a variant, the *Direct Sequence Spread Spectrum* (DSSS) technology [And97], all transmissions share a common carrier channel, which is furthermore exposed to environmental noise and various interferences. We can detect a parallel between the h-dimensional internal state layer of the MRNN that serves as state transition space $S \subset \mathbb{R}^h$ and the carrier medium in mobile communication.

In contrast to wireless signal transmission, the signal to be transmitted is intentionally changed by the forward propagation of the recurrent neural network (cf. formula 4.14) in order to match the desired target class $\mu(\vec{x}_t) \in C$ represented by $\vec{y}_{t+1}$. In terms of mobile communication, the sent signal carries the attribute values of the respective object $\vec{x}_t \in \mathbb{R}^{d_1}$ to be mapped onto its known class $\mu(\vec{x}_t)$. This has to be learned during the training phase by minimizing the Euclidean distance $\|\vec{o}_{t+1} - \vec{y}_{t+1}\|_2$. All input sequences $\vec{x}_{t-k}, \ldots, \vec{x}_t$ are propagated through the recurrent state layer $\vec{s}_{t-k}, \ldots, \vec{s}_t, \ldots, \vec{s}_{t+m}$ in forward direction. Subsequently, the deviations from the targets $\vec{y}_{t+1}, \ldots, \vec{y}_{t+m}$ to be learned by the MRNN are sent backwards. In case of object classification, the input-target sequences degenerate to input-target pairs $(\vec{x}_t \mapsto \vec{y}_{t+1}) \in TS$, where TS is the training set.

Given an input object $\vec{x}_t$, the associated class or type $\mu(\vec{x}_t) \in C$ should be recognized, given by the typing function $\mu : O \to C$. In the operative classification phase, the received signal has to be decoded to the correct class $\mu(\vec{x}_t) \in C$. This information is drawn from the spread output vector $\vec{o}_{t+1}$ (observed output), which has dimensionality $dim(\vec{o}_{t+1}) \leq d_2$. After having used the targets $\vec{y}_{t+1} = f(C\vec{s}_t)$ (see formula 4.14, section 4.4.1) for network training, d_2 is only an upper bound on the output dimensionality, since we allow variably dimensional vectors as encoding of the class labels. Therefore, the question is how to recover the class information from the output signal. A solution to this issue will be given by the despreading mechanism described in section 5.3.2.

5.3.1 Encoding of Node Types Using Spread Spectrum

The spread spectrum encoding of a target class label $C_i \in C$, $r(C_i) = \vec{b} = b_1 b_2 \ldots b_n$, $b_i \in \{0, 1\}$ is performed by applying an *XOR-operation* to the basic encoding (unary) of C_i. That is, $\vec{b}$ is *XOR*ed with a fixed binary code – the so-called *spreading code*[6], which imposes well-defined redundancy on the code vector $\vec{b}$. We chose *Barker codes* [Fak96] of different lengths as spreading sequences of the form $\vec{c} = c_1 c_2 \ldots c_\lambda$, $c_i \in \{0, 1\}$, $L = \lambda \cdot m$, $\lambda \in \mathbb{N}$, where λ is the *spreading factor* and L is the overall length of the resulting code.

---
[5]Utilized by *Code Division Multiple Access* (CDMA) in the *UMTS* standard.
[6]Also called *chipping* or *spreading sequence*.

Definition 5.3.1: Spreading Process

The spreading process is defined by the function spr, which convolutes an arbitrary bit vector $\vec{b}$ – that represents the object class, for example – with a well-defined spreading code $\vec{c}$.

$$spr(\vec{b}, \vec{c}) = xor(b_1, c_1), \; xor(b_1, c_2), \ldots, xor(b_1, c_\lambda),$$
$$xor(b_2, c_1), \; xor(b_2, c_2), \ldots, xor(b_2, c_\lambda), \qquad (5.4)$$
$$\vdots$$
$$xor(b_n, c_1), \qquad \ldots \qquad , xor(b_n, c_\lambda)$$

The resulting code is a bit string of length $n\lambda$; the xor-expressions are separated by commas to distinguish their concatenation from a multiplication. An example of spreading and despreading is provided in the next section. The spread spectrum technique is imposed as additional encoding to improve the type classification for the computed output signal $\vec{o}_{t+1}$. Each class label C_j is assigned to an own spreading sequence $\vec{c}_j$ such that all instances $\vec{y}_k \in C_j$ of the same class are encoded by $\vec{c}_j$.

5.3.2 Classification by Despreading

The data spreading in the form of an additional encoding causes redundancy, the amount of which depends on the fixed *spreading factor* $\lambda \in \mathbb{N}$ and thus reduces the computational efficiency. On the other side, the obtained *process gain* justifies the insertion of redundancy. The process gain PG, which is shown in figure 5.8, is defined as

$$PG := 10 \, \log_{10}(\frac{carrier\ bandwidth}{information\ bandwidth})[db] \qquad (5.5)$$

and is measured in decibel [Kü04]. When employed in terms of neural processing, the bandwidth is measured as the number of bits used to encode a class C_i, that is the dimensionality of the spread target vector $\vec{y}_{t+1}$.

Definition 5.3.2: Despreading Process

Let $\vec{o} := \vec{o}_{t+1} = (o_1 o_2 \ldots o_{d_2})$ be the observed output vector, $L \leq d_2$

$$\theta_\Delta(x) := \begin{cases} 1, & if \quad x > \Delta \\ 0, & else \end{cases} \qquad (5.6)$$

$\theta_\Delta(x)$ serves for digitalization of the numeric output signal, for the following equa-

CHAPTER 5. CONNECTIONIST LEARNING OF SYMBOLIC STRUCTURES   129

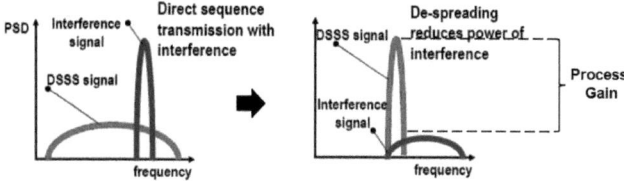

Figure 5.8: Visualization of the result of spreading and despreading and the obtained *process gain* in the analogy of signal transmission. The process gain becomes manifest in the amplitude of the despread signal in the right chart. *PSD* is the *Power Spectral Density* that specifies the power of a signal in an infinitesimal frequency band. The integral over all frequency proportions gives the power of the signal.

tions Δ will be set to 0.5 and the shortform $\theta(x) := \theta_{0.5}(x)$ is used.

$$despr(\vec{o}, \vec{c}) =$$
$$xor(\theta(o_1), c_1), xor(\theta(o_2), c_2), \ldots \quad , xor(\theta(o_\lambda), c_\lambda),$$
$$xor(\theta(o_{\lambda+1}), c_1), \ldots \quad , xor(\theta(o_{2\lambda}), c_\lambda),$$
$$\vdots \quad (5.7)$$
$$xor(\theta(o_{((n-1)\lambda)+1}), c_1), xor(\theta(o_{((n-1)\lambda)+2}), c_2), \ldots, xor(\theta(o_L), c_\lambda)$$
$$= \tau_1, \tau_2, \ldots, \tau_L, \quad \tau_i \in \{0, 1\}$$

The despreading is done λ-blockwise, because each block $\tau_{(k\cdot\lambda)+1} \cdots \tau_{(k+1)\cdot\lambda}$ of the spread output vector corresponds to a single bit of the original unspread representation.

Definition 5.3.3: Classification Certainty
The uniqueness of the decoding with respect to the original bit is considered as the distance of the prediction from the maximal entropy, where a clear decision can be made neither for 0 nor for 1. The relative *classification certainty* $cert$ for the k-th decoded bit is given by the distance from the mean value $minV$ (*minimum* number of *votes* required for a "1").

$$bitSum[k] := \sum_{i=((k-1)\cdot\lambda)+1}^{k\cdot\lambda} \tau_i \quad (5.8)$$

$$\hat{b}_k := \theta_{minV}(bitSum[k]), \quad (5.9)$$

$$minV := \frac{\lambda}{2}, \ k \in \{1, \ldots, n\}$$

$$cert := \frac{1}{n \cdot minV} \sum_{k=1}^{n} |bitSum[k] - minV| \quad (5.10)$$

The farther the result is separated from this mean value, which represents the maximal entropy where no decision can be made either for 0 or 1, the more unique the decoding is.

The relative classification certainty for a consensus $00\ldots 0$ or $11\ldots 1$ of all τ_i in a λ-block corresponds to a certainty of 100% for the bit b_k to decode as $\hat{b}_k = 0$ or $\hat{b}_k = 1$, respectively. Since different spreading codes $\vec{c}_i, \vec{c}_j$ may have different lengths $\lambda_i \neq \lambda_j$, the number of minimum votes $minV$ varies, but still does not influence the classification certainty of formula 5.10. Different code lengths are allowed, because the minimal number $n = \lceil \log_2 |C| \rceil$ of bits to represent all classes in the respective dataset is fixed and known a priori.

The overall certainty measure $\frac{1}{m}\sum_{k=1}^{m} cert[k]$ provides a tool for deciding between multiple matches, indicating the same original binary representation $\vec{b} = b_1 b_2 \ldots b_m$, $b_k \in \{0,1\}$. In this case, the type C_i with the highest certainty is chosen, which usually leads with a high certainty advance regarding alternatively matching types.

Figure 5.9 illustrates the complete despreading process, starting with the unclassified feature vector as input for the MRNN, the network prediction, and the subsequent digital despreading process. The downstreamed despreading through the

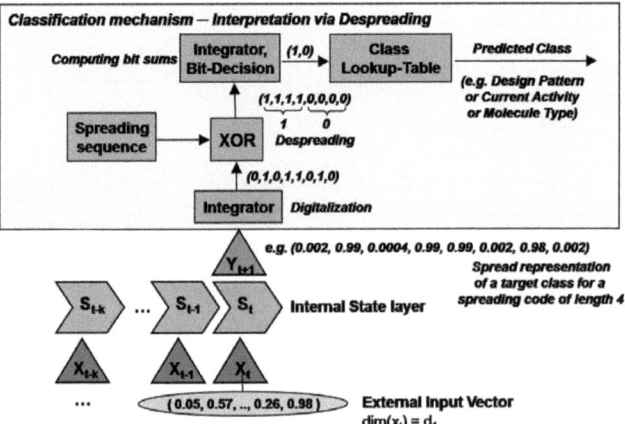

Figure 5.9: Schematic processing steps and gates required to despread the predicted numerical output signal $\vec{o}_{t+1}$. During the classification phase, the MRNN is fed with a domain-specific input vector to be classified, as for example with the representation of a class diagram, of an observed user behavior, or of a molecule. The predicted output signal $\vec{o}_{t+1}$ contains the class information that is reconstructed by the classification mechanism in the white box.

various xor-gates is repeated for all existing object classes. Thus, the output signal is despread with all spreading codes and each result is compared with the lookup-table that holds the basic encodings (unary) of all object classes C. If there is exactly one match $C_{hit} \in C$, then this class label is returned. Otherwise, it may be the case that none, one, or several of the despread sequences match one symbol from the lookup-table. Then, the most probable class label is predicted, which is determined by the certainty computed via formula 5.10. The certainty measure usually enables a clear decision between multiple decodings $\vec{b}'_{dec}$, $\vec{b}''_{dec}$, $\vec{b}'_{dec} = b'_1 b'_2 \ldots b'_n$, $b'_k \in \{0, 1\}$, $\vec{b}''_{dec} = \ldots$. The following despreading example will illustrate the used formulas.

Despreading Example When the network predicts the output vector $\vec{o} = (0.01, 0.9998, 0.00035, 0.9999, 0.9997, 0.0023, 0.9998, 0.0022)$, this vector is digitized by the *heaviside function* 5.6 at first: $\vec{o}_{\{0,1\}} = (0, 1, 0, 1, 1, 0, 1, 0)$. Then, $\vec{o}_{\{0,1\}}$ is despread with each of the existing spreading codes that represent the object classes.

$$despr((0, 1, 0, 1, 1, 0, 1, 0), (1, 0, 0, 1))$$
$$\stackrel{xor}{=} (\underbrace{1, 1, 0, 0}_{?}, \underbrace{0, 0, 1, 1}_{?})$$
$$despr((0, 1, 0, 1, 1, 0, 1, 0), (1, 0, 1, 0))$$
$$\stackrel{xor}{=} (\underbrace{1, 1, 1, 1}_{1}, \underbrace{0, 0, 0, 0}_{0})$$

Here a 100% certainty for class C_2 is reached by despreading with the spreading code $\vec{c}_2$, while the first code $\vec{c}_1$ does not allow a unique decoding at all (0% certainty). Thus, the classification is unique, a final table-lookup in table 5.3 revealing the predicted class label. The removal of the prior imposed redundancy results in

Class	Basic encoding	Spreading code
C_1	$\vec{b}_1$=(0,1)	$\vec{c}_1$=(1,0,1,0)
C_2	$\vec{b}_2$=(1,0)	$\vec{c}_2$=(1,0,0,1)

Table 5.3: Lookup-table containing the basic encoding and the assigned spreading codes that are unique for each class.

the main advantage of the spread spectrum technique, which is *robustness* against external interferences like noise blurring the input data. These effects are "spread out" (minimized) by the despreading process, which is also shown by the evaluation in the following section.

5.4 Rule Recognition Despite Heavy Noise

The inherent structure of a document can explicitly be specified by a grammar in a formal and hence machine-learnable way. Valid XML-based data is formed according to the rules of a context-free grammar (e.g. specified as *Document Type Definition* (DTD) or *XML Schema Definition* (XSD)). In this symbolic pattern recognition scenario, the rules of such a typed grammar are learned after a transformation to a context-sensitive form. In order to assess the *structure* as well as the *type learning performance* of the system, both functionalities are validated on the basis of an XML document as instance of the document grammar G. Thus, the concrete task is to continue a sentence from the defined language $L(G)$ according to the rules of G. Both the node name and its type should hereby be recognized by the classifier under the influence of different noise levels.

The grammar chosen for the evaluation is part of the *S1000D specification* for technical publications [Tec05]. These rules were derived from an XML document, a so-called *Data Module*, which formally describes the content of a self-contained technical issue enriched with meta information. An excerpt of this exemplary grammar is given by the following productions.

20-CFG rule set = {
avee ⇒ *modelic, sdc, chapnum, section, subsect, subject, discode, discodev, incode, incodev, itemloc;*
brexref ⇒ *refdm;*
content ⇒ *descript;*
descript ⇒ *para0;*
dmaddres ⇒ *dmc, dmtitle, issno, issdate, language;*
dmc ⇒ *avee;*
dmodule ⇒ *idstatus, content;*
figure ⇒ *title, graphic;*
idstatus ⇒ *dmaddres, status;*
status ⇒ *security, rpc, orig, applic, brexref, qa;*
...
}

Ten of the twenty learned context-free productions are listed, the first rule having the longest target sequence of eleven symbols to be learned and recognized correctly – even under the influence of noise on the left side variables. The left rule sides always consist of a single variable $A \in \mathcal{V}$, the right sides may contain terminal symbols or variables $\alpha_i \in \Sigma \cup \mathcal{V}$. The variables and terminal symbols are partitioned into four classes, the XML elements containing integer values are grouped to the type C_4=*XMLSimpleElement_Int* = {*chapnum, section, subsect, subject, discode*}, for example. Based on this grammar, the capability of the SYMBOCONN framework to learn typed context-free rules and to recognize them after distortion is evaluated in the following. Therefore the SYMBOCONN framework is faced with the following recognition and classification task. The trained machine learning engine is presented with a distorted representation of a left side variable, *dmodule*, for example. Based on that input, the engine should recognize the corresponding right side, in this case "*idstatus, content*", whose variables should furthermore be properly classified: $\mu('idstatus') = \mu('content') = $ *XMLComplexElement*.

CHAPTER 5. CONNECTIONIST LEARNING OF SYMBOLIC STRUCTURES 133

Simple Type Encoding The performance of the complex and non-intuitive spread spectrum process for encoding the variable type information should be compared with a straightforward approach. However, such a benchmark does not yet exist, because connectionist type learning is a new issue. Therefore, we implemented the following simple type encoding mechanism. A fixed intercept $(1, \ldots, r)$ of the node representation $(1, \ldots, d)$ is reserved for the node type, $r < d$, $d := \min(d_1, d_2)$ – comparable with a further type attribute for each node in the underlying knowledge base.

The simple approach unary encodes the $d_2 := r$ considered classes by d_2-dimensional target vectors $\vec{y}$, where $(y_i = 1 \wedge y_j = 0, \forall j \neq i) \Leftrightarrow \mu(\vec{x}) = C_i$. In this case the classification of the input object $\vec{x}$ via the output vector $\vec{o} := \vec{o}_{t+1}$ is achieved by selecting the maximum component o_{max}: $\mu(\vec{x}) = C_{max} \Leftrightarrow o_{max} = \max\{o_1, \ldots, o_{d_2}\}$.

Spread Spectrum Based Type Encoding The introduced simple type encoding is less powerful than the spread spectrum classification variant. To demonstrate this, we compared it with the spread spectrum based typing. Thereby, the main assessment criteria was *robustness* against noise in terms of absolute prediction accuracy on all rules of the learned grammar. The exemplary context-free grammar used for training the neural network consisted of twenty rules (*20-CFG rule set*), which contained four different types of symbols, namely

$\{C_1 = XMLElementRepresent, C_2 = XMLComplexElement,$
$C_3 = XMLSimpleElement, C_4 = XMLSimpleElement\_Int\},$

which were encoded by explicitly associated Barker codes [Fak96]. The alphabet Σ_G contained 41 symbols, which are mapped to bit vectors of length $6 = \lceil \log_2 41 \rceil$ by binary encoding. An exemplary training pattern for the spread spectrum mode is of the following form:

$$figure \mapsto title, graphic \qquad (5.11)$$

This context-free rule is transformed to a training pattern by component-wise basic encoding of the grammar symbols and by additionally encoding their types with the spreading function.

$$spr(\underbrace{(1,0,0,1,0)}_{Basic\ Encoding\ 'figure'}, \underbrace{(1,1,0,1)}_{Barker\ Code,\ \mu('figure')})$$

$$\mapsto spr(\underbrace{(0,1,0,0,1,0)}_{Basic\ Enc.}, \underbrace{(1,1,1,0)}_{\mu('title')}), spr(\underbrace{(0,0,0,1,1,0)}_{Basic\ Enc.}, \underbrace{(1,1,1,0)}_{\mu('graphic')})$$

Thereby, spr is the spreading function defined in section 5.3.1, so that the resulting pattern is a typed production with the symbol types $\mu('figure') = XML\-ComplexElement$ and $\mu('title') = XMLSimpleElement = \mu('graphic')$ both spread by the same spreading code $(1, 1, 1, 0)$. The spreading process computes one 24-bit

(6 · 4) left-side vector and two 24-bit right-side vectors. Since we are dealing with a context-free grammar, all input patterns consist of a single symbol in vector representation, while the length of the target patterns that correspond to the right sides of the productions may vary.

The reference value for measuring the accuracy is the number of right-side variables $s := \sum_{i=1}^{p} m_i$ of the p grammar rules $A_i \Rightarrow B_{i1}B_{i2}\ldots B_{im_i}$, which is $s = 46$ for the conducted evaluation. For each left-side variable A_i, the prediction of the corresponding right-side variables are checked, based on each target node B_{ij}. In order to achieve an accuracy of 100%, all s right-side variables have to be predicted correctly.

Table 5.4 shows the results of the evaluation process for different degrees of imposed uniformly distributed noise and different spreading factors. White noise[7] n interferes with the binary input pattern by adding a random value to each bit of the spread vector $\vec{d}$ (cf. formula 5.4): $d_i \pm n_i$, $d_i \in \{0,1\}$, $n_i \in [0.0, (n \cdot 1.0)]$, $n \in \{25\%, 50\%, 75\%, 95\%\}$, for example, $(1,1,1,0,1,0,0,0,1,0)$ is blurred to (1.34,0.71,1.05,-0.23,1.49,-0.17,0.15,0.39,1.09,-0.05).

Variant	Accuracy [%] of **Spread Spectrum** prediction for uniform noise n							
	n=0%	$n\leq$25%	$n\leq$50%		$n\leq$75%		$n\leq$95%	
	λ={5, 15}	λ={5, 15}	λ=5	$\lambda = \{10, 15\}$	λ=5	$\lambda = \{10, 15\}$	λ=5	λ=15
Node & Type	95.65	95.65	82.61	95.65	89.13	95.65	86.96	93.48

	Accuracy [%] of **Unary Encoding** prediction for uniform noise n				
	n=0%	$n\leq$25%	$n\leq$50%	$n\leq$75%	$n\leq$95%
Node	89.13	89.13	78.26	36.96	36.96
Type	95.65	95.65	95.65	84.78	78.26

Table 5.4: Comparison of the average classification accuracy for the rule-recognition and classification of right-side grammar symbols (target nodes) based on the 20-*CFG* rule set for different noise levels. For all predictions, the neural network was trained up to a residual training error of 3.6%. Since for the spread spectrum technique (with *spreading factor* λ) node and type prediction are intrinsically tied together, there is only one combined value for the accuracy.

In the case of spread spectrum learning, sequence and type prediction are one compound task only, since the respective node type is encoded in the spread node representation, while for the unary encoding approach, two separate tasks have to be fulfilled.

The grammar learning scenario demands the generalization capability of the neural network when presented with noisy input structures, whose target parts have to be recovered. In this case, there is no separation between training and test set as in conventional evaluations of classifiers, since the achievement is the successful

---

[7]Formally defined by Def. 8.2.4.

training and the recognition of symbols and their types under heavy noise, and not the classification of unseen entities.

The *extensibility* of the simple unary encoding technique is also far smaller than that by leveraging spread spectrum based classification, since each new type to be integrated requires a further vector dimension. Thus, the increment $k \to k+1$ of the typing intercept $1, \ldots, k$ implies an increment of the whole feature vector's dimensionality $\vec{x} \in \mathbb{R}^d$, $d \to d+1$. Such an incidence would require a retraining of all learned rules, since each node is thereby affected, which would be a significant drawback for a practical application. This is not the case for the spread spectrum based classification which only requires another spreading code. The already trained rules remain unchanged.

In summarizing the rule recognition scenario, we demonstrated that arbitrarily structured and typed contents can be learned and classified by the connectionist system. The MRNN succeeded in learning the document grammar and in recovering all target sequences of different length, when the symbol on the left rule side was presented. The results clearly indicate the high robustness of the spread spectrum based classification, which is nearly unaffected by an increasing noise level. Summing up the accuracy for all noise levels and taking the results for $\lambda=15$, the spread spectrum technique holds an overall accuracy of 95.2% and thus outperforms the simple approach that only holds an average accuracy of 78.0%. It is remarkable that even long target sequences of 11 nodes as in the case of the first grammar rule "$avee \Rightarrow \ldots$" are correctly predicted under heavy noise of almost 100%.

5.5 Holistic Learning of Structured Symbolic Contents

In the last sections, we have introduced grammar rules as one form of symbolic and structured knowledge representation, and have furthermore shown how they can be learned by the SYMBOCONN framework. As an augmentation, tree-shaped knowledge such as work breakdown structures [Hau03] should also be represented and learned with connectionist methods. Holism is the doctrine of *entireness*, which is originally a philosophical concept [Sch36, Smu38]. In computer science, holism represents an important pillar for the combination of symbolism and connectionism. The downside of holism is the lack of traceability, which means that the ensemble is not completely explicable by all of its parts[8]. This phenomenon is called *emergence*.

There are several forms of holism, such as structural or semantical holism. From the perspective of structural holism, the elements of a domain reveal themselves only by their reciprocal relationships. Semantical holism claims that the meaning of a phrase in a natural language cannot be determined on its own, but only by considering the language-specific context.

---

[8]A well-known and common characterization of holism is that "an ensemble is more than the sum of its parts".

Due to the importance of holism, especially in the case of structure encoding, connectionist methods must be able to support holistic representations: *"A consequence of the connectionist approach to artificial intelligence is the requirement for structured data to be encoded into fixed width vector representations."* [MV03]

This requirement can be fulfilled by a holistic representation[9] of compositional symbol structures. Holistic computation is a mechanism that builds a fixed-width representation of a compositional structure, while using each representation unit (e.g. a neuron) *for all* constituents of the structure to be encoded. When only one representation unit is changed, the whole encoded structure is affected – not only some of its components. Thus, symbol structures can be manipulated holistically, a decomposition being necessary neither for locating nor for accessing their constituents.

Recursive Auto-Associative Memory (RAAM) Recursive Auto-Associative Memory networks represent a bridge between connectionist and symbolic systems [MLP00] and are often applied to the field of *natural language processing*. These networks are able to process symbolic structures represented by trees with a fixed branching factor. Such a tree is generated by a set of *phrase structure rules* that are a type of formal grammar [CPB97] focusing on natural languages. The phrases are recursively composed by the RAAM in order to produce a compressed internal representation.

Both tree structures as well as sequences of terminal symbols and variables can be recursively encoded by RAAMs. The sequentially controlled presentation of the symbolic constituents to the network enables learning of complex symbolic structures. RAAMs create a fixed-width and lossy description of arbitrary tree structures which hides the details of the structure like the leaves of a tree. The created encoding is *holistically represented*, since the compressed representation can be used to classify complex structures without decomposing them beforehand. This technique is comparable to the look at a map from a wide angle where the details are not visible, but still available in a latent form. By looking at the map as a whole, humans can classify the respective map segment, considering its details without ever zooming in on the map [Neu01].

Any tree-structured knowledge, which is given as a subgraph of the knowledge model defined in section 3.2, for example, can theoretically be transformed into a holistical representation while keeping its structure. The produced fixed-width RAAM-representation works as a fingerprint of the fine-grained and unfolded structure and is used for the following main purposes:

- **Compression** (maybe lossy) and decompression of compositional symbolic structures to and from a fixed-width representation.

- Training of a connectionist classifier on the compressed representations to **quickly classify compressed structures** without decomposing them. An ex-

---

[9] In connectionism this term if often used as synonym for *distributed* representations.

ample is the holistical recognition of design patterns as an alternative to the approach presented in section 6.3. The correct tree-structured design patterns are recursively encoded into a RAAM-representation that is hence learned by a classifier. On the other hand, class diagrams that contain unknown design patterns are also compressed to a RAAM-representation, the classifier holistically recognizing their structure and similarity with the original design patterns. This procedure is very similar to the human way of recognizing and understanding design patterns – not by parsing each of their constituents but by looking at the structure as a whole.

- Direct **structure transformation** based on the compressed representations from a source structure to a target structure. An example is the transformation of *active* into *passive sentences* given in natural language.

Realization of RAAMs The SYMBOCONN framework supports RAAM networks as special configurations of the more generic MRNN. Its modular composition enables the reproduction of a RAAM network by setting appropriate input and target dimensionalities and presenting the training patterns in a prescribed order. Compositional structures as defined by the *composite design pattern* [GHJV95] that correspond to *unbalanced trees* with leaf nodes at different levels can be adequately expressed by a RAAM-representation. After completing the RAAM encoding process, the whole structure is *holistically* represented in a compound entity.

Aubyn and Davey [SAD97] applied a RAAM to encode rules of variable structure and content into a flat representation that can be fed into a conventional feed-forward network. The latter processed the holistically represented, context-free productions to perform simple operations upon bit strings. Thereby, the output of the RAAM was used as input for the downstreamed connectionist rule applicator, which interpreted the flattened rules as control information.

Chalmers also [Cha90] demonstrated the applicability of connectionist models to compositional structures. In his case, syntactic transformations were performed by a hybrid connectionist architecture consisting of a RAAM and a feed-forward network:

- A RAAM network encodes tree-shaped structures of variable length in a representation of fixed length [CPB97].

- A transformation network transforms the RAAM-encoded holistic representation into the target model again represented as RAAM-vector of fixed length.

- Finally, the transformed model is decoded in such a way that the tree structure is unfolded and the single constituents are regained.

Chalmers already successfully applied this setup to the transformation of *active* into *passive sentences* of natural language. The used sentences were quite simple, since the maximum depth of the representing trees was two and their valence (branching factor) was fixed to three.

A more recent approach called *Scaling Connectionist Compositional Representations* by Flackett et. al [FTL04] in 2004 tried to scale up RAAM en- and decoding to larger real-world datasets. The scalability is still a weakness of holistic computation, such that often only toy examples of structure encodings and decodings can be accomplished.

In general, there are many extensions of conventional RAAMs, like *Sequential RAAMs* (SRAAM) [LH03], *Labeling RAAMs* (LRAAM) [SS94] or *Bi-coded RAAMs* (BRAAM) [AD99], which try to improve the efficiency of the RAAM encoding process or to extend its applicability. In particular, these approaches aim at fewer training epochs, smaller hidden layers required for the internal representation, improved ability to represent long-term time dependencies in the input data and the reduction of the cumulative error effect during decoding [AD99].

Structure Encoding The central principle of encoding and decoding compositional structures with RAAMs is *recursion*. Assume the term $(a_1 + a_2) \cdot (b + (c_1 + c_2))$ should be represented by a compressed internal representation, then it is reasonable to first construct the corresponding *operator tree* to reveal the term structure, which is depicted by figure 5.10. The encoding process starts with the

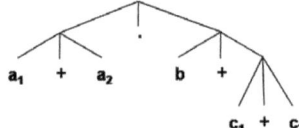

Figure 5.10: Ternary operator tree (valence 3) of depth 3 corresponding to the term $(a_1 + a_2) \cdot (b + (c_1 + c_2))$.

right-most subtree $(c_1 + c_2)$ with the tree terminal symbols c_1, $+$ and c_2, which are compressed into the internal representation $(c_1 + c_2)'$ by auto-associating them. This means that they are used both as input and target pattern for training the RAAM network. The encoding is recursive, since in the next step the resulting code vector $(c_1 + c_2)'$ is again encoded, this time together with the symbols b and $+$ of the next tree level. This process is recursively repeated until the root of the tree has been reached, which is encoded as ternary composition of its previously encoded children. The whole proceeding is schematically illustrated by figure 5.11.

The encoding of each n-ary tree can be formalized by *simultaneous recursion* using the n-ary constructor $cons_n$ that takes n subtrees as arguments. The following inductive definition of the operator $(\cdot)'$ gives the construction rule for the RAAM-representation $A := (A_1, A_2, \ldots, A_n)'$ of a tree with arbitrary depth, which consists of the subtrees $A_1, A_2, \ldots, A_n$.

$$(a)' := a \qquad (5.12)$$
$$(A_1, A_2, \ldots, A_n)' := cons_n((A_1)', (A_2)', \ldots, (A_n)') \qquad (5.13)$$

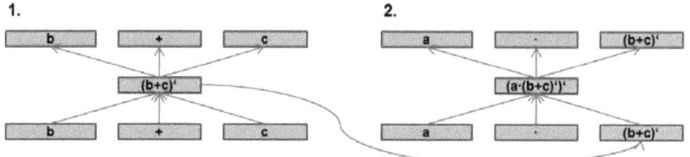

Figure 5.11: Schematic topology of a three-layered RAAM network. At first, the term $(b + c)$ is compressed to $(b + c)'$ by training the RAAM with the same input and target (auto-association). In a second step, this compressed vector of fixed length is combined with the uncompressed terminal symbols · and a of the higher level, which finally results in the holistic representation $(a \cdot (b + c)')'$ of the entire term.

The basis case holds for any terminal symbol a, which is atomic and therefore encoded by itself. The constructor $cons_n : [(\mathbb{R}^d)^n := (\mathbb{R}^d \times \ldots \times \mathbb{R}^d)] \to \mathbb{R}^d$ is practically realized by the auto-associative training procedure of the MRNN using the same input and target sequence $(A_1)', (A_2)', \ldots, (A_n)'$ of length n, respectively, as illustrated by figure 5.11 (see also section 4.2). From a theoretical point of view, the operator $(\cdot)'$ can be formulated according to the schema of primitive recursion.

$$f(A, 0) := A \qquad (5.14)$$
$$f(A, d) := h(f(A_1, d-1), f(A_2, d-1), \ldots, f(A_n, d-1)) \qquad (5.15)$$

The function f is called with the total tree depth $d := depth(A)$, which can be computed by a monadic primitive recursive function $depth$ in turn. In this schema, h represents the constructor $cons_n$ and the subtrees are encoded by simultaneous recursion via f.

5.5.1 Generating RAAM-Representations Using the MRNN

During the training phase, the internal representations denoted by $(\cdot)'$ change continuously, since the internal representations of their constituents are subject to change, as well. For instance, when the internal representation $(b + c)'$ changes during the first training epoch, the comprising structure $a \cdot (b+c)'$ is also affected by the change in its right-most subtree $(b+c)'$. Learning under these circumstances is called *moving target learning* [GK96], where only the vectors standing for the terminal symbols remain stable. In order to generate the training set for the RAAM, an auxiliary data structure is required, which supports the recursive *bottom-up construction* of the training samples, starting with the terminal symbols. It is not really surprising that such a data structure is once more a tree of adequate depth and valence which stores the current internal representations represented as inner tree nodes. For encoding a structured term, the corresponding operator tree of the form given in figure 5.12 is traversed beginning at its leaves. Note that the tree does not have to be

140 CHAPTER 5. CONNECTIONIST LEARNING OF SYMBOLIC STRUCTURES

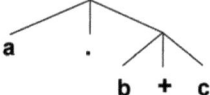

Figure 5.12: Ternary operator tree representation of the expression $a \cdot (b + c)$.

balanced, thus the training starts with the leaves at the bottom level.

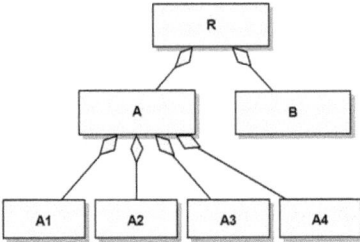

Figure 5.13: UML class diagram showing a tree-structure of three levels with varying branching factor corresponding to figure 5.14. The aggregation that belongs to class A consists of four constituents $A1$ to $A4$, while the root class R comprises only two classes.

Conventional RAAMs lack the capability of processing trees with variable valence, that is, parent nodes with different numbers of children. The MRNN is able to take the role of a RAAM and to work as a recurrent auto associator. Due to its modular design, the MRNN can even solve the problem of varying valence so that heterogeneous subtrees can be learned at the same time. Although dealing with varying tree valence is a contribution on its own to research in RAAMs, this is actually necessary for learning the structure of heterogeneous knowledge fragments (subgraphs) as they especially appear in software engineering. Figure 5.13 shows an UML class diagram representing an aggregation hierarchy with the root class R. The MRNN is capable of encoding such tree structures with varying branching factor, which is shown in the corresponding figure 5.14.

Training with Simultaneous Update There are several heuristics to treat the challenging *moving target effect* during training [SP03]. This effect is due to the recursive encoding process and always appears when computing RAAM-representations of structured knowledge. We chose the variant that requires a dynamic update of the training set (see Variant III. in [SP03]), since the training can be started with the full training set right from the beginning without the need for two different training phases. The current internal representations of level 1 that

CHAPTER 5. CONNECTIONIST LEARNING OF SYMBOLIC STRUCTURES   141

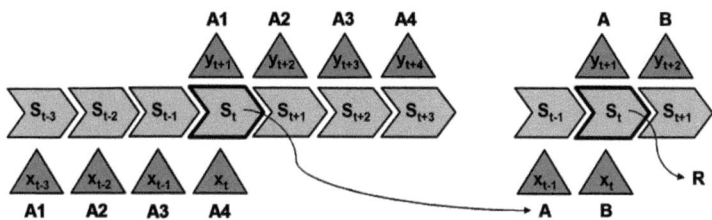

Figure 5.14: In this example, the MRNN auto-associates the elements that take part in an *aggregation* relationship as depicted by figure 5.13. The compressed result A participates again in another aggregation of two elements, which requires a flexible network topology that adapts to the respective branching factor. Finally, R is holistically represented as the hidden state s_t after finishing the training with the same network weights for both aggregations.

are computed from the terminal symbols at leaf level 0 are substituted in all higher levels after each training epoch, where they participate in the encoding of the superordinate structures again. We compared the simultaneous update with a training approach using static RAAM-representations for the reused subtrees (see Variant I. in [SP03]), which is less accurate than dynamic RAAM-representations. The static approach was outperformed by the approach with simultaneous update both in terms of manageability and speed of convergence.

The proceeding of the recursive training process is expressed by table 5.5.

Term Instance	RAAM Representation	Depth
$(b_1 + b_2)$	$(b_1 + b_1)'$	1
$a \cdot (b_1 + b_2)$	$(a \cdot (b_1 + b_2)')'$	2
$(a + (b_1 + b_2)) \cdot c$	$((a + (b_1 + b_2)')' \cdot c)'$	3

Table 5.5: Table showing the syntactical form of exemplary ternary terms and their encoded RAAM-representations (') formulated in infix-notation.

Structure Decoding Structure decoding is a top-down process that is almost a one-to-one inversion of the bottom-up composition described before. A compressed representation is directly fed into the the hidden layer of the network, and is propagated to the output layer, where the child nodes of the subordinate level are recovered. For each of these decoded output symbols, a decision rule determines whether the current output is already a terminal symbol or still a composed structure that has to be refed into the hidden layer for a further decomposition. This decision can be realized by an additional bit working as *structure-indicator*, which is represented by the function *isTerminal* in the pseudocode algorithm 1. Being able to refeed the structured output to the hidden layer as done in the recursive call of the

142 CHAPTER 5. CONNECTIONIST LEARNING OF SYMBOLIC STRUCTURES

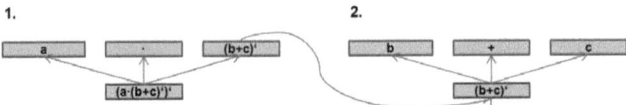

Figure 5.15: The compressed fixed-width term representation $(a \cdot (b+c)')'$ is decomposed into its constituents by the RAAM decoder. Therefore, it is fed into the hidden layer and is propagated to the output layer.

Algorithm 1 Recursive decoding algorithm to unfold the inherent structure of RAAM-representations. A "▷"-symbol indicates a comment.

function DECODEINTERNALREPR(double[] *internalReprToDecode*, int *treeValence*)
    decodedSequence ← raam.decode(*internalReprToDecode*, *treeValence*);
    for $\{i = 0; i < treeValence; i \rightarrow i + 1\}$ **do**   ▷ Depth-first search.
        outputVector ← decodedSequence[i];
        resolvedCode ← resolvePredictedSymbol(*outputVector*);
        resolvedSymbol ← null;
        if isTerminal(*resolvedCode*) **then**   ▷ Resolving the final terminal symbol.
            resolvedSymbol ← lookUpSymbol(*resolvedCode*);
        else   ▷ Recursive call of the decoding function upon the output.
            decodeInternalRepr(*resolvedCode*, *treeValence*);
        end if
    end for
    return *resolvedSymbol*;
end function

decoding algorithm, requires that the output and hidden representation are of equal width. Since the RAAM is an auto associator, the input, hidden, and output vectors hold the same dimensionality, which is reflected by the produced fixed-width representations.

5.5.2 Hybrid Structure Transformation System

In the following sections, we demonstrate that the SYMBOCONN framework is capable of higher level generalization in the case of symbolic knowledge. The unbalanced tree that was compressed by the RAAM in the previous section should be transformed according to the distributive law as shown by figure 5.16. Therefore, a hybrid connectionist system, which comprises both a RAAM network and a conventional neural network for the intended structure transformation, is set up. The training and application of the whole hybrid system is complex, since different network types and different training sets are involved in a prescribed order. Due

Figure 5.16: Tree-based representation of the *distributive law* as structure transformation applied to *operator trees*.

to the modularity of the SYMBOCONN engine, both types of neural networks can be realized by the MRNN, when configured appropriately. Two different instances of the MRNN realize the holistic encoding and decoding functionality – with the MRNN working as RAAM – as well as the transformation functionality as shown in figures 5.17 and 5.18.

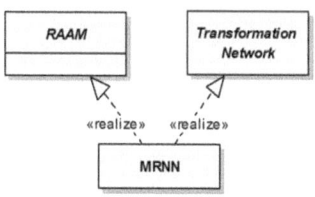

Figure 5.17: The MRNN network realizes both the required Recursive Auto-Associative Memory (RAAM) and the transformation network.

When an unseen compositional structure instance should be transformed, it must first be translated into an internal fixed-width RAAM-representation. This step is accomplished by creating a training set which only consists of the respective structure instance. The RAAM Encoder is then trained on this 1-element set until a remaining error of the same magnitude as for the structure instances encoded in the actual training phase (cf. previous section).

At this point, the hidden activation of the encoding RAAM network is taken as fixed-width input vector for the transformation network, which has already been trained and is ready to predict the hidden representation of the corresponding target structure. Finally, the predicted fixed-width activation becomes the input of the trained RAAM Decoder network that aims at properly unfolding the corresponding target structure. Therefore, the transformed vector (unseen) is fed as activation into the hidden layer of the decoder network, and the recursive decoding procedure is executed until it ends up in the predicted terminal symbols of the target structure.

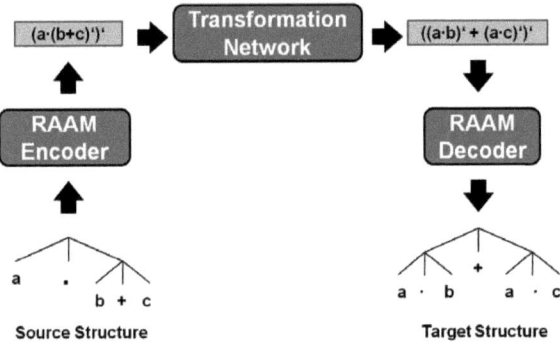

Figure 5.18: Hybrid architecture for structure transformations based on two RAAMs and one transformer network that are all realized by the MRNN.

Each source structure has to be encoded by the RAAM in order to obtain a fixed-width vector[10], which is the input part of a single training pattern for the transformation network. The target part of that pattern is again computed by RAAM-encoding the target structure. Thus, two encoding operations are required to generate one pair of RAAM-representations that serves as a single training pattern for the Transformation Network.

There are two possibilities to realize the encoding and decoding by the MRNN operating in RAAM-mode, shown by the rectangles on the left and right side of figure 5.18 named RAAM Encoder and RAAM Decoder. First, one RAAM instance can be trained on all structure samples such as $(a \cdot b) + (a \cdot c)$, $b \cdot (c + d)$ or $(b \cdot c) + (b \cdot d)$, no matter if these are source or target structures. In this case, only one instance is required that is responsible both for en- and decoding of the hidden representations processed by the transformation network.

---

[10]Representing the hidden network activation s_t, see section 4.4.

Second, two separate RAAM network instances are used, one for encoding and one for decoding. This time, the encoder network is only trained on the input structures and the decoder network is only used for decoding the target structures of the transformation. While both variants are admissible, the second one is usually easier to train, since each network has to process a less complex training set, and the encoder and decoder networks can be trained in parallel.

5.5.3 Structure Transform Prediction

In this section, the generalization hierarchy presented in section 3.1.1.2 is realized by the SYMBOCONN engine configured as RAAM network. We realize this generalization hierarchy by the hybrid architecture presented in the previous section. This theoretical application of our symbolic-connectionist architecture as part of SYMBOCONN supports the title of this dissertation, which emphasizes the duality of symbolic and connectionist information processing.

The difficult task of realizing the different levels of the hierarchy based on the leading example of the *distributive law* serves as theoretical proof of concept of the symbolic-connectionist learning and prediction capabilities of SYMBOCONN presented in section 3.3. We skip the rather trivial *memorization functionality* (Level 0), as well as Level 1, and start with generalization of Level 2. The application of the distributive law should be generalized both to elements in new syntactical positions and to completely new elements. The transformation of symbolic structures can be interpreted as a model transformation in terms of software engineering, since it can be used to describe the transformation of "bad design" into "good design" according to well-known conventions or design patterns. Figure 5.19 illustrates such a transformation using the *Bridge pattern*. The presented model transformation

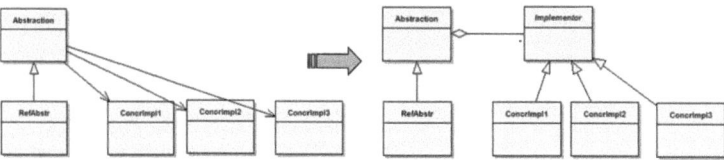

Figure 5.19: Transforming a delegation-based model with three concrete implementors into an easy-maintainable model according to the *Bridge pattern*.

can be formulated as a common training pattern $originalModel \mapsto targetModel$ learnable by the SYMBOCONN framework, where both models are holistically represented.

Generalization Level 2 Elements that occur in novel positions within the term to be transformed should be treated properly by the hybrid transformation system according to Level 2 of the hierarchy defined in section 3.1.1.2.

$$b \cdot (c + d) \quad \mapsto \quad b \cdot c + b \cdot d \tag{5.16}$$

During the evaluation, the hybrid structure transform system was presented with the left sides of 1,000 untrained expressions of the form 5.16. In about 960 cases, the system succeeded in generating the correct target structure, which corresponds to a generalization rate of 96.0%.

Generalization Level 3 We recall the training set from chapter 3:

$$a \cdot (b + c) \quad \mapsto \quad a \cdot b + a \cdot c$$
$$a \cdot (c + b) \quad \mapsto \quad a \cdot c + a \cdot b$$
$$b \cdot (a + c) \quad \mapsto \quad b \cdot a + b \cdot c$$
$$c \cdot (b + a) \quad \mapsto \quad c \cdot b + c \cdot a$$

From this training set, a new combination of elements can be found: $N := b \cdot (c + a) \mapsto b \cdot c + b \cdot a$; This term only contains elements that have already appeared in the given position for themselves, but not in this combination with other elements. Again we used a test set of 1,000 instances for evaluating the generalization rate in this difficult test case. The system accomplished the task with a generalization rate of 72.5%.

Generalization Level 4 Referring to Level 4 of the hierarchy, structure instances of higher complexity should be correctly transformed. Once more, the encoding process begins with the subtrees of highest depth.

$$b \cdot ((c_1 + c_2) + (d_1 + d_2)) \quad \mapsto \quad b \cdot (c_1 + c_2) + b \cdot (d_1 + d_2) \tag{5.17}$$

For example, the subtrees of highest depth are $(c_1 + c_2)$ and $(d_1 + d_2)$ in the case of test pattern 5.17. The three terminal symbols c_1, $+$ and c_2 are compressed to the internal representation $(c_1 + c_2)'$ by auto-associating them in the first logical step of RAAM training. The same is done for the triple $(d_1, +, d_2)$, which is combined with the first triple $(c_1, +, c_2)$ in the final logical step. Due to their interdependency, these three compositions are trained simultaneously and iteratively till the training error drops to an acceptable level. Unfortunately, we could not complete the evaluation of generalization Level 4 yet, since we were caught up in technical problems training the hybrid architecture shown in figure 5.18. We are confident of solving this problem in future work and the generalization results will be handed in later.

However, the presented connectionist realization of symbol manipulation serves as an example of how connectionist systems can be composed to provide explicit systematicity. We saw that connectionist generalization capability is not only an abstract concept, but can be systematically defined, especially in the case of symbolic knowledge. Due to the generality of the presented scenario and the flexibility of the hybrid transformation architecture, a concrete instantiation in one of the addressed domains should be feasible and is to be done in future work.

For example, in the field of software development, distributed representations can be used to learn process knowledge and to detect deviations between a given process model and the actual process execution according to best practice. In software engineering and agile development, project participants often ignore parts of the given process model bit by bit, so that after a while, the development process must be synchronized to adhere to the given process model. This could be done by learning a process model with all of its activities and sub-activities in the form of a possibly unbalanced tree, where the tree nodes represent the process activities – may be in form of a rich representation. A deviation from the process can be recognized by RAAM-learning the activities as they were actually carried out and applying an additional standard neural classifier on the computed RAAM-representation. The same concept is applicable to design patterns, which can also be incorporated into a RAAM-representation. Apart from software engineering, Hammerton has already substantiated the reconstruction of faded structures using RAAM networks in his paper *"Holistic Computation: Reconstructing a muddled concept"* [Ham97], which refers to the recognition and recovery of displaced structures.

5.6 Conclusion

In this chapter, we dealt with learning of compositional and typed (symbolic) contents. The SYMBOCONN framework is able to learn regular and context-free grammars even in the case of fuzzy rule constituents. This capability is useful to integrate prior domain knowledge or to learn structural knowledge such as design pattern definitions. In the case of business rules, robustness in recognizing left rule sides serves for handling incomplete decision tables with missing combinations of rule conditions.

There are many scenarios that do not allow to determine the value of a condition, which is part of the antecedent part of a business rule. The reason is often incomplete or contradictory information, which can be interpreted as noise upon the rule conditions that has been shown to be properly handled by the MRNN. The novel spread spectrum based classification mechanism enables the MRNN to robustly learn typed formal grammars describing structured contents or processes. In conclusion, we developed three main functionalities and integrated them into the SYMBOCONN framework:

1. **Structure Learning**
   The SYMBOCONN framework is able to learn arbitrary symbolic sequences such as context-free or context-sensitive production rules, which can be used to represent business rules or to describe the structure of XML documents, for example.

2. **Rule Recognition and Classification in face of Heavy Noise**

Heterogeneous rules composed of entities of different types can be learned and recognized by the neural network. Therefore, the SYMBOCONN framework is capable of classifying incomplete or blurred knowledge structures such as fuzzy business rules. Besides rule incorporation, the framework can be used to robustly classify multi-represented objects described by a set of feature values, as demonstrated in the case of molecule data. The high classification robustness is achieved by SYMBOCONN with the integration of a new data spreading mechanism, which is borrowed from state-of-art code multiplexing in mobile communication and is adapted to neural information processing. This spreading mechanism provides a bias and variance reduction and is a variant of error-correcting codes.

3. **Holistic Representation and Transformation of Symbolic Structures**
In the last section, the encoding of compositional symbol structures by connectionist methods was discussed and realized by means of the SYMBOCONN framework. So-called holistic representations are used to represent symbolic systematics by recursive auto associative neural networks (RAAMs). Symbol structures can be manipulated holistically without the need to decompose them, neither for locating nor accessing their constituents. Finally, elaborating on holistic transformation capability served as proof of concept of the generalization functionality defined in section 3.3.

Chapter 6

Application to Knowledge Engineering and Software Development

Software engineering involves a number of development activities such as analysis, design, implementation, and testing. During these activities, developers produce knowledge that describes different system aspects. For instance, a use-case specification is a system model describing a particular system functionality. A system architecture describes the knowledge about the components of the system and their relationships.

Traditionally, knowledge in software engineering is represented by *rationale* and *system knowledge*. Rationale is knowledge describing all significant decisions in a software project. It can be interpreted as meta system knowledge of the context in which design decisions were made [BD04]. Stakeholders such as project managers and developers generate knowledge about the system during its construction in the form of planned and unplanned communication regarding the elicited requirements, functionalities or bug fixes to be implemented. Unplanned communication includes requests for clarification, requests for change (RFC), and issue resolution. Each development activity requires knowledge about dependent activities from other work packages, which is delivered by supporting workflows such as project management. Rationale concepts like issues or decisions help to externalize the rationale that finally leads to a team decision[1]. The justification for a decision can be attached to specific artifacts as contextual information. According to Dutoit et al. [DMMP06](p. 91), rationale can be considered as a time-indexed sequence of elements visited during the developers' interaction with the system. Those sequences can be mapped onto SYMBOCONN node sequences that can be directly processed by the MRNN.

System knowledge is traditionally split up into a *functional model*, a *structural model*, and a *dynamic model* (cf. Rumbaugh [J.R90]). These models are work products that result from development activities usually accompanied by management

---
[1]Messages can be harvested in order to discover key issues within the project communication.

activities, especially in the case of complex projects such as distributed multi-team projects.

In the last decade, the trend of applying methods from artificial intelligence (AI) to the field of software engineering can be observed both in industry and academia. A capital reason for applying AI methods to knowledge-based areas is the increasing amount of rich information that becomes available during ongoing projects or by postmortem reviews [BD04] – both for successful and unsuccessful software projects. The amount and diversity of knowledge required by software engineering activities decrease the disability and ineffectiveness of current techniques for managing this knowledge. For these reasons, the application of machine learning to software engineering topics is considered to be increasingly relevant in the medium term.

Methods from AI such as fuzzy-logic models, decision and regression trees (cf. section 4.2), neural networks or case-based reasoning (cf. section 2.6.3) provide the means to mitigate this problem. Many research contributions that propose the prediction of the project success [Smi07], the project costs [She05, Pea97, Wil94], the project duration and so on. Especially cost and effort estimation are supported by two separate classes of methods, namely algorithmic models and machine learning. The trend of employing such methods is supported by providers of empirical software engineering data like the *PROMISE Repository of Software Engineering Databases* [SSM05], which is a collection of publicly available datasets and tools to serve researchers in building *Predictive Software Models* (PSMs).

The Rationale-based Uniform Software Engineering model (RUSE) [Wol07] is a graph-based knowledge model that integrates system models, collaboration artifacts, and organizational models in a uniform way [BDW06]. RUSE is used as the underlying knowledge model of the CASE tool UNICASE (also called SYSIPHUS), which supports the usage of rationale. The nodes in the project graph, as shown in figure 6.1, are called *model elements* and all modifications ever made to them are comprehensively captured. Links between entities are also represented by model elements; thus, they are made explicit as nodes themselves and links are assigned to a certain link type. UNICASE will serve as a provider of structured data for the SYMBOCONN framework.

The SYMBOCONN framework benefits from this graph-based knowledge model, since both content and structure are represented across all activities of the software development process – no matter which process model is employed [Hel08]. These activities produce cohesive artifacts which are directly mapped to node sequences in terms of the SYMBOCONN framework. Potentially, any observed software development process can be modeled and learned in form of node sequences by the MRNN for accomplishing either classification or prediction tasks.

We have chosen three areas in software engineering, in which we demonstrate the benefits of the SYMBOCONN framework. In section 6.1, we present an approach to the automatic classification of software artifacts, which can be used as a foundation for software metrics and is especially important for project management. This classification technique based on the SYMBOCONN framework gen-

APPLICATION TO KNOWLEDGE ENG. AND SOFTWARE DEVELOPMENT 151

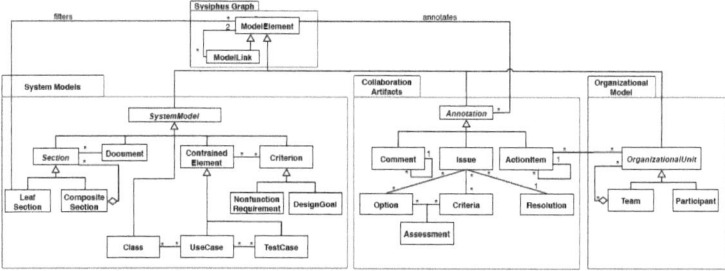

Figure 6.1: The project graph includes system models, collaboration artifacts, and the organizational model. Source: Dutoit et al. [BDW06].

erates knowledge about structure, since the activity classification can be used to identify a work breakdown structure. For example, tasks as constituents of the work breakdown structure are automatically classified according to their development activity, such that these tasks can be assigned to development teams by the project management[2]. This is especially useful for turning an empirical development process into an activity-oriented one such as the Rationale Unified Process (RUP). Time-dependent information elicited from the development artifacts can additionally be used to assign the predicted activities to the different RUP phases.

In section 6.2, we apply SYMBOCONN to reason about *causality*. In particular, we show how causality can be addressed by change impact analysis, which is concerned with learning the impact of changes in model elements by a set of training examples. We present two forms of change impact analysis implemented into SYMBOCONN: the first variant operates on a training set of change packages, the second variant uses the knowledge graph directly.

In section 6.3, we demonstrate the capability of the SYMBOCONN framework to process *structural knowledge* in form of design patterns. Design patterns are instances of structured knowledge, which are learned and discovered by the MRNN based on a grammar representation. The capability of learning and recognizing patterns is not restricted to software design patterns but can be extended to any patterns represented by subgraphs. The grammar productions are finally mapped onto pairs of node sequences $(v_{i_1}, \ldots, v_{i_m}) \mapsto (v_{j_1}, \ldots, v_{j_n}) \in (V^m \times V^n)$ again, which may be aggregated in order to describe the whole pattern.

In chapter 7, SYMBOCONN is applied to *procedural knowledge* providing navigation recommendation. This form of knowledge is also called *process* or *control knowledge*, since it can be used to describe the control flow of a predefined process. An example for procedural knowledge is the sequence of steps that an expert sys-

---

[2]Which is itself a development activity.

tem takes in the derivation of a conclusion[3]. Compared to knowledge of causality, functional knowledge is modeled by ordered node sequences $(v_1, v_2, \ldots, v_n) \in V^n$ instead of pairs of sets.

All of these applications benefit from an underlying project graph as given by the RUSE model shown in figure 6.1, which provides rich and interrelated knowledge fragments. Nevertheless, the machine learning functionality can also be applied to raw log data, instances of which are not linked together in form of a project graph of model elements. In this case, SYMBOCONN can be used to incorporate the tacit relationships between artifacts implicitly by learning from a set of examples – similar to association rule mining.

6.1 Classification of Software Development Artifacts

Software projects produce a variety of artifacts as outcome of different development activities, for example, use cases, components in system design, or action items in project management. These artifacts consist of a number of attributes; for example, a functional requirement could consist of a name and a description. Additional information is contained in associations between artifacts, e.g. when one requirement refines another requirement, or an action item is annotated with the task to be accomplished. Artifacts can be classified according to these attributes, e.g. the type or the priority of a certain requirement [SSL08]. We call them *classification attributes*. Classifications according to attributes of interest can be used as a foundation for metrics and analysis; Mockus [Moc08], for example, uses the attributes *state* and *resolution* of bug reports. Scrum [htt07] uses burn-down charts, which are based on the attribute *status* of ToDo items.

This type of classification relies on the availability and up-to-dateness of the classification attributes. However, up-to-date and available classification attributes are sometimes difficult to obtain. This can be the case when the need for a classification attribute was not anticipated and the attribute values were therefore not captured at artifact creation time. For example, one wishes to analyze the progress of different software engineering activities (e.g. requirements analysis), but the captured tasks are not categorized by activities. Furthermore, some attributes might not be entered appropriately by users. For example, we observed a significant number of users who are reluctant to close *irrelevant* tasks. An artifact becomes irrelevant in the following cases: 1) it is outdated, meaning that its due date has passed. 2) It does not contribute to the achievement of the project goals any longer or its priority has been downgraded to minor importance.

The process of manually completing and updating information that is required later on is often difficult to implement. Thus there are approaches that try to automatically classify artifacts. Hyatt and his colleagues [WRH97] developed an early life cycle tool for assessing requirements that are specified in natural language. The

---

[3]Procedural knowledge must not be constraint to algorithms only, since SYMBOCONN also supports fuzzy node sequences, which are accompanied by a degree of uncertainty.

tool searches the requirement specification document for terms that have been identified as quality indicators before and indicates, which statements need to be improved.

We employ the SYMBOCONN framework in combination with RUSE [Wol07] to automatically classify software engineering artifacts. This technique offers three major benefits compared to existing approaches: 1) It is capable of handling fuzzy, incomplete and partially incorrect data, which may result from incomplete and inaccurate user input. 2) It provides traceability between software engineering artifacts, which generates additional input information for the classification mechanism and therefore improves the quality of the classification result [PLD05, LM98]. 3) It is able to process different types of artifacts within the same classification task. Even more, SYMBOCONN is highly extensible with respect to additional artifacts. Thus our approach can be reused for classification problems in different projects regarding various types of software artifacts. One particular type of software artifact is an

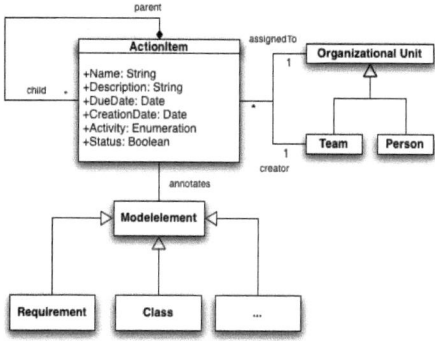

Figure 6.2: Class diagram showing the detailed ActionItem model adapted from [Wol07].

action item, which represents a task in RUSE. As shown in figure 6.2, an ActionItem consists of six attributes as well as five different links between ActionItem and other ModelElements. All information except CreationDate has to be entered manually by the developer or the project planner. Table 6.1 shows an overview of the six relevant attributes, table 6.2 shows the five links of interest.

6.1.1 Evaluation

The developed classification of model-based software development data based on a recurrent neural network is a new approach at the intersection of software engineering and machine learning. To evaluate the feasibility and performance of our approach, we conducted two classification experiments.

154   APPLICATION TO KNOWLEDGE ENG. AND SOFTWARE DEVELOPMENT

Attribute	Meaning
Name	A short and unique name for the represented task.
Description	A detailed description of the task.
DueDate	The deadline for the completion of the task, if there is one.
CreationDate	The date where the task was created in the system. This attribute is set automatically.
Activity	Classifies an ActionItem according to the software engineering activity it originated from. In our case, the considered activities are: *Analysis, System Design, Object Design, Implementation, Testing, Project Management*.
Status	Determines if the corresponding task is still in progress or already done, that is, *irrelevant*.

Table 6.1: Description of the attributes of an ActionItem.

Attribute	Meaning
parent	Link to a parent task. That is, a task that can be broken down to this child and other children.
child	Link to child tasks.
assignedTo	Link to a person or a team the task is assigned to.
creator	Link to a person or a team, which is the creator of the task.
annotates	Link to the object of the task, e.g. a requirement the task refers to.

Table 6.2: Description of the links between an ActionItem and other ModelElements.

APPLICATION TO KNOWLEDGE ENG. AND SOFTWARE DEVELOPMENT   155

The first one is to classify action items according to the activity in which they were formulated. In the second experiment, SYMBOCONN is employed to classify the status of ActionItems; that is, the machine learning engine decides whether they are still under examination or already completed.

The SYMBOCONN activity- and status-classification is independent from the concrete life cycle model. To show the feasibility and performance of the SYMBOCONN classification, we selected a real-world project with a particular life cycle model. This project used the activities *Analysis, System Design, Object Design, Implementation, Testing,* and *Project Management*. We used *five-fold cross-validation* to evaluate the performance of the SYMBOCONN classification. The performance was measured in terms of precision and recall, which are the standard metrics to assess the quality of a multi-class classifier.

The project was called DOLLI (Distributed Online Logistics and Location Infrastructure) [Dol07] and was carried out as a cooperation between the Technical University of Munich and the Munich Airport. The objective of DOLLI was to improve the airport's existing tracking and locating capabilities and to integrate all available location data into a central database; thereby, luggage tracking and dispatching of service personal as well as a 3D visualization of the aggregated data should be supported. More than 50 developers worked on the project for about five months. Their efforts resulted in a comprehensive project model consisting of about 15.000 model elements. The DOLLI project and the involved data collection were supported by the UNICASE tool [BDW06].

6.1.1.1 Activity Classification

In the first experiment, we added a new classification attribute Activity to the model element ActionItem. This classification attribute served as target feature for the supervised training of the SYMBOCONN machine learning engine. The project first followed a variant of a Unified Process for 4 months. The development activities were executed sequentially in the first part of the project. For the remainder of the project, the developers followed the Scrum methodology [htt07]. All ActionItems created during the project were manually classified into the predefined development activities. Figure 6.3 illustrates the development of open ActionItems over the project time classified by activity. The empirical dataset clearly showed an overlapping of these activities. In addition, it can be observed, that in the second part of the project, there was a significant rise of Analysis- and Implementation-related action items. Table 6.3 shows the distribution of ActionItems. Note that the ActionItems were rarely classified as belonging to *Testing* and *Project Management* activities.

As mentioned, the ActionItems were classified manually by the project participants. However, during the project, the requirement for an automatic classification arose for three reasons: (1) The manual input of the activity attribute was intrusive for the project participants as they had no obvious benefit from entering this information. It was necessary to continuously motivate the developers to fill out

156   APPLICATION TO KNOWLEDGE ENG. AND SOFTWARE DEVELOPMENT

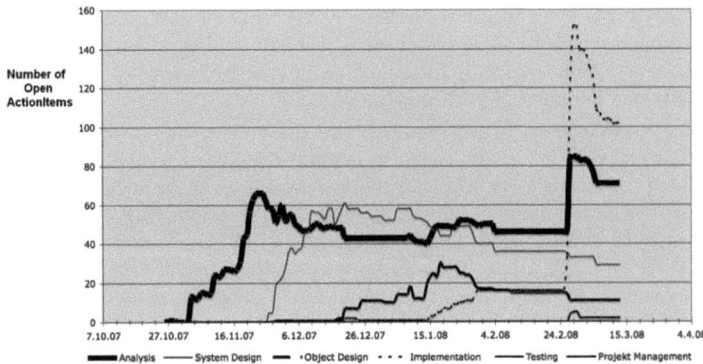

Figure 6.3: Number of open ActionItems managed in the DOLLI project, broken down by activity. Beginning from February 24th, the Scrum-oriented phase reveals itself by a momentary peak in the relative number of open ActionItems – especially in the activities Analysis and Implementation.

the activity attribute[4]. (2) ActionItems arising in meetings also need to be automatically classified according to their activity. This is especially important for the automatic capture of ActionItems using word spotting techniques. (3) In our case study, we started to work in a sequential- and activity-oriented approach and then switched to a more agile and Scrum-oriented process. In future projects, we plan to perform such a process shift also in converse order. Hence, when following an agile process, the ActionItems will not be classified by their activity. An automatic classification would help to retrospectively add this information whenever the process is turned into an activity-oriented process.

For an automatic classification, we trained the SYMBOCONN framework with data from the DOLLI project. The following paragraph describes the technical setup of the training patterns learned by the MRNN and reports on the results of the activity classification.

Training Data Representation For each of the 684 ActionItems, 13 attributes are captured in the UNICASE tool at the time of creation. These are Name, Team, Activity, State, DueDate, OrganizationalUnit, Description, ParentActionItem, ChildActionItems, Annotatables, URLElements, Attachments and CreationDate. The attributes of the ActionItems to be classified by the MRNN are described by 26 to 2536 feature dimensions, depending on the respective representation technique. As an example, a minimal training pattern with only two input attributes

---
[4]This is a common issue of research approaches, which need additional information to be captured.

Activity	Number of ActionItems
Analysis	258
System Design	158
Object Design	58
Implementation	202
Testing	7
Project Management	1
Total	**684**

Table 6.3: Distribution of ActionItems according to the activity they were assigned to by the project participants. The activities testing and project management were rarely assigned. We assume that project management tasks were mostly managed in the team wikis, whereas comprehensive testing was not in the scope of the DOLLI project.

results in the following straight-forward feature vector representation.

$$\vec{x}_t = (\underbrace{x_1, \ldots, x_{k_1}}_{Team}, \underbrace{x_{k_1+1}, \ldots, x_{k_2}}_{CreationDate}) \mapsto \underbrace{(a_1, \ldots, a_6)}_{\vec{y}_{t+1}}, \qquad (6.1)$$

where $x_i \in \mathbb{R}$, $a_j \in \{0, 1\}$. Categorical attributes such as Team or OrganizationalUnit are encoded in a unary form, that is, each symbol to be encoded is assigned to an orthogonal bit vector with a "1" at the ith component, $(0, 0, \ldots, 0, 1, 0, \ldots, 0)$. Numerical (metric) attributes such as CreationDate (relative point of time with respect to the beginning of the project measured in days) are assigned to a fixed-width intercept of the whole feature vector, for example, a numerical value is scaled to the range $[0, 1]$ and the respective value is replicated 10 times (as often as the width of the other attributes' representations). Even if a single feature dimension would suffice to represent a numerical value, due to balance reasons, the value is replicated in order to achieve the same weight than other types of represented attributes (e.g. categorical).

The training and test patterns both hold the form *input* $\mapsto$ *target* used in expression 6.1, while the test patterns were excluded from MRNN training. Five-fold cross-validation was used to obtain significant accuracy measurements, therefore the 684 objects were divided into 5 disjoint test sets. The standard measures precision and recall to assess the quality of a classifier were computed according to the following formulas:

$$Recall_i = \frac{|\{o \in C_i | K(o) = C(o)\}|}{|C_i|} \qquad (6.2)$$

$$Precision_i = \frac{|\{o \in K_i | K(o) = C(o)\}|}{|K_i|} \qquad (6.3)$$

158   APPLICATION TO KNOWLEDGE ENG. AND SOFTWARE DEVELOPMENT

C_i, $i = 1, \ldots, r$ is the ith class in the set of classes $C = \{C_1, \ldots, C_r\}$ and K_i is the set of objects that were predicted to belong to class C_i. $K(o) \in C$ is the classification of object o predicted by the machine learning engine. The classification $K(o)$ of unseen objects is compared with their actual class membership $C(o)$. The precision and recall values are weighted with the size $\alpha_i := |C_i|$ of each class by a weighted sum $precision = \sum_{i=1}^{r} \frac{\alpha_i}{n} \cdot precision_i$, $n = \sum_{i=1}^{r} \alpha_i$, analogously for the recall.

Variant	Input Attributes	LSI	Measure	Precision	Recall	F-Measure	Δ
1	Team, DueDate, CreationDate	–	Mean Variation	76.83 [75.11 - 78.93]	77.37 [74.51 - 79.21]	77.10 [74.81 - 79.07]	7.48
2	Name, Description	No	Mean Variation	50.78 [44.93 - 56.27]	53.73 [48.51 - 57.84]	52.21 [46.65 - 57.05]	1.58
3	Name, Description	Yes[1]	Mean Variation	48.71 [42.67 - 54.46]	52.37 [46.32 - 58.52]	50.47 [44.42 - 56.42]	10.27
4	All except Activity	Yes[2]	Mean Variation	80.64 [78.03 - 84.28]	80.38 [76.47 - 83.70]	80.51 [77.24 - 83.99]	7.60

[1] LSI using $\sigma^2 = 0.65$.
[2] LSI using $\sigma^2 = 0.35$.

Table 6.4: Average classification accuracy measured in terms of *Precision* and *Recall* for 684 ActionItems after *5-fold cross-validation*. The measure *Variation* indicates the range of the obtained accuracy values over the 5 individual test sets used for cross-validation. For all predictions, the network was trained until a residual error of Δ. Best accuracy is in bold, the F-Measure is a weighted mean of Precision and Recall: *F-Measure* = $\frac{2 \cdot Precision \cdot Recall}{Precision + Recall}$. If Latent Semantic Indexing (LSI) was used (only applicable in case of textual attributes), 35% and 65% of the variance σ^2 in the training set were kept, respectively. This implies that the dimensions corresponding to the 35% or 65% smallest eigenvalues, were discarded.

Table 6.4 shows the results of the evaluation process, which depend on the choice of attributes included in the training process (column *Input Attributes*). We see that the attribute CreationDate is highly significant for the classification of the activity that produced the respective artifact.

During the training phase, the machine learning engine is faced with incomplete data, for example, the values of the DueDate attribute are missing in 68.44% of the training examples. However, the MRNN machine learning engine is capable of handling fuzzy, incomplete and partially incorrect data. The MRNN coped with the incomplete attribute values, as shown by the evaluation variants 1 and 2 in table 6.4. Due to the additional DueDate attribute in variant 2, the accuracy could be slightly improved and stabilized (smaller variation) – despite the majority of missing Due-Date values.

In case of variant 2, the training error cannot be reduced as much as for variant 3 or 4, since the mapping from the input attributes to the classification attribute Activity is less unique than in the other cases. This is due to the lower discrimination provided by the attributes Team (categorical), DueDate and CreationDate (both numerical), which do not always uniquely determine the activity an artifact originated from. Since the neural network realizes a functional mapping, the training error does not vanish completely.

For activity classification, *overfitting* [KAD01] occurs very early when using textual attributes, such that the training procedure has to be stopped quite early. For example, reducing the training error to an amount of 3.14% leads to a 4.8% lower classification accuracy on unseen objects (generalization) than accepting a training error of 7.93% in case of variant 4.

The good classification result when using the attributes CreationDate and Team (variants 1,2,5, and 6) shows that certain periods of time in the project existed, in which certain teams worked in a specific activity.

The evaluation variants 3 and 4 showed that it is possible to classify ActionItems even without any time-related information, but in this case, the results are less accurate in an unproportional manner. Surprisingly, variant 4 using the advanced text representation LSI provides a slightly lower classification accuracy ($\delta = 1.74$) than variant 3 without using LSI and is considered to represent a statistical outlier. One reason for this might be the significantly higher training error Δ of variant 4, which is a sign of the less unique input-target (class) mapping that was more difficult to learn. The effect of hindered training progress in the case of latent semantic indexing is due to the lossy transformation ($\sigma^2 = 0.65$) of the input information, which discards both redundant information and information used to distinguish the artifact class. Normally, the improved representation (less redundant and more compressed) overcompensates the negative effect of loosing information which is usable for the class distinction.

6.1.1.2 Status Classification

All ActionItems in the DOLLI project were classified manually according to their status, which can be either open or closed. Figure 6.4 shows the distribution of open ActionItems over time. After the process shift from a sequentially oriented software life cycle model to an agile life cycle model, we observed that a large number of ActionItems was neither touched (read or changed) nor closed until the end of the project. A survey among the project participants revealed that 81% of these ActionItems were either irrelevant or were attached to a task which was already closed.

This implies that the respectiveActionItems should have been closed, too. Again, an automatic classification approach can support the user to mark these objects as irrelevant. In contrast to the classification of the artifact activity, the classification according to the status is a visible benefit to the project participants: the mechanism determines ActionItems, which are most likely irrelevant, and recommends to close or to delete them.

To gather trainings cases for our experiments, we used the change-based SCM approach [Koe08] to recreate the state of the DOLLI project before the process shift

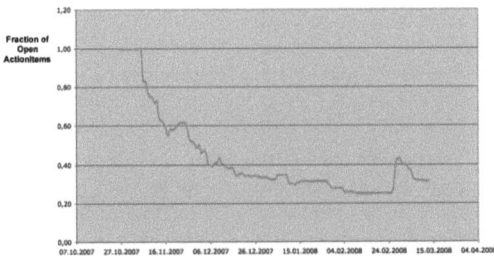

Figure 6.4: Fraction of open ActionItems with respect to the total number of ActionItems managed in the DOLLI project. Beginning from February 24th, the Scrum-oriented phase is revealed by a momentary peak in the relative number of open ActionItems.

to Scrum was done. As training set, we chose ActionItems which were not yet closed at this state. We then determined which ActionItems had not been closed until the end of the project. Under the assumption that all of the chosen ActionItems, which had not been closed at the end of the project, were irrelevant, we accordingly set the classification attribute Irrelevant of each ActionItem. As opposed to the activity classification with a target space consisting of six classes, the binary classification of the artifact status explicitly considers the development of an artifact over time, that is, the individual artifact history or life cycle.

For the classification of the artifact status, we again used a network topology with a hidden layer dimension of $h = 30$. Compared to the multi-class activity classification, the classification of the ActionItem status even shows a higher tendency to overfitting. To avoid an overadaption with respect to the training set, for each cross-validation we used a small auxiliary test set during training to check the current quality of the classification model. When the classification error on this test set started to rise, the training process was cut off. This is the reason for the higher level of the residual training error denoted by Δ in table 6.5.

Compared to the first experiment, status classification should only be used to provide the user with a recommendation, as it is not acceptable to wrongly classify an ActionItem as irrelevant (alpha error). For the purpose of recommendation, the given precision is sufficient to effectively support project participants. As shown in table 6.5, LSI had a positive effect on the classification accuracy, which is demonstrated by comparing variant three and four in table 6.5.

An interesting observation we made during the evaluation of the experimental data was the role of the attribute DueDate. One could expect that a defined and prompt DueDate tends to ActionItems which are not irrelevant and vice versa. However, we found out that the attribute DueDate had even a negative effect on the precision. To discover the reason behind that anomaly, we trained the MRNN only with the DueDate information without any further attributes. Due to the miss-

Variant	Input Attributes	LSI	Measure	Precision	Recall	F-Measure	Δ
1	Team, Activity, CreationDate	–	Mean Variation	74.30 [65.09 - 83.33]	71.20 [58.33 - 83.33]	72.65 [61.53 - 83.33]	22.01
2	Team, Activity, CreationDate, DueDate	–	Mean Variation	72.06 [59.35 - 84.72]	68.66 [54.17 - 83.33]	70.27 [56.64 - 84.02]	19.41
3	All Attributes	No	Mean Variation	78.18 [69.63 - 86.67]	75.36 [66.67 - 83.33]	76.74 [68.12 - 84.97]	12.33
4	All Attributes	Yes[1]	Mean Variation	81.13 [67.71 - 89.47]	80.47 [70.83 - 87.50]	80.79 [69.24 - 88.48]	22.87
5	All Attributes except DueDate	Yes[2]	Mean Variation	**85.49** [78.19 - 92.71]	**82.14** [73.91 - 91.67]	**83.72** [75.99 - 92.18]	16.31

[1] LSI using $\sigma^2 = 0.65$.
[2] LSI using $\sigma^2 = 0.85$.

Table 6.5: Average accuracy for the classification of the artifact status Irrelevant after 5-fold cross-validation. All values are given in percent [%], best accuracy is in bold.

ing values of the DueDate attribute in 54.24% of the training cases used for status classification, the training error stagnated on a high level of about $\Delta = 24\%$, because of the lack of information that could be used to distinguish and classify the respective ActionItems. This fact alone is not the reason for the repressed classification accuracy, since the neural classifier can deal with incomplete information, if further attributes are available. The main problem was that the DueDate attribute imposed contradicting time information. This means, for example, that there are 9 ActionItems which have the same DueDate value of 80 days since the first day of the project. However, in the first case they are irrelevant (5), while in the other case not (4). Of course, such ambiguous information is misleading and counterproductive for the classification (non-dichotomous or non-disjoint ActionItem distribution) and should be discarded. It argues for the robustness of the MRNN, that the classification accuracy is not even more distorted by the DueDate attribute.

6.1.2 Better Than Guessing?

In the previous section, we evaluated the performance of the SYMBOCONN framework, which is considerably high. But which practical benefit does this classification have, or in other words, how difficult is the activity classification task for humans? To figure this out, we conducted an experiment with developers, who should classify ActionItems according to their activity by hand. We chose three persons with different degrees of expertise in the project: The *Informed Outsider* knew the RUSE model and the information about the DOLLI project provided in this paper. The *Knowledgeable Observer* worked part-time in the DOLLI project as a teaching assistant. The *Expert* played a central role as an active project participant in DOLLI. We chose a layered single sample of $n = 70$ ActionItems from the basic

Expertise	Precision	Recall	F-Measure
Informed Outsider	38.07	32.86	35.27
Knowledgeable Observer	50.17	41.43	45.38
Expert	61.35	51.43	55.95

Table 6.6: Evaluation of the ability of humans to classify ActionItems. Three persons with different degrees of expertise and insight into the software project were compared.

population of $N = 684$ ActionItems to obtain significant results[5]. We conducted a random selection in groups, so that the class distribution of the objects in the sample was proportional to that in the basic population.

As shown in table 6.6, the quality of the classification significantly increases with the project-related expertise of the interviewee. Nevertheless, even the *Expert* was by far not able to match the classification accuracy of the machine learning system.

The demonstrated classification of software artifacts can be used as a foundation for software metrics and is especially important for project management. It enables the creation of knowledge about structure, since the activity classification can be employed to identify a work breakdown structure. In section 6.3, we show another application of the SYMBOCONN framework to structural knowledge, in particular, to design patterns. The following section demonstrates how the SYMBOCONN framework can be applied to causal knowledge of change, which is important predict the impact of changes in software projects with many interdependent artifacts.

6.2 Change Impact Analysis

As software systems become increasingly large and complex, the need increases to predict and control the effects of software changes [BA96]. Change impact analysis is an increasingly important activity of the change management process for handling change requests. Change impact analysis primarily concerns itself with determining which (software) entities of a system affect each other. During many software development activities, such as requirements elicitation or testing, change occurs frequently and its impact is generally not isolated to the source artifact, so that it is necessary to assess the impact of change. According to the chaos theory regarding nonlinear dynamical systems (dynamical system, cf. definition 4.4.1), the impact of a small local change may cause an exponential growth in the system's starting conditions and therefore lead to chaotic behavior. In a figurative sense, this also holds for software development to some extent, as almost every software developer

---

[5]The minimal sample size of $n_{min} \geq 30$ was met, which is the precondition for the samples' mean values to be normally distributed; though, in our case, there is only one sample and thus a meaningful distribution of several samples [vdL08, HEK99] does not exist.

with sufficient experience will agree. Thus, facing change and estimating its impact is essential in modern software engineering. Facing change is also a basic principle of *agile methods* [Amb06], which consider change to be omnipresent[6]. Change is not the exception and not an outlier[7] of the regular activity, but is envisioned by the development life cycle.

In the change management process described by the activity chart in figure 6.5, a *request for change* is created when existing software artifacts need to be changed. Besides determining the technical feasibility of the requested change, its costs and benefits have to be assessed, as well. Thus the *Analyze Change Request* segment of the change management process assesses the extent of the change; this activity is typically called change impact analysis and is addressed by the SYMBOCONN framework. During change impact analysis, the impact is analyzed in detail by

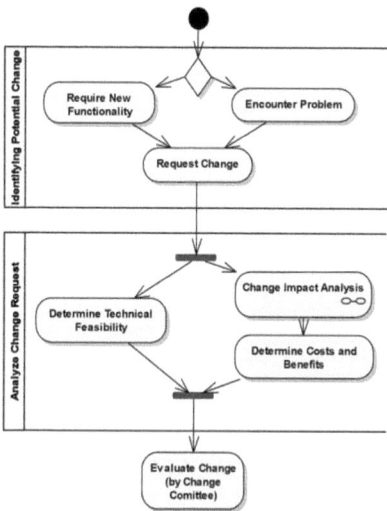

Figure 6.5: Activity diagram showing an excerpt of the change management process that clarifies the role of change impact analysis.

determining which other entities are affected by the change. *Change propagation* [HH04, Han97] represents the sequence of changes required to other entities of the software system to ensure their consistency after a particular entity is changed. Change propagation also proposes the locations in the project graph, where the corresponding changes are to be made.

---

[6] *"When the winds of change blow hard enough, even the most trivial things can be turned into deadly projectiles."*

[7] In terms of data mining, an outlier is a deviation from the typical object distribution.

Definition 6.2.1: Change-Impact Relation
The causality of changes, which is the relation between cause and impact, can formally be described as a partial order induced by the binary relation $R_{CI} \subset \mathcal{P}(V) \times \mathcal{P}(V)$ of change-impact dependency.
A change-impact pair $(\{c_1, c_2, \ldots, c_m\}, \{i_1, i_2, \ldots, i_n\}) \in R_{CI}$, $m, n \in \mathbb{N}$ is an element of the transitive relation on the power set of the artifact space (represented by nodes $v \in V$ of the SYMBOCONN knowledge model). The left hand side of this relation[8] represents one or many changes of software artifacts that have an impact on one or many other software artifacts.

The structural context of changed model elements in the graph should be exploited by machine learning equipped with an appropriate structural knowledge representation. Figure 6.6 illustrates the change of an artifact, which is captured together with its local neighborhood in the project graph. In order to generate training

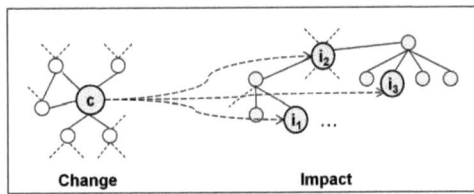

Figure 6.6: Structure-sensitive change of a model element c, which refers to other artifacts i_1, i_2, and i_3. Thus the local change is propagated from c to i_1, i_2, and i_3. The changed artifact and its impact are learned under consideration of the local neighborhood of the changed and impacted software artifacts in the graph.

examples for the SYMBOCONN engine, the changed artifact is considered together with its direct neighbors (linked via a single edge) in the graph. This subgraph is serialized and results in an input pattern for the MRNN. The model elements affected by the change are also captured together with their neighboring elements in form of the target subgraph; this target subgraph is serialized as a single target pattern. A structure-to-structure mapping has a higher potential to cover all aspects of cause and impact relationships than only considering isolated artifact changes.

Graph Serialization There are several methods stemming from knowledge discovery and discrete mathematics for the representation, comparison and search of graphs; these are used either for *graph mining* or for heuristic search, like the Warshal or Dijkstra algorithm. Graph nodes and links have to be serialized in the

---
[8]The change-impact relation R_{CI} can be compared with Lamport's *happened-before relation* $a \to b$ that is also transitive [Lam78]. $a \to b$ and $b \to c$ implies $a \to c$. If $a \to b$, where a and b are events of the same process, then a occurred before b. As opposed to R_{CI}, the happened-before relation imposes a logical time and must not be interpreted causally.

form of SYMBOCONN node sequences in order to be processable by the recurrent neural network. The literature on graph mining and representation often uses a triple-based approach in order to represent graph-structured knowledge [YH02]. In SYMBOCONN, a triple is of the form ($node_i$,$link\text{-}type_{ij}$,$node_j$), which represents two graph nodes as well as their connecting link. Thus, a subgraph is a set of triples transformed to an input pattern and mapped onto the subgraph of affected elements, which is also represented by a set of triples. Such a triple is considered as one node of the SYMBOCONN knowledge model (cf. section 3) and is realized by a multi-represented object with three complex features. The smallest structural entity, namely two nodes from the graph of figure 6.6 together with their connecting edge, are aggregated by one multi-represented object.

Unlike the rule-based design pattern representation, we have chosen an explicit representation of the graph links for change impact analysis. Since the links are also model elements, they carry important information such as the link type (createdBy, blockedBy, subclassOf, etc.) that should be directly bound to the source and target node and be incorporated into the machine learning process. Finally, a set of triples representing the change has to be mapped to a set of triples that stand for the impact. Both sets have to be transformed into ordered sequences that can directly be processed by the MRNN.

Change impact analysis is especially useful when traditional project and risk management approaches fail to assess the consequences of requested change packages in a timely fashion, due to lacking experience or expertise on the part of the project participants. Thus, change impact analysis is also related to the field of risk management [LSK04], since changes to sensitive software artifacts paired with an unfavorable timing imply risks for current development activities or even for the whole project. Risk is consensually interpreted as the *rate of change multiplied by its impact or severity* [GR05]. The risk graph depicted by figure 6.7 illustrates the different zones of danger resulting from the combination of change rate and change impact.

Traditional change management for software development supports the processing of changes and enables their traceability. In this dissertation, the SYMBOCONN framework uses history information [Per96] in the form of change logs to assess the impact of future changes. By applying this empirical variant of change impact analysis to software projects, the following benefits can be attained.

- **Preventing Incomplete Change.** Guidance of programmers by observing their working set and recommending related artifacts to prevent errors resulting from incomplete changes.

- **Pinpointing Entity Coupling.** Pointing out the implicit coupling of entities which is undetectable by conventional program analysis [ZWDZ04].

- **Cost and Time Metrics.** Cost and time metrics based on the result of change impact analysis can quantify the change impact for supporting a go/no-go decision of the change committee.

166   APPLICATION TO KNOWLEDGE ENG. AND SOFTWARE DEVELOPMENT

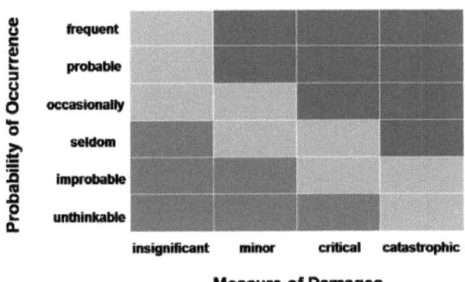

Figure 6.7: Risk graph showing three different risk zones. The green zone represents the *acceptable range*, while the red zone is *unacceptable*. The orange one is the so-called ALARP-range, which means *As Low As Reasonably Practicable*. The ALARP-range is flexible and may differ from institution to institution, depending on the sensitivity and maturity of the respective practice.

- **Enrichment of Burn-Down Charts**. Burn-down or Gantt charts that reflect the development progress can be enriched by grouping the results of change impact analysis according to the features to be implemented in the software release. The indicated change propagation caused by a feature implementation can help to improve the timely delivery of the desired product functionality and quality. At each stage of the development process, the apparently required changes of the current promotion can be confronted with the predicted time and resource constraints. Expensive changes to subsystems can be avoided.

- **Enabling Traceability of Changes Across Software Models**. From the history of a project and with the help of traceability, change propagation can be traced across different system models, such as class diagrams and use case diagrams, which reveals *inter-model* dependencies. On this basis, inter-model links can be categorized according to their probability to frequently propagate changes, which is useful to set up appropriate tool support for these change paths.

In this section, we exploit change information with the SYMBOCONN framework in order to recommend corresponding changes in accordance with the expected impacts.

APPLICATION TO KNOWLEDGE ENG. AND SOFTWARE DEVELOPMENT 167

6.2.1 Change Impact Analysis on Graph-Structured Data

In this section, we briefly present the principle of structure-based change prediction, while the evaluation of the technique will be carried out in future work within the scope of the DOLLI project [Dol07], which develops a tracking- and service system and was introduced in section 6.2.2.

The proposed change impact analysis is based on the UNICASE project graph shown in figure 6.1. The nodes in this graph are called *model elements* and all modifications applied to them are captured in a central repository. So-called inter-model links between *Actors* and *Use Cases*, or between *Use Cases* and *Classes* may propagate changes in one element even to elements of other models. The CASE tool user is able to follow these links forward and backward in order to assess the potential impact of a requirements change, or to validate the test results against a set of requirements. For example, a requirement change may affect a use case or a class diagram.

This task is automated by the SYMBOCONN framework, considering model element changes both in content and structure. This approach to change impact analysis may also detect link types that frequently propagate inter-model changes and are thus traceability links.

The project graph lays the foundations for structure-sensitive change impact analysis, as opposed to a content-based change analysis, which is merely based on repository transactions like those employed in section 6.2.2. UNICASE, for example, provides uniform mechanisms to trace changes to impacted design, implementation, or test elements in forward and backward direction, which is the precondition for a comprehensive change impact analysis.

Purely Structural Graph Representation Motivated by *frequent subgraph mining* [KK01], which is an extension of association rule mining and serves to discover structurally similar or equal subgraphs, an equivalence class of subgraphs is introduced. For consistency reasons, structurally equal subgraphs must be mapped to the same sequence of multi-represented objects learned by the MRNN, which can be achieved by *canonical labeling* [KK01, KK02]. A canonical label CL is an isomorphism-invariant normal form of a graph; thus, several distinct but isomorphic graphs are assigned to the same label. If two graphs G_1 and G_1 result in the same canonical label, then they belong to the same isomorphism class:

$$G_1 \cong G_2 \Leftrightarrow CL(G_1) = CL(G_2), \tag{6.4}$$

where $CL : \{V, E\} \to \Sigma^{\frac{1}{2}(n^2-n)}$, $V = \{v_1, \ldots, v_n\}$, $n = |V|$, E is the set of links (edges) in the change graph, and Σ is the alphabet of existing link type codes. Figure 6.8 shows a graph of typed nodes and links that is subject of change. For this example, the link type alphabet is $\Sigma = \{0, 1, 2, 3\}$, since a missing link is encoded by "0". The technical benefit of the canonical labeling consists in providing a well-defined transformation of isomorphic subgraphs to a unique code string that

168   APPLICATION TO KNOWLEDGE ENG. AND SOFTWARE DEVELOPMENT

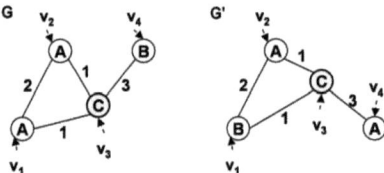

Figure 6.8: Exemplary change graphs G and G' consisting of the one-step neighbors of change node v_3. Node v_3 of type C is changed in its structural embedding in the graph. In the change impact analysis of SYMBOCONN, all graph nodes $v_1, \ldots, v_4$ are only considered by their type like A=Requirement, B=UseCase or C=Actor, but not as unique instances. The link types could be identified with associations like $1 = \text{createdBy}$, $2 = \text{blockedBy}$, or $3 = \text{changedBy}$.

stands for all graphs from the same isomorphism class. Canonical labeling was implemented into the SYMBOCONN framework for being capable of processing semantic graphs (see also section 3.2) such as the one in figure 6.8.

In the first step of canonical labeling, the adjacency matrix of the subgraph to be serialized is computed, which contains the link types encoded as integers; this is shown by the matrices 6.5.

$$M = \begin{matrix} A & A & B & C \\ \end{matrix} \begin{pmatrix} 0 & 2 & 1 & 1 \\ 2 & 0 & 0 & 1 \\ 1 & 0 & 0 & 3 \\ 0 & 1 & 3 & 0 \end{pmatrix} \quad M' = \begin{matrix} B & A & A & C \\ \end{matrix} \begin{pmatrix} 0 & 2 & 0 & 1 \\ 2 & 0 & 0 & 1 \\ 0 & 0 & 0 & 3 \\ 1 & 1 & 3 & 0 \end{pmatrix} \quad (6.5)$$

For n different nodes, $n!$ adjacency matrices are created and for each of them the upper triangular matrix is first read out column-wise and then row-wise. The resulting integer strings are sorted lexicographically, the lowest string being the desired canonical label. For the matrix M in expression 6.5, the resulting string is

$$CL(G) = \underbrace{210113}_{length\,=\,\frac{1}{2}(n^2-n)=\frac{1}{2}(16-4)=6},$$

which is one of 24 strings. The remaining 23 strings represent the other permutations of the node labels while preserving the graph structure. One isomorphism class consists of the different graphs arising from the permutations of the node labels of a specific change graph. Thus, the isomorphism class is determined by the structure of the graph, and not by its node labels. The class representative could be described in words by "there are two nodes of degree 2 and type A that are connected by a link of type 2. Both of these nodes are also connected to another node of degree 3 and type C by links of type 1...". In figure 6.8, graphs G and G' are not

APPLICATION TO KNOWLEDGE ENG. AND SOFTWARE DEVELOPMENT 169

isomorphic to each other, that is, $G_1 \not\cong G_2$, since $CL(G) \neq CL(G') = 200113$.

Content- and Structure-Based Graph Representation This form of graph representation is required to support change impact analysis in CASE tools, if they provide views onto the relevant subgraphs that enable the consideration of different levels of detail concerning the node or link type. For example, during a change impact analysis, one might want to ignore fine-grained node types (model element types) such as *NonfunctionalRequirement* or *DesignGoal* and, instead, only consider three types of nodes – *Issues*, *Requirements*, and *Activities*. Assume we are only interested in the influence of requirement changes on the duration of project activities, for example. In this case, coarse-grained node filtering results in several nodes of the same type (label), illustrated by figure 6.9. Now, the only remaining

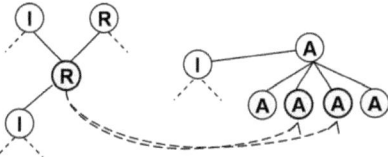

Figure 6.9: Excerpt of a project graph that was filtered according to the node types *Issues* (I), *Requirements* (R), and *Activities* (A) denoted as labels. Different link types were also filtered out here. The change in the marked requirement results in changes in two project activities with the same parent node.

fact is that the changed requirement is linked to another requirement, as well as to two annotations, which completely describes the relevant causal subgraph – regardless of its link types. Other filtering strategies lead to other node type partitions regarding the change and impact graphs. Then, nodes that have been of distinct types before filtering may afterwards be mapped onto the same type. To still obtain a fixed order of the triples that have to be transformed into SYMBOCONN node sequences, the graph nodes (model elements) are sorted by their degree[9] first and, in case of ambiguity, by their labels in a second step. The same applies to the order within the triples of the form $(node_i, link\text{-}type_{ij}, node_j)$.

Representing Changes in the Graph Structure In order to capture structural changes in the project graph such as the removal of a model element, as well, we optionally consider two change graphs instead of a single one as the input pattern

---
[9]The number of incoming and outgoing links.

for the neural network.

$$(CSG_1, CSG_2) \mapsto ISG$$
$$CSG_1 \Rightarrow (i_1, (ij)_1, j_1), (i_2, (ij)_2, j_2), \ldots, (i_m, (ij)_m, j_m)$$
$$CSG_2 \Rightarrow (i_1, (ij)_1, j_1), (i_2, (ij)_2, j_2), \ldots, (i_n, (ij)_n, j_n)$$
$$ISG \Rightarrow (k_1, (kl)_1, l_1), (k_2, (kl)_2, l_2), \ldots, (k_r, (kl)_r, l_r),$$

where the source node i_k and target node j_k linked by $(ij)_k$ are ordered according to their degree within one triple and across triples: $deg(i_k) \leq deg(j_k)$, $k = 1, \ldots, \max(m, n)$ and $deg(j_1) \leq deg(j_2) \leq \ldots \leq deg(j_{\max(m,n)})$. If this orderrule does not produce unambiguousness, then the nodes are additionally sorted by their label as mentioned before. The change subgraph CSG_1 is a snapshot of the structural situation before the change and CSG_2 is the snapshot after the respective change, both of which are mapped to the impact subgraph ISG during the training phase. This way, the removal or addition of a node can be detected by machine learning[10]; this would not be possible if only a single change graph is considered.

Beyond learning the structure of changes, the SYMBOCONN framework even has the capability of learning structural changes that lead to a change in the content of the impact subgraph (effect). An example is the addition of a new actor to a use case, which requires a description of the actor in the use case model. This change in the model is hidden behind the triple components, such as $(k_2, (kl)_2, l_2)$ modified to $(\hat{k}_2, (kl)_2, l_2)$ within the ISG, for example. To learn the correlations between change and impact graphs by the MRNN, a set of training patterns of the form $(CSG_1, CSG_2) \mapsto ISG$ is used.

Causal relationships are often not explicit and are thus not represented in the knowledge graph that determines the structure of the available project knowledge. Therefore, in the following section, we apply the change impact analysis of the SYMBOCONN framework to software artifacts that are not linked by an explicit graph structure, but which show an implicit coupling through their occurrence within the same checkin transactions.

6.2.2 Recommending Software Changes

In this section, we present the results of our approach to content-based change impact analysis, which were already discussed in detail in [Dav08c]. The central goal of recommending software changes is to predict software artifacts that are frequently changed together by a developer due to their explicit or latent interdependencies. The software repository receives a set of artifact changes within one commit transaction. This implicit knowledge of interdependent changes can be exploited in order to recommend likely further changes, given a set of already changed artifacts.

---

[10]The technique of employing two subgraphs can also be used to represent structural changes on the impact side, of course.

Developers deal with a work package of a software project and complete each of their working steps with a checkin operation on the artifact repository. A *Configuration Management aggregate* (CM aggregate) [BD04], or shortly *commit set*, is a composite of configuration items that are checked in within the same repository transaction. The software developers' working focuses should be learned from their interaction with the artifact repository by means of *learning by example*. The working focus of a developer is considered as the union of all commit sets within the time frame T. In particular, two distinct tasks are to be solved by learning from the repository transaction data.

1. **Recommending further changes**: Guiding a beginner or an experienced programmer who is unfamiliar with a certain subsystem and its configuration items. When a developer is working on a programming task, *relevant software artifacts* such as documentation, UML diagrams, code, multimedia files, etc. that might require corresponding changes should be proactively recommended: *"Programmers who changed these artifacts also changed.."* [ZWDZ04].

2. **Generalization**: The connectionist system should go beyond the state-of-art in guiding programmers, which is mostly based on symbolic association rules. The recommendation of related artifacts should even work for completely unlearned configuration items, which have not been under version control at the time of training. Based on their textual and conceptual similarity, the neural network provides a *content-based* assessment of unseen artifacts.

The procedure for recommending software changes is very similar to the navigation recommendation functionality introduced before, since many settings, such as the structure of the training patterns, hold for both applications. In the case of navigation recommendation, the recommended subjects are web pages or documents, while in change impact analysis, they are software artifacts changed together with high probability. Again, a hybrid approach based on *Latent Semantic Indexing* (LSI) and on the Modular Recurrent Neural Network (MRNN) is used to recommend software development artifacts; that is, predicting a sequence of configuration items that were checked in together. In both cases, textual attributes of the entities to be predicted are analyzed and transformed by LSI, as described in section 7.3.

As opposed to related approaches to repository mining, which are mostly based on symbolic methods like *Association Rule Mining*, our connectionist method is able to generalize to unseen artifacts. Compared to association rule mining, which is a purely symbolic approach operating on atomic artifact identifiers, our connectionist technique – paired with text mining methods – is able to incorporate actual content into the learning and recommendation process. The association rule mining approach often used in related work [ZWDZ04] is, in principle, not able to assess changes or visits of *new* artifacts, since their (latent) semantics are ignored by the symbolic representation[11].

---

[11]We did not address source code fragments, as did Zimmermann et al. [ZWDZ04], but focused

The combination of neural networks with Latent Semantic Indexing is a new and promising approach to change impact analysis, which has hardly been investigated so far [SLD96, DDF+90].

Navigation and artifact recommendation as well as change impact analysis are highly relevant areas of research [GHJ98, CM03, ZWDZ04]. In *"Mining Version Histories to Guide Software Changes"*, Zimmermann et al. [ZWDZ04] applied association rule mining to the analysis of artifact changes that frequently occur together and thus are empirically related to each other. The current *situation* of a software developer is considered as a set of file changes that is used for mining association rules with a corresponding antecedent part *on the fly* (only on demand). The consequent parts of length one of all matching rules are ranked by confidence and are presented to the user. The implementation was carried out as an *Eclipse* plugin, so that the recommendations appear as a list in an integrated window of the development environment.

The industrial paper [SLW07] demonstrates the use of the Singular Value Decomposition (SVD) to analyze the changes in software project files that occur together. These are counted in a quadratic frequency matrix, which is then decomposed by Singular Value Decomposition in order to obtain the significances of the *association clusters*. These clusters indicate the strength of the associations between files. As in the work at hand, a frequency matrix of keyterms and text units is computed and analyzed by SVD (only as preprocessing), which is a powerful method for removing redundancy and for eliciting the correlated latent concepts from an empirical dataset.

In [ZWDZ04], the recommendation of software artifacts or web pages, respectively, is based on association rule mining. Thus, useful *predictive information* in the form of artifact contents is given away when relying solely on symbolic items without consulting the similarity between artifacts. This drawback can be avoided by considering a rich representation of the visited entities, instead of reducing them to meaningless unique identifiers.

In the following case study, the technique was applied to three publicly available datasets from the *PROMISE Repository of Software Engineering Databases*.

Case Study: Exploiting Repository Transaction Data The change recommendation technique described in this chapter was applied to repositories of versioning data from three independent projects, namely *Nickle, XFree86,* and *X.org*[12]. The used datasets stem from the *PROMISE Repository of Software Engineering Databases* [SSM05], which is a collection of publicly available datasets and tools to serve researchers in building predictive software models. Massey [Mas05] has logged and analyzed the publicly available CVS archives of these projects resulting in datasets with the same structure for different projects, so that we could conduct a uniform evaluation for the three projects.

---

on versioned files in general, which are distinguished by type as listed in table 7.2.

[12]http://{nickle.org, xfree86, x}.org

The value of the attribute *FilePath* is to be predicted by the SYMBOCONN framework, which is considered as a change recommendation for this item. The file names as suffix of the attribute *FilePath* take values such as *"INSTALL-X.org"* or *"Makefile"* (see table 7.2). *FilePath* is the only text-based attribute of the CVS transaction data and its values are considered as text units in terms of section 7.3 for constructing the vector space model. The remainder of the attributes, such as *external* (boolean, author is different from submitting person), are mostly nominal and thus do not provide the possibility of computing similarity among their discrete values. The metric attributes *lines_added* and *lines_removed* proved to be hardly significant and were thus excluded. Table 7.2 shows the schema of the logged repository transactions.

The commit records were grouped according to their checkin dates, thereby obtaining sets of artifacts that were checked in by a specific author at the respective point of time. The contents of each CM aggregate were split into input and target sequences, one pair making up a single training pattern for the neural network.

FileType	FilePath	AuthorID	Revision	Commit Date
"code"	"config/imake/imake.c"	1	2.0	"2004-04-03 22:26:20"
"devel-doc"	"INSTALL-X.org"	1	1.6	"2005-02-11 03:02:53"
"doc"	"config/cf/Fresco.tmpl"	1	1.2	"2005-02-11 03:02:53"
"unknown"	"LABEL"	2	1.2	"2003-07-09 15:27:23"

Table 6.7: Excerpt of the data schema of the *repository transactions* from the XFree86 project, concerning the committed configuration items with some of their attributes.

For our case study we chose arbitrary subsets of 2,970 to 5,350 commit actions by up to 39 anonymous developers, depending on the respective project: Nickle, XFree86, or X.org. The generalization accuracy for the target attribute *FilePath* was evaluated by arbitrary test sets with different numbers of configuration items from the three projects. The repository transaction data was arbitrarily split up into a training set of $\frac{7}{8}$ and a test set of $\frac{1}{8}$ of the relevant commit actions by interleaving (taking each 8th pattern). Since no internal order is specified on the CM aggregates, the artifacts of one commit set C are represented by the possible combinations of ordered input and target sequences making up one training pattern $(input \mapsto target)$.

We trained the network on up to 455 training patterns resulting from a basic set of 3,000 commits. The MRNN learns the committed items as subsequences of the form $(C \supset (item_{i_1}^C, item_{i_2}^C, \ldots, item_{i_n}^C) \mapsto item_{j_1}^C)$, where the target sequence only consists of one item. Despite the relatively short sequences of 3.3 configuration items per CM aggregate on average (*min* 1, *max* 34), we use a neural network for predicting related software artifacts because of its *generalization capability* [Sch97], which reveals its effect when visiting *unseen* artifacts that were not part of the training sequences.

A successful recommendation is given if a set of items $H := \{item_{i_1}, item_{i_2}, \ldots, item_{i_m}\} \subset C$ that was not trained before is presented, and if the network predicts one or several items of the complementary set $T := C \setminus \{item_{i_1}, item_{i_2}, \ldots, item_{i_m}\}$. In general, all items $u \in H$ of the input set are presented and one or several items $v \in T$ of the target subset are expected as correct recommendation, which counts as a hit and is summed over all test cases.

The singular value decomposition of the term-document matrix successfully discovered the latent semantic concepts of the textual attribute *FilePath* and thus optimized the term-frequency based *bag-of-words* approach. The *FilePath* attribute indicates the relative path of the configuration item within the versioned project. We were able to reduce the vector space dimensionality to $d'_1 = d_1 - k = 159$ by $k = 7$ while loosing only 1.06% of the variance in the XFree86 training set, which represents a nearly lossless transform. This was possible because high-dimensional bag-of-words vectors are usually *sparse*, that is, they contain many 0-entries. More formally, the term-document matrix $M \in \mathbb{R}^{d_1 \times |V|}$ (d_1 is the number of keyterms in the knowledge base) does not have full rank, but only $rank(M) = d_1 - k$. We did not conduct an actual dimension reduction with information loss by $k > 7$, because any removal of further dimensions led to a significant downgrade of the prediction accuracy[13].

Before presenting the quantitative results of our recommendation technique, we show two exemplary item recommendations generated from partially *unseen* commit histories of the XFree86 project. Both recommendations were validated by hand, using appropriate queries on the transaction database.

- *1 input, 1 target item*: ***config/cf/xfree86.cf*** $\mapsto$ ***config/cf/xf86site.def***
  The item *config/cf/xf86site.def* was predicted due to its conceptual similarity to the input item *config/cf/xfree86.cf* residing in the same subdirectory *config/cf*, which is detected by LSI-based text mining.

- *2 input, 1 target item*: ***Makefile.std, registry*** $\mapsto$ ***Imakefile***
  In this case, the item *Imakefile* of type *build* was recommended to be changed, since the neural network had learned that checking in the items *Makefile.std* and *registry* mostly implies checking in the *Imakefile*, as well.

The target items in all test sets could be inferred with a maximal accuracy of 72.72% in the case of the X.org project. For the Nickle dataset, we achieved an accuracy of 61.29%, compared to 69.23% for the XFree86 dataset. Note that the residual training error could not be minimized completely (relative training error $0.25\% \leq \delta \leq 0.75\%$) and still might leave room for improvement. In order to avoid overfitting, we did not strive for a perfect mapping of all training sequences.

The significance of all results is quite high, since the dependent variable *FilePath* can take 167 (XFree86) to 1047 (X.org) different values, depending on the project. Assuming an equal distribution of these values, guessing a single target item based on a given set of committed X.org project items would result in an average hit probability of $1/1047 = 0.096\%$.

We think that even better results would be achieved in the presence of more meaningful and more predictive attributes than the path of a software artifact, which does not offer a variety of meaningful keyterms to form a broad basis for textual

---

[13]The smallest kept singular value $\sigma_{159} = 0.999 \approx \frac{6}{100}\sigma_1$ was still significant (X.org).

similarity. The lack of rich content in the *FilePath* attribute, whose values mostly consist of only one to three terms (e.g. "config", "cf", and "xfree86.cf"), provides less predictive information compared to richer multi-represented domain objects.

To summarize, the case study demonstrates that the connectionist LSI-approach achieves a significantly higher recommendation precision than existing methods based on association rule mining. Even for unseen artifacts our approach still provides a precision of up to 72.7% on the given datasets. This means that for 72.7% of the presented test patterns a correct change recommendation was generated. One reason for these results is the inclusion of domain content by the attributes *FileType*, *FilePath*, *AuthorID*, and *Revision* that is exploited as predictive information.

6.3 Design Pattern Discovery

Machine learning can support modeling activities in software engineering by recognition and recommendation of potential design patterns during analysis. Software design patterns were originally defined by Gamma et. al: *"Design patterns are partial solutions to common problems, such as separating an interface from a number of possible implementations. A design pattern is composed of a small number of classes that, through delegation and inheritance, provide a robust and modifiable solution."* [BD04, GHJV95].

Modeling activities are facilitated by design patterns, which are templates to solve well-known design problems. They often improve a software system in terms of expandability, simplicity or reusability. *"In the course of development, software engineers build many different models of the system and of the application domain."* [BD04]. The impacts of design patterns on software development have been empirically analyzed by means of criteria established by Guhneuc and Khomh [GK07].

In the following, the SYMBOCONN classification capability – additionally improved by the introduced spread spectrum mechanism – is applied to the recognition of design patterns. Malformed or partial design patterns, which have been learned according to their original definition but are presented in noisy or incomplete form, should be reliably recognized in the operative phase. Design patterns can be hidden in complex class diagrams, which do not necessarily provide an indication of where to start the discovery process. This is primarily a weakness of purely *symbolic pattern discovery methods* that handle software classes as variables of grammar productions, as accomplished by Costagliola et al. in *"Design Pattern Recovery by Visual Language Parsing"* [CDLD+05]. The *holistic* [Cha90] neural network approach considers class diagrams as a whole and therefore avoids this problem in principle.

6.3.1 Classification Based on Decision Trees

Before developing a symbolic-connectionist method for design pattern discovery, a preliminary but also simple alternative is given, which has not been presented so far. In this section, we adapt the approved information-theoretic method of decision trees for the discovery of design patterns. Table 6.8 defines several design patterns by the number of contained *Aggregation*, *Composition*, *Inheritance*, and *Association* relationships. These frequency attributes are used as naive heuristics to construct a decision tree for classifying class diagrams according to the contained design patterns. As demonstrated by figure 6.10, an initial decision tree is computed that serves for classifying an unknown class diagram.

ID	#Aggregation	#Composition	#Inheritance	#Association	DP
A	0	0	1	1	Adapter
B	1	0	3	0	Bridge
C	0	1	1	0	Composite
O	1	0	2	0	Observer
P	0	0	2	1	Proxy
⋮					

Table 6.8: Naive definition of several design patterns (DP) based on the number (#) of contained *Aggregation*, *Composition*, *Inheritance*, and *Association* relationships.

The building of a decision tree by recursively splitting the respective dataset is completed when all leaf nodes stand for the instances of a single class and thus are homogeneous. Figure 6.10 and 6.11 both depict decision trees for the same design pattern classification problem, but only the second tree is optimal with respect to the entropy information criterion. The first split by the attribute *Inheritance* results in a higher information gain than a first split by the attribute *Aggregation* (Aggr). The reason for this is the created partitioning, which is purer when split based on the question of how many *Inheritance* (Inh) relationships exist in the class diagram. A split according to the number of inheritance relationships results in one homogeneous leaf node for $Inh = 4$ at once, isolating two realizations of the Bridge pattern. The remaining three child nodes have to be split further.

At the root of decision tree 6.10, the design patterns $DP = \{A, B, C, O, P\}$ already show different prior frequencies; thus, the entropy of DP is not maximal, since we approximate the prior probabilities of single design patterns in the basic population of class diagrams by the given frequencies. The assumption of D representing the basic population leads to the following probability approximations: $\mathbb{P}(A) = \frac{5}{20}$, $\mathbb{P}(B) = \frac{3}{20}$, $\mathbb{P}(C) = \frac{5}{20}$, $\mathbb{P}(O) = \frac{3}{20}$ and $\mathbb{P}(P) = \frac{4}{20}$. Formula 6.6 defines the conditional entropy of the two random variables X and Y, which gives the uncertainty of Y when X is already known.

$$H(Y|X) = \sum_{x \in X} \mathbb{P}(x) H(Y|X = x) \qquad (6.6)$$

Apparently, it holds $H(Y|X) = H(Y)$, if X and Y are uncorrelated.

The information gain given by formula 6.7 can be interpreted as the decrease of

ID	#Aggregation	#Composition	#Inheritance	#Association	DP
1	0	0	1	1	Adapter
2	1	0	1	3	Adapter
3	0	1	1	2	Adapter
4	2	1	1	4	Adapter
5	1	1	2	3	Adapter
6	1	0	3	0	Bridge
7	1	1	4	0	Bridge
8	2	1	4	2	Bridge
9	0	2	1	0	Composite
10	0	1	2	2	Composite
11	1	2	2	1	Composite
12	1	2	2	4	Composite
13	1	2	3	3	Composite
14	1	0	2	0	Observer
15	1	1	2	0	Observer
16	1	0	3	1	Observer
17	0	0	2	1	Proxy
18	1	0	2	2	Proxy
19	0	0	2	3	Proxy
20	0	1	3	1	Proxy

Table 6.9: Exemplary dataset D containing realizations of several class diagrams that contain (at least) one concrete design pattern (DP). The descriptive attributes stem from the schema defined by table 6.8.

178   APPLICATION TO KNOWLEDGE ENG. AND SOFTWARE DEVELOPMENT

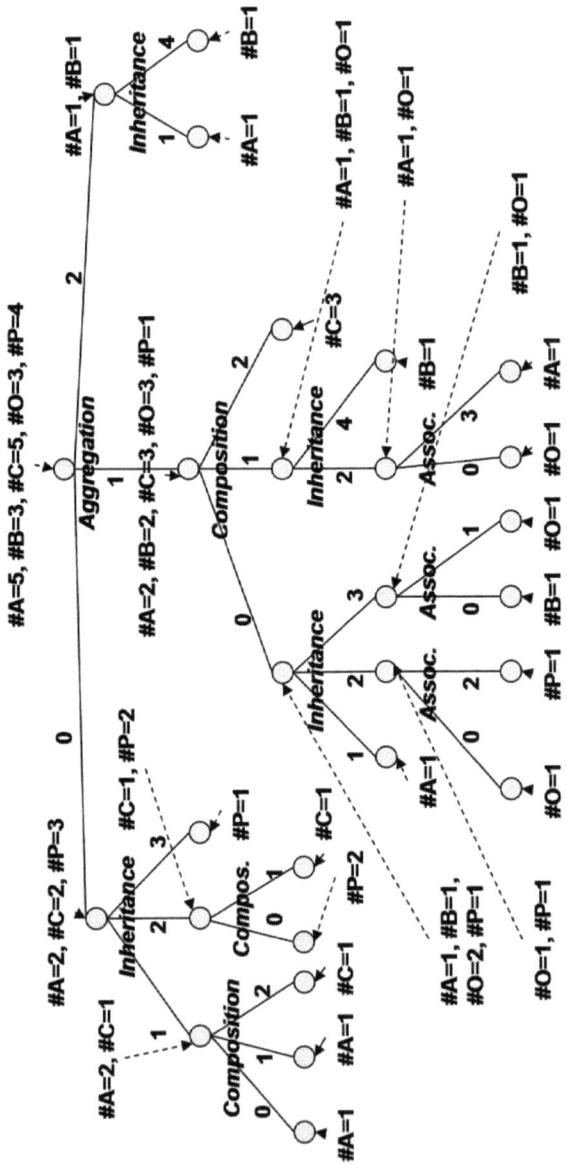

Figure 6.10: Decision tree for the naive classification of class diagrams according to the predefined design patterns *Adapter*, *Bridge*, *Composite*, *Observer*, and *Proxy*. The number of relationships of the respective type T at each decision node is given by the notation "#T=n".

the uncertainty $H(Y)$ after a split by the attribute X.

$$IG(X) = H(Y) - H(Y|X)$$
$$= H(Y) - \sum_{i=1}^{n} \mathbb{P}(i) \cdot H(Y|X = i) \qquad (6.7)$$

Following this, we will exemplarily compute the information gain when splitting the dataset D of table 6.9 by the attribute *Aggregation* at first, which is represented by the root node of the decision tree 6.10. Therefore, the (absolute) entropy of the instances contained by the dataset D before any split needs to be calculated.

$$H(D) = -\sum_{i=1}^{5} \frac{|C_i|}{|D|} \log_2 \frac{|C_i|}{|D|}$$
$$= -(\frac{5}{20} \log_2 \frac{5}{20} + \frac{3}{20} \log_2 \frac{3}{20} + \frac{5}{20} \log_2 \frac{5}{20} \qquad (6.8)$$
$$+ \frac{3}{20} \log_2 \frac{3}{20} + \frac{4}{20} \log_2 \frac{4}{20}) \approx 2.29$$

Subsequently, the conditional entropy values for all realizations of the variable *Aggr* must be determined.

$$H(D|Aggr = 0) = -\sum_{i=0}^{2} \frac{|C_i|}{|D|} \log_2 \frac{|C_i|}{|D|}$$
$$= -(\frac{2}{7} \log_2 \frac{2}{7} + \frac{2}{7} \log_2 \frac{2}{7} + \frac{3}{7} \log_2 \frac{3}{7}) \qquad (6.9)$$
$$\approx 1.56$$

$$H(D|Aggr = 1) = \ldots \approx 2.23 \qquad (6.10)$$
$$H(D|Aggr = 2) = \ldots \approx 1.0 \qquad (6.11)$$

$$IG(D|Aggr) = H(D) - \sum_{i=0}^{2} \frac{|Aggr = i|}{|D|} H(D|Aggr = i)$$
$$= 2.29 - (\frac{7}{20} \cdot 1.56 + \frac{11}{20} \cdot 2.23 + \frac{2}{20} \cdot 1.0) \qquad (6.12)$$
$$\approx 0.413$$

We see that the information gain $IG(Aggr)$ for the first split of the whole dataset by the ternary attribute *Aggregation* amounts to 0.413, which is quite low. Now, we compute the information gain for another split attribute, the 4-valued *Inheritance*,

180 APPLICATION TO KNOWLEDGE ENG. AND SOFTWARE DEVELOPMENT

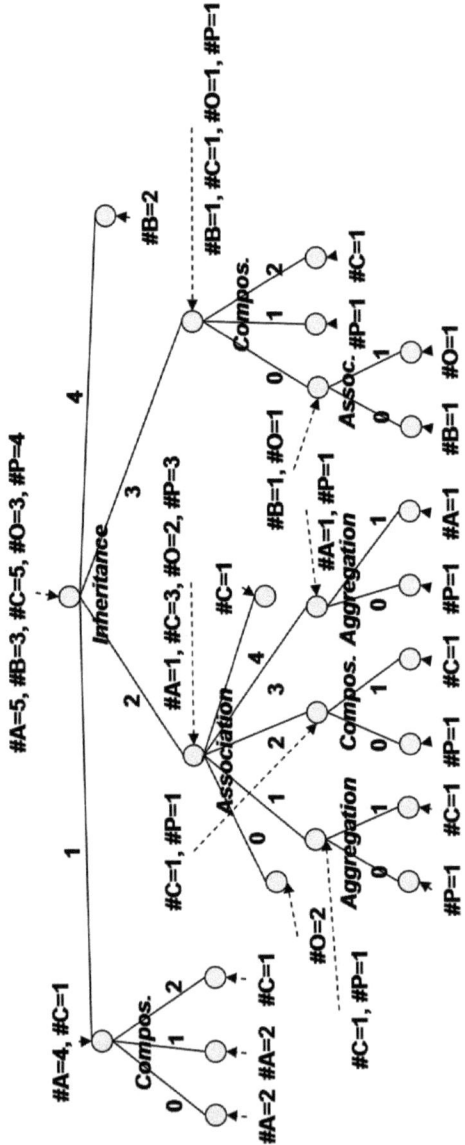

Figure 6.11: Optimal decision tree for the same classification problem as addressed by the suboptimal decision tree of figure 6.10.

for example.

$$IG(D|Inh) = H(D) - \sum_{i=1}^{4} \frac{|Inh = i|}{|D|} H(D|Inh = i)$$
$$= 2.29 - (\frac{5}{20} \cdot 0.722 + \frac{9}{20} \cdot 1.89 + \frac{4}{20} \cdot 2.0 + \frac{2}{20} \cdot 0.0) \quad (6.13)$$
$$\approx 0.854$$

The result is rather illustrative, since the information gained by the split attribute *Inheritance* amounts to more than double of that gained by *Aggregation*. The split of the tree root by the inheritance attribute leads to an information gain of $IG(D|Inh) = 0.854$, while a split by the attribute *Aggregation* only attains a gain of $IG(D|Aggr) = 0.413$. The first split of the second tree is more discriminative and leads to a 5-9-4-2 partitioning, which has a lower entropy than the 7-11-2 partitioning from the first tree – additionally considering the degree of homogeneity in the created child nodes.

It is intuitively feasible that the second decision tree provides the better problem solution, since the Bridge design pattern B can, in several cases, be directly classified by a single decision starting from the root, and the patterns A and C require only one additional decision in the best case. The total number of decisions to be made for classifying all instances of the dataset D according to the five design patterns amounts to $9 + 15 + 3 = 27$ (left, middle and right subtree) in the case of the first tree, while the second tree only requires $4 + 18 + 1 = 23$ decisions.

To obtain the globally optimal decision tree for this small design pattern discovery problem, an exponential number of information gain computations has to be accomplished. In addition to the information gain, an optimal choice of the respective split attribute can be computed using the *Gini Index* criterion [RS04]. Building an optimal decision tree requires splitting the root by all possible attributes and computing the information criteria such as the information gain or the Gini index each time. When the split with the highest information gain or the lowest Gini index is found, the same procedure is recursively repeated at the next tree level for the remaining attributes, and so on.

Some drawbacks of decision trees include their tendency towards overfitting and the high number of required training examples due to their exponential number of leaf nodes. The created decision trees, including the optimal one, will show a low generalization capability when applied to unseen class diagrams, since most of their leaf nodes are supported by only one class diagram instance, which is far too little.

In the following section, we introduce a symbolic encoding schema for aggregated types, advancing the typing function μ defined in section 5.3.

6.3.2 Complex Types

A complex type is an aggregation of simple node types that are used to formally represent a software design pattern, consisting of several pattern constituents such as classes or associations. Thus, a complex type is represented as a sequence of simple types

$$\mu_c : \underbrace{(C \times C \ldots \times C)}_{k\times} \to \mathcal{Z}, \ |\mathcal{Z}| = |C|^k. \quad (6.14)$$

The k-ary typing function μ_k is used for assigning a complex type z to a structure that consists of k already typed nodes. For example, a design pattern that captures the meaning of a special class diagram consisting of k classes (types) represents such a $z \in \mathcal{Z}$. For the exemplary case of software design patterns, the assigned spreading codes [Fak96] are shown in figure 6.12. An instance of the

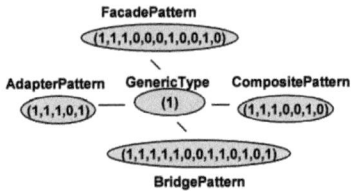

Figure 6.12: *Barker* spreading codes of different lengths for discriminating among the *non-hierarchical target types* z to be classified by the MRNN. Here, each type code encodes the name of a characteristic software design pattern shown as node label in the graph. This class-label allocation is arbitrary but fixed, so *OVSF*-codes (cf. section 5.2) could also be used again.

multi-dimensional domain $C \times C \ldots \times C$ of the function μ_k can be seen in the *signature* of the respective complex type. This signature is learned by the neural network in the following *input* $\mapsto$ *target* form:

$$r[(A_1 \Rightarrow \alpha_{11} .. \alpha_{1k_1}), .., (A_l \Rightarrow \alpha_{l1} .. \alpha_{lk_l})] \mapsto spr(\vec{e}_i, \vec{c}_i) \quad (6.15)$$

Each component $(.. \Rightarrow ..)$ of the input pattern describes the relationship between two classes of the respective class diagram by a context-free rule. The function r substitutes each symbol by its code vector through a hash table and subsequently sorts the resulting vector series by a predefined order. The function spr of formula 5.4 spreads a canonical basis vector $\vec{e}_i$ as unary encoding (also called *orthogonal encoding*) of the target type z with the assigned spreading code. The entire result of expression 6.15 represents a final training pattern *<input $\mapsto$ target>* for the neural network.

6.3.3 Symbolic Representation of Design Patterns

In the case of symbolic-connectionist machine learning of software design patterns, these patterns are formalized and typed by a context-free grammar together with the typing mechanism presented in section 5.2. In order to illustrate the preprocessing steps for obtaining a training set that contains the design patterns to be learned, the transformation of an exemplary design pattern into a machine-processable representation is demonstrated. The *Bridge pattern* depicted in figure 6.13 is mainly characterized by an aggregation and several inheritance relationships. It is meant to "decouple an abstraction from its implementation so that the two can vary independently" [GHJV95]. Thus, the *Bridge pattern* leads to the following grammar

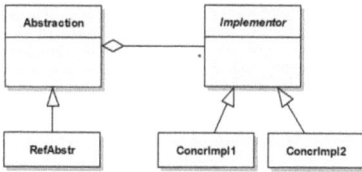

Figure 6.13: *Bridge pattern* with abstract *Implementor* class and refining implementations.

productions, which are incorporated by the neural network:

$$RefAbstr \Rightarrow Abstraction \quad (6.16)$$
$$Abstraction \Rightarrow T \quad (6.17)$$
$$T \Rightarrow Implementor\, T \quad (6.18)$$
$$T \Rightarrow \epsilon \quad (6.19)$$
$$ConcrImpl1 \Rightarrow Implementor \quad (6.20)$$
$$ConcrImpl2 \Rightarrow Implementor, \quad (6.21)$$

where $\mu(RefAbstr) \leq_S \mu(Abstraction)$, $\mu(ConcrImpl_i) \leq_S \mu(Implementor)$, $i = 1, 2$, where "$\leq_S$" is again the subtype-relation. The regular rules 6.18 and 6.19 are artificially introduced in order to generate 1..* *Implementor* classes required by the aggregation relationship. The number of required production rules to describe the *Bridge pattern* is $p = 6$ and the number of comprised symbols is $k = 13$. Each symbol is encoded according to the code tree of figure 5.6. Except the one-to-many relation between *Abstraction* and *Implementor* expressed by rule 6.18 and 6.19, each directed association is determined by one context-free production.

Now, the new *spread spectrum classification* technique defined in section 5.3 is applied to software design patterns based on their structural characteristics. The MRNN serves as classifier K with the signature

$$K : (\mathbb{R}^{m_1} \times \mathbb{R}^{m_2} \times \ldots \times \mathbb{R}^{m_k}) \to \mathbb{R}^{d_j}, \quad m_i, d_j \leq d, \quad (6.22)$$

$k \in \mathbb{N}, j \in \{1, \ldots, |Z|\}$, that maps a sequence of heterogeneous node vectors onto a type representation vector. Thereby, the type $C_j \in C$ to be classified is represented by the spread target vector $\vec{y}_{t+1} \in \mathbb{R}^{d_j}$, where $d_j = n \cdot dim(\vec{c}_j) = n \cdot \lambda_j, n = |C|$ in the case of unary type encoding.

A design pattern is modeled as a *complex type* consisting of production rules, which represent the relationships between the involved classes. The following complex rule stands for the *Adapter pattern* (AP) depicted in figure 6.14:

$$r[(SubClass \Rightarrow AbstrClass), (SubClass \Rightarrow NonhierarchClass)]$$
$$\mapsto spr(\underbrace{(0,1,0,0)}_{AP\ basic\ enc.}, \underbrace{(1,1,1,0,1)}_{AP\ spreading\ code}\ )$$

The production symbols are substituted by their codes and the right side is spread

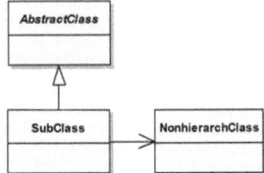

Figure 6.14: *Adapter pattern* with abstract superclass *AbstractClass* and directed association between *SubClass* (Adapter) and *NonhierarchClass* (Adaptee). The *client* that accesses the superclass is omitted here.

to obtain the final training pattern:

$$((1,1,1,1) \Rightarrow (1)), ((1,1,1,1) \Rightarrow (1,0)) \qquad (6.23)$$
$$\mapsto spr((0,1,0,0),(1,1,1,0,1))$$

$$(1,1,1,1),(1),(1,1,1,1),(1,0) \qquad (6.24)$$
$$\mapsto (1,1,1,0,1,0,0,0,1,0,1,1,1,0,1,1,1,1,0,1)$$

All codes are taken from the prefix-based code tree depicted in figure 5.6; the design pattern codes stem from figure 6.12. The decomposition of the single context-free rules implies that only one complex rule of the resolved form 6.24 is learned by the MRNN for each design pattern, instead of learning all single rules.

6.3.4 Design Advice Upon Complex Design Patterns

For the recognition of more complex design patterns such as the *Template* or the *Observer Pattern*, it is no longer sufficient anymore to consider only classes and the associations between them, ignoring methods and attributes. This issue is addressed in the next sections. Furthermore, the question of how to turn the developed pattern recognition technique into an actual design adviser arises. On top of the classification functionality presented in the previous sections, such an adviser should indicate which classes and associations belong to the respective design pattern or have a high significance for them.

The proposed DesignAdviser is a subsystem consisting of four major components:

1. **Design Pattern Representation**
   Each design pattern supported by SYMBOCONN has its internal rule-based representation as depicted by figure 6.17:
   AdapterPatternRepresent, BridgePatternRepresent, CompositePattern-Represent, FacadePatternRepresent, TemplatePatternRepresent, ObserverPatternRepresent, and StrategyPatternRepresent.

2. **XMI Analyzer** (XML Metadata Interchange)
   The XMIAnalyzer imports and parses exported class diagrams in the XMI format. Therefore, it walks through the serialized system model along its associations and analyzes their source and target entities.

3. **Source Code Analyzer**
   The source code is only analyzed when the hypothesis for a *Template Pattern* was not discarded during the analysis of the XMI representation of the class diagram by the XMIAnalyzer. In this case, the code may be scanned for actual method calls within a *template method*, for example. At the time of writing this document, the source code analyzer was not yet implemented.

4. **Prediction Interpreter**
   The PredictionInterpreter actually carries out the discovery of design patterns within a given class diagram and invokes the rule checking by the XMI-Analyzer, if needed. Furthermore, the interpreter has access to the neural network engine MRNN in order to repeat predictions with varying subsets of the original class diagram. This is necessary for determining which classes are indicators for the predicted design patterns and their certainties (cf. paragraph *Identifying Design Pattern Constituents*).

Figure 6.15 shows the DesignAdviser subsystem. The abstract class PatternRepresent is the software representation of a design pattern; concrete patterns are defined as extensions. All supported design patterns are converted into a machine-processable form; that is, these patterns are transformed into typed grammar rules, which is elaborated upon in section 6.3. Figure 6.17 shows all software design patterns supported by the implemented prototype.

Intermediate Representation by XMI The rule-based intermediate representation of SYMBOCONN matches the standardized schema language representation

APPLICATION TO KNOWLEDGE ENG. AND SOFTWARE DEVELOPMENT

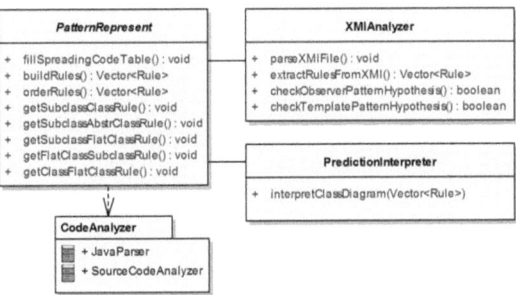

Figure 6.15: DesignAdviser subsystem consisting of the components PatternRepresent, XMIAnalyzer, CodeAnalyzer, and PredictionInterpreter.

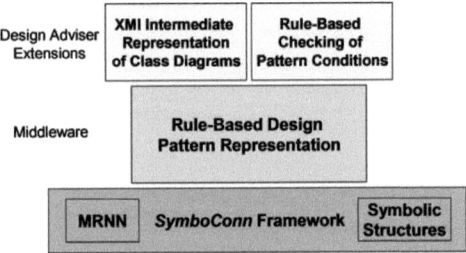

Figure 6.16: Modular architecture of the DesignAdviser component of SYMBOCONN that is based on the connectionist framework engine, but is extended by a symbolic middleware layer ensuring interoperability with CASE tools and enabling rule-based checking of elimination criteria for design pattern hypotheses.

of class diagrams used by most of the available CASE tools, hence fostering interoperability with these. Since design patterns are usually denoted in UML, the graph-based class diagrams (*source model* of transformation) are transformed into a grammatical representation (*target model*). The desired target model is a set of productions that can be directly processed by the SYMBOCONN framework. Fortunately, extensive research has already been conducted on uni- and bi-directional model transformations involving UML and the schema languages XMI and XSD. Certain CASE tools allow to directly export XMI documents from UML diagrams, as accomplished by the commercial product *Enterprise Architect*[14]. A system model represented by XMI is closest to the required target model, since we are interested in the structural relations (associations) and methods of the class diagram. Source code is not addressed by an XMI representation; however, an in-depth source code analysis is not required for the majority of design patterns. If source code analysis is needed, as in the case of the *Observer Pattern*, an additional mechanism addressing source code has to be downstreamed, as presented in section 6.3.4.

Identifying Design Pattern Constituents As mentioned in the beginning of this section, holistic classification of structural patterns induces a lack of traceability with respect to the identification of those class diagram elements that are responsible for the "winner pattern" of the accomplished classification. The MRNN is usually a sequence processor, which means that an order on the node sequences representing the single components of a design pattern, which are transformed into numerical training patterns, is assumed. For design pattern discovery based on a rule-based representation, an order of these rules is undesirable, because this recalls the problem of *multiple starting symbols* normally attached to symbolic methods. To avoid this effect, the rules in the input sequence that are fed into the MRNN are rotated, as described in the appendix A.2.2. Hence, the classification result is an average over all k-1 phase shifts, which corresponds to the number of external inputs $\vec{x}_{t-k}, \vec{x}_{t-k+1}, \ldots, \vec{x}_t$ minus one.

Since a neural network generates a *distributed representation* of the learned patterns, it is generally a difficult task to determine the single constituents of an input pattern which are responsible for the classification output that corresponds to the recognized design pattern. The central idea is to decrease the input node sequence (and thereby the corresponding input pattern) rule by rule, as long as the predicted class, which is a design pattern here, does not change. For each input sequence, the neural classification is computed as long as the originally classified design pattern is still assessed to be the most probable. When this kind of backtracking technique is fully developed, an integration into a CASE tool would be useful for highlighting the responsible classes in the respective class diagram.

The SourceCodeAnalyzer component is responsible for the rule-based recognition of design patterns that require a source code analysis.

---

[14]http://www.sparxsystems.com.

188 APPLICATION TO KNOWLEDGE ENG. AND SOFTWARE DEVELOPMENT

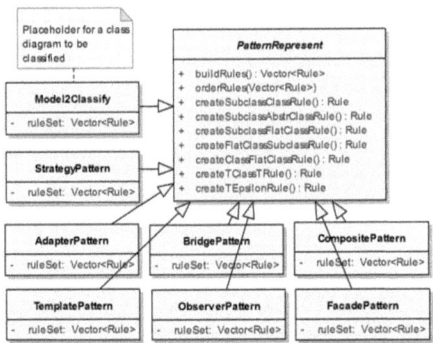

Figure 6.17: Extendable class representation of the supported design patterns that are all subclasses of an abstract PatternRepresent class. All concrete design patterns are children of the abstract PatternRepresent class, which provides methods for generating the rule-based internal representation of the respective pattern. Model2Classify is a placeholder for the that is dynamically filled with the concrete classes and relations of the diagram to be classified. The common attribute ruleSet is not pulled out as superclass attribute in order to emphasize that each concrete design pattern has its specific rule set. Further design patterns that should be recognized can be defined and plugged-in by using the buildRules method of the superclass.

Control Flow of Design Pattern Learning and Classification Again, the control flow is divided into a preprocessing and training phase on the one hand and the subsequent operative phase on the other hand. In the first phase, an internal representation of all design patterns is generated, which is basically a set of grammar productions. Subsequently, these are transformed to the final vector-valued training patterns that can be learned by the MRNN.

When employing the trained system, the classification process begins with an unknown UML class diagram. The class diagram to be classified is assumed to follow yet unknown design patterns and is therefore exported as a standardized XMI 1.0 document. Then, it is fed into the system as an XMI file and is parsed by the XMIAnalyzer component. The XMIAnalyzer analyzes this file and for each pair of associated classes, an internal context-free grammar rule is built. The resulting set of rules is transformed to input patterns according to the left side of formula 6.22 in section 6.3, so that the MRNN classifier can numerically process them. Figure 6.18 shows the control flow of the whole design pattern discovery process.

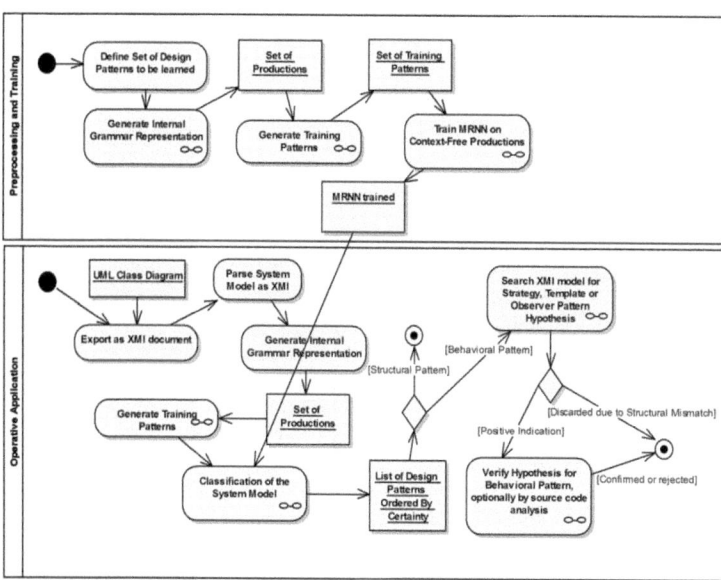

Figure 6.18: Activity diagram showing the training and application of the design pattern discovery process as upper and lower *swimlane*.

6.3.4.1 Recognition of the Template Pattern

The representation of the *template pattern*, belonging to the group of behavioral patterns, is different from the four purely structural design patterns *Composite*, *Bridge*, *Adapter* and *Facade*. The template pattern is employed when several subclasses share the same algorithm but differ regarding the specific realization, which is often relevant, for example, in the implementation of software frameworks. Since common process steps should not be duplicated in the subclasses, these are sourced out and placed in the abstract superclass to define the abstract control flow of the procedure.

Hence, a mechanism is required to access the fine-grained representation of model elements within class diagrams. For this purpose, an XMI export of UML class diagrams from a standard CASE tool is conducted. The XMIAnalyzer parses this XML file and provides methods to create the internal production rule based representation of a class diagram defined in section 6.3. The serialization of an UML class diagram as XMI comprises method declarations as well as other required meta information, e.g. whether a class is *abstract* or not, the direction of associations, or the name of the encompassing subsystem.

When the MRNN prediction indicates a high certainty for the template pattern at least one inheritance relation with an abstract superclass exists, the XMIAnalyzer is invoked to search for identical method declarations in all classes participating in the inheritance relations. This proceeding can be considered as a *beam search*, since the prediction by the neural network reduces the number of cases which demand for an actual search for the template pattern. Since the neural prediction is a search with linear time-complexity $O(n)$ in the number of classes $n = |V|$, this is a heuristic method to decide whether a full search of all associations in the diagram should be conducted. Therefore, the actual search has a linear time complexity $O(m)$ in the number of generalizations $m = |E_{gen}|$ in the class diagram, which is less than or equal to the number of all associations since $E_{gen} \subseteq E$.

To satisfy the criteria of the template pattern, there has to be one additional non-abstract method in the superclass, called *template method*, which invokes the methods implemented in the concrete subclasses. If this template method does not exist, the TP-hypothesis is discarded. Since the abstract superclass calls the generic implementation-invariant steps of the procedure, the template method must not be missing in the superclass. Figures 6.19 and 6.20 show the difference between an incomplete and a complete template pattern. The logical expert rule or heuristics for the *Template Pattern* (TP) is

$$TP := \exists x_1, x_2 \; isa(x_2, x_1) \wedge \exists m_1, m_2 \; hasMethod(x_1, m_1) \wedge hasMethod(x_2, m_2)$$
$$\wedge \; isAbstract(x_1) \wedge isAbstract(m_1) \wedge \neg isAbstract(m_2)$$
$$\wedge \; equalSignature(m_1, m_2)$$

(6.25)

This strong indicator solidifies the TP-hypothesis in the following way: it is unlikely

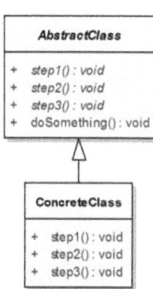
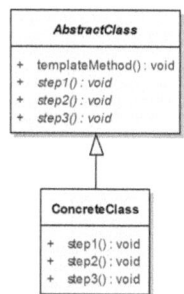

Figure 6.19: Incomplete *Template pattern* due to missing template method in the abstract superclass.

Figure 6.20: Structurally complete *Template pattern* with template method in the superclass, which calls the abstract methods step1, step2, step3 representing sequential work steps.

to find identical method signatures in two or more classes, these methods being abstract in the superclass and non-abstract in the subclasses, without a template pattern being on hand in the respective model.

More formally, we claim that the posterior probability $\mathbb{P}(\neg TemplPatt|TP)$ for a *false positive* that satisfies the criteria of the TP-hypothesis without a template pattern actually being existent, is very low.

The complementary probability $\mathbb{P}(TemplPatt|TP)$ for the positive case does not turn zero if the probability of the condition $\mathbb{P}(TP) > 0$ is non-zero, due to the fact that TP is a *required condition*[15] for the presence of a template pattern. The actual method call in the body of the template method

public void templateMethod() { ... step1(); ... step2(); ... step3(); ... } ,

which is mandatory for a complete template pattern, is not represented by a class diagram. For simplicity reasons, no program code should be processed by the DesignAdviser at first, so that the content of the template method cannot be considered. However, due to the low probability of a *false positive*, the resulting incompleteness of information has an empirically marginal impact. The *sensitivity* of the test, which is the probability $\mathbb{P}(TP|TemplPatt)$, remains unaffected by this limitation and is constantly 1.

6.3.4.2 Recognition of the Observer Pattern

The *Observer Pattern* – sometimes also known as *publish/subscribe pattern* – is also a behavioral pattern which designs an indirect communication between subjects and

---

[15]However, TP is not a *sufficient condition*.

their observers. It can also be used for event handling, especially in combination with the architectural pattern *Model-View-Control*, since it facilitates a loose coupling between the model and the view.

To recognize the observer pattern without a loss of generality, it is essential to allow arbitrary method names for the registration of the *Observer*. In the observer pattern of figure 6.21, these methods are called *attach* and *detach*, but they could also be denoted as *subscribe* and *unsubscribe*. Furthermore, the abstract *Observer*

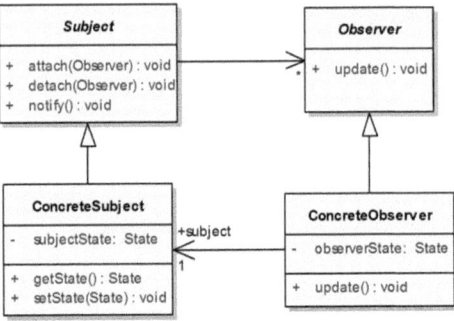

Figure 6.21: *Observer Pattern* with its typical division into abstract *Subject* and *Observer*, which are both realized by concrete implementors.

is required to provide a public *update method* that can be accessed by the abstract subject after the concrete subject has *notified* a change via the public *notify method*. The existence of these methods is essential and supports the hypothesis for an observer pattern. A violation of one of these constraints leads to a rejection of the hypothesis; thus, each constraint has to be checked either in the XMI class diagram representation or in the source code. This is either the task of the *XMIAnalyzer* component or of the *SourceCodeAnalyzer*.

The observer pattern exists in a few variants that differ in the way of communication between subject(s) and observer(s). There are *push* and *pull* communication paradigms[16]. Since the subject should not know about the individual information needs of its observers, it cannot decide which observer requires which subset of the updated information. This is to be considered especially in *push communication* mode, where the subject emits the update information regardless of whether the particular observer needs the whole update or not. In *pull communication* mode, the observers are only notified that a change has occurred; they are responsible themselves for pulling the required information via the getState method of the ConcreteSubject. The latter mode is to be preferred when vast amounts of data, such as BLOBs[17] or multimedia files, should be transmitted.

---

[16]Hybrid notification.

[17]*Binary Large Object.*

6.3.5 Evaluation

The generalization capability of the neural classifier was tested with different fragments of well-known design patterns which held characteristic relationships like the widely used *aggregation* link, but missed some aspects of the original design pattern. In this way, the system cannot exclusively rely on the learned pattern structure but has to generalize the pattern fragment in order to determine the *nearest neighbor* among the known design patterns. Furthermore, the presented fragments offer the chance to evaluate the *design advise* functionality by pointing to the elements missing to complete the design pattern.

6.3.5.1 Classification of Unknown System Models

In this section, different class diagrams are processed and the contained design patterns should be discovered by the framework to evaluate the provided generalization capability. Thereby, each result is classified according to the abstract generalization hierarchy of section 3.3.

The basic use case for the classification of a class diagram that follows a yet unknown design pattern is depicted in figure 6.22. The proceeding corresponds to

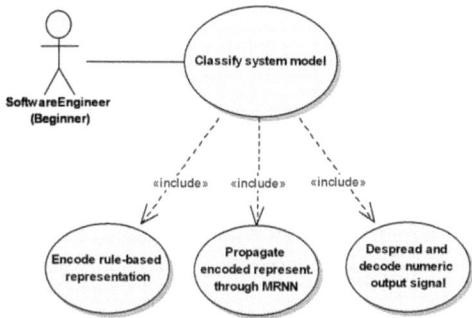

Figure 6.22: Use case for the classification of a system model.

the lower swimlane of figure 6.18. First the unknown class diagram is transformed to a set of context-free productions which is numerically encoded and spread by the *spread spectrum* technique. Then, the numeric output is computed by a single forward propagation through the network; finally, the output vector is despread and its distance to the known pattern representations is determined.

Example 6.3.1: Partial Composite Pattern
Assume that the system was trained on the exact form of the *Adapter*, *Bridge* and *Composite* design pattern. Now a scenario, in which a class diagram as a mixture of these design patterns is presented to the classifier, is considered and depicted in

figure 6.23. Although the used classes were already part of the training set, this was only in the form of constituents of different patterns. The NonhierarchClass is part of the *Adapter pattern*, while Class and Subclass appear both in *Bridge* and *Composite pattern*. Hence, there are no new elements, but the known classes participate in different associations which require generalization to novel element positions.

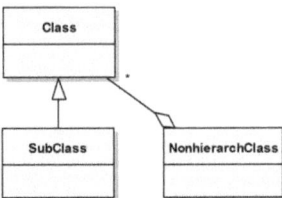

Figure 6.23: Partial *Composite pattern* with non-abstract (non-italic) superclass Class and missing inheritance between Class and composite class NonhierarchClass.

The partial design pattern of figure 6.23 was classified to be a *Composite pattern* with an average certainty of 70.3%, while *Bridge* and *Adapter pattern* were ranked second (54.5%) and third (43.8%), which is indeed correct. When the class diagram is changed towards the original *Composite pattern* by setting the *abstract* property of Class and introducing inheritance between Class and NonhierarchClass, the certainty increases to 78.1%.

New methodologies are often tested by applying them to their own concepts. Therefore, the design pattern discovery is self-applied to the ConnectionistModels subsystem described in section 4.4.3.

Example 6.3.2: Strategy Pattern
The class diagram corresponding to the abstract training algorithm architecture shown in figure 6.24 is presented to the classifier. This class diagram partially resembles the *strategy pattern* excluding the missing client class usually accessing the Context class, whose role is taken by the MRNN here.

The strategy pattern is both related to the *bridge* and to the *template pattern*, since all of them provide abstract definitions of a concept or an algorithm as well as concrete implementations. This similarity is also reflected in the classification result of table 6.10, which foremost indicates a strong compliance with the strategy pattern that still precedes the similar patterns *Bridge* and *Template*.

6.3.5.2 Transforming an Adapter Pattern into a Composite Pattern

In this section, we illustrate the strength of the connectionist approach to design pattern discovery by means of a classification scenario aiming at toy class diagrams.

APPLICATION TO KNOWLEDGE ENG. AND SOFTWARE DEVELOPMENT

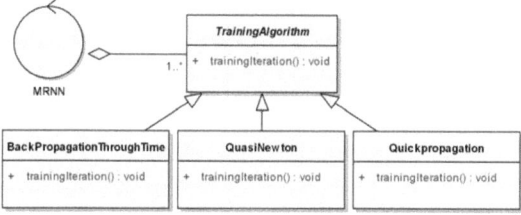

Figure 6.24: Generic plug-in architecture for training algorithms partially resembling the *strategy pattern*.

Rank	Design Pattern	Certainty [%]
1	Strategy	66.67
2	Bridge	60.95
3	Template	58.33
4	Facade	53.33

Table 6.10: Classification result for the TrainingAlgorithm class diagram of figure 6.24 including the independent certainties for each detected pattern. The neural network was trained on the six original design patterns *Adapter*, *Bridge*, *Composite*, *Facade*, *Strategy*, and *Template* till a residual error of 0.03%.

Dealing with incomplete and partially incorrect knowledge requires fuzzy knowledge representation instead of purely symbolic methods. This is made especially apparent by the following stepwise classification of toy examples. For this purpose, the MRNN was trained on four design patterns: *Composite*, *Adapter*, *Bridge* and *Facade*. These were jointly and successfully learned up to a relative training error of 0.03%. Now, we show a concrete classification scenario in which a software engineer adds new model elements in each design step, thereby transforming an initial class diagram into an adapter pattern and, subsequently, into a composite pattern. Starting with two classes, the scenario incrementally leads through several stages of an analysis object model, while the respective system model is classified by the connectionist classifier in each step. Even slight changes in the class diagrams will result in observable changes of the computed certainties for the classified design pattern candidates.

Starting from Scratch Figure 6.25 shows an initial classification task in the form of a class diagram consisting of only two classes. The classification result of figure 6.26 favors the *Adapter pattern* here, since this is the only pattern that comprises such a structure with a directed association.

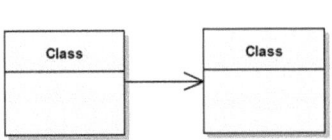

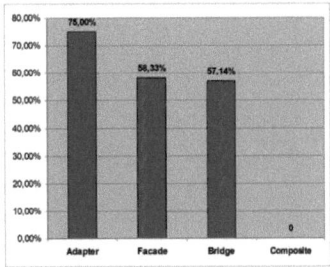

Figure 6.25: Initial design consisting of two associated classes on the same hierarchy level.

Figure 6.26: Classification result indicating a tendency towards the adapter pattern, since this pattern is the most similar.

Partial Adapter Pattern Except for the missing abstractness of the superclass Class, this system model represents the original *Adapter pattern*. Small imponderabilities like the increased certainty of the *Bridge pattern* (78.57% oppposed to 67.86%) compared to the previous scenario have to be accepted when employing fuzzy connectionist techniques.

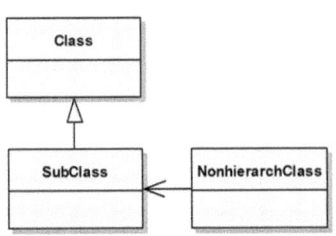

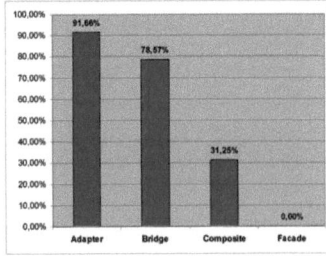

Figure 6.27: Class diagram that almost corresponds to the adapter pattern (Scenario *Partial Adapter Pattern*).

Figure 6.28: Certainty distribution with a maximal value for the adapter pattern. The bridge pattern follows up as *false positive* here.

Mixture of Adapter and Bridge Pattern The third scenario illustrated by figure 6.29 adds a superclass and an aggregation to the initial diagram. This situation leaves a lot of room for interpretation by the classifier, since many design patterns have to be considered closely. Hence, the certainties for the three most probable design pattern *Composite*, *Bridge*, and *Adapter* are more closely aligned. Still, the similarity to the *Composite pattern* is highest, since for its completion mainly an inheritance relation is missing and the association between SubClass and NonhierarchClass is out of place. The present aggregation relationship provides strong evidence for either the *Composite* or the *Bridge pattern*, which is reflected by the bar chart 6.30. Finally, the *Facade pattern* is rather unlikely in this constellation, because the classical *star schema* starting from the *Facade class*, which would be the SubClass in this case, is not at hand here.

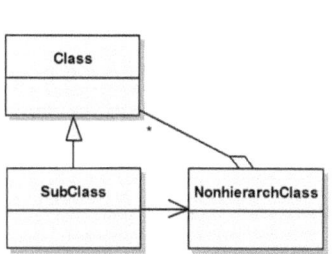

Figure 6.29: Class diagram showing the scenario *Mixture of Adapter and Bridge Pattern*.

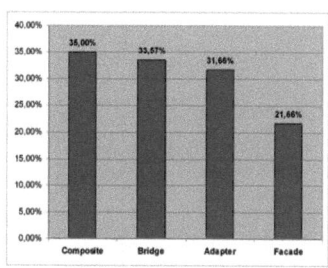

Figure 6.30: This class constellation results in a high information entropy with respect to the classification certainty that implies low preference for a specific pattern. Only the facade pattern is disqualified to a certain degree.

Partial Composite Pattern The fourth scenario represents a strong shift towards the *Composite pattern*, which is also expressed by the results in diagram 6.32. The *Facade pattern* is nearly discarded, while elements of both *Adapter* and *Bridge pattern* are contained in the class diagram 6.31; these make for similar certainties of about 42%.

Penultimate Transformation Step: Making Superclass *abstract* The next to last snap-shot of the changing class diagram shows a nearly complete composite pattern. The only change, compared to the previous scenario, is the *abstract* superclass, which prevents an instantiation when actually implemented. Adding the abstractness property again results in a higher probability (about 10% increase) of the composite pattern, as is shown by figure 6.34.

Complete Composite Pattern Compared to the previous scenario, the final system model depicted by figure 6.35 holds a further inheritance relationship between the composite class and the superclass. This is the final state of the stepwise transformation towards the composite pattern, resulting in a classification certainty of 89.06% for the *Composite* structure. The connectionist classifier provides a discrimination degree of almost $\delta = 50\%$ compared to the second probable candidate

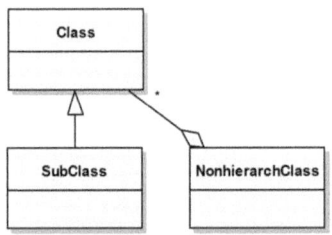
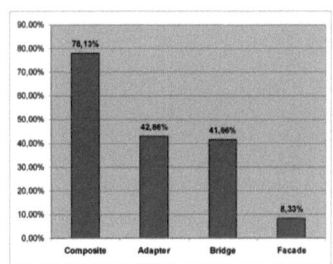

Figure 6.31: Generic class diagram showing elements of *Composite*, *Bridge*, and *Adapter pattern* that imply a strong tendency towards the composite pattern (Scenario *Partial Composite Pattern*).

Figure 6.32: The degree of similarity to the original shape of the composite pattern is about 36% higher than to adpater and bridge pattern.

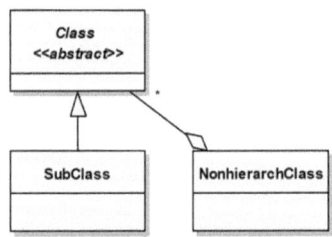
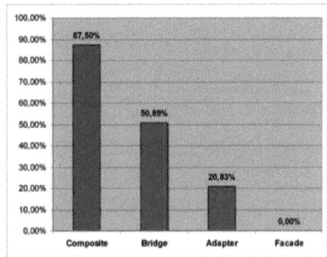

Figure 6.33: Nearly completed composite pattern still missing the inheritance between Class and NonhierarchClass.

Figure 6.34: The higher compliance with the original composite pattern leads to an increase of the respective certainty of almost 10%.

and furthermore completely excludes the *Facade pattern* from the set of possible pattern candidates.

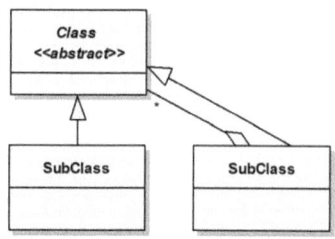

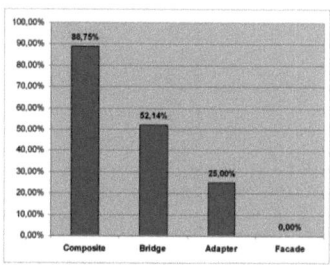

Figure 6.35: Complete *Composite pattern* with abstract superclass (Scenario *Complete Composite Pattern*).

Figure 6.36: Final classification result with maximal certainty for the composite pattern. As in the step before, the facade pattern hypothesis is completely discarded.

To fully exploit the strength of the connectionist methodology for classifying incomplete or partially incorrect design patterns, the classifier should be trained on a corpus of actual class diagrams, representing imperfect instances of the original design pattern definitions. Only in this sense, learning by example is performed, which is far more suitable for training a connectionist system than learning only the pure pattern definitions without concrete occurrences. In further work, the technique will be evaluated by a full benchmark for design pattern discovery in order to determine the scalability of our approach, as well as its *precision* and *recall*.

6.3.5.3 Generalization to Novel Complexity

Connectionist methods represent the structure of a design pattern in a *holistic* way distributed across their interconnected neurons. This internal representation partially solves the problem of interleaved and hidden design patterns, which is demonstrated by the class diagram in figure 6.37. Thereby, the task is to classify a pattern conglomerate with classes that participate in different design patterns. For example, the Implementor class is both part of the *Bridge* and of the *Adapter pattern*. The difficulty consists in seeing, which patterns occur to which extent in the entire system model. As becomes apparent from two different aspects, this class diagram exhibits novel complexity with respect to the less complex patterns that have been discovered before:

1. **Number of Elements**
   The number of classes (9) exceeds the number of classes participating in each of the trained design patterns, where the maximal number is given by the *Bridge pattern* (5).

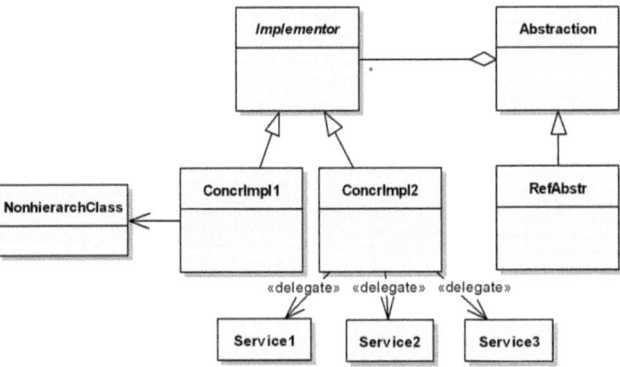

Figure 6.37: Conglomerate of three design patterns. The class Implementor participates in the *Adapter pattern* as the *Adapter's target* (client interface) and in the *Bridge pattern* as implementation interface. Furthermore, there is a partial *Facade pattern* based on the delegations from the *Facade* class ConcrImpl2 to the entity classes Service1 till Service3.

2. **Structural Relationships**

The class ConcrImpl2 is involved in the *Bridge* as well as in the *Facade pattern*. Altogether, this class participates in four relations, one inheritance relationship and three directed associations. Furthermore, the Implementor superclass is also part of two design patterns (*Adapter* and *Bridge*).

Obviously, novel complexity requires a much higher generalization ability than varying element positions.

The MRNN has succeeded in recovering the correct pattern and provides a *degree of certainty* for each detected class. The *Bridge pattern* was assessed to be superior in this class diagram with a certainty of 56.1%, as shown by the classification results in table 6.11. The connectionist classifier was able to handle multiple patterns within a single class diagram, which is demonstrated by the non-exclusive classification[18] of both *Bridge* and *Adapter pattern* with high certainties. In the case of the *Facade pattern*, the stereotype *delegate* was not represented in the typed formal grammar, while the direction of associations plays an important role in learning pattern semantics. If this simple evidence for a *Facade pattern* needs to be avoided, one would additionally have to claim an exclusive invocation of the *Facade class* from other system components as single point of access; however, considering associated system components is out of scope, here.

The consideration of structural properties alone has already led to a high generalization ability of the classifier. The *Composite pattern* was clearly rejected by assigning a certainty of only 3.1%; thus, no *false positives* were found. We note that

---
[18] Therefore, the certainties must not be forced to sum up to 100%.

Rank	Design Pattern	Certainty *Spread Spectrum* [%]
1	Bridge	56.1
2	Adapter	50.0
3	Facade	38.8
4	Composite	3.1

Table 6.11: Classification result for the pattern conglomerate of figure 6.37 including the independent certainties for each detected pattern. The neural network was trained up to a residual error of 0.03% on the four correct pattern definitions, but has never seen this conglomerate of classes nor a class diagram of more than five classes during training.

the certainty calculation of formula 5.10 in section 5.3.2 is very conservative and hence leads to moderate certainty values below 100%. Its expressiveness is given by the distance between two subsequently ranked classes. This distance is a result of the despreading and its process gain, which is $PG_{Facade} = 10\log_{10}\frac{44}{4} = 10.41\,db$ for the *Facade pattern* encoding, for example. The signal amplification in the range of $7.0 - 11.1\,db$ entails an advantage over the non-spread classification. The result

Rank	Design Pattern	Certainty - *Unary* [%]
1	Bridge	31.2
2	Adapter	30.8
3	Facade	18.4
4	Composite	13.6

Table 6.12: Classification result for the pattern conglomerate based on the simple *unary type encoding* without data spreading. The classifier was trained in the same manner until stagnation with a residual error of 0.05%. The result distinguishes less accurately between correct, partially correct and incorrect types (*Composite* is a *false positive* here).

for the classifier without spread spectrum extension is less accurate, as shown in table 6.12. The simple encoding approach fails to disqualify the *Composite pattern* on the basis of the absent inheritance $\mu(Abstraction) \leq_S \mu(Implementor)$. Moreover, it suffers from a far fuzzier classification with lower discrimination between the fully and partially detected patterns. The predominant *Bridge pattern* is only classified with 17.6% advance compared to the non-occurring *Composite pattern*, while the spread spectrum-enabled classification results in a very strong difference of 53.0%.

The recognition of unseen structures as an instance of one or several design patterns requires a generalization capability of level 4 according to the hierarchy presented in section 3.1.1.2. The SYMBOCONN framework generalizes to novel complexity in this case, since a conglomerate of three design patterns consisting of nine classes was never present in the training set.

6.3.6 Advantages and Disadvantages of the Connectionist Approach

The symbolic-connectionist approach to design pattern recognition realized by the SYMBOCONN framework implies several advantages over a purely symbolic approach. A precondition for these advantages is the provision of an implicit similarity measure $sim: Z \times Z \to \mathbb{R}$:

$$sim(X_1, X_2) := 1 - \frac{\sum_{i=1}^{m} \sum_{j=1}^{d_2} (o_j(i, X_1) - o_j(i, X_2))^2}{m \cdot d_2}$$
$$\stackrel{m=1}{=} 1 - \frac{\sum_{j=1}^{d_2} (o_j(X_1) - o_j(X_2))^2}{d_2}, \quad d_2 \neq 0, m \geq 1 \quad (6.26)$$

$X_1, X_2 \in Z \supset DP$ among all class diagrams as superset of all supported design patterns DP (Z is the space of complex types). Due to this similarity measure, the symbolic-connectionist approach possesses the following benefits:

- *Discovery of Incomplete Design Patterns Based on Similarity*
  The *nearest neighbor* of an unknown class diagram is computed based on similarity by formula 6.26; thus, diagrams that resemble an incomplete design pattern can also be interpreted by the system. The certainty *cert* of a class diagram X to contain a design pattern Y is computed based on sim and the most similar design pattern Y_{max} out of the trained patterns DP, which serves as a reference:

$$Y_{max}(X) := \arg\max_{Y \in DP} \{sim(X, Y)\} \quad (6.27)$$

$$cert(X) := 1 - \frac{\sum_{j=1}^{d_2}(o_j(X) - o_j(Y_{max}))^2}{d_2}, \quad (6.28)$$

  where $o_j \in [0, 1]$, $j = 1, \ldots, d_2$. Moreover, the certainty gives a useful assessment of the system's confidence in the provided classification by looking at the difference $\delta_{X,Y'} := cert(X) - \max_{Y \in DP \setminus Y_{max}}\{sim(Y', Y)\}$ to the second likely design pattern Y'. If the difference is high, then the respective design pattern is likely to be classified properly.
  In the case of missing elements or associations (model elements), the symbolic approach will fail to recognize the most similar pattern, leaving out useful information for domain experts or software developers who are unaware of this. Related work such as *"Design Pattern Detection Using Similarity Scoring"* from Tsantalis et al. [TCSH06] show that similarity-based approaches are very promising. In this article, the pattern structure of class diagrams is represented by association graphs, generalization graphs, abstract classes graphs, etc. which are described by corresponding matrices.

- *Dealing with Pattern Overlapping and Multiple Starting Symbols*
  Overlapping patterns and multiple starting symbols are primarily a problem

of symbolic methods such as *LR-Parsing* [CDLD+05]. Holistic methods are less affected by overlapping design patterns and by the question of where to begin the discovery, since the class diagram is not parsed symbol by symbol but from a global perspective. The holistic view onto the class diagram is comparable to the wide-angle look at a picture. Its meaning is not realized by taking a locally restricted view at the details and by moving from one picture segment to the other, but by comprehensively perceiving all of its aspects such as structure, color, and proportions, at once.

- *Linear Time-Complexity*
  The spread spectrum-enabled classification used for design pattern recognition is efficient, since, in principle, the despreading step itself can be performed in $O(|C|) = O(r)$, where r is the number of classes – in comparison to $s_r := \sum_{i=0}^{r} |C_i|$ as the number of instances in all classes of the given dataset ($r << s_r$).
  Furthermore, the number N_{comp} of weighted sum ($\sum_{i=1}^{d} x_i w_{ij}$), $w_{ij} \in M \in \{A, B, C\}$, $d \in \{d_1, d_2\}$ computations in the (trained) neural network to compute the classification increases linearly in d_1. The growth is dependent on the fixed dimension h of the hidden state layer, which is constant: $N_{comp} = h \cdot d_1 + h \cdot d_2 = h \cdot (d_1 + (\lambda_{max} \cdot r))$. The factor λ_{max} is the length of the longest assigned spreading code. As described in section 5.3.1, $d_2 = \lambda_{max} \cdot r$ is the upper bound on the number of required bits to represent all target classes. The despreading process of figure 5.9, which itself requires $d_2 = \lambda_{max} \cdot r$ computations, has to be performed r times, once for each class. Thus, the entire complexity to classify an input sequence is

$$\begin{aligned} O((N_{comp} + d_2) \cdot r) &= O((h(d_1 + d_2) + d_2) \cdot r) \\ &= O([hd_1 + (h+1)d_2] \cdot r) \\ &\stackrel{const.\,terms}{=} O((d_1 + d_2) \cdot r) \\ &= O(d_1 r + \lambda_{max} r^2), \end{aligned}$$

since the constant h determines the network resources and is largely independent of the object representation (with dimensionality d_1). Compared to a nearest neighbor approach, the term s_r for calculating all neighbor distances is omitted, while the factor r is added to the complexity and d_2 becomes λ_{max}-times bigger.

However, there are also drawbacks of the connectionist approach to design pattern recovery. We present three main weaknesses:

- *Sensitivity of the training error and the hidden layer dimension*
  The amount of the remaining error $E = \sum_{p \in TS} E_p$ (bias) according to section 4.4.3 after training the neural network almost until convergence has an impact on the classification result. The sensitivity of the classification result to the network bias depends on the respective machine learning task, its difficulty,

and the provided training samples. This is typical for neural networks, which partially buy their capability of processing fuzzy and incomplete data with a manual decision when to stop the training process. Moreover, the hidden layer dimension has a certain influence on the classification result.

- *Low traceability and rationale of the classification*
  This is a consequence of the *holistic* and distributed representation that takes into account the class diagram structures a whole. This drawback is addressed and diminished by the technique proposed in section 6.3.4, where the responsible elements for the respective classification are traced back by a workaround.

- *Recognizing multiple instances of one design pattern*
  Several instances of the same design pattern within one class diagram cannot be recognized yet, because the number of existent classes and their associations is not taken into account during training. Instead, concrete classes are reduced to proxy types such as Class, AbstractClass, or SubClass.

Due to the complementary weaknesses and strengths of the symbolic and the connectionist approaches, we think it is advisable to aim for a hybrid system that uses a connectionist engine for discovering incomplete and partially malformed design patterns, as well as a symbolic component. The latter provides symbolic representations for structural patterns and supports rule-based approval or rejection of design pattern candidates in advance, as done by De Lucia et. al [CDLD$^+$06, DLDGR07].

6.4 Conclusion

In the first part of this chapter, we applied the SYMBOCONN framework to the classification of software development artifacts. We demonstrated that the MRNN machine learning engine is able to classify complex artifacts, which may even be afflicted with fuzzy, incomplete, or partially incorrect attributes. In particular, the SYMBOCONN framework succeeded in classifying action items according to the development activities in which they were formulated. Furthermore, we classified the status of action items; that is, to decide whether they are still under examination or already irrelevant. Five-fold cross-validation of both applications resulted in classification accuracies of 80.51% (six categories) and 83.72% (two categories), respectively. In future work, we will also classify the status of ActionItems, that is, deciding whether they are still under examination or already irrelevant. Additionally, the spread spectrum technique will be used to further improve the accuracy of the activity classification (cf. section 5.3).

Secondly, we introduced a connectionist approach to change impact analysis, which covers two variants: a structure- and content-based as well as a purely content-based one. As decision support service, our change impact analysis allows an ad hoc overview on the impacts of planned changes during an ongoing project. The first variant considers changes upon graph-structured data, whose impacts are structure-sensitive and cannot be predicted, for example, from changes in attribute-value pairs of software artifacts alone. This hybrid structural and content-based change impact analysis integrated into SYMBOCONN has not been applied yet, but will be used within UNICASE-projects in future work. Thus we could not evaluate the impact prediction accuracy yet, since software project data has not been available therefor so far.

Within the scope of the second variant, the SYMBOCONN framework was used for semantic learning and prediction of co-occurring artifact changes. The MRNN was trained on the cohesive items of configuration management aggregates in a supervised manner, leading to a recommendation system that fulfills the following tasks:

- *Preventing Incomplete Change.* Guidance of programmers by observing their working set and recommending related artifacts in order to prevent errors resulting from incomplete changes.

- *Inference of Related Artifacts.* The learned dependencies among the items of each commit set are exploited by the MRNN, which *generalizes* onto *unseen* histories of committed software artifacts and thus even provides advice for newly added artifacts.

For both functionalities, a knowledge representation based on Latent Semantic Indexing of text attributes builds the foundation for semantic recommendation. The evaluation was conducted by three independent datasets from the *PROMISE Repository of Software Engineering Databases* and revealed a total prediction precision for partially unseen artifact sets of 67.75% (maximum of 72.72% for the XFree86 project), based on a result space of 167 to 1047 different artifacts. Compared to existing methods based on association rule mining, whose authors report precision values of about 26% to 50% [ZWDZ04], the connectionist approach achieves a higher accuracy even when applied to untrained item sets, which is not possible with symbolic techniques at all. Unfortunately, there exists no one-to-one comparability with Zimmermann, since the evaluations used different projects[19]. Another reference value is provided by the evaluation of the *NavTracks* algorithm based on the logged navigation pathways of three developers, conducted by Singer et al. [SES05], which led to a precision of about 29%.

Finally, we developed a robust connectionist classification aimed at structured and typed contents – especially design patterns. This classification is again based on the MRNN, which is able to learn context-sensitive production rules that represent structured contents. Therefore the grammars' symbolic entities, such as terminal symbols and variables, are arranged in the form of an input sequence representing, for example, a specific design pattern. To recapitulate, we developed two main functionalities that were wholly integrated into the MRNN:

---

[19]The trial to obtain the original dataset from Zimmermann [ZWDZ04] failed.

1. **Structure and Type Learning**
   The capability of learning arbitrary sequences of typed nodes, such as the left and right hand sides of context-free or context-sensitive production rules.

2. **Discovery of Design Patterns in Class Diagrams**
   Totally heterogeneous knowledge structures containing instances of different types can be interpreted by the neural network. The MRNN is further able to classify partial or distorted knowledge structures, as well, such as design pattern fragments; this is done according to the learned complex type.

The proposed classification technique is efficient, since the computational effort for a classification only linearly increases in the size of the class diagram. The major effort has to be accomplished during the training phase.

Chapter 7
Navigation Recommendation

Navigation recommendation is a form of user assistance that assists the user with the search for relevant artifacts or the exploration of an artifact space. Normally users prefer or require certain types of artifacts such as documents, multimedia items, etc., while disliking or ignoring others. The users exhibit individual behaviors when traversing the navigation space, driven by different information needs and intended tasks. In the narrower sense, a navigation is a path of nodes in the application domain. However, navigation recommendation is not restricted to paths, but can also be applied to sets of articles in e-Commerce or to sequences of actions as part of a certain business process, for example. From a technical point of view, navigation recommendation is a generalization to new elements, which corresponds to level 3 generalization according to the generalization hierarchy presented in section 3.1.1.2.

Navigation recommendation systems are a special type of information filtering systems. Information filtering deals with the retrieval of relevant products, services or information selected from a large collection that the user is likely to find interesting or useful. Thus, recommendation can be modeled as a classification task that distinguishes between potentially relevant and irrelevant entities. The field of recommendation systems is mainly determined by information filtering methods such as collaborative and content-based filtering, whose functionalities are covered by the connectionist machine learning framework. Content-based and collaborative filters, as well as similar techniques described in section 7.1, currently represent *best practice* solutions for recommendation functionality, as is also repeatedly claimed in literature [ALJ].

In this chapter, we demonstrate that a better recommendation capability including relationships can be achieved by exploiting both content and structure of the underlying knowledge base. So far, there are hardly any connectionist systems that provide recommendation functionality. By combining aspects of content-based and collaborative filtering, the connectionist approach is able to achieve a higher recommendation accuracy than most of the mentioned traditional methods; this was reported by Nasraoui et al. [NP04]. The combination of a recurrent neural network and latent semantic indexing is a novel and promising hybrid approach, as shown by the navigation and artifact recommendation in section 7.2. To improve the recommendation capability even further, the support of the entity contents is enhanced by latent semantic indexing, which elicits the latent semantics from textual contents as described in sections 7.3.

Intelligent navigation recommendation can improve the quality of knowledge portals and information services provided via intranets and the internet. There are numerous overlapping techniques that realize navigation recommendation, such as *web user session clustering*, *web page clustering*, *association rule mining* [AS94], or *frequent navigational path mining*.

The main purpose of all recommendation systems is to discover the underlying functional interests that lead to common navigational activity among several users. Thereby the central problem is to provide generic navigation recommendation on nodes of a knowledge graph. Actual navigations on these graphs, which reflect the browsing behavior and interests of many users, are captured and taken as training patterns for the *Modular Recurrent Neural Network* (MRNN). Cohesive nodes sequences are learned by the MRNN in a supervised training process. We suggest a hybrid approach based on *Latent Semantic Indexing* (LSI) and machine learning methods to provide navigation recommendation. The neural network generalizes the observed navigation histories to proactively guide beginners through a sequence of web pages, for instance.

7.1 Required Data Mining Techniques

Exploiting intrinsically associated and unstructured contents for navigation recommendation requires methods from data mining, which are able to discover and represent potentially useful knowledge and patterns. Being intrinsically associated means that similar or complementary contents coexist without being explicitly linked by semantic relationships. This problem can be addressed by Association Rule Mining (ARM), which discovers intrinsic associations between symbolic contents, such as items in a shopping cart, and makes them explicit in form of association rules. The carrier of the associated entities are unstructured text documents organized in a knowledge base that represents the domain of discourse. Two fundamental data mining techniques for different kinds of knowledge, textual and symbolic, are introduced here, since both of them are used and extended by the SYMBOCONN framework.

7.1.1 Text Mining

Text mining is a subarea of the knowledge discovery process introduced earlier (see section 2.4), aiming at unstructured or low-structured textual data. The main purposes of text mining are, among others [Bö03]:

- *Analysis of content* and *structure* of text documents. Frequency measures are computed for each document and for each comprised term in order to numerically represent the document base and to compute the significance of all keyterms. This process is described in section 7.1.1.

- *Usage analysis* of a set of text documents as described in section 7.1.2.

- Analysis of the *link structure* of a set of text documents. This is often called *web mining* and one method is the popular *Page Rank* algorithm introduced in section 7.2.

In the case of text mining, each node in the knowledge graph that stands for unstructured text has to be transformed into a multi-represented object (see Def. 3.2.2, 3.2). The framework engine operates only on the content representation of each node and is hence decoupled from their symbolic and unsubstantial identifiers within the knowledge base.

Document Representation Using a Vector Space Model For each knowledge node a feature vector $\vec{v}_i \in \mathbb{R}^d$ is computed. In the case of textual content, we apply well-known text mining methodologies for computing a low-redundancy numerical representation – including *stemming* and *stop-word lists*[1]. Stemming is the process of reducing inflected or derived words to their stem (root form). Stemming aims at natural languages, especially English, which can even be stemmed algorithmically (Porter-Stemmer algorithm [Por80]). Tokens that are contained in the respective *list of stopwords* are removed and not considered for text mining, especially meaningless terms such as articles or sometimes pronouns.

By means of the *term frequency – inverse document frequency* (TF-IDF) we now give a procedure that computes a characteristical vector for each document in the knowledge base $KB = \{doc_1, \ldots, doc_n\}$ by rating the relevance of all existing keywords via the following measures.

Definition 7.1.1: Term and Document Ratios

$$df(t_i) := \frac{|docs(t_i)|}{|KB|} \tag{7.1}$$

$$tf(t_i, doc) := \frac{n(t_i, doc)}{\sum_{t \in doc} n(t, doc)} \tag{7.2}$$

$$tf\_idf(t_i, doc) := \frac{n(t_i, doc)}{\sum_{t \in doc} n(t, doc)} \cdot \frac{|KB|}{|docs(t_i)|}, \tag{7.3}$$

where $i = 1, \ldots, m$ runs over all terms in the entire knowledge base. The *document frequency* $df(t_i)$ counts the number of documents that contain a term t_i related to the number n of existing documents in a certain knowledge base *KB*. The measure $n(t, doc)$ counts the frequency of occurrence of a term t_i in a single document *doc*. The *term frequency* $tf(t_i, doc)$ gives the relative frequency of a term t_i within a single document *doc*. As stated in formula 7.3, TF-IDF is composed of the formulas 7.1 and 7.2, while inverting the document frequency.

---

[1]The preprocessing steps *stemming* and *stop-word removal* are realized by the *Apache Lucene* indexing and search framework[2].

The idea behind TF-IDF is to assign a higher relevance to terms that occur often within a single document. At the same time terms, which appear less often in the entire repository *KB*, are rated higher. The reason is that globally frequent terms are not valuable for differentiating between the documents $doc_1, \ldots, doc_n$, because they are contained in most of these documents.

To be useful for the SYMBOCONN framework, a *fixed number* d of most significant terms has to be selected that is less than the total number n_{tot} of occurring terms in *KB*. Thus, a global term significance measure is required, which rates terms according to their occurrences in *all* documents of *KB*.

An adequate way to determine the globally most relevant terms is to compute the TF-IDF measure for all documents in *KB*. Then the term t_{max} with maximum tf_idf value is identified and, in case of ambiguity, the maximal number of all term occurrences $\max_{t_i, doc} tf(t_i, doc)$ in the entire knowledge base is also calculated.

Definition 7.1.2: Globally Significant Terms
Let $t_{r\_1} := t_{max}$, which results from expression 7.5:

$$T_{max} := \{\arg \max_{t_i \in doc \in KB} \sum_{doc \in KB} tf\_idf(t_i, doc)\} \qquad (7.4)$$

$$t_{max} := \arg \max_{t_i \in T_{max}} \sum_{doc \in KB} tf(t_i, doc) \qquad (7.5)$$

Expression 7.5 is evaluated d times, while the most relevant term t_{r_1} is globally removed from *KB* by a *pop-operation* each time, then the second relevant term is determined and so on.

Now, the feature vector $\vec{v}_i$ that describes a document is locally computed by the TF-IDF of the d globally most significant terms for the respective document $doc \in KB$:

$$\vec{v}_i := (tf\_idf(t_{r\_1}, doc), tf\_idf(t_{r\_2}, doc), \ldots, tf\_idf(t_{r\_d}, doc)). \qquad (7.6)$$

This computation is different from the common *bag-of-words* approach based on TF-IDF, since we represent each document by the $d < n_{tot}$ globally top-ranked terms that are locally rated via $tf\_idf(t_{r\_i}, doc)$. This global vector space model [SWY75] captures the semantics of each document and enables the MRNN to uniformly learn the complete textual content of a knowledge base.

7.1.2 Association Rule Mining

Association rule mining (ARM) is a data mining technique usually applied to large databases that contain sets of co-occurring items. This technique originally was first introduced by Argawal, Imielinski, and Swami [AIS93], who used it market basket analysis. Its goal is to discover buying patterns of the form *"85% of the transactions that contained purchasing diapers also contained purchasing beer"*. Such probabilistic rules can then be used for decision support systems regarding price promotion or store layout. Figure 7.1 shows the functioning of ARM from a blackbox perspective, receiving item sets as input and providing discovered rules as output.

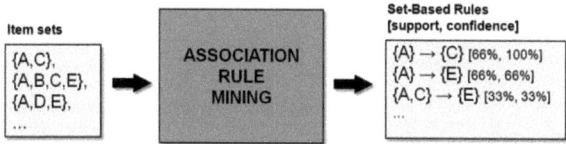

Figure 7.1: Blackbox view of association rule mining with generic input and output representation that is applicable to many different domains and their problems.

Recently, association rule mining has also been applied to software engineering, in particular to *mining of version histories to guide software changes* [ZWDZ04]. When a developer works on a programming task, relevant software artifacts such as documents, source code, multimedia files, etc. that might require corresponding changes, can be proactively recommended: *"Programmers who changed these artifacts also changed ..."*.

The ARM technique based on the apriori algorithm [SON95] has been implemented and integrated into the SYMBOCONN framework as a symbolic data mining technique. It was used for the following purposes:

- The TEAM project [TEA09] on knowledge management in software engineering uses the ARM implementation of SYMBOCONN as one component of rule-based activity classification and user assistance regarding software developers. Further details on activity classification in general were given in section 6.1.

- **Navigation Recommendation**

    – Symbolic realization of navigation recommendation by association rule mining, section 7.2.

    – Connectionist and content-based realization of navigation recommendation leveraged by mining the associations between keyterms in unstructured text. The resulting technique is a combination of text and association rule mining, which makes up a preprocessing to obtain a content-based training set for the neural network engine of SYMBOCONN (see also appendix A.1.2.2).

- **Recommending Software Changes**
  Recommending further changes to guide software developers can be realized by association rule mining as done by Zimmermann et al. [ZWDZ04]. ARM

is simpler but less powerful than the competing connectionist technique. Furthermore, ARM is relatively simple to implement and especially easy to use, which nominates it for a universal plug&play-like data mining technique.

ARM works upon unordered sets and not upon ordered sequences, which is a fundamental premise and constraint of this technique. The following terminology defines the fundamental concepts of association rule mining [Bö03].

- *Items* $I = \{i_1, i_2, \ldots, i_m\}$: The set of all existing items each represented by a unique symbol.

- *Itemset* $X \subseteq I$: A subset of the globally available items, e.g. a shopping cart of goods to be bought. For facilitating the mining process, the items are ordered lexicographically, $(x_1, x_2, \ldots, x_n)$ with $x_1 \leq x_2 \leq \ldots \leq x_n$. A k-itemset is an itemset containing k items $x_1, \ldots, x_k$.

- *Transaction* $T = (tid, X)$: Each transaction is a 2-tuple consisting of a tid and an itemset X.

- The *Cover* of an itemset X_T is the set of transactions T that contain X_T: $cover(X) := \{tid | (tid, X_T) \in D, X \subseteq X_T\}$.

- The *Frequency* of an itemset X in the database D is the probability of its occurrence within a transaction $T \in D$: $frequency(X) = \frac{support(X)}{|D|} = \mathbb{P}(X)$, where $support(X) = |cover(X)|$.

- Itemsets $X \in D$ that satisfy a given frequency threshold t, $frequency(X) \geq t$, $t \in [0, 1]$, are of special interest.

All of these concepts are typically measured by means of a transaction database, which represents the dataset to be analyzed, as shown in table 7.1.

Starting out with these fundamental concepts, there are two main problems addressed by ARM:

1. **Mining of Frequent Itemsets**
   There are $\binom{|I|}{k}$-many k-itemsets that all have to be checked for minimum support in case of a naive approach to itemset mining. Thus the total costs sum up to $O(\sum_{k=1}^{|I|} \binom{|I|}{k}) = O(2^{|I|} - 1)$. Frequent itemset mining is formally stated as function a) in algorithm 2.

2. **Association rule mining**

   - An association rule is an implication of the form $X \Rightarrow Y$, $X \cap Y = \emptyset$. X is the rule's *body*, Y is the *head*.

   - The *Support* of an association rule $A \equiv X \Rightarrow Y$ is computed based on the support of (frequent) itemsets:
   $supp(A) = supp(X \cup Y)$.

CHAPTER 7. NAVIGATION RECOMMENDATION

Itemset	Frequency
$\{A\}$	0.25
$\{B\}$	0.5
$\vdots$	
$\{A,B\}$	0.25
$\{E,F\}$	0.5
$\vdots$	
$\{A,B,C\}$	0.05
$\{C,D,E\}$	0.03
$\{A,B,D,E\}$	0.01
$\vdots$	

TID	Itemset
1	$\{A,B,D,E\}$
2	$\{C,D,E\}$
3	$\{B,D,E,F,G,H\}$
4	$\{F,G,H,I,J\}$
$\vdots$	

Table 7.1: Example of a database of items that appeared together in common transactions, for example, articles bought together. The left table gives the frequencies of several 1-, 2-, 3-, and 4-itemsets. The right table contains itemsets of different size that were accessed within transactions (buying articles) of domain users.

- *Confidence* of an association rule $A \equiv X \Rightarrow Y$: $conf(A) = \frac{supp(X \cup Y)}{supp(X)}$. The confidence can also be interpreted as *conditional probability* of the rule's head: $\mathbb{P}(Y|X) = \frac{\mathbb{P}(Y,X)}{\mathbb{P}(X)}$, $\mathbb{P}(X) \neq 0$. The desired minimal confidence is set by domain experts before starting the frequent itemset mining.

The problem of association rule mining is superimposed on frequent itemset mining and is formally stated as function b) in algorithm 2.

Both problems are solved by the ARM implementation of the SYMBOCONN framework.

Mining Association Rules Based on the discovered k-itemsets, which are frequent in the underlying database, association rules A of the form

$$A := (Y \Rightarrow X - Y) \tag{7.7}$$

are computed, where the minus operator signifies the difference between sets ("\"). Only rules with the desired minimal confidence are considered. The confidence $conf(A)$ can be calculated in the following simple way:

$$conf(A) = \frac{supp(Y \cup (X - Y))}{supp(Y)} = \frac{supp(X)}{supp(Y)}. \tag{7.8}$$

Apriori Algorithm To solve the frequent itemset problem in a more efficient way than checking each k-itemset $X = \{(x_1, x_2, \ldots, x_k)\}$ for $k = 1, \ldots, m$ regarding its support (a total of $2^m - 1$ evaluations), a dynamic programming approach is carried out. This technique is known as the apriori algorithm for ARM, which exploits a *monotony property*. The monotony property states that all supersets X' of an itemset X, $X \subset X'$, cannot be frequent, if X is not frequent. This property narrows the search space significantly and thus speeds up the computation of frequent itemsets. The constrained search space corresponds to the set of *candidate itemsets*, whose support has to be computed. Algorithm 2 provides a pseudocode formulation of the apriori algorithm.

Algorithm 2 Pseudo code formulation of the *apriori algorithm*, which consists of two main functions: *a) mining frequent itemsets* and *b) compute association rules.*

    function APRIORI_ARM(database D, double $minSupp$, double $minConf$)
        $CS_1 \leftarrow$ computeFrequentOneItemsets($minSupp$);
        $FS_{total} \leftarrow \{\emptyset\}$;
        $RES \leftarrow \{\}$;
        for ($k = 2; k < m; k \rightarrow k + 1$) **do**
            $CS_k \leftarrow$ generateCandidateSet(CS_{k-1});   ▷ *Join based on the (k-1) candidates.*
            $CS_k \leftarrow$ removeNonFrequentItemsets($k - 1, minSupp$);   ▷ *Pruning of invalid candidates.*
            $FS_k \leftarrow$ computeFrequentItemsets($CS_k, minSupp$);
            $FS_{total} \leftarrow FS_{total} \cup FS_k$;
        end for   ▷ *Compute association rules based on frequent itemsets.*
        for ($i = 1; i < |FS_{total}|; i \rightarrow i + 1$) **do**
            $Y \leftarrow FS_{total}[i]$;
            for ($j = 1; j < \binom{|Y|}{j}; j \rightarrow j + 1$) **do**
                Choose subset $Y \subset X$;
                Split X into body and head: $A := (Y \Rightarrow X - Y)$;
                $conf_A \leftarrow \frac{supp(X)}{supp(Y)}$;
                if $conf_A \geq minConf$ **then**
                    $RES \leftarrow RES \cup A$;
                end if
            end for
        end for
        return RES;
    end function

The frequent 1-itemsets are directly computed by the procedures contained in the *Apache Lucene* library, since these frequencies are exactly the document frequencies $df(t_i)$ as introduced in section 7.1.1. Besides the apriori algorithm, there are also other algorithms for association rule mining such as *Eclat* [Zak00] and *Eclat II* [LZZZ05], which choose a depth-first search for frequent k-itemsets instead of completing all itemsets of size k first before proceeding to the next tree level k+1.

7.2 Existing Recommendation Approaches

Since the connectionist approach to navigation recommendation uses principles of content-based and collaborative filtering techniques, we describe relevant research findings in these areas. In addition, there are already commercial products like the *Navigation Predictor* [Int07] that claim to generate real-time recommendations for products that are most relevant to the customer.

Symbolic Recommendation Based on Association Rule Mining The functionality of navigation recommendation can solely be realized by employing association rule mining without using a connectionist prediction model. Fu and his colleagues have attempted to exploit the tacit knowledge incorporated in the navigation history of web users [BFH00]. They propose an information recommendation system called *SurfLen*, which suggests interesting web pages to users. The underlying data mining technique is association rule mining, which is used to discover *frequent 2-itemsets* containing web page URLs like $\{\{p, p_1\}, \{p, p_2\}, \ldots, \{p, p_n\}\}$. When the user is reading page p, then the associated pages $\{p_1, \ldots, p_n\}$ are recommended. Hence, the items stand for URLs here, itemsets being ranked by an intersection measure

$$rank(U_i, S_j) = |U_i \cap S_j|$$

between users' browsing histories $U_i = \{p_1, \ldots, p_m\}$ and mined frequent itemsets $S_j = \{p'_1, \ldots, p'_m\}$. The best k itemsets according to the $rank$-measure are recommended when the current browsing history matches one of the stored ones. The software architecture of the recommendation system is depicted in figure 7.2. Such

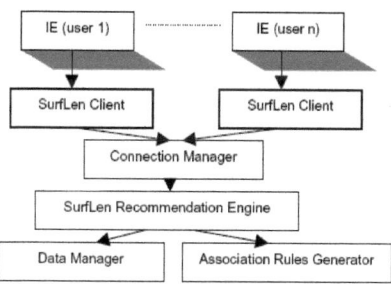

Figure 7.2: The client-server architecture of the *SurfLen* recommendation system.

a symbolic approach cannot incorporate the semantics of the entities to be recommended, since the content of the web pages is not considered by the URL-based representation. No similarity measure is implied on web pages either. This deficiency can be solved by considering a rich representation of artifacts instead of reducing them to meaningless identifiers. The danger of recommending misleading symbolic associations can be avoided by considering the meaning of the visited nodes (e.g. web pages or text documents), for example by means of their textual content. The work at hand addresses this problem by multi-represented objects that incorporate textual descriptions or other attributes.

Navigation Recommendation by a Connectionist Architecture A central problem of association rule mining, especially on sparse web data, is the difficulty of setting suitable support and confidence thresholds to yield reliable and complete web usage rules. So far, there are hardly any connectionist methods that accomplish navigation recommendation; one of the few approaches is the paper *"A Connectionist Approach to Accurate Web Recommendations based on a Committee of Predictors"* [NP04]. Taking a closer look at the purpose of neural networks in this concept, we see that they are used for profile-based URL recommendation. The architecture of this connectionist system is rigid, since unlike in our MRNN-based approach, a fixed number of input and output URLs are required for network training, which renders the session sizes static. The proposed recommendation process consists of

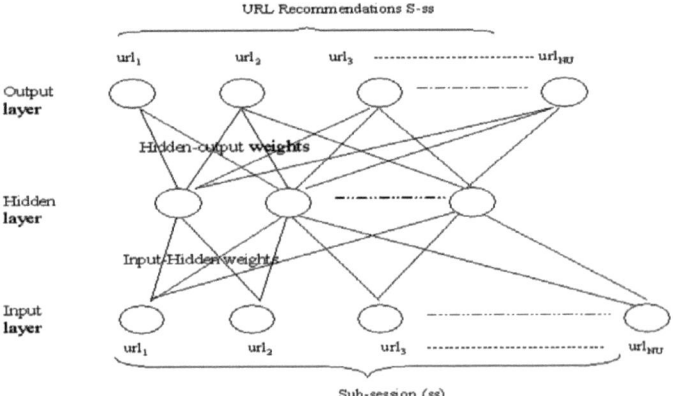

Figure 7.3: Two-step recommendation process based on 20 user profiles and on an ensemble of 20 specialized back-propagation neural networks (MLPs).

two integral steps as depicted by figure 7.3. First, both the highest cosine similarity between all sub sessions and the static profile vectors are computed. After a blackbox indexing activity, the indexing result is fed into each of the 20 individual back-propagation neural networks, which have been trained on profile-specific sub session-to-URL mappings before. The 20 profile-specific URL-predictor multilayer perceptrons have to recommend further web pages not yet contained in a single user session. Since the URLs of the web pages were not learned in a content-based way and no completely unseen pages had to be handled (as is the case in the study using the SYMBOCONN framework, which is presented in section 7.5), neither the results nor the underlying datasets are comparable. The committee of predictors called accomplished the recommendation task with a precision of 74.2% on average.

Structural Recommendation – Google PageRank Internet search engines require a ranking mechanism to prioritize the results consisting of a vast amount of retrieved keyword hits. One very popular ranking algorithm that considers the structure of the navigation space (interlinked nodes) is *PageRank*, named for its inventor Lawrence Page [BP98]. This algorithm is based on a directed graph $G = (V, E)$ as a model for the internet and its purpose is to assess the relevancy of web pages.

The distinctive feature of PageRank is conducting a theoretically infinite *random walk* on the graph, which finally reflects the *prestige* of the visited websites represented by graph nodes. The prestige is the state probability of a certain node

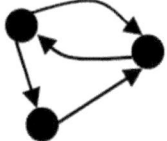

Figure 7.4: Exemplary directed and non-symmetric graph consisting of three websites.

in iteration t of the random walk. The asymmetrical adjacency matrix A describes the edges of the strongly connected graph, taking into account their direction. A so-called random-surfer starts at an arbitrary node and navigates according to the transition probabilities $A'[u, v]$, which are the entries of the normalized adjacency matrix A'.

Example 7.2.1: Random Walk Graph

$$A = \begin{pmatrix} 0 & 1 & 1 \\ 1 & 0 & 0 \\ 0 & 1 & 0 \end{pmatrix} \qquad A' = \begin{pmatrix} 0 & \frac{1}{2} & \frac{1}{2} \\ 1 & 0 & 0 \\ 0 & 1 & 0 \end{pmatrix}$$

The normalization $A'[u, v] = \frac{A[u,v]}{\sum_k A[u,k]}$ is performed row-wise in order to induce a probability measure $\mathbb{P}: \mathcal{F} \to \mathbb{R}$ with the σ-algebra $\mathcal{F} = \mathcal{P}(V)$, $\{u\} \in \mathcal{F}$, $\mathbb{P}[u] := \mathbb{P}(\{u\}) \in [0, 1]$.

In a further step, the following recursive transition equations are applied to compute the probability vector $\vec{p}[u_1, u_2, \ldots, u_n](t)$ of the pages u_i, $i = 1, \ldots, n$ at time

t. $\mathbb{P}[u](t)$ is the random surfer's probability of visiting page $u \in V$ at time t.

$$\vec{p}(0) = \frac{1}{|V|} \quad (7.9)$$

$$\vec{p}(t) = A^T \vec{p}(t-1) \quad (7.10)$$

$$\vec{p}(t) \xrightarrow[t \to \infty]{} (\mathbb{P}[u_1], \ldots, \mathbb{P}[u_n]), \quad (7.11)$$

The uniform distribution computed by formula 7.9 serves as initial node probability, which depends on the number of nodes in the graph. The computation normally converges after a decent number of so-called *power iterations* defined by equation 7.10. The iterative probability computation is similar to the forward propagation of signals in the recurrent layer of the MRNN. In the case of example 7.2.1, the final probabilities approach $\mathbb{P}[u] = 0.4$, $\mathbb{P}[v] = 0.4$, $\mathbb{P}[w] = 0.2$ for $t \to \infty$. This behavior can already be observed after about 30 iterations.

If the random surfer ends up on a page without any outgoing links, then a page among the remaining ones is picked randomly as next browsing target. In light of the performed random walk, web pages can be classified according to two types of graph nodes, called *authority* and *hub*, which are characterized by the number of incoming and outgoing links. A good authority is linked by many hubs and a good hub refers to many authorities. In example 7.2.1, v represents a hub and u an

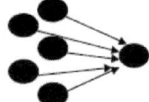

Figure 7.5: An *authority* is a web page that is referred to by many web pages.

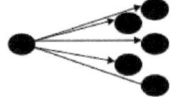

Figure 7.6: A *hub* is a web page that holds many outgoing links to other web pages.

authority. w is neither hub nor authority, coherently resulting in the lowest stopover probability $\mathbb{P}[w] = 0.2$, which is often denoted as *score* of a web page.

7.3 Knowledge Representation for Navigation Recommendation

In chapter 3, the knowledge model of SYMBOCONN was defined, including the notion of multi-represented objects. In the case of navigation recommendation, the multi-representation is tailored to the content of the nodes to be learned and recommended. Either, the nodes are taken as atomic symbols merely possessing unique names such as URLs, called symbolic node representation below, or the nodes provide textual content to be considered by a text mining approach.

Symbolic Node Representation Symbolic node representation solely relies on the string-based naming schema used by the knowledge base to administer its entities – comparable to a directory of files. This syntactical approach follows the paradigm of collaborative filtering and is far easier to implement and computationally less complex than a full text representation; it might still provide an acceptable recommendation accuracy in the individual case.

A unary encoding approach maps a node identifier $v_i \mapsto (0, 0, \ldots, 0, 1, 0, \ldots, 0)$ to an orthogonal bit vector with a "1" at the ith component, but does not consider any content of the knowledge nodes at all – if available. Compared to a binary encoding of all node identifiers that requires $\lceil \log_2 n \rceil$ bits to represent $n = |V|$ nodes, the unary encoding provides a much better discrimination between the represented node IDs by its strictly orthogonal vectors. This simple approach unarily encodes n-many nodes by n-many n-dimensional vectors $\vec{x}_1, \ldots, \vec{x}_n$. The purely symbolic approach is comparable to the URL-based navigation recommendation by association rule mining, described in section 7.2.

Rich Representation Based on Text Mining Navigation recommendation may be enhanced by text mining capabilities, because the navigation space often provides rich textual contents for machine learning and enable to apply the generalization capability of the connectionist system.

According to the vector space model presented in section 7.1.1, a feature vector $\vec{x}_i \in \mathbb{R}^d$ is computed for each knowledge node v_i. A simple way of obtaining a vector space model [SWY75] is to count the keyterms for each text unit, creating so-called bag-of-words vectors. These vectors can be arranged in a *term-document matrix* M of keyword frequencies per text unit (e.g. sentences, paragraphs, sections, documents). The entry $M_{i,j}$ denotes the frequency of occurrence for term i in text unit j, which is the textual content of a node in the knowledge graph.

When applying this text mining approach to unstructured text in order to obtain a knowledge representation for neural processing, several lingual and statistical problems remain:

- *Synonymy*: Synonymy is the phenomenon of several distinct words holding the same linguistic meaning.

- *Polysemy*: Polysemy describes the phenomenon, that the same expression has different meanings in different linguistic contexts; polysemy is contrary to synonymy.

- *No VSM-term orthogonality*: The vector space model (VSM) used to numerically describe text documents makes the implicit assumption of uncorrelated terms by assigning each of them to a single vector space dimension. This assumption does not hold for natural languages in general. Linguistic constructs such as "change management" are not only composed of the independent terms "change" and "management" that would be represented by independent dimensions, but are highly correlated when they occur together in a text document. Mathematically spoken, the probabilities for the event A_1 that the word "change" occurs, and the event A_2 that the word "management" occurs are not stochastically independent: $\mathbb{P}(\bigcap_{j \in \mathcal{J}} A_j) \neq \prod_{j \in \mathcal{J}} \mathbb{P}(A_j)$, $\mathcal{J} = \{1, \ldots, k\}$.

Refinement by Latent Semantic Indexing The vector space model can be refined by applying *Latent Semantic Indexing* (LSI) [DDF+90] to the set of obtained feature vectors $\{\vec{x}_1, \ldots, \vec{x}_n\}$, which determines the inherent key concepts characterizing all d-dimensional feature vectors $\vec{x}_i$. LSI is capable of dealing with problems such as polysemy and synonymy by analyzing the latent semantics of interdependent concepts. As an advanced text analysis method, LSI is employed on top of the term-document matrix $M_{i,j}$ discovering the correlations between text units and the contained terms. The matrix is decomposed by *Singular Value Decomposition* (SVD), which is a generalization of the *Principal Component Analysis* (PCA). While PCA compares equal objects by setting up a quadratic and symmetric matrix, SVD is able to analyze the relations between terms and text units by a non-quadratic matrix.

Based on SVD, we reduce the dimensionality and thereby the redundancy of the term-document matrix M, which is usually sparse. The matrix is decomposed $M = UDW^T$ into two orthonormal matrices U and W and one diagonal matrix D. This decomposition is called *diagonalization*. After diagonalizing the matrix M, the singular values $\sigma_j = D_{j,j}$ in the diagonal of the matrix D reveal the insignificant dimensions to be discarded. The k least informative dimensions with singular values $\sigma_{d-k}, \sigma_{d-k+1}, \ldots, \sigma_n$ are ignored by the transformation to a $(d-k)$-dimensional subspace. The result are feature vectors $\vec{x}_j \in \mathbb{R}^{d-k}$ that represent the content of a node $v_j \in V$:

$$\vec{x}_j^T := (W_{1,j}^T, W_{2,j}^T, \ldots, W_{d-k,j}^T), \qquad (7.12)$$

where $W_{i,j}^T$, $i = 1, \ldots, d\text{-}k$, $j = 1, \ldots, |V|$ are the entries of the transposed right-singular matrix. The dimension-reduced document representation based on the subspace $\mathbb{R}^{d-k}$ represents an input source of higher quality for connectionist prediction by the MRNN, since it provides a lower rank approximation of the original vector set. Generally, the high-dimensional bag-of-words vectors are *sparse*; that is to say, they contain many 0-entries. More formally spoken, the term-document matrix $M \in \mathbb{R}^{m \times |V|}$ (m is the number of keyterms in the knowledge base) does not have full rank, but only $rank(M) = m - k$. In this case, even a dimension reduction without information loss can be accomplished, keeping nearly the whole variance of the original vector set. The practical benefits of SVD, the increased input quality for neural processing, and the existence of lossless lower rank transformations, are empirically shown in section 7.5.

The benefit of latent semantic indexing applied to raw text is the transformation 7.12 of the original term frequency vectors into a more meaningful and – in addition – more compact representation. The resulting feature vectors are less noisy than the

original data, capturing the latent association between the terms and documents.
Carthy and his colleagues also used the SVD technique in the field of intelligent recommendation [SCD05]. They developed an intelligent online recommendation system, which uses a *Singular Value Decomposition-Collaborative Filtering* (SVD-CF) method to represent the latent associations between users and recommended items while reducing the dimensionality of the user-item space. Their approach demonstrates the adequacy of SVD-based techniques for recommendation tasks concerning associations between two sorts of entities, like customers and products or terms and documents. Similarly, the SVD-based rich representation of SYMBOCONN also exploits the latent associations between terms and the items to be recommended, which are, for example, web pages in the case study presented in section .

7.4 Navigation Recommendation in SymboConn

When users navigate in an associative way by performing sequences of navigation operations to solve a knowledge-driven problem [SS05], their behavior is observed by the SYMBOCONN framework and modeled as a navigation through the graph. The navigation recommendation technique presented in this section is an extended version of [Dav08a] and applies to beginners, advanced learners and domain experts.

In SYMBOCONN, the goal of navigation recommendation is to proactively predict a sequence of relevant nodes based on the observation of the user navigation on the knowledge graph. These target nodes are predicted to be associated most strongly with the history sequence of observed nodes. The abstract model of the respective knowledge base uses the graph defined in section 3.2, but this time in the shape of an unbalanced tree with arbitrary valence and nodes of possibly different types, as shown in figure 7.7.

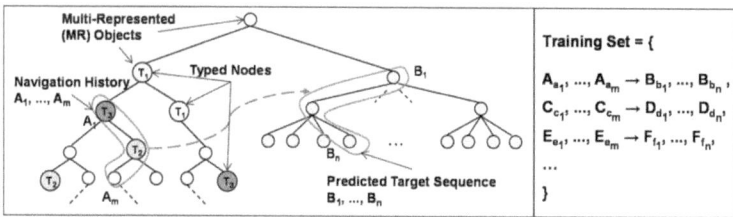

Figure 7.7: Exemplary navigation history together with the predicted target sequence on a tree-shaped knowledge base. The nodes may be of different types, for example, $\mu(A_1) = T_3$. Nodes without a type label $T_1, T_2, \ldots$ are considered as untyped.

Since, in general, no behavioral rules are available which reveal the browsing behavior of users on the knowledge base in form of explicit control knowledge, learning from examples is the only way of incorporating knowledge about the users and the application domain. The interests and expertise of users become partially manifest in their navigation behavior on the respective knowledge base. The users implicitly reveal their interests and furthermore produce new associations by actually using the system.

Before navigation recommendations can be generated, the system has to be trained on observed navigations through learning by example (see the requirement introduced in section 3.1.1.1). Assume that the system has learned the relationship between history and target sequences on a knowledge graph by supervised training. Now, a navigation sequence generated by a beginner consisting of yet unseen nodes,

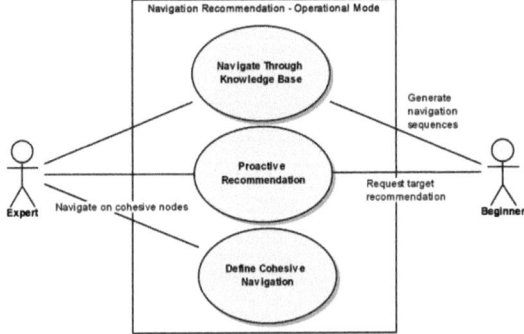

Figure 7.8: Use case diagram showing the operational mode of navigation recommendation in SYMBOCONN. The third use case, which can only be executed by an expert user, can be interpreted as *programming by example*, where the user plays the role of a teacher.

is presented to the system. In this case, the SYMBOCONN framework provides two forms of recommendations, which are condensed in the use case Proactive Recommendation in figure 7.8:

1. *Recognition and Recovery*: When presenting a navigation history to the MRNN which equals the *history part* of a learned training pattern, its *target part* can be fully recovered. An example that can be widely interpreted as navigation recommendation are the working steps that an expert technician performs when confronted with a malfunctioning thermostat. The fault diagnosis represents the history part and the repair actions to be carried out represent the target part.

2. *Generalization*: A virtually unknown sequence of navigation operations is fed into the MRNN, which is able to predict the target nodes most likely

related. An example is the recommendation of related pages in a documentation. When presented with an unseen documentation page, the SYMBOCONN recommendation engine is able to recommend (using LSI) a sequence of pages that contain related explanations on the same topic, but with the use of synonymical terms. Such a recommendation cannot be provided by a simple full-text search.

Expert-Defined Associations Users might adopt different roles, such as beginner or expert, with characteristic degrees of knowledge demand and provision, as described by the use case diagram of figure 7.8. In terms of *end-user programming* [EUD02], experienced users should be able to define cohesive navigations by visiting nodes that semantically belong together due to their conceptual similarity. Expert-defined navigations, denoted by the use case Define Cohesive Navigation in figure 7.8, allow for the direct insertion of domain knowledge into the recommendation engine. The user notifies the SYMBOCONN framework to capture the current navigation with explicit history and target part, which is then added to the set of navigation sequences to be learned (training set).

The great benefit of expert-defined node associations is their multiplier effect, which only evolves from the proposed connectionist realization of a content-based[3] machine learning system. Other users of the information system benefit from this kind of *programming by example*[4] by following analogous procedures in new navigation scenarios. Since the content of each node participating in the captured navigation is considered as multi-represented object (see also section 3.2) by the connectionist approach, its latent semantics are also learned with respect to other nodes. Thus by means of a structural and content-based similarity of history node sequences, supported by the sequential state layer of the MRNN, unseen but similar history sequences can be assessed and carried forward. Metaphorically speaking, each meaningful and cohesive navigation sequence that was explicitly defined by a knowledgeable user has a multiplying effect on the domain understanding of the neural network, since the exemplified content correlation "emits" onto untrained contents.

The usual and more unobtrusive way of learning from users is to automatically trace and incorporate the navigation behavior of experts, without requiring them to explicitly declare cohesive navigation sequences. However, a beginner should not explicitly define a navigation due to his lack of domain knowledge; nevertheless, beginners are traced by the system in order to be proactively assisted with recommendations of potentially relevant target nodes. An expert on a specific domain might lack expertise in foreign domains and thus might behave like a beginner or an informed outsider needing to be assisted in this case.

---

[3] The *collaborative* aspect is of minor relevance here.
[4] Also called *programming by demonstration*.

7.4.1 Adapting Principles from Content-Based and Collaborative Filtering

The connectionist approach to learning of user navigations benefits both from aspects of content-based and of collaborative filtering. As introduced in section 1.2, content-based filtering exclusively takes into account the preferred entities of a single user and analyzes[5] their content for similarity-based recommendations.

Instead of considering the carried content, most collaborative filtering systems solely rely on symbolic relationships: the node content is neglected and the relationships between nodes are reduced to the fact that a set of users has visited sets of symbols, like the URL identifiers of web pages. These systems compute the recommendation for the current user based on the degree of compliance of his interest profile with the profiles of all other users, assuming that this coincidence also holds for further nodes. The class diagram in figure 7.9 shows the combination of content-based and collaborative filtering.

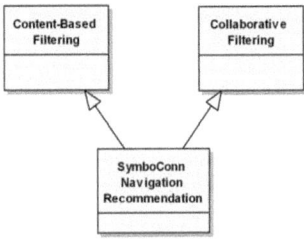

Figure 7.9: Multiple specification inheritance from content-based and collaborative filtering combining the advantages of both methods. The SYMBOCONN framework learns both the node contents (such as the titles of web pages or even their content) as well as user-to-node relations.

When the navigation behavior of more than one user is learned, the connectionist machine learning transcends the purely content-based approach and additionally becomes collaborative. The SYMBOCONN framework learns both the node contents, such as the titles of web pages or even their content, as well as user-to-node relations. The question to be resolved is whether the neural network can benefit from the integration of other users' preferences when predicting the subsequent nodes based on the previously visited ones, which is empirically answered in section 7.5.

Since collaborative filtering is also tailored to the individual user, we need a mechanism to bind the user to his specific navigation sequences. Therefore each navigation sequence is contextualized with the respective user, which allows for tailored navigation recommendations that may deviate from the mean user preferences. Users who have visited the same subset of nodes so far may vary in the

---
[5] By Latent Semantic Indexing (LSI).

subsequently visited nodes. Therefore, a representation of each user together with the visited nodes is learned in the **contextualized learning** mode.

This contextualization is especially useful in guaranteeing a unique mapping of visited nodes to target nodes, which makes for a consistent training set according to condition A.2.1 explained in the appendix A.2.1. Otherwise, many ambiguous navigation sequences would have to be removed from the training set in order to obtain an unambiguous functional mapping of navigation sequences learnable by the MRNN. For this reason, the mappings of visited and recommended nodes are tailored to the respective user resulting in user-specific and thus context-sensitive node mappings; this allows to consider a broader set of unambiguous navigation sequences. Navigations with equal history but different target parts have to be excluded from training in the case of the context-free mode. They can be considered, however, when using the additional context nodes that guarantee the required uniqueness.

For the contextualized learning of navigation sequences, it is necessary to train a recurrent neural network on the productions of a context-sensitive grammar $\mathcal{G}_1$ of type 1, according to the Chomsky-hierarchy [Sch01]. Context-sensitive rules like $\alpha B \gamma \Rightarrow \alpha \beta \gamma$ can be recognized by neural networks with the appropriate learning algorithm. Without contextualization, functional associations like $node_j \mapsto node_k$, $j \neq k$ would have to be substituted by relational associations in the sense that a visited $node_j$ maps to $node_k$ for user u_1, but maps to $node_l$ for user u_2:

$$u_1 : node_j \mapsto node_k$$
$$u_2 : node_j \mapsto node_l$$

Since this is not a functional mapping, it is not representable by the MRNN. On the other hand, relational associations of the form $(node_j \mapsto \{node_k, node_l\})$ are not desired either, because user u_1 should not be presented with $node_l$ and user u_2 not with $node_k$. A solution to this problem is given by the proposed contextualization with the user identities, which corresponds to the functional requirement of context-sensitivity (cf. section 3.1.1.4) and is therefore supported by the SYMBOCONN framework. The user identities provide a *navigation-context* for the determination of the target nodes to be recommended upon the knowledge graph:

Content-based filtering becomes collaborative by exploiting the user identity as navigation context.

Adding the respective user ID as an atomic node (without content) to the beginning of the history results in two functional and hence unambiguous mappings $(u_1, node_j) \mapsto node_k$ and $(u_2, node_j) \mapsto node_l$, which are illustrated by figure 7.10. These contextualized training patterns can be expressed by context-sensitive productions

$$(u_1, node_j) \Rightarrow node_k, \quad u_1, u_2 \in \Sigma, \; node_j, node_k \in V,$$

where Σ is terminal alphabet and V is the set of variables. The usage of multi-represented nodes as described in section 3.2 allows to treat users as nodes with a single categorical attribute that represents their identity. These inherently heteroge-

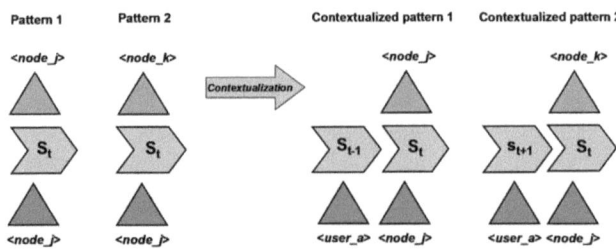

Figure 7.10: Contextualization of two training patterns for navigation recommendation shown together with the corresponding network topology. The pairs of correlated nodes $(node_i, node_j)$ and $(node_j, node_k)$ are *contextualized* from the left by the respective user identity.

neous training sequences can only be processed due to the modular architecture of the MRNN, which enables joint learning of different node types.

Independent from the decision of whether using a content-based representation or a symbolic one, navigation sequences of many users can be learned independently from the behavior of the individual user. We denote this variant as **context-free learning**. In the context-free learning approach, a median navigation behavior of all considered users is incorporated into the SYMBOCONN recommendation engine, while ignoring possibly given user-to-navigation mappings that represent the visited nodes for each user. Navigation sequences are not bound to specific users, but are representative of all of them. The content of the visited nodes is carried by multi-represented objects as defined in section 3.2. Users are either represented by arbitrary symbols that do not carry any information – as in the following case study –, or they are described by profiles consisting of name-value pairs, for example.

An advantage of context-free learning is its higher extensibility regarding further users. If new users should be provided with recommendations which have not been hitherto represented in the training set of navigation sequences, the uncontextualized prediction model can be used without adoption. In the case of symbolic user identities, this extensibility does not apply to contextualized navigations: since the user identities are not represented in a content-based way, a new user identity does not stand in any relationship to the trained set of user behaviors and thus cannot be assessed by means of similarity to already incorporated behaviors.

7.4.2 Control Flow of Navigation Recommendation

The abstract control flow of navigation recommendation integrates all the activities and techniques presented in the previous paragraphs into a cohesive machine learning process applicable to text-based and non-textual knowledge bases. The activity diagram depicted in figure 7.11 illustrates the dynamic model of generic learning

CHAPTER 7. NAVIGATION RECOMMENDATION

and recommendation in an arbitrary domain. The upper *swimlane* shows the activ-

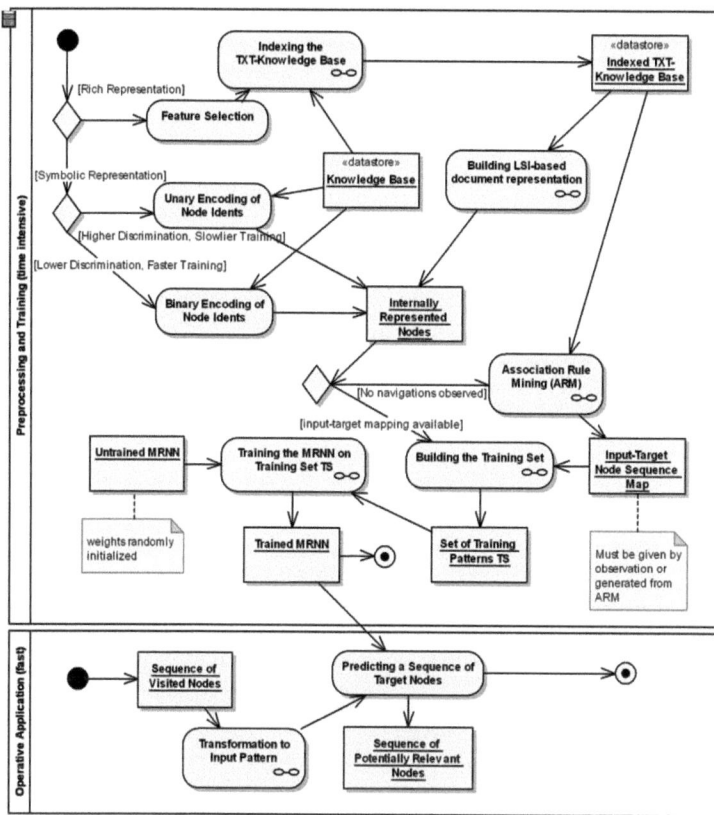

Figure 7.11: Activity diagram for navigation recommendation on the knowledge graph, either based on symbolic or rich content representation.

ities, decisions and work products required for preprocessing the data and training the system. The lower swimlane represents the actual recommendation process after the system is already trained.

During preprocessing and training, several expert decisions concerning the type of knowledge representation have to be made and the adequate encoding technique. Feature Selection is the activity of deciding which features or attributes within the existing data schema contribute significantly to an ex-post prediction of the observed target sequence (observed variables in terms of statistics); that is, these features explain the target sequence and are called *predictor variables*. The node representation as defined in 3.2 is set up in a symbolic or rich way, which both call for different preprocessing and data encoding activities. In each case, the resulting work product Internally Represented Nodes represents the basis for Building the Training Set.

If no navigations can be captured beforehand, an initial training set (Input-Target Node Sequence Map) can be generated by the combination of text and association rule mining in order to enable a preliminary training of the system – as described in the appendix A.1.2.2.

If there is no content-based information, the symbolic representation is applied; that is, the payload of all nodes is null and only their name or identifier is taken into account. An example is a sequence of visited URLs, which represent meaningless but unique identifiers. In this case, observed navigations must be available to build the training set because there is no similarity measure between nodes to derive sequences of related nodes. Both symbolic and rich knowledge representation result in sequences of input and target nodes that make up the training set for supervised training.

The operative application of the system shown in the lower *swimlane* of figure 7.11 is triggered by the observation of a user navigation manifesting itself as a node sequence, which is transformed to a single input pattern for the neural network. The MRNN is fed with a sequence of preprocessed input vectors and predicts the most probable target sequence. The resulting work product is a list of recommended target nodes to be visited by the user. This recommendation requires a generalization of Level 3 (cf. section 3.1.1.2), since new nodes may be observed in the application phase.

7.5 Case Study: Web Navigation

In this section, we apply the connectionist recommendation technique described in the beginning of section 7.4 to a publicly available dataset of web page navigations based on representative log files. Figure 7.12 shows a prototypical user front-end for receiving recommendations and defining cohesive navigations according to the use cases of figure 7.8. After visiting a fixed but definable number of documents, the system computes a recommendation of an arbitrary number of related documents with decreasing relevancy estimates.

Microsoft logged web access data relating to its portal *www.microsoft.com* by sampling and processing the server log files, resulting in 32,700 user navigations on 329 different web pages [BHK98, WI01] involving different topics called *Vroots*. The data reflects the usage of the internet portal by 38,000 anonymous, randomly selected users. For each of these users, the set of all visited web pages within one week was stored as the user's navigation. In the terminology of the SYMBOCONN framework, such a navigation is a node sequence and the nodes represent Vroots. Unfortunately, the given web log data has two deficiencies:

CHAPTER 7. NAVIGATION RECOMMENDATION

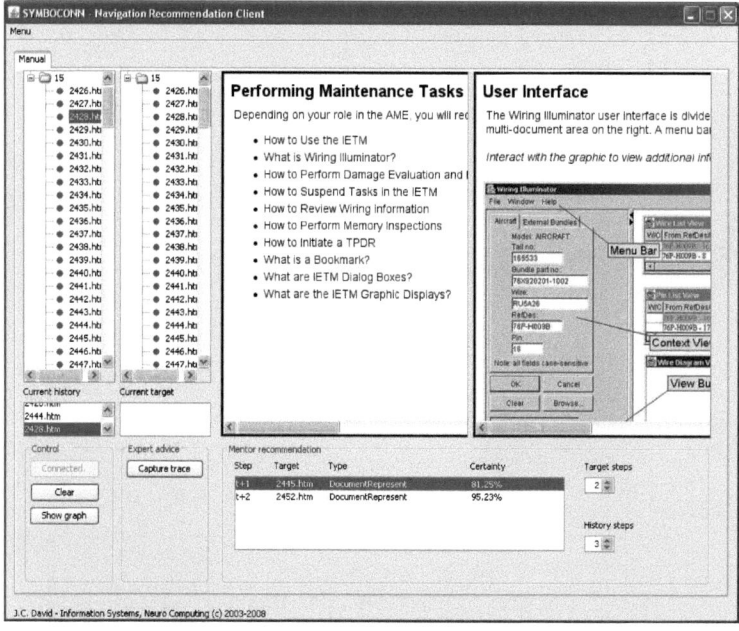

Figure 7.12: Prototypical user front-end of the SYMBOCONN framework for navigation recommendation. The two browser frames display the current page in the navigation history (2428.htm) and the recommended target page (2445.htm), respectively [Boe06]. In this case, two documentation pages with the titles "Performing Maintenance Tasks" and "User Interface" are in focus of the user – guided by the recommendation engine. The *Mentor recommendation* frame displays the recommended documents together with a degree of *Certainty*, which can be interpreted as a relevancy estimate. This snapshot shows the 2-step recommendation result (*Target steps* = 2) after having observed a 3-step navigation history (*History steps* = 3). The recommended objects of type DocumentRepresent are clickable and are thereupon shown in the right browser frame.

- The order of the web page visits within one user navigation is not apparent from the record-based dataset; thus, the navigations represent node sets instead of node sequences.

- Only the title of the visited web page (Vroot) is available, but not its actual content. This is reminiscent of collaborative filtering, where only the identities of the user and the visited node are considered, while the nodes' content is neglected.

Page titles like *"MS Office"* or *"Professional Developers Series"* are the *Vroots* of an access case and are considered as text units in terms of section 7.3 for constructing the vector space model. Table 7.2 and 7.3 show the schema of the captured web access data. The visited nodes are modeled as multi-represented objects with two

VrootID	Web Page Title	URL Suffix
1287	"International AutoRoute"	"/autoroute"
1215	"For Developers Only Info"	"/developer"
1083	"MS Access Support"	"/msaccesssupport"
1026	"Internet Site Construction for Developers"	"/sitebuilder"

Table 7.2: Excerpt of the web data used in this case study. The table shows the existent web page topics together with their relative address.

CaseID	VrootID	Number of Nodes
10127	{1081, 1082, 1040, 1001, 1018, 1083}	6
12879	{1026, 1041}	2
13999	{1008, 1020, 1003, 1018, 1004, 1215}	6
14000	{1008, 1027, 1123, 1007, 1026, 1172, 1004}	7

Table 7.3: Case-to-Vroot mapping concerning the observed navigations of 38,000 anonymous users. A single case consists of one ore more web page visits shown in the column *VrootID*.

textual attributes *Web Page Title* and *URL suffix*[6].

Evaluation An evaluation of the trained prediction model should substantiate the assumption that user preferences can be incorporated from the contents of the web pages logged in the navigation histories (content-based). Learning the preferences of other users as well (collaborative aspect) should result in a superior recommendation performance to that of learning only the navigations of a single user who is isolated from others. Secondly, we evaluate the introduced contextualized learning in direct comparison to the uncontextualized variant on the same test cases.

In addition to these two variants of recommendation, the two proposed knowledge representations are individually considered with regard to the input and output

---
[6]Type *Textual Feature* in definition 3.2.2.

space of the network, resulting in a total of six competing variants in scope of this evaluation. We compare the symbolic prediction model with the text mining based model. The web page access data is split up into an arbitrary training set of about 2,500 cases and a test set of 1,250 cases for evaluating the generalization capability of the SYMBOCONN framework. Since no visitation order is specified for the user navigations, the visited web pages are learned pair-wise with a fixed length three of the history and length one of the target sequence, respectively. The different training patterns resulting from a single navigation case (of one user) like $\{1081, 1082, 1040, 1001, 1002\}$ are given by the possible combinations of ordered input and target sequences with the predefined lengths.

Thus, the MRNN was trained on navigation sequences such as $(1081, 1082, 1040 \mapsto 1001)$ or $(1082, 1040, 1001 \mapsto 1002)$, where the integers in each sequence identify a single web page and their Vroots are represented using *latent semantic indexing*. After training the system up to a final training error in the range of $0.15\% \leq E \leq 1.0\%$, about 80% of the navigation sequences could be successfully recovered on average when using the learned history sequences[7].

In the ex-post evaluation, a set of visited nodes not used for training is presented to the network, where the associated target nodes are known for each user and are expected as navigation recommendation by the MRNN. A successful recommendation is given if a web page visit from the exemplary subset $H := \{1081, 1082, 1040\} \subset TC$ of a single test case, e.g. $TC := \{1081, 1082, 1040, 1001, 1018, 1083\}$, is presented and the network predicts one node of the complementary set $T := \{1001, 1018, 1083\}$. In general, one node $u \in H$ is presented and one node $v \in T = TC \setminus H$ of the target subset is expected as correct recommendation, which counts as a hit and is summed over all test cases[8].

Despite of the relatively short training sequences of 2.83 nodes on average (*min* 1, *max* 35), we use the MRNN as sequence predictor because of its approved generalization capability [Dav08c, Sch97], which reveals its effect when visiting unseen artifacts that were not part of the training sequences – at least in the case of content-based node representation. This is superior to association rule mining which is only able to discover association rules such as $(node_i, node_j \mapsto node_k)$, which can be used for a static recommendation of $node_k$, when the navigation history $(node_i, node_j)$ was observed. Due to the symbolic approach, no deviations from the history part of the discovered rule are allowed. As a consequence, adding a node with index h to the history, resulting in the sequence $(node_h, node_i, node_j)$, would not trigger the desired recommendation of $node_k$.

The recommendation accuracy was calculated by formula 7.13:

$$\frac{1}{n \cdot \sum_{i=1}^{n} |pred_i|} \sum_{i=1}^{n} \sum_{j=1}^{|pred_i|} (\mathcal{I}_{A_i}(pred_{i_j})), \quad A_i := \{target_{i_j}, 1 \leq j \leq m\}. \quad (7.13)$$

---

[7]We did not strive for a perfect training of all sequences in order to avoid overfitting [KAD01], which diminishes the generalization capability upon unseen entities.

[8]Wong et al. [WSP01] refer to H as the *problem* and to T as the *solution part* of a test case.

$pred_i = (pred_{i_1}, \ldots, pred_{i_m})$ is the sequence of predicted nodes based on the history of the ith test case and $\mathcal{I}_A(x)$ is an indicator function that returns 1 if x is in the set A, otherwise 0. The order of the prediction is not considered, which is in accordance with the set-based navigation cases.

The consideration of a broad basic population of navigations is crucial for the predictability of single user navigation operations, as assumed in the beginning of this section. To test this hypothesis, we first trained the system on the largest navigation case (*case ID* 40310) of the MS web log dataset only, which reflects the behavior of a single user by 35 page visits. Secondly, we used about 1,000 arbitrary training cases in order to resemble collaborative filtering. In both cases, the prediction accuracy was only measured on untrained patterns generated from the same case with the ID 40310. The result favors collaborative training: in the first case, not a single recommendation out of 12 test patterns is correct, since the few training examples (23) are not sufficient to assess this user's navigation behavior. In the second case, 12.5% of the presented test histories were exploited by the MRNN and led to correct recommendations, that is, the target parts of these test patterns were predicted properly. This result illustrates the impact of the collaborative aspect: Unobserved navigation operations of a single user can actually be assessed and continued by exploiting the behavior of a whole group of users[9].

Of course, this generalization was only possible due to the content-based training mode enhanced by LSI. For this case study, the vector space dimensionality could be reduced to only $d' = d - k = 253$ by $k = 41$ while keeping more than 99.98% of the variance in the training set (nearly lossless transform). An actual dimension reduction with information loss by $k > 41$ was not conducted, because any removal of further dimensions led to a significant downgrade of the prediction accuracy[10]. Unlike real documents, the web page titles do not offer a variety of meaningful keyterms that form a basis for document similarity, but are often arbitrary symbols like *"Windows Family of OSs"*, *"isapi"* or *"regwiz"* (registration wizard). This lack of content leaves further potential of the LSI method unused, which can, however, be exploited in other applications of the SYMBOCONN navigation recommendation.

In the context-free learning mode, navigation histories are not bound to specific users, but nevertheless representative for all users. As shown in table 7.4, the SYMBOCONN framework is able to deal with sequences of unseen web pages[11]. Without contextualization but with the support of the LSI representation for both input and output space, the best recommendation accuracy of 35.57% was achieved.

Thus the singular value decomposition of the term-document matrix succeeds in discovering the latent semantic concepts and optimizes the text representation. The highest prediction accuracy of all proposed methods was achieved when using

---

[9]The recommendation upon unseen nodes can be considered as a statistical inference – an out-of-sample prediction (see also chapter 8, page 237).

[10]The smallest kept singular value $\sigma_{253} = 0.205 \approx \frac{1}{36}\sigma_1$ was still significant, since keeping the corresponding feature space dimension improved the prediction accuracy.

[11]An unseen web page has never been presented to the neural network during training.

LSI without contextualization, as shown by table 7.4. The global LSI vector space model enables the MRNN to capture the latent concepts of the whole text base and thus leverages the best prediction results.

In contrast to context-free learning, the described contextualized learning still considers the textual content by latent semantic indexing; however, it additionally binds the user identity to a specific navigation history. The expected benefit of contextualized learning is that the machine learning engine also considers the individual users and tailors the recommendation according to their past behavior (content-based filtering). This extends the mere incorporation of mean user preferences based on an average of all users' interests (collaborative filtering).

Unfortunately, the precision on average suffers from the contextualization, as listed in table 7.4. The contextualized prediction based on LSI that considers the respective user is ranked second with 30.05% accuracy on average. Context-free recommendation works slightly better than the contextualized counterpart for all evaluated training configurations. We conjecture that the reason for this empirical fact is the lack of explicit information about user preferences (user profiles), since users are only represented by symbols.

Accuracy [%]	Rich Representation		Contextualized Learning
	Input	Output	
35.57	yes	yes	no
33.50	yes	yes	yes
28.99	yes	no	no
26.60	yes	no	yes
27.13	no	no	no
23.94	no	no	yes

Table 7.4: Prediction accuracy for the application of SYMBOCONN to the recommendation of *msn.com* web pages. The accuracy was determined using an arbitrary test set of 1,250 untrained web navigations with **histories of length three**. The column *Rich Representation* indicates whether the textual node descriptions were included in the training process – separately for the input and output space; that is, the nodes of the input and target sequences were either represented in the content-based way (yes) involving Latent Semantic Indexing (LSI) or in the symbolic way (no). The combination of symbolic input nodes and content-based target nodes is not reasonable and was therefore excluded from the evaluation. In the case of symbolic representation, the node names have been numerically represented by *unary encoding*. All evaluations are based on a hidden layer dimension of $h = 35$.

For recommendations based on symbolic node representation, the target nodes in all test sets could be inferred with an accuracy of 27.13% without contextualization and 23.94% in the case of contextualized learning. Thus, the simpler recommendation model, which is only built of sequences of node identifiers, is inferior to the content-based recommendation model that takes into account the textual content by latent semantic indexing. The performance advance of LSI of more than 8% is significant here, due to the low expressiveness of the web page titles that are not rich in content and thus prevent an even higher level of recommendation accuracy.

Surprisingly, the Microsoft dataset allowed for a higher prediction accuracy when shortening the navigation histories of the training examples to the length one, so that the prediction model becomes comparable to a Markov model of order one. This means that the prediction of the next node only depends on the previous node and not on the whole navigation history, which is known as *Markov property*:

$$\mathbb{P}(Y = o_{t+1}|X = x_t) = \mathbb{P}(Y = o_{t+1}|X_t = x_t, X_{t-1} = x_{t-1}, \ldots, X_{t-k} = x_{t-k}),$$

where o_{t+1} is the network prediction (see section 4.4.1), Y is a random variable standing for the correct node to be recommended and $X_t, \ldots, X_{t-k}$ represent the variables for the actually visited nodes, respectively. By contrary, in the case study at hand, the additional history nodes serving as content-based navigation context even corrupt the prediction accuracy. If o_{t+1} is the correct target node to be recommended, the longer history decreases the success probability:

$$\mathbb{P}(Y = o_{t+1}|X = x_t) > \mathbb{P}(Y = o_{t+1}|X_t = x_t, \ldots, X_{t-k} = x_{t-k}).$$

According to table 7.5, the target nodes of 1,250 test sets could be inferred with an accuracy of 50.00%, which is 14.43% higher than for histories consisting of three nodes. Hence, for the web log dataset, learning context-free navigations works better than considering longer navigation histories. This is empirical evidence that only

Accuracy [%]	Rich Representation	Contextualized Learning
50.00	yes	no
46.59	yes	yes
48.94	no	no
44.44	no	yes

Table 7.5: Prediction accuracy for the application of SYMBOCONN to the recommendation of *msn.com* web pages. The accuracy was determined using an arbitrary test set of 1,250 untrained web navigations with **histories of length one**. Similar to table 7.4, the column *Rich Representation* indicates whether textual node descriptions have been used. Since the best results were obtained before when representing both input and output space by the LSI-based text mining approach, the individual distinction between them has been omitted here. In the case of symbolic representation, the node names have been numerically represented by *unary encoding*. All evaluations are based on a hidden layer dimension of $h = 35$.

holds for the evaluated dataset and cannot be generalized. Otherwise, all navigation patterns with a history part $x_{t-k}, x_{t-k+1}, \ldots, x_t$ longer than one could be always cut off except for the last node x_t – loosing context-sensitivity with respect to the preceding nodes. Such a simplification obviously does not allow for a meaningful navigation recommendation.

Results From Other Recommendation Techniques   There are two comparable navigation recommendation approaches, namely *NavTracks* and *Intention Modeling for Web Navigation*.

The *NavTracks* approach keeps track of the navigation history of software developers by forming associations between related files, as described by Singer et al. [SES05]. Its symbolic algorithm is based on navigation events and constructs associations between visited nodes. In the case study conducted by Singer, the navigation patterns of three users performing their everyday software maintenance tasks were captured. The NAVTRACKS algorithm achieved an accuracy of 29% on average; that is, the next file was correctly recommended in 29% of the presented event streams, respectively.

The n-gram model approach from Sun and his colleagues is based on frequent substrings of the entire navigation path in order to predict further user navigation [SCWM02]. The last n node visits are considered by computing and maximizing products of conditional probabilities. In the best case, the provided performance amounts to about 37% based on a dataset of NASA web server logs (NASA Kennedy Space Center web server logs [SCWM02]). The specialty of this approach is the computation of the maximum probability of the entire navigation path. Like the SYMBOCONN framework, the n-gram model is not only capable of one-step predictions, but can even predict theoretically infinite sequences of hyperlinks, which is achieved by a global optimization. Sun and his colleagues consider this as an advantage, because the user is not misled to a local optimum due to the unconsidered remaining navigation space.

The performance[12] reached by the SYMBOCONN framework is, in the best case, both higher than the one of NAVTRACKS and of the n-gram recommendation conducted by Sun et al..

7.6 Conclusion

In this chapter, we introduced a recommendation engine based on the SYMBOCONN framework. This engine enables the learning of variably long node sequences on graph-based and domain-specific knowledge repositories. The navigation behavior of different users is modeled as a path through the graph that can be described by the rules of a formal grammar. The MRNN network is trained on navigation sequences in a supervised manner. Nodes that carry textual contents are provided with latent semantics by utilizing text mining methodologies, which extract the significant latent concepts from unstructured text.

The navigation recommendation system fulfills two main tasks. The first one is **Learning and Recovering of Navigation Sequences** on graph-based knowledge bases. Arbitrary navigations in form of node sequences can be learned by the SYMBOCONN framework. During the operational application of the trained MRNN, the

---

[12]In appendix A.1.2.1, a technical method for improving the prediction accuracy for prediction horizons of more than one target node is given.

incorporated target sequences are recovered and proactively recommended when a learned navigation history has been recognized.

The second task is the **Recommendation of Node Sequences According to the Users' Preferences**. Under consideration of the multiple node contents, the learned user preferences are exploited by the MRNN, which generalizes onto unseen navigation histories. We compared different knowledge representations for navigation recommendation based on the SYMBOCONN framework engine: Symbolic versus rich node representation and context-free versus contextualized learning.

To evaluate our approach, we conducted a case study based on Microsoft web log data. The most sophisticated model with text representation by latent semantic indexing (LSI) achieved the best prediction accuracy of 35.57% on a test set of 1,250 navigation patterns. A simpler model based on symbolic prediction provided a prediction accuracy of 27.13% at maximum. Thereby, each navigation pattern consisted of three history nodes and one target node.

The results for latent semantic recommendation are promising, since more than every third node that was recommended in the evaluation matched the users' interests for navigation histories of length three[13]. Surprisingly, the performance could be significantly increased to 50.00% when using shorter histories of length one, so that every second node was recommended properly.

---

[13] In light of the sparse content of the Microsoft dataset, the achieved performance on unseen web pages shows the generalization capability of the SYMBOCONN framework.

Chapter 8
Time Series Prediction

In this chapter, we demonstrate the applicability and power of the SYMBOCONN framework in the area of time series prediction. We show that the MRNN recommendation engine subsumes two statistical regression methods. In the first part from section 8.1 to 8.3, we present the basic theory of time series required to compare the connectionist engine of SYMBOCONN with established statistical prediction techniques.

In section 8.4 and 8.5, the framework is applied to non-symbolic but real-valued economical data, which mostly takes the form of time series. Time series are the basic representation used for predicting financial and economical data that varies over time. The field of time series prediction is considered to be of significant industrial relevance [Inv08]; it is, however, completely unrelated to the domains treated earlier and thus underpins the domain independence of the developed framework.

In general, forecasting generates an estimation of a future state of a time-dependent process using mathematical and non-mathematical methods. We use the term *prediction* for the forecast of a dependent variable based on one or many independent variables (*predictors*) using mathematical methods. A principal element of every prediction is an analysis of the past development of the variable of interest. To a certain extent, the predictors correlate with the dependent variable and their correlation in the past should enable a prediction of the dependent variable's future development. The past and present realizations of the predictors are known when computing the prediction.

In contrast to classification, the value space for the quantitative prediction of time series is usually continuous. If time series are afflicted with coincidence or uncertainty, they are commonly considered to be the representation of *stochastic processes* that follow certain probability distributions. The realizations of real-valued time series reflecting the underlying stochastic process are learned, and their future realizations are predicted by SYMBOCONN. The machine learning-based prediction is compared with a choice of statistical techniques such as autoregressive models or exponential smoothing.

Besides quantitative time series prediction, there are also decision problems which can be supported with a *qualitative trend prediction*. An example is the short-term decision problem of whether the stock price increases or decreases in the course of the next day [Sch89] – given the open-high-low-close data (OHLC) of the previous days. This task is formally equivalent to a binary classification, which can be solved by methods such as linear discriminant analysis [McL04] – stemming from the intersection of machine learning and statistics.

Another subject of time series analysis out of scope of this chapter are simulations of stochastic processes, which must not be misunderstood as predictions. As opposed to prediction, simulation tries to resemble a random process with its intrinsic characteristics most appropriately. Simulation is not meant for an extrapolation of the process beyond the observed period, which would represent a prediction of its future realizations (out-of-sample). In this chapter, we show that the generic machine learning functionality of SYMBOCONN can also be applied to the prediction[1] of time series.

There exists a strong correspondence between statistical methods for modeling time series and the modular recurrent neural network used as the framework engine. In section 8.4, we point out that the MRNN subsumes existing statistical methods for time series analysis and prediction, as indicated by figure 8.1. The RNN, a

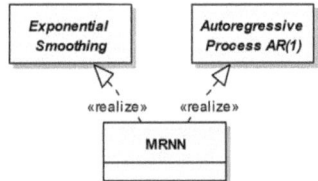

Figure 8.1: The abstract statistical techniques *Exponential Smoothing* and *Autoregression* of order one can be realized by the MRNN, due to its generic and recurrent composition.

predecessor of the MRNN, has already been used and evaluated in an industrial environment for a large telecommunication company in 2005. These results are presented in section 8.5.2. Furthermore, we conducted a direct comparison of the status quo MRNN framework engine with statistical methods on real-world time series from that company.

8.1 Stochastic Processes and Time Series

Before introducing the statistical and connectionist prediction of continuous variables, their structure must be formalized. The theory of stochastic processes is a discipline of probability theory, which elaborates on the structure and characteristics of random variables $\psi : \Omega \to \mathbb{R}$, such as continuity, differentiability, or measurability. These formal concepts are subject to a broad stochastic analysis, which

---

[1] *"Prediction is very difficult, especially if it's about the future."* - Niels Bohr.

CHAPTER 8. TIME SERIES PREDICTION

is based on *measurable mappings* (such as random variables) on probability spaces $(\Omega, \mathcal{F}, \mathbb{P})$, where Ω is an event space, $\mathcal{F}$ is a sigma algebra, and $\mathbb{P}$ is a probability measure.

In contrast to this, time series analysis and prediction is considered as a statistical discipline, which uses the same model for time series as is used for stochastic processes. However, time series prediction focuses on practical modeling of time series in order to simulate the underlying process or to predict their future realizations[2]. This data-driven approach tries to fit time series models to given, temporally ordered feature vectors in order to predict their future development. Only the latter area is in the scope of this chapter, in which the MRNN is used to model and to predict time series as an alternative to traditional statistical methods.

Definition 8.1.1: Stochastic Process
A stochastic process Z is a family of time-dependent random variables[3] on an event space Ω into a state space S: $Z(t) : \Omega \to S, t \in T$:

$$Z = \{Z(t),\ t \in T\}$$

A stochastic process can be seen as a function of two variables, $Z_t(\omega) := Z(\omega, t)$, $\omega \in \Omega$. In many cases, the state space S is identified with the continuum $\mathbb{R}$.

There are continuous and discrete stochastic processes, so that the corresponding timeline is either $T = (-\infty, \infty)$ or $T = \mathbb{Z} = \{\ldots, -2, -1, 0, 1, 2, \ldots\}$.

Definition 8.1.2: Time Series
A time series $\{X(t)\}_{t \in T}$ can be decomposed into a *trend component* $m(t)$, a *periodic component* (seasonal) $s(t)$, and a *stochastic component* $Y(t)$, which is often given by *white noise* (see Def. 8.2.4, [Pru05]).

$$X(t) = m(t) + s(t) + Y(t),\ t \in T$$

These components may be instantiated several times for a single process; for example, if two seasonal effects – a short term and a long term one – are observed. Thus, a time series is modeled as an additive superimposition of statistical sub-processes[4].

This generic decomposition can be applied to all types of time series and is visualized in figure 8.2. We give an example for a time series model from the field of financial mathematics.

Example 8.1.1: Simplified Stock Price $X(t)$

$$X(t) = X(0) \cdot e^{(b \cdot t)} \tag{8.1}$$

---

[2] The observations or measurements of a stochastic process.
[3] More formally, Z is defined on a measure space $(\Omega, \mathcal{F}, \mu)$ with values in a measurable space $(S, \mathcal{F}')$. It is claimed that $Z_t : \omega \to Z_t(\omega)$ is $\mathcal{F}$-$\mathcal{F}'$-measurable for all $t \in T$.
[4] In case of absence of one or several components, these are formally represented by the constant null-function $f_0(t) = 0,\ \forall t$.

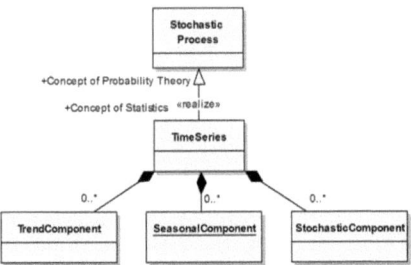

Figure 8.2: Decomposition of a time series into a trend component, a seasonal component, and a stochastic component.

$$\log X(t) = \log x_0 + (b \cdot t) + Y(t), \quad (X(0) := x_0) \quad (8.2)$$
$$Y(t) := \log X(t) - (\log x_0 + b \cdot t), \quad (8.3)$$

where b is the constant trend, $X(0)$ is the initial value and $Y(t)$ is the stochastic component. $Y(t)$ represents the stochastic deviation of the stock price from the predisposed development given by the trend component $e^{(b \cdot t)}$. Equation 8.1 is logarithmized to the log-linear equation 8.2, since the following requirements on the distribution of the stochastic component should be met:

$$Y(t) \sim \mathcal{N}(0, \sigma^2 t) \quad (8.4)$$
$$Y(t) - Y(s) \sim \mathcal{N}(0, \sigma^2(t-s)), \quad \forall s, t, \ s < t \quad (8.5)$$

The stochastic component of the log-linear model is normally distributed with time-dependent variance $\sigma^2(t)$. Moreover, formula 8.5 states that increments of the stochastic component are variance-stationary (see section 8.2).

The goal of time series prediction is to construct *unbiased estimators* for the future realizations $y_{t+1}, y_{t+2}, \ldots$ of a time series Y, whose past realizations $y_0, \ldots, y_t$ are known. The bias of an estimator represents its systematic error, meaning the deviation from the actual process parameter $\theta \in \Theta \subset \mathbb{R}^n$. Unbiased signifies that the expectancy of the estimator equals the true parameter value, at least when the size of the data sample approaches infinity (asymptotically unbiased). The entire risk of an erroneous prediction should be minimized, which is equivalent to minimizing the mean error squares $\widehat{MSE} = \frac{1}{n} \sum (\hat{y}_i - y_i)^2$ of the prediction deviations. $\widehat{MSE}$ is the estimator for the mean squared error MSE, which is defined as follows.

Definition 8.1.3: Mean Squared Error (MSE), Bias
The mean squared error of an estimator $\hat{\theta}$ with respect to the actual process param-

eter θ, which is to be estimated, is defined as

$$MSE_\theta(\hat{\theta}) := \mathbb{E}((\hat{\theta} - \theta)^2)$$
$$= Var(\hat{\theta}) + Bias(\hat{\theta}, \theta)^2$$

$$Bias(\hat{\theta}, \theta) := \mathbb{E}(\hat{\theta}) - \theta$$

The process parameter $\theta = (\theta_1, \ldots, \theta_n) \in \Theta$ stems from a multi-dimensional parameter space Θ, since a stochastic process is determined by a whole set of unary parameters in general.

In the case of time series, θ determines the usually unknown stochastic process $Y(\theta)$, which generates the time series $y_0, \ldots, y_t$. As opposed to the variance $Var(\hat{\theta})$ of the estimator $\hat{\theta}$, the bias is the degree of systematic error in the estimation process[5].

The goal of most statistical methods is not to generate accurate predictions for each single point in time (point predictions), since this is not possible for non-deterministic processes in general. Such a proceeding always implies risking a higher mean squared error for the predicted period.

The higher the variance $Var[Y(t)]$ of the underlying random process $Y(t)$, the higher the risk $\int_T (\hat{Y}(t) - Y(t))^2 dt$ of a misclassification or misprediction[6]. The formal properties of the variance of stochastic processes, which are important for building an appropriate prediction model, are discussed in the next section.

8.2 Covariance and Stationarity

Covariance and autocovariance are central characteristics of stochastic processes in general, but are especially important for the analysis of time series. The autocovariance function is often used to determine periodicities or the signal-to-noise ratio of time series. Furthermore, the validity of a prediction model can be examined by analyzing its residuals with respect to their autocorrelation, which is the normalized autocovariance.

Definition 8.2.1: Covariance Function

The covariance of two random variables X and Y is defined as

$$Cov(X, Y) = \mathbb{E}[(X - \mathbb{E}[X])(Y - \mathbb{E}[Y])]$$

This definition requires X and Y to be quadratically integrable, meaning that both $\mathbb{E}[X^2]$ and $\mathbb{E}[Y^2]$ must exist, that is, $\mathbb{E}[X^2] < \infty$ and $\mathbb{E}[Y^2] < \infty$.

---

[5] A bias can be caused by a random error ϵ_t with an expected value of $\mathbb{E}[\epsilon_t] \neq 0$, which distorts the realizations of the dependent variables.

[6] In the continuous case.

Definition 8.2.2: Stationarity
A stochastic process which has the same expected value and the same variance at all points in time $t \in T$ is called *stationary*. Covariance-stationarity is given if there is a unary function $r(.)$, so that holds:

$$\begin{aligned} Cov(X(s), X(t)) &= r(|s-t|),\ s, t \in T \\ R(h) &:= Cov(X(s), X(s+h)),\ \forall s \in T \end{aligned} \quad (8.6)$$

If stationarity is given, the prior unknown unary function r can be identified with the covariance $R(h)$ for the *time lag* h; thus, the second variable t of the covariance function can be omitted. In the case of stationarity, the covariance only depends on the absolute difference $|s - t| = h$ of the two points of time s and t, which is called time lag. Therefore, the dependency of $X(s)$ and $X(t)$, $h = |t - s|$ is equal for all realizations of the random variable X with the same time lag h.

Stationarity is one of the most important properties of time-indexed processes which enables to transform a time series $X(t)$ to a new *centered* time series $X(t) - \mathbb{E}[X(t)]$ with $\mathbb{E}[X(t) - \mathbb{E}[X(t)]] = 0$. Many economic time series are not stationary, but most statistical methods assume stationarity as a precondition for their applicability. Two non-stationary time series may seem to strongly correlate, relying on a first analysis using the squared correlation coefficient R^2, due to a common linear trend. After removing the linear trend by a 1-fold differentiation, the two time series may not be correlated any longer. This effect is called *spurious regression* (see also [Has03]). Building statistical prediction models upon non-stationary time series can be misleading, since the generated predictions are often distorted.

In the following, we define the autocovariance and declare its properties, which are applied to the case study in section 8.5.1 to analyze the provided real-world time series.

Definition 8.2.3: Autocovariance Function R

$$\begin{aligned} R(s,t) &:= \mathbb{E}[(X(s) - \mu)(X(t) - \mu)] & (8.7) \\ R(h) &\stackrel{8.6}{=} \mathbb{E}[(X(t) - \mu)(X(t+h) - \mu)],\quad s,t \in T & (8.8) \end{aligned}$$

where $\mu = \mathbb{E}[X(t)]$. $R(h)$ determines the covariance in the case of a stationary time series $X(t)$, otherwise $R(s,t)$ has to be applied. The autocovariance function $R(h)$ has the following properties:

Property 8.2.1: Autocovariance

$$\begin{aligned} Var[X(t)] &= R(0) & (8.9) \\ R(-t) &= R(t) & (8.10) \\ |R(t)| &\leq R(0),\ \forall t \in T & (8.11) \end{aligned}$$

The *Cauchy-Schwarz's inequality* $Cov(X,Y) \leq \sqrt{Var(X) \cdot Var(Y)}$ is used to prove equation 8.11, the remaining properties being trivial.

CHAPTER 8. TIME SERIES PREDICTION

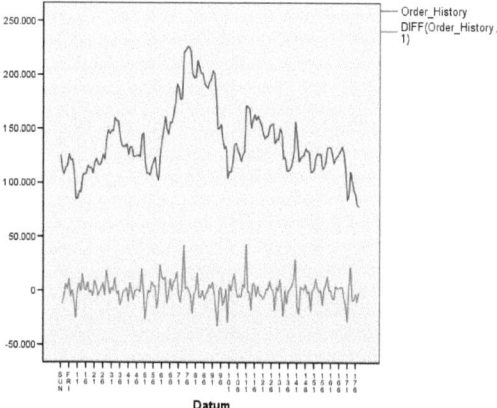

Figure 8.3: Non-stationary time series (top) of the incoming orders concerning an industrial product together with its stationary pendant (bottom) for a period of 180 days. Empirical stationarity with respect to the expectation was achieved by computing the difference of first order of the original time series by computing $X'(t) = X(t) - X(t-1)$, $t \in T$.

Proof 8.2.1: (Equation 8.11)

$$|R(t)| = |Cov(X(s), X(s+t))| \leq \left|\sqrt{Var(X(s)) \cdot Var(X(s+t)))}\right| \\ \stackrel{*}{=} |Var(X(s))| = R(0) \quad (8.12)$$

(*): A shift of the random variable by t does not change the variance.

Definition 8.2.4: White Noise
White noise is the classical example of a stationary stochastic process.

$$Y = \{Y(t),\ t \in T\},\ Y(t)\ independent,\ \mathbb{E}[Y(t)] = 0.$$

White noise is an elementary model for the construction of further types of time series, which itself is stationary and centered with the covariance function $R(0) = \sigma^2$ and $R(t) = 0$, $\forall t \neq 0$.

8.3 Statistical Models for Time Series

In practice, the process that generates a time series is mostly unknown and only some of its realizations are available for analysis. Often one has to assume that a selected sample of these realizations is representative for predicting the future development of the time series.

The development of a dependent variable Y (target variable, variable of interest) can be predicted using one or several explaining predictor variables. For an accurate prediction, the predictor variables and the dependent variable have to be significantly correlated in the observed past. The degree of correlation can be determined by the *correlation coefficient* ρ by Pearson

$$\rho(X,Y) = \frac{\mathbb{E}[(X - \mathbb{E}[X])(Y - \mathbb{E}[Y])]}{\sigma_X \sigma_Y} = \frac{Cov(X,Y)}{\sigma_X \sigma_Y} \in [-1,1], \quad (8.13)$$

where $\sigma_X = \sqrt{Var[X]}$ is the standard deviation of the variable X. For two concrete realizations $\vec{x}$ and $\vec{y}$, the correlation coefficient $\rho(X,Y)$ can be determined by the estimator $r_{\vec{x},\vec{y}} = \hat{\rho}(X,Y) = \frac{\sum(x_i - \mu_x)(y_i - \mu_y)}{(n-1)s_x s_y}$, where s_x and s_y are the estimators for the standard deviations. To determine the correlation of two time series $X(t)$ and $Y(t)$, the cross-correlation $\rho(X(t), Y(t+h))$ is computed for the time shifts $h = -k, \ldots, -1, 0, 1, \ldots, k$ (cf. Def. 5.2.2).

The development of a time series can also be predicted based solely on itself and without any predictor variables, which we call *endogenous prediction*. This method can be used if predictor variables $X_1, \ldots, X_n$ are not or only partially available, if they are assessed to be unreliable, or if their correlation with the dependent variable $Cov(X_i, Y) < \tau$, $i = 1, \ldots, n$ is below some threshold τ and thus too marginal. Then, the future development of the time series can only be explained by its own history as done by exponential smoothing.

Regression Regression is a statistical analysis mechanism that aims at actually discovering the correlation between a dependent variable $Y = (Y_1, \ldots, Y_n) \in \mathbb{R}^n$ (multivariate case), which is typically metric, and a multi-dimensional variable $X = (X_1, \ldots, X_m)$, whose components X_i, $i = 1, \ldots, m$ are stochastically independent. In a deterministic setting, the predictors $X_1, \ldots, X_n$ are instead assumed to be linearly independent[7].

There are several linear and nonlinear regression models which can be used to model the realizations of a time series $\{Y(t) \mid t \in T\}$. The purpose of regression models $m_{\vec{\beta}}$ is to explain the dependency between the predictors and the realizations $Y(t)$ of the time series, so that the mean squared error $\frac{1}{|I|}\sum_{t \in I}(Y(t) - m_{\vec{\beta}}(X,t))^2$, $I \subset T$ is possibly minimized. Therefore, the regression coefficient $\vec{\beta} \in \mathbb{R}^k$, $k \in \mathbb{N}$ has to be determined, which can be achieved by computing the null of the first derivation of the MSE. In the case of time series prediction, the realizations can be split into a known history part $Y(0), Y(1), \ldots, Y(t_0)$ and a future part, $Y(t_0 + 1), Y(t_0 + 2), \ldots, Y(t_0 + \gamma)$, which is to be predicted by the regression model. The constant γ is called the *forecast horizon* [BFO02].

---

[7]It must not be possible to express any predictor as a linear combination of the others.

CHAPTER 8. TIME SERIES PREDICTION

Linear Regression Models (LRM) There are deterministic and stochastic regression models that can be solved linearly. We give an example of a deterministic linear regression model which is only dependent on the time, but not on any further independent variables X_i, $i = 1, \ldots, m$.

Example 8.3.1: Polynomial Trend
A polynomial regression model is linear with respect to the coefficients β_i, which have to be determined in order to fit the polynomial of the variable t to the time series.

$$m_\beta(t) = \sum_{i=1}^{k} \beta_i t^{i-1}, \ t \in T \tag{8.14}$$

Polynomial regression should be performed hierarchically, in such a way that each increment in the power of the time variable is only accepted as a new model if the new one significantly improves the fit to the observations measured by the MSE. Usually, the predictors $t^0, t^1, t^2, \ldots$ are highly correlated to each other, hence their coefficients β_i must not be assumed to be linearly independent.

Polynomials are often not flexible enough to capture the trend of certain classes of phenomena, as shown by the following example. The order history of an industrial product and two regression models are drawn in the same chart in figure 8.4.

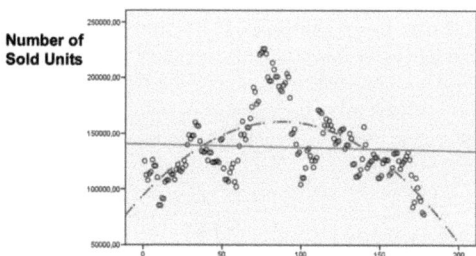

Figure 8.4: Scatter plot of the number of sold units of an industrial product indexed by time on a day-scale. The two polynomials of degree one (green, solid) and two (blue, dashed) overlayed onto the scattered points are both incapable of explaining the whole variance of the given realizations of the underlying stochastic process.

Nonlinear Regression Models (NRM) Although many scientific and engineering processes can be described well with the use of linear models, there are many other processes which are inherently nonlinear. An example of these are autoregressive processes that exponentially propagate the regression parameter α, which determines the influence of the past.

Nonlinear regression must not be misunderstood as a regression model such as $Y = \alpha + \beta_1 \cdot X + \beta_2 \cdot X^2 + \beta_3 \cdot X^3$, which is only nonlinear in the dependent variable X. Such a model can be analytically solved by a transformation into a multiple linear regression problem $Y_{mult} = \alpha + \beta_1 \cdot X_1 + \beta_2 \cdot X_2 + \beta_3 \cdot X_3$ with the new variables $X_1 := X$, $X_2 := X^2$ and $X_3 := X^3$. Actual nonlinear regression models are nonlinear in their parameters and are therefore difficult to solve; their solution has to be computed by numerical optimization algorithms. The following generic model of a nonlinear random process can be taken as a foundation for all nonlinear regression models.

Definition 8.3.1: Nonlinear Random Process

$$X(t) = m(t) + \epsilon(t), \quad t \in T, \, m(.) \in M$$
$$M = \{m_\gamma(t), \, t \in T, \gamma \in \Gamma\}$$

M is called model space and Γ represents the parameter space. The regression function $m_\gamma(t)$ depends *nonlinearly* on the regression coefficient γ. Alternatively, the notation $m(\gamma, t)$ is used, since the function is differentiated with respect to γ during the parameter estimation, based on given observations.

Both classes of regression, linear and nonlinear, are used to determine the parameters of the respective time series model. Of all statistical techniques, nonlinear regression models are most similar to the connectionist way of time series processing, which also uses a nonlinear relationship between the parameters, the independent variables (input data), and the dependent variables (target data). In the following, we present established models for stochastic processes used also for time series. Given the realizations of such a process, these models can be *fitted* to the data by linear regression. After this parameter estimation, they can be used for the prediction of future realizations.

8.3.1 Moving Average Process (MA)

A moving average process is the result of a white noise process by a *filtration*, that is, the MA-process is obtained by a linear combination of a sequence of white noise realizations with filter weights $(b_j)_{j \in T} \in \mathbb{R}$.

Definition 8.3.2: MA-process of order q (MA(q))

$$X(t) = Y(t) + \sum_{j=1}^{q} b_j Y(t-j), \, t \in T$$

Moving average processes are often used as smoothing models in the financial sector, since they can, for example, represent smoothed series of stock prices. The development of commercial papers is often described by several moving average views, e.g. MA(38), MA(200) – indexed by days [Dek08].

CHAPTER 8. TIME SERIES PREDICTION

The MA(q)-process is stationary with expectation $\mathbb{E}[X(t)] = 0$, since it is defined as a linear combination of white noise. If the white noise components $Y(t\text{-}q)$, $Y(t\text{-}q\text{+}1)$, ..., $Y(t\text{-}1)$ are seen as external shocks, then they take $1 \leq i \leq q$ time steps to fade away.

Figure 8.5 and 8.6 show how an MA(5)-process is generated from white noise.

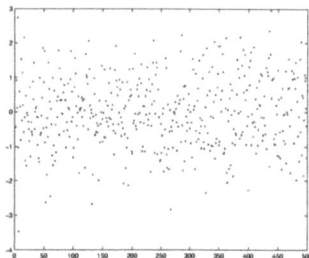 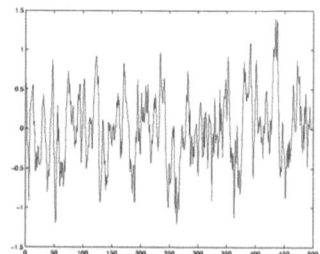

Figure 8.5: 500 realizations of white noise $Y(t)$ that spread around the expected value $\mathbb{E}[Y(t)] = 0$.

Figure 8.6: MA(5)-process of white noise $Y(t)$ corresponding to figure 8.5 with identical weights b_j, $\forall j = 1, \ldots, 5$.

8.3.2 Autoregressive Process (AR)

An *autoregressive process* at time t is defined as the sum of its p preceding values plus a stochastic component $Y(t)$. In contrast to moving average processes, an AR process is deterministically dependent on its own history, which implies that earlier (white) noise terms $Y(t - k)$, $k > 0$, are reproduced in the present.

Definition 8.3.3: AR-process of order p (AR(p))

$$X(t) = \sum_{j=1}^{p} a_j X(t-j) + Y(t),\ t \in T$$

8.3.3 ARMA Process

The *Autoregressive Moving Average* (ARMA) process is the sum of an auto regressive component and a moving average component.

Definition 8.3.4: ARMA-process of order p, q (ARMA(p, q))

$$X(t) = \sum_{j=1}^{p} a_j X(t-j) + Y(t) + \sum_{j=1}^{q} b_j Y(t-j),\ t \in T$$

The ARMA model is frequently used for the purpose of modeling economical and financial time series, and as a foundation for their prediction. If the time series to be modeled is not stationary or shows non-seasonal trends, then ARIMA models that perform an additional differentiation of order i of the non-stationary time series[8] should be used. After differentiation, the time series can be explained by an usual ARMA(p, q) model, which is combined to an ARIMA(p, i, q) model.

Concrete ARMA models are estimated by nonlinear regression, that is, the appropriate coefficients a_i and b_j, $i = 1, \ldots, p$, $j = 1, \ldots, q$, are determined by numerical optimization algorithms.

8.3.4 Exponential Smoothing

An important extrapolation method stemming from time series prediction is *exponential smoothing*, which is used when the respective time series does not show any systematics that could be directly modeled, but rather behaves chaotically. Such systematics may be a linear trend or a seasonal component, for example. The future realizations of a time series are predicted using its past values, assuming that there is an auto-dependency[9]. Exponential smoothing is an endogenous technique, because the time series Y is continued with no means of external predictors X explaining its behavior due to their correlation $\rho(X, Y)$ with Y. Given a time series $x_0, x_1, \ldots, x_t$, the exponential smoothing technique is defined as follows:

$$x_t^* := \alpha x_t + (1-\alpha) x_{t-1}^* \qquad (8.15)$$

$$= \alpha \sum_{i=0}^{t-1} (1-\alpha)^i x_{t-i} + (1-\alpha)^t x_0, \quad 0 \leq \alpha \leq 1. \qquad (8.16)$$

x_0^* is the arbitrarily definable starting value of the smoothed time series at the fixed point of time $t = 0$ that is normally chosen as the first observed value, $x_0^* := x_0$. By unfolding the recursion, as done by equation 8.16, the smoothed value x_t^* is computed. The smoothing factor α determines the impact of the past values; for $\alpha = 1$, no smoothing is done and the predicted value equals the currently observed value. This appears to be reasonable: if no information about the process systematics is available, the best prediction of the future realization x_{t+1} is the present observation.

The factor α can be fixed in advance, e.g. $0.2 \leq \alpha \leq 0.3$, or it is determined by an additional optimization process with respect to the estimation $\widehat{MSE} = \frac{1}{t}\sum_{i=0}^{t-1}(x_i^* - x_i)^2$, $t > 0$, of the mean squared error of the smoothed past values and the actual past values. The first prediction of the unknown value x_{t+1} is provided by the smoothed value x_t^*, which is computed based on the last available observation x_t. In order to extend the forecast horizon to more than one step, the predicted value is taken as a new observation by setting $x_{t+1} := x_t^*$; subsequently, formula 8.18 is applied again.

---

[8]See also section 8.5.1 for a practical example of differentiation.
[9]A random walk process, for example, does not fulfill this assumption.

Exponential smoothing has already been used for warehousing and demand planning [Bec03]. The swiss army, for example, applied this method for the prediction of the number of required rifles in the subsequent year, based on the development of the previous years.

There are further time series models from econometrics that are relevant for the prediction of financial derivatives, for example, which are not detailed in this chapter. ARCH (Autoregressive Conditional Heteroscedasticity) and GARCH (Generalized ARCH) are linear models [HAM05] which address the problem of time-variant process variance $\sigma^2(t)$, meaning that the variance changes over time. This *heteroscedasticity* often applies to financial derivatives and their underlyings. Besides statistical methods, neural networks are also able to model time series with conditional variance [SDD99]. In the following section, we especially apply the machine learning engine of SYMBOCONN to the prediction of time series – also to those showing heteroscedastic developments.

8.4 Neural Networks Applied to Time Series Prediction

Both connectionist and statistical methods can be used for business forecasting, and especially for time series prediction. The connectionist approach to time series prediction is similar to the statistical approach, because the series of past values is considered as a noisy signal which can be cleaned and continued into the future [Kra91] by a neural network. During the training phase, the structure of the underlying stochastic process is either learned by means of exogenous predictors (regressors) that correlate with the dependent variable, or by the endogenous dynamics of the process itself. During neural information processing, a cleaning of the signal from its noise portions is performed, partially or fully masking out the noisy and redundant information by inhibitory network weights.

Correlations among different random variables, which cannot be discovered by humans due to their multi-dimensional character or the vast amount of given realizations, should be exploited by our connectionist learning algorithm. In this chapter, we only focus on *out-of-sample* predictions, meaning that all information used to generate a prediction at time t must be available until that point of time – no future information may be assumed or used to build the prediction model [CW05].

Multilayer Perceptron (MLP) The *Multilayer Perceptron* has already been successfully applied to the prediction of business figures. Its rigid topology demands for a *moving time window* approach in order to process time series of variable length. The diagram in figure 8.7 illustrates the time series capturing process by a moving time window that operates on the known history and pseudo-future data providing the target values for training. In order to enable a plausible prediction of the time series' future values, the network must be trained with representative data over a long time range, compared to the prediction horizon to be forecasted.

250 CHAPTER 8. TIME SERIES PREDICTION

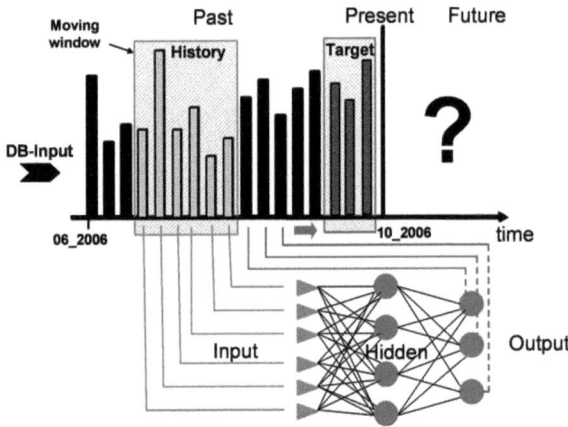

Figure 8.7: Schematic mapping of a time series to the input and target part of a training pattern for the Multilayer Perceptron. The topology is chosen for a prediction horizon of three steps based on a moving time window of 6 time steps.

The feed-forward architecture of the MLP without recurrent connections does not allow to directly represent a time line as given by the hidden state layer of the MRNN. In particular, an MLP does not implement a dynamic system as defined in section 4.4 (see Def. 4.4.1). The temporal relation between the history and target periods of a time series neither becomes manifest in the network topology of the MLP nor in its output computation. Also the time lag between the last index of the input sequence and the first index of the target sequence may be arbitrarily defined to be more than one time step.

Modular Recurrent Neural Network When applying the MRNN to time series prediction, the entities to be processed are time-indexed numerical vectors. The notion of *node sequences* from section 3.2, while still being valid, is nonessential here, because no symbolic data has to be transformed to a content-based feature vector representation. Instead, the vectors are directly given as multi-dimensional time series $\vec{x}_{t-k}, \ldots, \vec{x}_t$. The control flow of connectionist time series prediction, which is structurally similar to that used for navigation recommendation, is depicted by figure 8.8. Again, the machine learning process is split into a training and an operative application phase.

CHAPTER 8. TIME SERIES PREDICTION

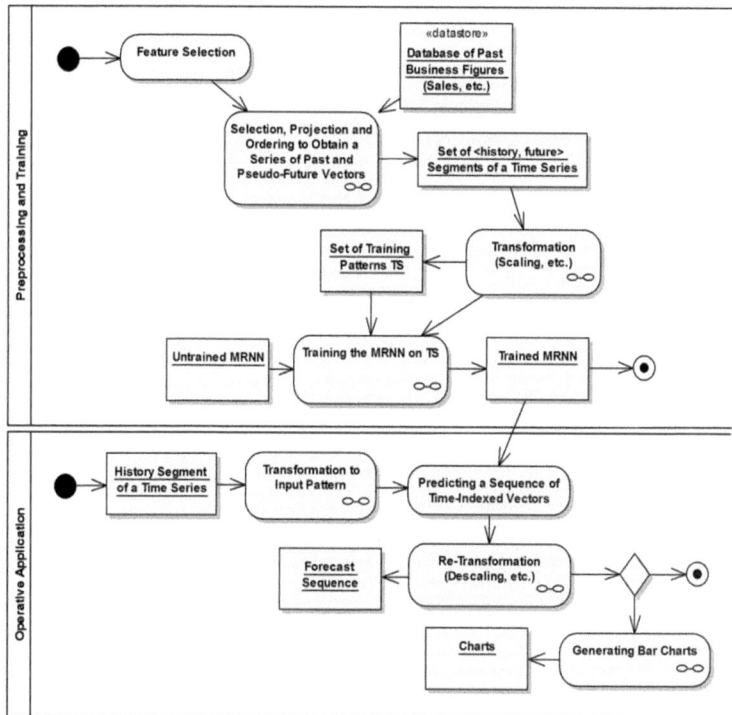

Figure 8.8: Activity diagram illustrating the entire forecast process from training to prediction of a time series' future period.

8.4.1 MRNN Implementing Exponential Smoothing (ES)

Least squares methods typically use the mean squared error of the estimations x_t^*, $x_{t+1}^*, \ldots$ as objective function for computing a prediction model. Since the modular recurrent neural network has a flexible architecture and is based on a variant of the least squares method, it can be used to learn the parameter α from the given realizations of a time series. Therefore, the weight matrix B is degenerated to a scalar by setting $B := (1 - \alpha) \in \mathbb{R}^{1 \times 1}$, while the remaining matrices A and C are fixed to their arbitrary initialization. The instantiation of the MRNN to implement exponential smoothing is given in figure 8.9, which illustrates the required configuration and topology of the recurrent network.

The MRNN directly computes the exponential smoothing of the given time series $(x_t)_{t \in \mathbb{N}}$ without learning from a set of examples, which would require many realizations of the underlying random process $X(\theta)$ – as was the case for the other applications in this dissertation. Here, the training phase is used for optimizing the smoothing factor α, because the actual smoothing function does not have to be learned, but is given by the recurrent equation 8.18 beneath. The MRNN actually implements the exponential smoothing method when configured according to the following setup[10]: $A := \alpha$, $B := (1 - \alpha)$, $C := I$.

$$s_0 := 1 \cdot x_0 \qquad (8.17)$$

$$\begin{aligned} s_t &:= \alpha \cdot x_t + (1 - \alpha) s_{t-1} \\ &= A x_t + id(B s_{t-1}) \end{aligned} \qquad (8.18)$$

$$\tau_i := 0, \quad i = 0, \ldots, t \qquad (8.19)$$

$$f_B := id_\mathbb{R}^\mathbb{R} \qquad (8.20)$$

$$f_{C,\alpha} := f(s_{t-1}, X_t) \stackrel{C=I}{=} (I s_{t-1} - x_t)^2 \qquad (8.21)$$

Since the state s_{t-1}, which is interpreted as the estimation x_t^* of x_t, depends on the current value of α, the activation function $f_{C,\alpha}$ also depends on α. This activation function in the output layer of the network plays the role of the error function $\widehat{MSE}$ defined above, which is minimized by setting the training targets τ_i to zero. The weight scalars A and $B = 1 - A$ are linked in this setting, which additionally constrains the possible weight space of the MRNN, besides the fixed assignment of the output matrix to the identity matrix by $C := I$.

When the parameter α is adapted during the training phase, the current output $o_t = (s_{t-1} - x_t)^2$ of f_C changes. For $i = 0, \ldots, t$ the outputs o_i are minimized such that $o_i \xrightarrow{n \to \infty} \tau_i := 0$. The reason that the ES-process is called exponential is the

---

[10] I represents the identity matrix.

CHAPTER 8. TIME SERIES PREDICTION

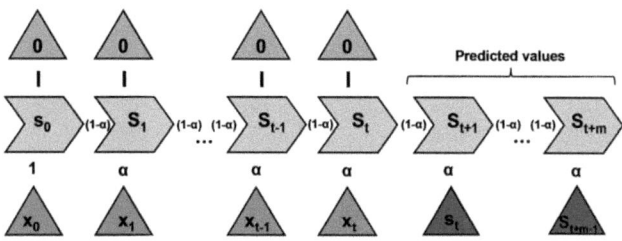

Figure 8.9: Topology and weight configuration of the modular recurrent neural network (MRNN) to implement the exponential smoothing method from statistics. The predicted values $s_{t+1}, \ldots, s_{t+m}$ are computed without external inputs x_t or targets τ_t. For $t+1$, $t+2$, ..., the external inputs are substituted by the respectively predicted (smoothed) values for these future time steps.

decay in the contribution of its past values, which is exponential:

$$s_t = \alpha \cdot x_t + (1-\alpha)(\alpha \cdot x_{t-1} + (1-\alpha)s_{t-2})$$
$$= \alpha[x_t + (1-\alpha)x_{t-1} + (1-\alpha)^2 x_{t-2} + (1-\alpha)^3 x_{t-3} + \ldots] + (1-\alpha)^t x_0$$

For $(1-\alpha) < 1$, the influence of the past exponentially decreases in t, which clarifies the notion of an *exponentially weighted moving average*. The constraint $B := (1-\alpha) < 1$ is not mandatory for a time series modeled by the MRNN, since in general, the weight scalar $B \in \mathbb{R}^{1 \times 1}$ or the norm $\max\{\frac{\|Bv\|}{\|v\|}, Bv \in \mathbb{R}^m, \mathbb{R}^n \ni v \neq 0\}$ of the weight matrix $B \in \mathbb{R}^{m \times n}$ may be bigger than one, respectively.

Overall, the MRNN is more powerful than the classical exponential smoothing method, since it completely subsumes the ES-process and furthermore automatically optimizes the required parameter α, a feature which is not provided by the original method.

8.4.2 Connectionist Implementation of Autoregressive Processes

In addition to exponential smoothing as a prediction technique, the MRNN can also be set up to model an *Autoregressive Process* $AR(1)$ of order one, which was defined in section 8.3.2.

$$\begin{aligned} s_t &:= a \cdot s_{t-1} + \epsilon_t \\ &\stackrel{MRNN}{=} B \cdot s_{t-1} + x_t \end{aligned} \qquad (8.22)$$

The optional second summand stems from a white noise process $(\epsilon_t)_{t \in \mathbb{N}}$ with stationary expectation and variance (see section 8.2, Def. 8.2.4), which can be fed into the network as external input at time t. Normally, ϵ_t is an interference component contained in the observations as an extrinsic noise portion that is not part of the actual random process to be modeled. In this case, no realizations of white noise would be fed into the network as external input $(x_t)_{t \in \mathbb{N}}$, but the input would be set to zero ($x_t := 0$). In this configuration, the recurrent network directly resembles an autoregressive process of order 1.

To model AR processes of a higher order, we use the multi-layer perceptron (MLP) of the SYMBOCONN framework, which allows for having different weights to implicitly model time-dependent processes. Figure 8.10 shows a moving time window approach based on a 2-layered feed-forward network. The number of input units corresponds to the length of the time window, which in turn equals the order p of the AR process. The parameter p must be determined during model building by significance tests with varying past window sizes [FF98]; these tests determine the explanatory power of the past realizations with regard to the future ones.

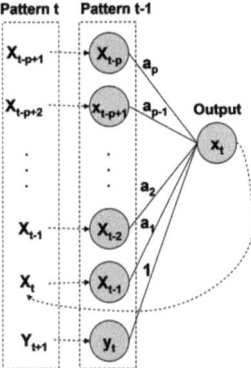

Figure 8.10: Topology and weight configuration for a 2-layered MLP network that resembles an autoregressive (AR) process of order p. The depicted network is not recurrent, since it holds a common feed-forward topology with a single output neuron. There is no recurrent connection in the network, the dashed backward link only illustrates the shift of the input pattern by one time step.

The patterns t-1 and t of figure 8.10 are two subsequent samples of the training set that are used to learn the network weights $a_1, a_2, \ldots, a_p$. The white noise term y_t can be interpreted as an external error signal that is constantly fed into the network via a fixed connection of weight 1. The depicted AR realization can be trained by a conventional backpropagation algorithm which automatically approximates the weights depending on the chosen window size. When used for prediction, the last p observations $x_{t-p}, \ldots, x_t$ are presented to the network, while the computed output value x_{t+1} represents the first predicted value. Further future values are obtained by refeeding the last predicted value as last observation, while shifting the rest of the input sequence by one – this is similar to the recursive prediction accomplished by exponential smoothing.

Both the realization of exponential smoothing and of autoregression shows that the SYMBOCONN framework is able to subsume approved statistical methods for time series analysis and prediction.

8.5 Application to Business Forecasting

Business forecasting has evolved into the practice of supply chain and asset management, especially in the case of manufacturing companies. Demand planning and consensus forecast, which are sub-disciplines of supply chain management, rely on statistical forecasting of the expected demand, as well as on consensus processes. Demand planning coordinates the demand of the various business units which is aggregated and submitted to the production facilities in regular intervals. The consensus forecast is the mean of all forecasts given by analysts who consult the respective company. In case of the telecommunication company supplied with our decision support service, the coordination activities culminate in monthly decision rounds of experts in demand planning, who require the prediction of the expected customer orders to make their final decisions.

As mentioned in the beginning of this chapter, forecasting, seen from the statistical perspective, is the prediction of future realizations of a dependent variable based on one or many explaining variables, which are also called predictors. This type of forecasting was done for a large telecommunication company as a monthly decision support service from January 2005 to September 2006. The ancestor of the machine learning framework at hand, namely the recurrent neural network RNN, was applied to the operative business forecasting at the telecommunication company in order to predict the aggregated number of units sold per product line on a world-wide scale. The portfolio comprised several product lines of component parts for fixed-network telecommunication infrastructures.

8.5.1 Applied Time Series Analysis

Time series analysis can be accomplished in the frequency-domain or in the time-domain. In this chapter, we only use time-domain methods such as the analysis of auto- and cross-correlations. Periodogram or spectral analyses could be employed in a second step, which are out of scope of this chapter.

The prediction task at the telecommunication company was to machine learn the order and planning history stored in a multi-dimensional data cube since the end of 2002. The number of *actual orders*[11] (I) for each month and each product line, as well as the *planned orders* (P), served as predictor variables. The actual orders turned out to be nearly equivalent to the actually sold units. Table 8.1 shows the

---

[11] Incoming orders from customers.

schema of the time-indexed data that was processed for providing business forecasts.

Region	Country	Site	Plantitle	Type	Date	Value
AME	USA	DET	868	Is (I)	12-2004	xxx
EUROPE	GER	BSL	868	Plan (P)	12-2004	xxx
APAC	HAW	A	868	A	01-2005	xxx
APAC	HAW	B	868	A	02-2005	xxx
EMEA	TH	U	808	D	02-2005	xxx
EMEA	TH	O	886	Plan (P)	03-2005	xxx

Table 8.1: Excerpt from the data schema of the worldwide sales figures of a large telecommunication company. "xxx" represents a placeholder due to nondisclosure agreements. The column *type* indicates the type of the sales figure, such as actual orders (Is) or planned value according to different degrees of ripeness (A till F), which are a refinement of the *Plan* magnitude. A *plantitle* is an abstraction for the subject of planning, such as a single product or a product group.

There were two main reasons for applying connectionist methods to the business forecast for the telecommunication company. First, the used statistical methods[12] did not succeed in improving or refining the by-hand planning. The second reason was the assumed systematic over- or underplanning of the demand planning experts, which was expected to be discovered and cleared by the neural network. Such a systematic planning error is represented by the systematic part of the mean squared error MSE, which is the bias of the prediction model.

If the mean squared error $MSE(P) = \mathbb{E}[(P - I)^2] = Var[P] + Bias(P, I)^2$ of the by-hand demand planning not only consists of a random variance component, but also of a $Bias(P, I) \neq 0$, then machine learning by neural networks can implicitly retrieve the intrinsic correlation $\rho(I(t), P(t))$ between demand planning and actually sold units. Thus, systematically incorrect planning of domain experts can be exploited by connectionist methods in order to provide an improved prediction of future sales figures. The systematic planning error, which can be discovered from the measurable *residuals*[13] $I(t) - P(t)$, may still contain useful information both about the prediction model and the modeled process – as opposed to a random error. The residuals represent the fraction of the process variance which cannot be explained by the constructed model. For our case study, we compute the linear differences $\delta(t) = I(t) - P(t)$ for two exemplary product lines (*plantitles*), which are, again, time series shown in figure 8.11 and 8.12.

Ideally, the residuals of a regression or prediction model should represent a white noise process, which means they are assumed to be *identically and independently distributed* (IID) with constant expectation and variance. If any systematics, such as significant autocorrelation, remain in the residuals, the chosen model is not able to explain the full variance of the dependent variable.

---

[12] Probably, a *moving average*-based technique was used; there was no assured information on the kind of prediction models used as decision support.

[13] In general, the difference between the predicted values and the observed values.

CHAPTER 8. TIME SERIES PREDICTION

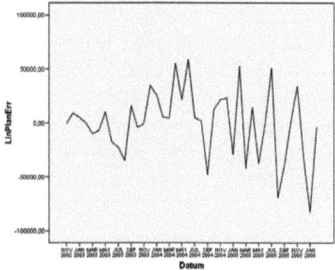
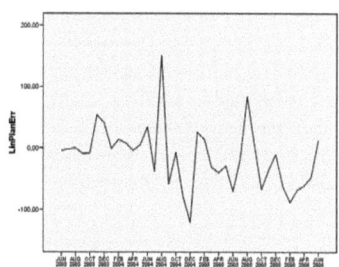

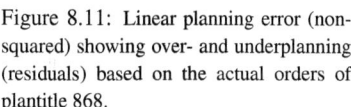

Figure 8.11: Linear planning error (non-squared) showing over- and underplanning (residuals) based on the actual orders of plantitle 868.

Figure 8.12: Linear planning error for plantitle 886. The variance is not constant over time, which is a sign for heteroscedasticity.

As shown, for example, in figure 8.11, the variance of the residuals for the plantitles 868 and 886 is not constant over time, meaning that the residuals are *heteroscedastic* [Ham94]. Heteroscedasticity of the error term violates the precondition of many statistical techniques to operate on independently and identically distributed observations. This was a further reason for applying the RNN as a refinement of the manual expert planning given by the time series $P(t)$.

In the following, we present a qualitative analysis of the statistical properties of the given time series $I(t)$ and $P(t)$. We limit the analysis to the exemplary plantitle 886, while three different plantitles are considered for the quantitative evaluation. To decide whether the planning time series $P(t)$ should be used to build a prediction model, its correlation coefficient with respect to $I(t)$ is computed, which reveals a strong correlation of both time series $\rho(I, P) = 0.807$. Such a strong dependency on a predictor variable is not very common in practical applications, such as business forecasting, and fans the expectation of finding a sound prediction model. If the coefficient ρ was below 0.3, for example, one would rather decide to exclude the planning variable P from the prediction model. In this case, the orders time series $I(t)$ would have to be predicted endogenously, which means an extrapolation beyond the known period without any predictors would have to be accomplished.

Another important aspect of the dependency between the planning and orders time series is their cross-correlation. There may be a time lag h in the correlation $\rho(I(t), P(t+h))$, $t, h \in \mathbb{N}$ of planned and actual orders. For example, for $h = -1$, $\rho(I(t), P(t-1)) \geq \tau$, the planned orders $P(t)$ would follow the actual orders $I(t)$ with a delay of one month. We computed the cross-correlation of both time series to discover such a dependency, which revealed that the highest correlation is obtained for $h = 0$, $\Phi_{I,P}(h) = \rho(I(t), P(t)) = 0.807$. Thus, all shifts $h = -7, \ldots -1, 1, \ldots, 7$ led to a lower correlation of both time series (highest cross-correlation for $h = 2$: $\Phi(I(t), P(t+2)) = 0.481$), meaning that they should be processed in the unshifted form by the MRNN or by statistical methods.

In the third step, the dependent variable $I(t)$ and the independent variables should be tested for stationarity as defined in section 8.2, in order to determine if statistical prediction models can be directly applied or whether the variables first have to be transformed. Time series may show a deterministic or a stochastic trend, sometimes even showing both, which have to be removed by appropriate transformations in advance. In time series analysis, two basic types of processes are distinguished: those growing over time and those randomly distributed around a constant mean value.

The observed period of the time series $I(t)$ describing the orders of plantitle 886 seems to grow in the long term, which can either be caused by a deterministic or by a stochastic trend. A known deterministic trend (linear, quadratic, exponential) is eliminated by analytical operations such as subtracting, taking the square root or the logarithm, respectively. Stochastic trends can be removed by k-fold differentiation[14] of the time series.

In economics, the presence of both a deterministic and a stochastic trend is unlikely, and is normally excluded by the various regression models. The following *mixed regression model* stated in formula 8.23 will be the basis of the *Dickey-Fuller* (DF) test for determining the type of time series, which is a so-called unit root test [FHH03]. The model consists of an autoregressive part X_t and a deterministic trend $\beta \cdot t + \gamma$. The null hypothesis H_0 of the DF-test assumes that the considered time series is a non-stationary *random walk process with drift*. If H_0 is rejected, then the alternative H_1 is assumed, indicating a trend-stationary process. The regression equation is given by the following equivalent formulations

$$Y_t := X_t + \beta \cdot t + \psi_t + \gamma + \eta_t \qquad (8.23)$$

$$X_t := \begin{cases} \alpha \cdot X_{t-1}, & t > 1 \\ \psi_1 \in \mathcal{N}(0,1), & t = 1 \end{cases}, \quad -1 < \alpha < 1 \qquad (8.24)$$

$$\Leftrightarrow \Delta X_t = (\alpha - 1)(X_{t-1}), \qquad (8.25)$$

where $\Delta X_t := X_t - X_{t-1}$, α is the influence of the past term, β is the linear trend factor, γ is the drift-generating constant (level) and η_t represents the stochastic error component. The factor α is restricted to the unit circle, since $|\alpha| > 1$ would result in an explosive process that cannot be used to model the behavior of the considered time series. Equation 8.25 is the reason why a random process, that is $\alpha - 1 = 0$, is also called difference-stationary.

The random variables ψ_i, $i = 1, \ldots, n$ are independent and identically distributed (IID) with expected value $\mathbb{E}[\psi_i] = 0$ (centered) and variance $Var[\psi_i] = 1$, which are considered as white noise. The sum $\sum_{i=1}^{t} \alpha^{t-i} \cdot \psi_i$ represents a stochastic trend generated by cumulation of the previous random variables. The stochastic components η_t are the perturbation factors of the regression model; they represent

---

[14]Differentiation means computing the difference between realizations of different time indices, but must not be misunderstood as the derivative of a function. Differentiations of an order greater than $k = 2$ are unusual.

the non-explainable variance of the stochastic process and are meant to be stationary.

To check the time series corresponding to plantitle 886 for (trend-) stationarity, we use an alternative test called KPSS-test of Kwiatkowski, Phillips, Schmidt, and Shin [HFO98]. The KPSS-test inverts the hypotheses of the DF-test, since the null hypothesis H_0 of the KPSS-test assumes stationarity. By means of a nonlinear least squares optimization, we approximate the coefficients[15] α, β and γ and obtain the following model $\hat{I}(t)$ for the orders time series of plantitle 886.

$$\hat{I}(t) := Y_t := X_t + 5.303 \cdot t - 5.370 \tag{8.26}$$

$$X_t := \begin{cases} 1.042 \cdot X_{t-1}, & t > 1 \\ \underbrace{0.491}_{\psi_1}, & t = 1 \end{cases} \tag{8.27}$$

The approximated value of $\alpha = 1.042 \approx 1$ is a sign of a random process ($\alpha = 1$). The slight delta of $\alpha - 1 = 0.042$ is the result of approximation errors caused by the nonlinearity in α; its mere positivity argues for a non-stationary process. This first hint regarding the process type is formally checked by the Dickey-Fuller test in the following. The test statistic $\hat{t}_n$ for the DF-test is based on the Dickey-Fuller distribution [DF79], whose limit distribution is a composite of Wiener processes[16].

$$\hat{t}_n = \frac{1 - \hat{\alpha}}{\sqrt{\hat{\sigma}^2 (\sum_{t=2}^{n} Y_{t-1}^2)^{-1}}}, \tag{8.28}$$

where $\hat{\alpha}$ is the estimated value for the parameter α and $\hat{\sigma}^2 = \frac{1}{n-1} \sum_{i=1}^{n} (\hat{\eta}_i - \mathbb{E}[\eta_i])^2$ is the variance estimator for the residuals $\hat{\eta}_i$ [FHH03].

Only by looking at the chart in figure 8.13, we see that the variance of the depicted process is not constant over time, but increases in the long term. This fact rather argues for a stochastic trend generated by the time-dependent cumulation of a white noise random variable. This is confirmed by the DF-test, since the test statistic returned the value $\hat{t}_{37} = -0.740$ (critical value $DF = -3.41$ to the significance level 0.05). Thus trend-stationarity based on a non-integrated model according to equation 8.23 with $\alpha < 1$ is discarded by the test. If the covariance $Cov(I(t), I(t + h))$ was equal for all t and depended only on the time lag h, then $I(t)$ would be stationary. In this case, the test statistic would normally evaluate to $\hat{t}_{37} \leq -3.41$.

When testing for stationarity, attention must be paid to autocorrelated residuals, which can distort the significance level. To exclude this effect, we first calculate the autocorrelation function (ACF) for the series of residuals $\hat{\eta}_t$, $t = 1, \ldots, n$, which shows that the deviations of the estimated values from the observed values are not significantly autocorrelated, but widely independent from each other (white noise).

---

[15]The concrete regression model was computed with the computer algebra software Maple 11 by means of the function *NonlinearFit*.

[16]A Wiener process W_t is the standard model to describe a Brownian motion. W_t has independent, stationary and normally distributed increments: $W_t - W_s \sim \mathcal{N}(0, t-s)$.

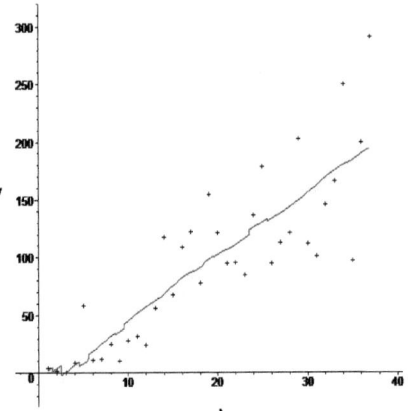

Figure 8.13: Scatter plot of the realizations for $t = 1, \ldots, 37$ of the orders series $I(t)$ of plantitle 886 together with the estimated regression model of formula 8.26.

The maximal autocorrelation amounts to $R_{max} := R_{\hat{\eta}}(6) = -0.322$, while the average ACF value is -0.047. This first check is confirmed by the *Durbin-Watson* (DW) test [Ver04], which provides information whether the residuals tend to be autocorrelated or not. The critical values for the test statistic 8.29 can be taken from tables [UoSCCC08] that give the lower and upper values for rejecting or accepting the null hypothesis of non-autocorrelated residuals.

$$DW_n = \frac{\sum_{i=2}^{n}(\hat{\eta}_i - \hat{\eta}_{i-1})^2}{\sum_{i=1}^{n} \hat{\eta}_i^2}, \quad n \in \mathbb{N} \qquad (8.29)$$

For the regression of formula 8.23, the value of the test statistic amounts to $DW_{37} = 1.973$; thus, our hypothesis of a random walk process with drift, is valid.

As detected by the DS-test, the time series $I(t)$ is not trend-stationary, but shows a stochastic trend in its expected value[17] and variance. The trend in the expected value of $I(t)$ can be removed by 1-fold differentiation, as depicted by figure 8.14. Likewise, the plan time series $P(t)$ used as predictor variable shows both a trend in expectation and variance. This behavior is typical for time series on industrial products, since these normally follow a life cycle model that includes phase-in and phase-out of the product line.

---

[17]This type of process is also called *difference stationary*.

CHAPTER 8. TIME SERIES PREDICTION 261

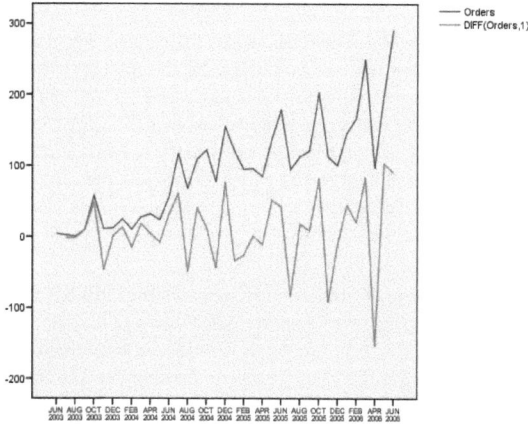

Figure 8.14: Plot of the time series $I(t)$ for plantitle 886 (top) together with its differentiated pendant (bottom, 1-fold). We see that both time series still show a non-stationary variance, while the empirical average value of the differentiated series is now nearly constant.

8.5.2 Quantitative Results

The results of the operative prediction that were submitted to the telecommunication company as a business intelligence service were quantified by an ex-post evaluation for the year 2005; they are listed in table 8.2. At that time, a predecessor of the MRNN, the RNN, had been especially developed to provide business forecasts. Since the incoming orders planned by the experts were not only comparative values, but also served as input features for the neural network, the connectionist prediction is a matter of refinement here.

Period of Time	Business Area	Experts Plan $P(t)$	RNN	Delta
01 - 06/2005	C	51.04	59.31	+8.27
01 - 06/2005	T	49.40	52.51	+3.11
07 - 12/2005	C	51.87	56.01	+4.14
07 - 12/2005	T	42.23	54.89	+12.66
Total		**48.64**	**55.68**	**+7.04**

Table 8.2: Quantitative results of demand planning at a large telecommunication company for the year 2005. The decision support service realized by the recurrent neural network (RNN) is compared with the by-hand forecast of domain experts in terms of prediction accuracy in percent. The result is distinguished by the respective business area – and is averaged over all predicted product lines and all planning months.

262   CHAPTER 8. TIME SERIES PREDICTION

The previous generation of the modular recurrent network already achieved a high generalization capability. The RNN enabled a forecast accuracy, which was, on average, 7% higher than that accomplished by the domain experts, who were leading in knowledge gained by informal communication and expertise acquired by every day planning. We assume that the MRNN, as the advanced engine of the SYMBOCONN framework, would have provided an even higher forecast quality. To validate this hypothesis, in the following paragraph we compare the performance of the MRNN with advanced statistical regression models on time series data obtained from the telecommunication company.

Experimental Comparison of Statistical Regression and MRNN Prediction By an ex-post analysis, the performance of statistical and connectionist prediction is evaluated on real time series from demand planning, in order to assess their adequacy for practical business forecasts. Both methodologies are compared on the basis of three time series from different business areas of the telecommunication company such as carrier and transport telecommunication infrastructure. The three quantities to predict, which are again plantitles, represent the time-indexed planned and actual orders (Plan and Is) of three different product lines named 868, 808, and 886.

Due to the highly non-continuous graphs of both planning and the orders time series, which are reminiscent of the development of stock prices, simple statistical models like polynomial regression models of first or second degree are dropped from the candidate methods. A *best fit straight line*, for example, is not able to explain the variance of the non-differentiable[18] orders graph.

One strength of connectionist methods is their ability to process high dimensional data sources, which also turned out to be an advantage in this case study. The MRNN processed 383 to 479 input features that were mapped onto a single output feature, the univariate time series $I(t)$. The network exploited the fine-grained information given by the order and planning figures for each country according to the column *Country* in table 8.1.

All values of the prediction accuracy PA are calculated according to the standard definition of the relative error with respect to the prediction p and the reference value r.

$$PA(p,r) = 1 - \frac{|p-r|}{|r|}, \quad r \neq 0 \qquad (8.30)$$

Statistical Analysis In the following, we analyze the statistical properties such as stationarity, autocorrelation, etc., of the plantitle time series in order to build an appropriate prediction model, which is directly compared with the MRNN prediction. After 1-fold differentiation, the order time series of plantitle 868 is modeled surprisingly well by an integrated autoregressive process of order one (ARIMA(1,1,0)), as shown by the plot of figure 8.15. In contrast to this, exponential

---
[18]Here, the first derivative of the orders curve is meant.

smoothing completely fails to model both the undifferentiated and the differentiated time series $I(t)$; hence, an out-of-sample prediction is impossible. In the case of MRNN prediction, differentiating the predictor and dependent time series was not necessary, but was even counterproductive. Since it is not quite feasible to process

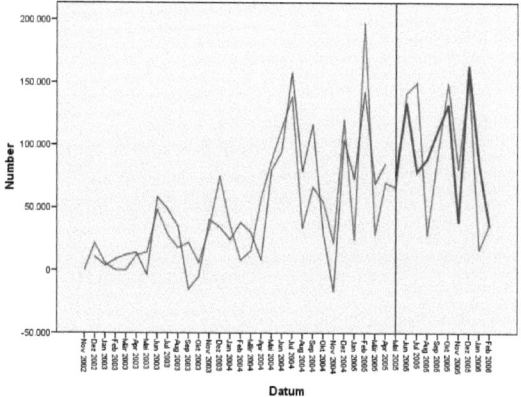

Figure 8.15: Plot of the time series $I(t)$ (red) for the plantitle 868 together with the ARIMA(1,1,0) prediction model (blue). The time line of the chart (x-axis) is divided into an estimation and a prediction period left and right besides the vertical line.

383 predictors with an ARIMA model, the history of product sales was aggregated. The aggregation was carried out based on the countries where the sales took place and the type of planning distinguished by various degrees of ripeness. Table 8.3 shows the results of the MRNN prediction and the statistical prediction. The higher performance achieved by the MRNN is an empirical evidence of its capability of predicting multi-variate time series.

The second row of table 8.3 confirms the detected correlation between the planning and orders time series, since a prediction without the plan variable led to a worse model and, consequently, to an inferior accuracy for the statistical and especially for the connectionist method. The *Expert Modeler* of the statistical software SPSS[19] has chosen an *Additive Winter model*, instead of an ARIMA process, to predict the orders time series in the case of plantitle 886. The additive winter model is an extension of exponential smoothing including level, trend, and season parameters. When using the Additive Winter model, the planning time series $P(t)$ was not employed as predictor due to its insufficient correlation with the orders time series of $\rho(I, P) = 0.557$ in the estimation period.

---

[19]SPSS is the *Statistical Package for the Social Sciences* with user interface and high-quality graphical output in form of a variety of diagrams. It belongs to the field of predictive analytics and is widely used for all kinds of statistical analyses.

Predictor	Plantitle	PA **MRNN**	PA **Statistical**	**Stat. Model**
Plan (P)	868	70.53	63.65	ARIMA(1,1,0)
-	868	32.48	55.26	Add. Winter
Plan (P)	808	69.01	46.00	ARIMA(0,1,0)
-	808	56.13	55.75	Add. Winter
Plan (P)	886	76.32	64.02	ARIMA(1,1,2)
-	886	54.73	67.14	Add. Winter
Total		**70.71**	**62.18**	

Table 8.3: Accuracy PA of the connectionist MRNN prediction compared with the statistical prediction (ARIMA, Add. Winter) measured in percent for the prediction period 05-2005 until 02-2006. A "-" indicates that no predictor variable was used for that prediction variant. The topology of the MRNN was configured for 9 history months mapped onto 1 future month using a hidden layer dimensionality of $h = 15$ (except for the prediction of plantitle 886, where we chose $h = 5$). As opposed to the ARIMA prediction, the predictor *plan* was not aggregated across the *countries* and the *planning type*, but was learned in broken down form by the MRNN. All used ARIMA models, which consist of auto regressive and moving average terms, were set up without seasonal components.

We observed a significant trend in the correlation of $I(t)$ and $P(t)$, which increases with the time on market of the respective product line within its life cycle. If the correlation analysis is extended to the full time line of plantitle 886 (estimation period plus out-of-sample period), the correlation coefficient increases to $\rho(I, P) = 0.738$. At the time of a product's market launch (phase-in), the experts learn to deal with the new product and are still able to tune their planning actions; this leads to a lower planning quality than in the middle or end of the product life cycle, when the experts have gained more experience.

Figure 8.16 and 8.17 graphically compare both prediction models based on the estimation and prediction periods for the orders time series of plantitle 886. For training the MRNN, a validation set was harnessed, containing patterns that are not used for training but for validating the current prediction model on the fly (during the ongoing training process). Therefore, the strong adaption of the neural network to the history series is interrupted by these validation targets at the points Mar. 04, May 04, Aug. 04, Jan. 05, and Jun. 05, which were excluded from training. In figure 8.17, the adaption curve for the first nine months is missing (Jun. 03 until Feb. 04), since the MRNN was trained with a past window of nine months. In consequence, the first trained target value was May 04 (Mar. 04 was part of the validation set).

8.6 Conclusion

In this chapter, the SYMBOCONN framework was employed for time series prediction, which is a traditional application area for neural networks in general – unlike

CHAPTER 8. TIME SERIES PREDICTION

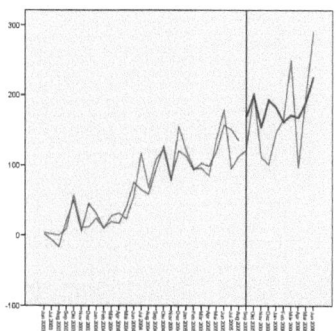 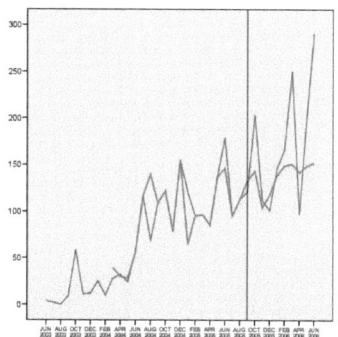

Figure 8.16: Plot of the estimation and prediction periods regarding the orders time series $I(t)$ (red) for the plantitle 886 by the Additive Winter model (blue) from statistics. The vertical line divides the estimation (left) from the prediction period (right).

Figure 8.17: Plot of the estimation and prediction of the MRNN (green) with respect to the orders time series $I(t)$ (red) for the plantitle 886. The connectionist prediction is almost 10% more accurate when compared to the statistical one (left figure 8.16).

the knowledge-based domains that were elaborated upon in the previous chapters. In the first part, we introduced the theoretical fundamentals of time series modeling, which were directly implemented and applied to real-world datasets in the subsequent sections.

First, the predecessor of the MRNN, the RNN, was applied to datasets of the telecommunication company in order to machine learn the orders and planning history. The RNN prediction was compared to the planning activities of the human domain experts, who were leading in expertise and knowledge. The results of the planning year 2005 show that our connectionist method provides an improvement in prediction accuracy of more than 7% compared to human experts.Secondly, within the scope of an industrial case study, the SYMBOCONN framework was compared with advanced statistical prediction methods using an ex-post evaluation. The prediction accuracy of the MRNN and of ARIMA as well as Additive Winter models was measured based on a pseudo-future prediction period. The MRNN showed a 10% higher performance than the statistical methods and was, furthermore, much more robust against non-stationarity in expectation and variance; hence, no prior time series transformations, such as differentiation, were necessary.

Chapter 9

Conclusions

This dissertation addresses connectionist and symbolic machine learning focusing on practically relevant applications mainly in the area of knowledge and software engineering. As shown in this dissertation, symbolic methods contain deficiencies regarding intelligent recommendation – at least in knowledge-intensive areas such as knowledge engineering or software development – which can be ameliorated by a hybrid approach. Symbolic machine learning methods, like association rule mining, are unable to incorporate rich content represented by categorical, metric, or textual attributes [Dav08c]. Recommendation systems realized by symbolic rule-processors still lack important capabilities that prevent their broader and more successful application. Amongst others, missing properties are function- and domain-comprehensive applicability, handling incomplete, uncertain, heterogeneous, or changing knowledge as well as the ability to learn from examples.

Our hypothesis stated that, especially for intelligent recommendation, combining the connectionist and symbolic concepts is superior to applying each of them individually. So far, most recommendation systems are based on symbolic concepts like association rules [ZWDZ04]. We developed a framework for domain-independent machine learning called SYMBOCONN which represents a new approach to intelligent recommendation. As integral constituent of this framework, we employed a recurrent neural network to process heterogeneous information, which can be symbolic or non-symbolic, as well as structured or unstructured. We applied this framework to *new domains* and to *new problems*, which have not been addressed in a connectionist way before. Thereby we demonstrated that value can be added to knowledge-driven processes [Deb00] by intelligent recommendations – requiring only a basic data history to learn from.

However, the SYMBOCONN framework still lacks the ability to be seamlessly integrated into a knowledge or software engineering process, in a way that it could be operated by knowledgeable outsiders. Furthermore, the framework has to be applied during an ongoing software project to empirically evaluate its actual usefulness for the different types of project participants, such as requirements engineers, developers, or project managers.

The benefits of our hybrid symbolic-connectionist approach are confirmed by evaluations on concrete datasets. In the following, we present its main contributions and the planned directions our research will take in the future.

9.1 Contributions

The SYMBOCONN framework developed in this dissertation is a contribution to symbolic-connectionist processing in practical applications. The following concepts and implemented functionalities represent the main contributions of this dissertation.

Bringing Together Concepts from Software Development and Artificial Intelligence The recent trend to support software development by methods taken from artificial intelligence [BW08, DD08, LKB06, Nav97] raises the problem of an unambiguous and efficient communication between software engineers and researchers in artificial intelligence. The terminology of both areas is often conflicting and many technical terms are overloaded with different meanings. An example of this is the usage of the term *feature* in both communities: when software engineers use this term, they usually mean a functionality or a characteristic of a software program. By contrast, those who deal with artificial intelligence mostly speak of an attribute or a feature space dimension when using the term *feature*.

Against this background, we took another step to apply artificial intelligence to knowledge-based systems and processes, while clearly distinguishing the concepts of both worlds. This dissertation contributes to the understanding of concepts from machine learning and knowledge discovery by people who work in the field of software engineering. In a similar way, researchers in artificial intelligence are familiarized with fundamental concepts from software engineering. Thereby, the high potential of machine learning methods to solve knowledge- and software engineering problems is highlighted.

Framework for Domain-Independent Machine Learning The "touchable" outcome of this dissertation is a new machine learning framework named SYMBOCONN, which provides intelligent recommendations in various domains. This framework is a meta-domain framework [EB07] that provides *functions* and *knowledge structures* required to conduct classification and prediction in general, without a constraining focus on a specific application or even on a specific domain. Thus, independence from concrete applications and from domains is one of the contributions of this dissertation. Therefore, this work goes beyond the scope of domain frameworks that provide the generic control flow and service interface for a specific problem domain, which is called a *vertical slice* [Pre97].

In terms of extensibility, SYMBOCONN can be classified as a blackbox framework, because external systems that intend to use SYMBOCONN have to comply with an interoperability interface SymboConnInterop and are integrated using delegation [BD04]. The extensibility of the framework and its adequacy for domains yet unconsidered is specifically shown by including the separate domain of time series prediction in chapter 8. Altogether, three different domains are considered in this dissertation, making a fundamental contribution to applied machine learning in each of these areas. The viability of the SYMBOCONN approach, based on the modular recurrent neural network (MRNN) as framework engine, was empirically shown.

The Modular Recurrent Neural Network (MRNN) The development of the framework engine had already begun in 2004. At that time, predecessors of the MRNN, namely a multi-layer perceptron (MLP) and a recurrent variant (RNN), had been developed especially to provide business forecasts for a large telecommunication company. Since 2006, the network was completely redesigned to fulfill the requirements of the SYMBOCONN framework formulated in section 3.1.

An integral part of the MRNN is a new backpropagation algorithm tailored to the modular structure of the neural network, which enables to process incomplete and heterogeneous inputs and targets. Due to the flexibility of the network topology and the new *Backpropagation Through Time* (BPTT) algorithm, it was possible to realize and advance two different statistical prediction techniques using the MRNN. These techniques, exponential smoothing and auto-regression, are subsumed by the SYMBOCONN machine learning engine only by means of an appropriate configuration of its topology and parameters. Thus, for time series applications, the SYMBOCONN framework can replace these statistical methods by a more generic prediction mechanism.

Navigation Recommendation The field of navigation recommendation is primarily addressed by content-based filtering and collaborative filtering. Both techniques are combined by the hybrid navigation recommendation technique of the SYMBOCONN framework. Still, recommending commercial products or learning of consumer buying habits are not the focus of this dissertation and hence are not instantiated as specific applications; however, they could be addressed in the future.

In the conducted case study on navigation recommendation based on Microsoft web log data, the most sophisticated model with text representation based on latent semantic indexing (LSI) achieved the best recommendation accuracy of 35.57% on a test set of 1,250 navigation patterns [Dav08a]. The results for latent semantic recommendation are promising, since more than every third recommended node matched the users' interests in the case of navigation histories of length three. The performance could even be increased to 50.00% when using histories of length one, instead.

Application to Knowledge Engineering and Software Development Developing software through an engineered process generates work products together with considerable amounts of software development data, e.g. data produced by planned and unplanned communication. Thus, *system knowledge* in the form of system models and *meta knowledge* of project stakeholders are potential targets of machine learning.

In the first part of chapter 6, we demonstrated that the SYMBOCONN framework is able to classify complex artifacts, which may even be afflicted with fuzzy, incomplete, or partially incorrect attributes. In particular, the SYMBOCONN framework succeeded in classifying action items according to the development activities in which they were formulated: the classification accuracy for six categories amounted to an average of 80.51%. Furthermore, we classified the relevance of action items for the accomplishment of the project with an accuracy of 83.72%.

Secondly, we introduced a connectionist approach to change impact analysis, which considers changes upon graph-structured data whose impacts are structure-sensitive and thus cannot solely be predicted, for example, from changes in attribute-value pairs of software artifacts. Moreover, the SYMBOCONN framework was used for content-based learning and for the prediction of co-occurring artifact changes. The MRNN was trained on the cohesive configuration items of each CVS commit set in a supervised manner in order to prevent incomplete changes and to recommend related artifacts.

The evaluation conducted by three independent datasets from the *PROMISE Repository of Software Engineering Databases* revealed an average prediction precision for partially unseen artifact sets of 67.75%, based on a result space of 167 to 1047 different artifacts. Compared to existing methods based on association rule mining, whose authors report precision values of about 26% to 50% [ZWDZ04], our connectionist approach achieves an even higher accuracy when applied to untrained item sets. This is not possible with symbolic techniques at all.

Thirdly, we developed a robust connectionist classification aimed at structured and typed contents. The created capability of structure and type learning was applied to the discovery of design patterns in class diagrams. The MRNN was also able to classify partial or distorted design pattern instances within given class diagrams.

Transfer of the Spread Spectrum Information Encoding The crucial problem of any classification lies in the sharp discrimination between the existing classes in the underlying feature space and, in determining the significant (discriminating) features. For this reason, we adapted the *spread spectrum* method from signal transmission technology to the classification of multi-represented objects[1], which are encoded for neural processing by means of unique spreading sequences. The spread spectrum technique originally stems from mobile communication and was first investigated around 1908. Data is spread over a wide bandwidth for transmission via the air interface. The energy of the signal that was generated in a particular bandwidth is deliberately spread in the frequency domain, resulting in a signal with a wider bandwidth.

Originating from a completely different discipline, the abstract spread spectrum

---

[1] Represented by feature vectors.

principle can also improve the robustness and precision of classifiers. Spread spectrum encoding facilitates the classification through its process gain (see section 5.3.2), which results in a higher discrimination between different classes than in the case of a classifier trained in the same way, but without data spreading. This spreading mechanism provides a bias and variance reduction and is a variant of *error-correcting output coding* [Gha00, Liu06].

The new technique was evaluated on the basis of sequence prediction and design pattern classification. In both cases, a context-free and typed grammar was successfully learned by the network with integrated spread spectrum encoding. Compared to a simpler type-encoding schema, the proposed solution was superior with respect to robustness against noisy input sequences. We conjecture that its error-correcting effect can be used to improve the robustness and accuracy of further connectionist or statistical classifiers.

The contributions to navigation recommendation, as well as to knowledge engineering and software development, are directly based on the symbolic-connectionist machine learning capabilities which are provided by the SYMBOCONN framework. By contrast, the spread spectrum contribution is self-contained and, in principle, also applicable to non-connectionist classifiers.

9.2 Future Work

We believe that the potential of the SYMBOCONN framework will especially unfold in knowledge-driven and empirical domains, such as software development. As mentioned in the beginning of this dissertation, the availability of empirical evidence, while having low insight into the driving activities and processes behind an artificial or natural system, calls for the employment of connectionist methods:

"If we have more knowledge than data, then 'hard' operators are proper[2]. Alternatively, if we have more data than knowledge, then fuzzy or neural operators are more adequate." [BBK02]

9.2.1 Activity Classification Based on User Behavior

As opposed to the static activity classification of artifacts presented above, the current activity of the user of a development environment, or of a knowledge-based system in general, can be determined by means of the generated stream of events; this, again, is a classification task. An unordered set or a ordered sequence of events should be assigned to a certain activity by a classifier K, $K : \{E_1, E_2, ..., E_n\} \rightarrow \{A_1, A_2, ..., A_n\}$. Coding, testing, collaborating or debugging are seen as interesting activities, for example. Since it is not known which sequences of events are characteristic for a certain activity, we have to learn the regularities from given examples. The project progress can be observed through the emitted events, which

---

[2]Here the 'hard' operators are such as symbolic inference rules that hold a discrete definition and value space.

indicate transitions between different project phases, as well as the execution of activities within those. The accomplished activities leave their mark as streams of observable events that can be processed as node sequences by the MRNN. The behavior of software developers is often spontaneous, and not all produced events, such as opening, reading and writing a document or committing source code to a repository [Dav08c], are significant to their current activity – many of these events merely represent outliers.

The work on event-based activity classification is not substantiated yet, requiring further investigation by means of concrete project observations. Actual software development data stemming from the European project on knowledge management in software engineering called TEAM [TEA09] was not available during the completion of this dissertation. However, the TEAM-infrastructure logging event streams generated from software development activities already existed. Thereupon, the conceptual design of activity classification can be sketched out, which consists of two decoupled phases:

1. **Clustering**
   The event history has to be clustered in order to obtain the training cases for the classifier. This can be done by density-based clustering in conjunction with a compactness measure on the resulting clusters that decides which event to activity mappings $\{E_1, E_2, \ldots, E_m\} \mapsto A_i$, $i = 1, \ldots, n$ represent valid training cases. A density-based clustering algorithm like DBSCAN [EKSX96] can be applied to the captured events. The predefined activities (classes) might be extended by further intermediate activities that have been discovered during the clustering process (hierarchical clustering, dendrogram).

2. **Classification**
   After determining the existing classes of user activities by phase one, unknown user behavior can be recognized through the interaction with the system. The user-generated events are captured, preprocessed and subsequently used for activity classification. The computed class probability for the respective event sequence is compared to all existing classes and mapped onto the most similar class characteristic.

As introduced in section 4.1.3, there are types of neural networks that are capable of clustering data sets. The Self-Organizing Map (SOM), which is part of the SYMBOCONN framework implementation, is able to cluster feature vectors.

The benefit of activity classification accomplished by the SYMBOCONN framework is the order-sensitivity of the sequence processing machine learning engine. The classification $\{E_1, \ldots, E_m\}^k \mapsto \{A_1, \ldots, A_n\}$, $k \geq 1$ depends on a whole sequence of events, instead of depending only on isolated or unordered events; this is appropriate to properly reflect the context-sensitive user behavior. Single events are often not meaningful with respect to the determination of the current user activity. For example, first editing a source code file and then running the corresponding program in debug mode indicates a debugging activity, while the mere editing of program code does not allow the conclusion that the developer is debugging.

9.2.2 Further Applications in Software Engineering

Model elements created during a software project can be automatically annotated with quality criteria or characteristical attributes, whose values are assessed by machine learning. Those criteria are represented by categorical, ordinal or metric attributes like *Feasible, Correct, Unambiguous, Testable, Modifiable, Complete, Traceable, Concise,* or *Understandable*. Having a completed project captured by the CASE tool UNICASE available, the contained model elements have to be valuated once by hand, according to the classification criteria in order to build a training set for the SYMBOCONN framework. Then, the machine learning task is to classify given model elements, such as requirements, regarding the chosen quality criterion, based on their content and their neighborhood in the project graph. The surrounding nodes indirectly provide information (e.g. the *completeness* of a requirement) about the linked artifact. If a requirement deals with functionality, for example, it should be associated with the respective use cases in the project graph. Therefore, the artifact to be assessed is considered together with its direct neighbors in the graph. This kind of structure-sensitive artifact classification, based on heterogeneous pieces of information, extends the activity classification presented in section 6.1.

There are further possible applications of the SYMBOCONN framework for exploiting software development knowledge via the blackbox integration of SYMBOCONN into the CASE tool UNICASE. One example is the prediction of burn-down charts, which are a method of the agile project management methodology Scrum. Burn-down charts reflect the project progress and the features to be implemented for each planned release. The prediction of the remaining implementation time can answer the question of whether the planned release will be on time, and whether it will meet the functionality and quality requirements of the client.

Appendix A

Framework Extensions and Details

In this supplemental chapter, three concrete improvements and extensions of the framework implementation are outlined, which concern the object design on the one hand and the functional model of SYMBOCONN on the other hand. Finally, a few technical issues regarding the training of the machine learning engine are mentioned.

A.1 Future Implementation

In this section, we provide a selection of concrete improvements currently being implemented or to be implemented in future promotions of the SYMBOCONN framework. The following section restructures the object model to improve the extensibility of the framework.

A.1.1 Decoupling of Domain-Specific Subsystems

Since the SYMBOCONN framework should support the integration of further domains, the coupling between the abstract node representation and the domain-specific classes must not be strong. Unfortunately, the *implementation inheritance*, used in the subsystem NodeRepresent depicted in figure A.1, introduces a certain coupling along the type hierarchy. When the superclass NodeRepresent changes, all implementing subclasses are affected, even if the change is not required by one or several application domain implementations.

By using delegation instead of inheritance, this effect can be diminished or even avoided. For each domain-specific set of subclasses encircled in figure A.1, an *adapter* that performs the necessary conversions is defined. Using the *Adapter Pattern* (cf. section 6.3), the domain-specific subsystems take the role of *legacy systems*. The refined model is represented by figure A.2. To make the framework truly extensible, the architecture can be moved to the delegation variant in future work.

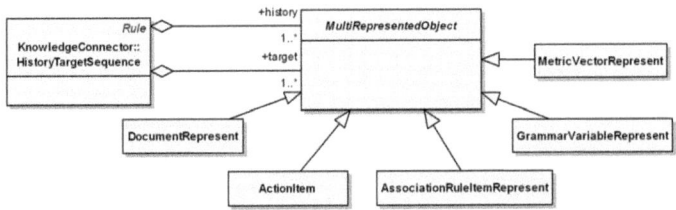

Figure A.1: NodeRepresent subsystem using implementation inheritance to integrate the application-specific representations.

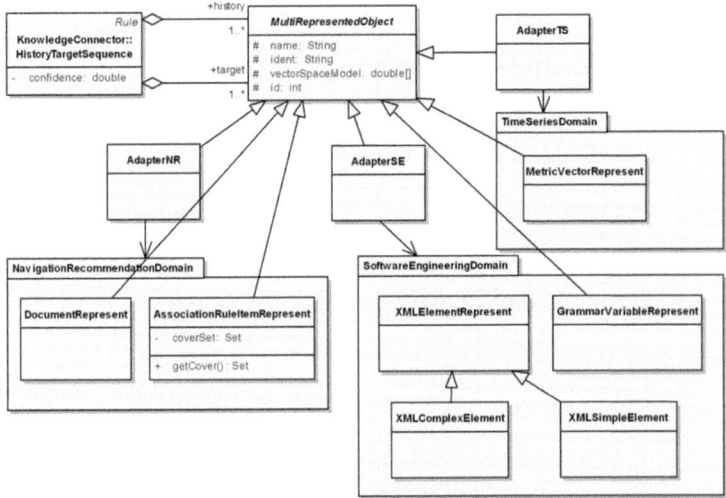

Figure A.2: *Delegation variant:* NodeRepresent subsystem refined by a delegation mechanism via three adapter classes that decouple the domain-specific subsystems from the abstract knowledge representation.

A.1.2 Extensions of the Framework Functionality

A.1.2.1 Output-Input Refeeding for Navigation Sequences

Refeeding of a one-step prediction output as input of the next single step prediction is a method for improving accuracy in the case of context-free grammars. Let m be the length of the node sequence to be predicted, which is also called the prediction horizon. The MRNN is able to predict the whole sequence at once, due to its modular composition that theoretically enables an infinite prediction horizon.

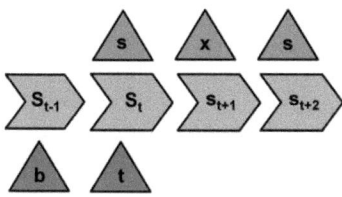

Figure A.3: Immediate prediction of the three subsequent symbols in a word of the Reber language. The prediction takes to input symbols "b" and "t" and continues this sequence with three valid symbols "sxs". The resulting training pattern is embedded in the required topology of the MRNN. The generated partial Reber word is "$btsxs$".

Alternatively, the target sequence can be predicted step-wise, that is, in m-many single predictions of length one. Thereby, the respective output $\vec{y}_{t+i}$ is re-fed as input for the prediction of $\vec{y}_{t+i+1}$. The training setup required for stepwise prediction is visualized in figure A.4.

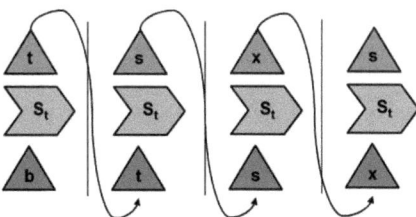

Figure A.4: Four productions of the Reber grammar 5.3 in the form of training patterns embedded in the respective topology of the MRNN. The previous output is fed into the network as input of the subsequent prediction. The resulting partial Reber word is again "$btsxs$".

The refeeding technique has the strong advantage of implicitly correcting the neural predictions at each time step. Since the prediction is, to some extent, always an uncertain approximation of the unknown right side symbol, a code table lookup has to be conducted in order to obtain the actual symbol from the numeric prediction $\vec{y}_{t+1}$. The original encoding of the resolved symbol is then used as new input $\vec{x}_{t+1}$ of the subsequent prediction $\vec{y}_{t+2}$, instead of refeeding the fuzzy and unresolved prediction $\vec{y}_{t+1}$.

The effect that should thereby be avoided is comparable to the momentous accumulation of rounding errors in a complex computation, which consists of sequential computations each taking the previous result as own input.

Similar techniques are known from mobile communication, where transmitted signals are freed from noise at intermediate stations before they are redirected.

A *chain of single node recommendations* can be derived by refeeding the previous recommendation $\vec{y}_{t+1}$ as input $\vec{x}_{t+1}$ for the subsequent network prediction $\vec{y}_{t+2}$. The refeeding technique for navigation recommendation is only possible for context-free productions (otherwise the context is lost) and is visualized by figure A.5. It is obvious that an infinite recommendation chain can be obtained by continu-

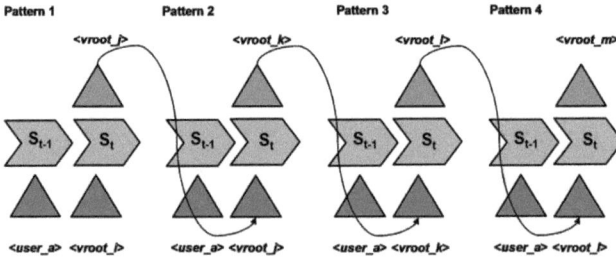

Figure A.5: Stepwise prediction of the subsequent web page based on the previous prediction.

ously refeeding the previous prediction as input for the next one. Such an arbitrarily long sequence can also be generated at once (immediate prediction), without refeeding, only by use of the hidden network layer S as depicted in figure A.6. In both cases, the recommendation certainty declines with the length of the recommendation sequence. The question is whether the refeeding technique is superior to an at-once prediction, due to its correction properties described before. In section 5.1, we have seen the benefit of the refeeding technique compared to the direct completion (by prediction) of partial words from the Reber grammar.

A.1.2.2 Combining Text and Association Rule Mining

Navigation recommendation can be done either in a *cold-start* or a *warm-start* scenario. In cold-start, the system comes from an untrained state and has not yet learned any navigations. To provide recommendations, the information system has

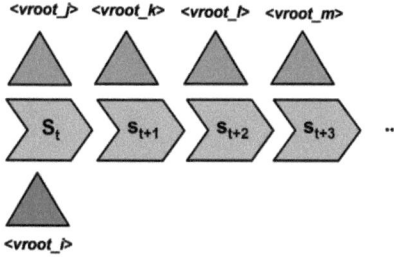

Figure A.6: At-once prediction of arbitrarily many sequential pages based only on the current web page.

to first be used in order to capture actual navigations, since meaningful recommendations require a critical mass mass of observed user behavior to learn from.

To provide warm-start capability without gathering a representative set of user navigations, a means for discovering cohesive navigations is required. In addition to capturing navigations with the help of the respective user, correlated node sequences can be automatically discovered by association rule mining (ARM) [AS94]. The precondition for applying this kind of preprocessing is that the nodes from the navigation space carry textual contents.

This discovery approach does not focus on the whole document representation, but instead aims at co-occurring keyterms in single documents. These terms mostly stand in a semantical relation, since all analyzed text corpora stem from the same domain. We have adapted the well-known *a priori algorithm* for association rule mining to this keyterm-association problem, which now computes *frequent keyterm sets* of increasing size. Based on these sets, the *cover* of each *frequently co-occurring* keyterm is identified, which is the non-empty *set of documents* containing these terms. Finally, a mapping from association rules to document sequences is conducted, which was also implemented in the SYMBOCONN framework. The result of the ARM procedure is a set of document sequences containing cohesive keyterms. Now, a warm-start scenario is enabled by training the system on this result set. The cohesive node sequences discovered by ARM are used to equip the system with a basic domain expertise that can be exploited by the user immediately, without any latency period.

A.2 Technical Issues in Training the Framework Engine

There are several technical issues in the context of training the MRNN and neural networks in general. At first, we explain some limitations of connectionist learning that have been reported to occur in a similar way before.

A further peculiarity of recurrent neural networks concerns the implicit weighting of the constituents of the input sequence, which is slightly unbalanced, while the last aspect emphasizes the ability of the MRNN to process heterogeneous feature vectors.

A.2.1 Limitations of Connectionist Learning

There are several limitations of connectionist learning, mainly concerning the kind of data that is learnable by the framework engine. Long-term sequences and relational data cause problems such as decaying error flow and ambiguity of training patterns during network training, which are explained in the following.

The Problem of Decaying Error Flow Hochreiter and Schmidhuber [Hoc91] analyzed the error flow in recurrent neural networks trained with the conventional backpropagation algorithm (BPTT) and came to the conclusion that the error flow decays exponentially in relation to the modeled time line. This problem is illustrated by the following, seemingly simple classification task. Only two symbolic input sequences over the alphabet $\Sigma = \{a, b, x_1, x_2, \ldots, x_n\}$ should be mapped onto two target classes "0" and "1":

$$a\, x_1 x_2 \ldots x_n \;\mapsto\; 0 \tag{A.1}$$
$$b\, x_1 x_2 \ldots x_n \;\mapsto\; 1, \tag{A.2}$$

where $y_1 = 0$ or $y_1 = 1$, respectively. The longer the time lag n between the first symbol a or b, respectively, and the last symbol x_n, the harder the learning task. The reason for this effect lies in the exponentially decreasing error flow during the backpropagation phase, which especially reveals its effect for long input sequences with $n > 100$. This limitation also applies to the MRNN in principle, as we checked by using the given simple grammar.

Schmidhuber and his colleagues solved this problem with their *Long Short-Term Memory* (LSTM) network [SH97], which possesses so-called *constant error carousels* (CEC) that prevent the error flow from completely diminishing. The error information is needed to adapt the network weights in order to match the desired output. Thereby, especially the input units with the longest distances (here a and b) to the source of the error flow at the target units (here y_1) suffer most from the decaying corrective information. So far, a component like the CEC has not been necessary for the applications addressed by the SYMBOCONN framework, but might be part of future work on the framework engine.

Learning Relational Data A far-reaching constraint of all neural networks is their inability to directly learn mathematical relations, since they typically realize functional mappings. Thus, neural networks can only learn mappings of objects resembling a (partial) mathematical function, without the need for being *injective* or *surjective*. An example is the function $f : x \mapsto \frac{1}{x^2}$. f is neither injective nor surjective on $\mathbb{Q}$ (e.g. $\nexists x \in \mathbb{Q} : -1 = f(x)$), but it is still learnable by a neural network, because all x are mapped to their uniquely determined image $f(x)$.

If the network is meant to learn a binary relation $\{(x_i, y_j) \in D_1 \times D_2 \mid i \in I \subseteq \{1, \ldots, |D_1|\}, j \in J \subseteq \{1, \ldots, |D_2|\}, |D_1| < |D_2|\}$ in the valid training set form $\{x_i \mapsto y_i\}$, the network training will definitely be unsuccessful and stagnate on a high error level. The network will fail to minimize the training error, no matter which training algorithm is used. This is intuitively plausible because neural networks are in principle deterministic information processors[1]. The figures A.7 and A.8 show relational and functional mappings in the case of node sequences. The

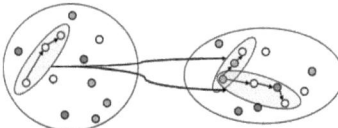
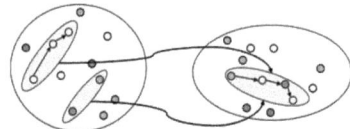

Figure A.7: A relation is on hand if the same entity is "mapped" onto two or more different entities of the value space. In the case of node sequences, the same history sequence is mapped onto several target sequences, which cannot be learned by a neural network.

Figure A.8: A non-injective functional mapping of two input sequences onto one target sequence that resembles a mathematical function. Thus, *one* entity from the definition space is only mapped to *one* entity of the value space, which can easily be learned.

training set is consistent if the following condition is met.

Condition A.2.1: Uniqueness of Training Patterns

$$\forall y_1, y_2 \in D_2 \; \nexists x \in D_1 : (x \mapsto y_1) \wedge (x \mapsto y_2),$$

where x, y_1, y_2 are nodes of the definition space D_1 and value space D_2, respectively. Of course, $x \mapsto y_1 \wedge x \mapsto y_2 \wedge \ldots \wedge x \mapsto y_n$ is not allowed either, but this case directly follows from the case with two target variables. The uniqueness condition A.2.1 is checked by the framework in the preprocessing phase.

The apparent problem of not being able to learn relational data can always be solved by transforming the relation into a functional mapping. For example, the relation $\{(a, b_1), (a, b_2), \ldots, (a, b_n)\}$ can be transformed into a training pattern $a \mapsto b_1, b_2, \ldots, b_n$ with an input sequence of one node and a target sequence of n nodes.

Prediction Convergence When operatively applying (cf. Def. 3.2.5) the recurrent neural network to prediction problems, the behavior of the MRNN itself for the predicted node sequence should be mathematically foreseeable. Due to the

---
[1] Except the random weight initialization and the presentation order of the training patterns.

generality of the network architecture, this is only conditionally applicable: is the prediction converging or diverging?

In contrast to the training phase, an oscillating network behavior is not likely to occur in the prediction phase with frozen weight matrices $A,B,C = const.$. The prediction horizon, i.e., the number of reliably predictable target nodes m_0, can normally be recognized by means of the output behavior $\vec{y}_{t+m}$, which attains to a *steady state* $\vec{y} \in \mathbb{R}^d$ for $m > m_0$, $m_0 \in \mathbb{N}$ and $m \to \infty$ in practice.

The autonomous part of the network dynamics without external inputs for $t < \tau \leq m$, defined by the recurrent equation 4.14, determines the prediction convergence. This equation can be written as composition

$$f(B(\ldots f(B(f(B\vec{s}_t)))\ldots))$$

if unfolded over time. In theory, the operator $(fB) : \mathbb{R}^h \to \mathbb{R}^h$, $(fB)(x) \mapsto f(Bx)$, $x \in \mathbb{R}^h$ is not always a contraction which would converge to a *fixpoint* $\vec{s} \in \mathbb{R}^h$ for $m \to \infty$, according to the *Banach fixed-point theorem*. If we tried to show the convergence, the state transition would have to contract in the way $d(f(B\vec{s}_t), f(B\vec{s}_{t+1})) = d(\vec{s}_{t+1}, \vec{s}_{t+2}) \leq \lambda \cdot d(\vec{s}_t, \vec{s}_{t+1})$, $\forall t \in T \subset \mathbb{N}$, $0 \leq \lambda < 1$, which is obviously *not true* $\forall B \in {}^h\mathbb{R}^h$, $\vec{s}_t, \vec{s}_{t+1}$ and a metrics d. However, a simplified form of prediction convergence, $\|Tx - Ty\| \leq C \|x - y\|$, can be shown.

Proof A.2.1: Simplified Convergence
Let $T := fB, f : S \to S, S = \mathbb{R}^h, \sup_{x \in S}\{f(x)\} = \vec{1}$. For T being a contraction that converges to a fix point $\vec{s}$, the constant C has to be less than 1 for all $x, y \in S$.

We can show a simplified form of convergence when choosing the transition matrix B as identity matrix $B := I$. The sigmoidal activation function $f(x) = \frac{1}{1+\exp(-x)}$ with $0 < f(x) < 1$, $\forall x \in \mathbb{R}^h$ makes for a convergence

$$\left\| \frac{1}{1+e^{-x}} - \frac{1}{1+e^{-y}} \right\| \stackrel{?}{<} \|x-y\| \quad (A.3)$$

$$c(x,y) := \left\| \frac{e^{-x} - e^{-y}}{(1+e^{-x})(1+e^{-y})} \right\| - \|x-y\| < 0, \forall x,y \in \mathbb{R}^h \quad (A.4)$$

Figure A.9 illustrates the inequality A.4 for the case of a one-dimensional state layer S. In practice, the normalized input data and the smooth initialization of the weight matrices, especially the matrix B, nevertheless fosters reaching a steady state $\vec{s} \in \mathbb{R}^h$ for $m > m_0$ also for B being of non-canonical form. This fact was also validated during our intensive work with the implementation of the recurrent network.

A.2.2 Implicit Weighting of the Input Nodes

Since the *timely unfolded* modular recurrent network is a sequence processor, there is a minor shortcoming when processing unordered sets of input nodes. The MRNN

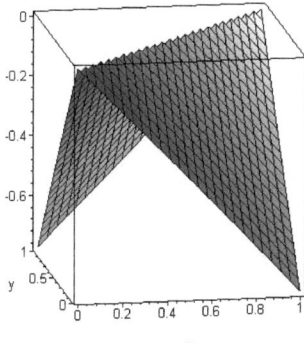

Figure A.9: Visualization of the function of convergence $c(x, y)$ based on the difference of pairwise activations. The non-differentiable break that realizes the maximal value results from the absolute value function.

tends to focus more strongly on the nearer history $\ldots, \vec{x}_{t-2}, \vec{x}_{t-1}, \vec{x}_t$ w.r.t. t than on its more distant part $\vec{x}_{t-k}, \vec{x}_{t-k+1}, \ldots$ in order to explain the dependent variable[2] $\vec{y}_{t+1}$. This effect of oddly weighted input units has already been described for other types of recurrent neural networks by Hochreiter [Hoc91].

An example in which ordered input nodes are unwanted is the design pattern recovery, elaborated upon in section 6.3. Since the MRNN processes the pattern signature consisting of context-free rules as an ordered input sequence, a stronger focus on the more recent rules (fed in at first) may occur, which is undesired. To eliminate this order-dependency, the input sequence representing the design pattern signature, for example, is rotated k times by $\vec{x}_i \mapsto \vec{x}_{(i+1) mod(t-k)}$ in the classification phase, and the final classification is the winning class averaged over k. This method facilitates the classification and adds only a factor of k to the complexity, which corresponds to the number of components in the class diagram to be classified.

A.2.3 Processing Arbitrarily Dimensioned Vector Sequences

In conventional neural network models with fixed topology, it is neither possible to process variably long training patterns $<\vec{x}_{t-k}, \ldots, \vec{x}_t \mapsto \vec{y}_{t+1}, \ldots, \vec{y}_{t+m}> \in$ TS (training set) with free k and m, nor to process vectors $\vec{x}_i \in \mathbb{R}^{d'_i}$ or $\vec{y}_j \in \mathbb{R}^{d'_j}$ with arbitrary dimensionality $d'_i \neq d'_j$. Due to the modular design of the MRNN model, it is not only possible to treat variably long training sequences, but even to handle arbitrarily dimensioned input and target vectors. The functional requirement for the processing of heterogeneous data implies different vector dimension-

---

[2] In the case of classification, there is only one output signal indexed by $t+1$

alities, because different content types may lead to a different number of bits required for the encoding of multi-represented contents. In other words, feature vectors representing different domain objects can belong to different subspaces $U_j \subseteq \mathbb{R}^d$, $j \in I = \{1, 2, \ldots, n\}$, $dim(U_j) \leq d$, $d \in \{d_1, d_2\}$ (cf. section 4.4.1). In a concrete domain, it might hold $\forall i, j \in I$, $i \neq j : U_i \nsubseteq U_j$.

In the case of spread spectrum encoding, the type information is implicitly carried by all components of the respective input or target vector $\vec{x}_{t-k}, \vec{y}_{t+m}$. After the forward propagation through the state layer S, the computed output vector $\vec{o}_t = (o_{t_1}, o_{t_2}, \ldots, o_{t_{d_2}})^T$ must be related to the original node representation $\vec{y}_t$, which was fed into the neural network as training target. Due to the possibly different dimensionality of nodes from different types, the original vector $\vec{y}_t \subseteq \vec{o}_t$ must not have exploited the entire dimensionality of the state space S.

This is also the case for the spread spectrum encoding, where the output dimensionality $d := \max_{\vec{x} \in KB} dim(\vec{x})$ is set to the maximal dimensionality of all multi-represented objects occurring in the domain $\mathcal{D}$. Note that heterogeneously dimensioned input vectors slightly hamper the error minimization process.

A.2.4 Principal Component Analysis

In this dissertation, the *Principal Component Analysis* (PCA) and its generalization, the *Singular Value Decomposition* (SVD), are used for building a vector space representation of unstructured text in terms of text mining. The general purpose of the principal component analysis is to determine the principal components of a set of vectors in $\mathbb{R}^d$. The original vector space is transformed into a new vector space with another basis, which reveals the significance of the vector space features via their characteristic eigenvalues. Therefore, the computation of the eigenvalues and eigenvectors of a matrix M plays an important role in the PCA, which is first explained.

Let φ be a linear mapping $\varphi : \mathbb{R}^d \to \mathbb{R}^d$, $\varphi(\vec{x}) := M\vec{x}$ and M a quadratic matrix, then we consider the equation

$$\varphi(\vec{x}) = \lambda \vec{x}, \quad \vec{x} \in \mathbb{R}^d. \tag{A.5}$$

All vectors $\vec{x}$ and scalars λ, which fulfill equation A.5, are called eigenvectors and eigenvalues of the matrix M, respectively. This means that the eigenvectors $\vec{x}$ do not change their direction under the mapping φ, but are transformed into a λ-fold multiple of them.

The null vector $\vec{0}$ also fulfills A.5, but this special case cannot be used for a meaningful transformation of the set of feature vectors. In our case, M is the covariance matrix of all input vectors.

$$\begin{aligned} M_{(i,j)} &= \mu((x_i - \mu(x_i))(x_j - \mu(x_j))) \\ &= \frac{\sum_{\vec{x} \in D}[(x_i - \frac{1}{|D|}\sum_{\vec{x} \in D} x_i) \cdot (x_j - \frac{1}{|D|}\sum_{\vec{x} \in D} x_j)]}{|D|}, \end{aligned} \tag{A.6}$$

where $1 \leq i, j \leq d$.

For computing the PCA, M has to be diagonalized in the following way

$$M = V^T \Lambda V,$$

where Λ is a diagonal matrix $\begin{pmatrix} \lambda_1 & 0 & \cdots & 0 \\ 0 & \lambda_2 & \ddots & \vdots \\ \vdots & \ddots & \ddots & 0 \\ 0 & \cdots & 0 & \lambda_d \end{pmatrix}$ and $V = (\vec{v}_1, \ldots, \vec{v}_d)$ consists

of the eigenvectors of M written as column vectors $\vec{v}_i = \begin{pmatrix} v_{i1} \\ \vdots \\ v_{id} \end{pmatrix}$.

The diagonalization is a well-known mathematical method which can be accomplished with JAMA[3] [HMW+05].

Existence of the diagonal matrix Λ. The existence of Λ is assured, because the covariance matrix M to be diagonalized is always symmetric. The symmetry of a matrix guarantees its diagonalizability (cf. [MW99], p. 215).

Summarizing the stated fundamentals, a set of feature vectors $\{\vec{x}\}_{i \in \mathbb{N}}$ can be transformed into an equivalent vector-set $\{\vec{x}^*\}_{i \in \mathbb{N}}$ with a basis $(\vec{v}_i)_{1 \leq i \leq d}$ of eigenvectors, also called *principle components*, which spans a new vector space. Hence, the principal component transformation can be considered as a 'shift' of the original Cartesian coordinate system or as a change of the generating vector system $(\vec{v}_1, \ldots, \vec{v}_d)$, $\vec{x}^* = \sum_{i=1}^{d} \lambda_i \vec{v}_i$. In principle, this transformation does not lead to any loss of information.

By applying the PCA, we want to create a new dimension-reduced subspace $U \subset \mathbb{R}^{d-k}$. The k-many least significant features with eigenvalues λ_i are determined via their contribution to the information loss $\mathcal{X}^2$ given by

$$\mathcal{X}^2 = \sum_{i=1}^{k} \lambda_i \quad (A.7)$$

Since $\mathcal{X}^2$ should be minimized, the k-many eigenvectors with the smallest corresponding eigenvalues are discarded in order to obtain a new eigenvector matrix $\hat{V} = (\vec{v}_1, \ldots, \vec{v}_{d-k}) \in {}^d\mathbb{R}^{d-k}$. $\mathcal{X}^2$ represents the accompanying information loss by removing k-many data dimensions.

Now, the eigenvector matrix $\hat{V}$ is used to transform the original feature vectors into the new subspace U by a simple multiplication:

$$\hat{\vec{y}}_j = \hat{V}^T \vec{y}_j, \quad j \in \{1, \ldots, n\}, \, \hat{\vec{y}}_j \in U \quad (A.8)$$

It is crucial to transpose the matrix $\hat{V}$ before developing the feature vectors $\vec{y}_j$ ac-

---

[3] JAMA is a basic linear algebra package for Java.

cording to this new basis of U; otherwise, the dimensions will not match.

The result is a set $\hat{Y} = \{\hat{\tilde{y}}_1, \ldots, \hat{\tilde{y}}_n\}$ of transformed feature vectors, which hold the dimensionality $(d\text{-}k)$, where k is determined via a fixed threshold for the sum of the remaining eigenvalues $\sum_{i=k+1}^{d} \lambda_i$. For latent semantic indexing, which is based on a singular value decomposition as described in section 7.3, a lower bound of $\sigma^2 := 0.95$, $k = \max\{k \mid (\sum_{i=k+1}^{d} \lambda_i) \geq \sigma^2\}$ could be chosen, for example.

Acknowledgements

I would like to thank *Prof. Bernd Brügge, Ph.D.* for his visions and his great support with regard to my research at the intersection of software engineering and machine learning. This dissertation would not have been possible without his enduring commitment and mentorship. Especially, the frequent review meetings with Prof. Brügge in the last half-year of my doctorate contributed a lot to the success of this dissertation.

Furthermore, I wish to thank *Prof. Dr. Dr. h.c. Wilfried Brauer* for his in-depth review of my dissertation and his early support of my work on neural information processing.

List of Figures

2.1 Connectionist disease classification by means of a feed-forward neural network. 31
2.2 (a) Form of a neurule, (b) Corresponding adaline unit. 33
2.3 Two concrete arithmetical expressions that require the correct insertion of parentheses. 35
2.4 Forms of knowledge representation together with their fields of application. 36
2.5 Use case diagram showing top-level services provided and used by knowledge-based systems. 38
2.6 UML class diagram illustrating the associations and dependencies between functions of knowledge-based systems and the responsible disciplines relevant for this dissertation. 41
2.7 Machine learning, inference, and their interrelations expressed by *specification inheritance*. 42

3.1 UML class diagram showing a tree-structure of three levels with varying branching factor. 55
3.2 Layered model of a rich representation, which can be based on an ontology defining the available features. 58
3.3 *Knowledge Graph* of *Multi-Represented* (MR) objects. 60
3.4 Use case diagram of the main functions offered to framework users such as experts in the respective application domain. 64
3.5 Activity diagram showing the training phase and the operative application of the SYMBOCONN framework. 65
3.6 Three-layered application architecture of the SYMBOCONN framework with flexible MRNN Machine Learning Engine. 67
3.7 System decomposition of the SYMBOCONN framework as UML component diagram. 68
3.8 Control subsystem containing the ControlLogic subsystem. 68
3.9 KnowledgeConnector subsystem. 69
3.10 *NodeRepresentation* subsystem using implementation inheritance to integrate the domain-specific knowledge representation. 70
3.11 DesignAdvise subsystem that defines several software design patterns by a rule-based representation. 71
3.12 ConnectionistCore subsystem. 72

3.13 FrontEnd subsystem implementing the user front end that provides access to the learning and recommendation functionality. 73
3.14 External COTS components used by the SYMBOCONN framework. 73

4.1 Example of a Multilayer Perceptron (MLP) with input, hidden, and output layer consisting of 3, 4, and 2 neurons. 77
4.2 Dynamic model of the basic signal processing by a single neuron. 78
4.3 Schema of an Elman network with recurrent connections that feed the hidden activations back the input layer. 79
4.4 Hopfield network consisting of four fully interconnected units without reflexive connections. 80
4.5 Exemplary topology of a Radial Basis Function network consisting of three layers. 81
4.6 Machine learning, information theory, computational intelligence, and their interrelations. 83
4.7 *Auto-associative network* that encodes and decodes a given feature vector. 84
4.8 Exemplary data table and corresponding decision tree for the classification of software developers according to the types *beginner* and *expert*. 85
4.9 Three-dimensional illustration of the *XOR-problem*. 92
4.10 Schematic topology of the modular recurrent neural network MRNN used in SYMBOCONN. 94
4.11 UML representation of the Modular Recurrent Neural Network (MRNN). . 95
4.12 Two neurons interacting via a direct connection. 99
4.13 Generic plug-in architecture for training algorithms. 99
4.14 Copy of figure 4.10 recalling the three-layered structure of the MRNN. . . 100
4.15 Assignment of the formulas to the schematic network topology for one time step of the forward propagation phase. 102
4.16 Backward information propagation in the MRNN. 103
4.17 Assignment of the (error) gradient computation formulas to the schematic network topology for one time step. 104
4.18 Visualization of the training process showing the temporal development of the vector-valued training error. 106
4.19 Training setup of the MRNN for the learning experiment (easy task). ... 108
4.20 Second input node carrying the vector representation of an exemplary molecule (Corresponding to figure 4.19). 108
4.21 Training setup with single input node that carries both the feature values and the class information of the respective molecule. 110
4.22 Vector representation $\vec{x}_t := \vec{d}$ of molecule features. 110

5.1 Graphical representation of an instance of the *HTML-Table* schema. ... 116
5.2 Topology of the SYMBOCONN machine learning engine for context-sensitive learning of the production $\alpha B \gamma \rightarrow \alpha \beta \gamma$. 117
5.3 Exemplary and simplified decision table for the business process *cash check* of a bank. 118

LIST OF FIGURES

5.4	Deterministic finite state automaton for the *Reber grammar*.	119
5.5	Set-theoretic interpretation of symbol types.	123
5.6	Prefix-based type taxonomy exemplarily labeled with generic classes (types) of an UML model.	123
5.7	Recursive generation schema for OVSF codes in bipolar denotation.	125
5.8	Visualization of the result of spreading and despreading and the obtained *process gain* in the analogy of signal transmission.	129
5.9	Schematic processing steps and gates required to despread the predicted numerical output signal $\vec{o}_{t+1}$.	130
5.10	Ternary operator tree (valence 3) of depth 3 corresponding to the term $(a_1 + a_2) \cdot (b + (c_1 + c_2))$.	138
5.11	Schematic topology of a three-layered RAAM network.	139
5.12	Ternary operator tree representation of the expression $a \cdot (b + c)$.	140
5.13	UML class diagram showing a tree-structure of three levels with varying branching factor corresponding to figure 5.14.	140
5.14	MRNN auto-associating the elements that take part in an *aggregation* relationship as depicted by figure 5.13.	141
5.15	The compressed fixed-width term representation $(a \cdot (b + c)')'$ is decomposed into its constituents by the RAAM decoder.	142
5.16	Tree-based representation of the *distributive law* as structure transformation applied to *operator trees*.	143
5.17	MRNN network realizing both the required Recursive Auto-Associative Memory (RAAM) and the transformation network.	143
5.18	Hybrid architecture for structure transformations based on two RAAMs and one transformer network that are all realized by the MRNN.	144
5.19	Transforming a delegation-based model with three concrete implementors into an easy-maintainable model according to the *Bridge pattern*.	145
6.1	Project graph including system models, collaboration artifacts, and organizational model.	151
6.2	Class diagram showing the detailed ActionItem model.	153
6.3	Number of open ActionItems managed in the DOLLI project, broken down by activity.	156
6.4	Fraction of open ActionItems with respect to the total number of ActionItems managed in the DOLLI project.	160
6.5	Activity diagram showing an excerpt of the change management process that clarifies the role of change impact analysis.	163
6.6	Structure-sensitive change of a model element, which refers to other artifacts.	164
6.7	Risk graph showing three different risk zones. The green zone represents the *acceptable range*, while the red zone is *unacceptable*.	166
6.8	Exemplary change graphs G and G' consisting of the one-step neighbors of change node v_3.	168
6.9	Excerpt of a project graph that was filtered according to the node types *Issues* (I), *Requirements* (R), and *Activities* (A) denoted as labels.	169

6.10 Decision tree for the naive classification of class diagrams according to the predefined design patterns *Adapter, Bridge, Composite, Observer*, and *Proxy*. 178
6.11 Optimal decision tree for the same classification problem as addressed by the suboptimal decision tree of figure 6.10. 180
6.12 *Barker* spreading codes of different lengths for discriminating among the *non-hierarchical target types* z to be classified by the MRNN. 182
6.13 *Bridge pattern* with abstract *Implementor* class and refining implementations. 183
6.14 *Adapter pattern* with abstract superclass *AbstractClass* and directed association between *SubClass* (Adapter) and *NonhierarchClass* (Adaptee). ... 184
6.15 DesignAdviser subsystem consisting of the components PatternRepresent, XMIAnalyzer, CodeAnalyzer, and PredictionInterpreter. 186
6.16 Modular architecture of the DesignAdviser component based on a connectionist core engine. 186
6.17 Extendable class representation of the supported design patterns that are all subclasses of an abstract PatternRepresent class. 188
6.18 Activity diagram showing the training and application of the design pattern discovery process as upper and lower *swimlane*. 189
6.19 Incomplete *Template pattern* due to missing template method in the abstract superclass. 191
6.20 Structurally complete *Template pattern* with template method in the superclass, which calls the abstract methods step1, step2, step3 representing sequential work steps. 191
6.21 *Observer Pattern* with its typical division into abstract *Subject* and *Observer*, which are both realized by concrete implementors. 192
6.22 Use case for the classification of a system model. 193
6.23 Partial *Composite pattern* with non-abstract (non-italic) superclass Class and missing inheritance. 194
6.24 Generic plug-in architecture for training algorithms partially resembling the *strategy pattern*. 195
6.25 Initial design consisting of two associated classes on the same hierarchy level. 196
6.26 Classification result indicating a tendency towards the adapter pattern, since this pattern is the most similar. 196
6.27 Class diagram that almost corresponds to the adapter pattern (Scenario *Partial Adapter Pattern*). 196
6.28 Certainty distribution with a maximal value for the adapter pattern. The bridge pattern follows up as *false positive* here. 196
6.29 Class diagram showing the scenario *Mixture of Adapter and Bridge Pattern*. 197
6.30 Class constellation resulting in a high information entropy with respect to the classification certainty and thus implying low preference for a specific pattern. 197

6.31 Generic class diagram showing elements of *Composite*, *Bridge*, and *Adapter pattern* that imply a strong tendency towards the composite pattern (Scenario *Partial Composite Pattern*). 198
6.32 The degree of similarity to the original shape of the composite pattern is about 36% higher than to adpater and bridge pattern. 198
6.33 Nearly completed composite pattern still missing the inheritance between Class and NonhierarchClass. 198
6.34 The higher compliance with the original composite pattern leads to an increase of the respective certainty of almost 10%. 198
6.35 Complete *Composite pattern* with abstract superclass (Scenario *Complete Composite Pattern*). 199
6.36 Final classification result with maximal certainty for the composite pattern. 199
6.37 Conglomerate of three design patterns. 200

7.1 Blackbox view of association rule mining with generic input and output representation that is applicable to many different domains and their problems. 211
7.2 The client-server architecture of the *SurfLen* recommendation system. . . 215
7.3 Two-step recommendation process based on 20 user profiles and on an ensemble of 20 specialized back-propagation neural networks (MLPs). . . 216
7.4 Exemplary directed and non-symmetric graph consisting of three websites. 217
7.5 An *authority* is a web page that is referred to by many web pages. 218
7.6 A *hub* is a web page that holds many outgoing links to other web pages. . 218
7.7 Exemplary navigation history together with the predicted target sequence on a tree-shaped knowledge base. 221
7.8 Use case diagram showing the operational mode of navigation recommendation in SYMBOCONN. 222
7.9 Multiple specification inheritance from content-based and collaborative filtering combining the advantages of both methods. 224
7.10 Contextualization of two training patterns for navigation recommendation shown together with the corresponding network topology. 226
7.11 Activity diagram for navigation recommendation on the knowledge graph, either based on symbolic or rich content representation. 227
7.12 Prototypical user front-end of the SYMBOCONN framework for navigation recommendation. 229

8.1 The abstract statistical techniques *Exponential Smoothing* and *Autoregression* of order one can be realized by the MRNN, due to its generic and recurrent composition. 238
8.2 Decomposition of a time series into a trend component, a seasonal component, and a stochastic component. 240
8.3 Non-stationary time series (top) of the incoming orders concerning an industrial product together with its stationary pendant (bottom). 243

8.4 Scatter plot of the number of sold units of an industrial product indexed by time on a day-scale. 245
8.5 500 realizations of white noise $Y(t)$ that spread around the expected value $\mathbb{E}[Y(t)] = 0$. 247
8.6 MA(5)-process of white noise $Y(t)$ corresponding to figure 8.5 with identical weights b_j, $\forall j = 1, \ldots, 5$. 247
8.7 Schematic mapping of a time series to the input and target part of a training pattern for the Multilayer Perceptron. 250
8.8 Activity diagram illustrating the entire forecast process from training to prediction of a time series' future period. 251
8.9 Topology and weight configuration of the modular recurrent neural network (MRNN) to implement the exponential smoothing method from statistics. 253
8.10 Topology and weight configuration for a 2-layered MLP network that resembles an autoregressive (AR) process of order p. 254
8.11 Linear planning error (non-squared) showing over- and underplanning (residuals) based on the actual orders of plantitle 868. 257
8.12 Linear planning error for plantitle 886. 257
8.13 Scatter plot of the realizations for $t = 1, \ldots, 37$ of the orders series $I(t)$ of plantitle 886 together with the estimated regression model of formula 8.26. 260
8.14 Plot of the time series $I(t)$ for plantitle 886 together with its differentiated pendant (1-fold). 261
8.15 Plot of the time series $I(t)$ (red) for the plantitle 868 together with the ARIMA(1,1,0) prediction model (blue). 263
8.16 Plot of the estimation and prediction periods regarding the orders time series $I(t)$ (red) for the plantitle 886 by the Additive Winter model (blue) from statistics. 265
8.17 Plot of the estimation and prediction of the MRNN (green) with respect to the orders time series $I(t)$ (red) for the plantitle 886. 265

A.1 NodeRepresent subsystem using implementation inheritance to integrate the application-specific representations. 276
A.2 *Delegation variant:* NodeRepresent subsystem refined by a delegation mechanism via three adapter classes that decouple the domain-specific subsystems from the abstract knowledge representation. 276
A.3 Immediate prediction of the three subsequent symbols in a word of the Reber language. 277
A.4 Four productions of the Reber grammar 5.3 in the form of training patterns embedded in the respective topology of the MRNN. 277
A.5 Stepwise prediction of the subsequent web page based on the previous prediction. 278
A.6 At-once prediction of arbitrarily many sequential pages based only on the current web page. 279

A.7 A relation is on hand if the same entity is "mapped" onto two or more different entities of the value space. 281

A.8 A non-injective functional mapping of two input sequences onto one target sequence that resembles a mathematical function. 281

A.9 Visualization of the function of convergence $c(x, y)$ based on the difference of pairwise activations. 283

List of Tables

2.1	Truth function for the *logical implication*.	25
3.1	Meta model showing the multi-representation of objects by different features.	61
4.1	Exemplary look-up table that contains different representations of symbols from an arbitrary alphabet.	89
4.2	Evaluation matrix comparing several fundamental techniques from machine learning and statistics.	93
5.1	Words of different lengths generated by the Reber automaton depicted in figure 5.4.	120
5.2	Results of partial word completion according to the Reber grammar.	121
5.3	Lookup-table containing the basic encoding and the assigned spreading codes that are unique for each class.	131
5.4	Comparison of the average classification accuracy for the rule-recognition and classification of right-side grammar symbols (target nodes) based on the 20-*CFG* rule set for different noise levels.	134
5.5	Table showing the syntactical form of exemplary ternary terms and their encoded RAAM-representations (') formulated in infix-notation.	141
6.1	Description of the attributes of an ActionItem.	154
6.2	Description of the links between an ActionItem and other ModelElements.	154
6.3	Distribution of ActionItems according to the activity they were assigned to by the project participants.	157
6.4	Average classification accuracy measured in terms of *Precision* and *Recall* for 684 ActionItems after *5-fold cross-validation*.	158
6.5	Average accuracy for the classification of the artifact status Irrelevant after 5-fold cross-validation.	161
6.6	Evaluation of the ability of humans to classify ActionItems. Three persons with different degrees of expertise and insight into the software project were compared.	162
6.7	Excerpt of the data schema of the *repository transactions* from the XFree86 project, concerning the committed configuration items with some of their attributes.	173

6.8 Naive definition of several design patterns (DP) based on the number (#) of contained *Aggregation, Composition, Inheritance,* and *Association* relationships. ... 176
6.9 Exemplary dataset D containing realizations of several class diagrams that contain (at least) one concrete design pattern (DP). ... 177
6.10 Classification result for the TrainingAlgorithm class diagram of figure 6.24 including the independent certainties for each detected pattern. ... 195
6.11 Classification result for the pattern conglomerate of figure 6.37 including the independent certainties for each detected pattern. ... 201
6.12 Classification result for the pattern conglomerate based on the simple *unary type encoding* without data spreading. ... 201

7.1 Example of a database of items that appeared together in common transactions, for example, articles bought together. ... 213
7.2 Excerpt of the web data used in this case study. The table shows the existent web page topics together with their relative address. ... 230
7.3 Case-to-Vroot mapping concerning the observed navigations of 38,000 anonymous users. ... 230
7.4 Prediction accuracy for the application of SYMBOCONN to the recommendation of *msn.com* web pages. The accuracy was determined using an arbitrary test set of 1,250 untrained web navigations with histories of length three. ... 233
7.5 Prediction accuracy for the application of SYMBOCONN to the recommendation of *msn.com* web pages. The accuracy was determined using an arbitrary test set of 1,250 untrained web navigations with histories of length one. ... 234

8.1 Excerpt from the data schema of the worldwide sales figures of a large telecommunication company. ... 256
8.2 Quantitative results of demand planning at a large telecommunication company for the year 2005. ... 261
8.3 Accuracy PA of the connectionist MRNN prediction compared with the statistical prediction (ARIMA, Add. Winter) measured in percent for the prediction period 05-2005 until 02-2006. ... 264

List of Algorithms

1 Recursive decoding algorithm to unfold the inherent structure of RAAM-representations. 142
2 Pseudo code formulation of the *apriori algorithm*. 214

List of Abbreviations

ACF .... Autocorrelation Function
AR .... Autoregressive
ARIMA ...... Autoregressive Integrated Moving Average
ARM .... Association Rule Mining
ARMA .... Autoregressive Moving Average
BPTT .... Backpropagation Through Time
BRAAM ..... Bi-coded RAAM
CASE .... Computer-Aided Software Engineering
CB .... Content-Based
CBR .... Case-Based Reasoning
CEC .... Constant Error Carousel
CF .... Collaborative Filtering
CIA .... Change Impact Analysis
CM .... Configuration Management
COCOMO .... COnstructive COst MOdel
COTS .... Commercial-off-the-Shelf
CRC .... Cyclic Redundancy Check
CSG .... Change Subgraph
CTLK .... Connectionist Temporal Logic of Knowledge
CVS .... Concurrent Versions System
DC .... Dublin Core
DF-test .... Dickey-Fuller test
DL .... Description Logics
DOLLI .... Distributed Online Logistics and Location Infrastructure
DP .... Design Pattern
DSSS .... Direct Sequence Spread Spectrum
DTD .... Document Type Definition
DW-test ...... Durbin-Watson test
ECOC .... Error-Correcting Output Coding
ERM .... Entity Relationship-Model
ERP .... Enterprise Resource Planning
ES .... Exponential Smoothing
FOL .... First Order Logic
FSA .... Finite State Automaton
HRR .... Holographic Reduced Representations

LIST OF ABBREVIATIONS

HTML	Hypertext Markup Language
IBIS	Issue-Based Information System
IG	Information Gain
IID	Independent and Identically Distributed
IR	Information Retrieval
ISG	Impact Subgraph
ITS	Intelligent Tutoring System
KDD	Knowledge Discovery in Databases
KE	Knowledge Engineering
KM	Knowledge Management
KPI	Key Performance Indicator
KPSS-test	Kwiatkowski, Phillips, Schmidt, and Shin test
LRAAM	Labeling RAAM
LRM	Linear Regression Model
LS	Least Squares
LSI	Latent Semantic Indexing
LSTM	Long Short-Term Memory
MA	Moving Average
MDL	Minimum Description Language
MLP	Multilayer Perceptron
MMH	Maximum Margin Hyperplane
MR	Multi-Represented
MRNN	Modular Recurrent Neural Network
MSE	Mean Squared Error
NAND	Not AND
NLP	Natural Language Processing
NRM	Nonlinear Regression Model
ODBC	Open Database Connectivity
OVSF	Orthogonal Variable Spreading Factor
OWL	Web Ontology Language
PCA	Principal Component Analysis
PSM	Predictive Software Model
RAAM	Recursive Autoassociative Memory
RBF	Radial Basis Function
RDF	Resource Description Framework
RFC	Requests For Change
RL	Reinforcement Learning
RNN	Recurrent Neural Network
RTRL	Real-Time Recurrent Learning
RUSE	Rational-based Uniform Software Engineering
SE	Software Engineering
SOM	Self-Organizing Map
SPSS	Statistical Package for the Social Sciences
SRAAM	Sequential RAAM

LIST OF ABBREVIATIONS

SRN .... Simple Recurrent Network
SVD .... Singular Value Decomposition
SVM .... Support Vector Machine
SWRL .... Semantic Web Rule Language
TF-IDF .... Term Frequency - Inverse Document Frequency
UML .... Unified Modeling Language
XMI .... XML Metadata Interchange
XML .... Extensible Markup Language
XOR .... Exclusive OR
XSD .... XML Schema Definition

Bibliography

[ABD+08] Elke Achtert, Christian Böhm, Jörn David, Peer Kröger, and Arthur Zimek. *Noise Robust Clustering in Arbitrarily Oriented Subspaces.* In Proceedings of SIAM Conference on Data Mining, SDM 08, Society for Industrial and Applied Mathematics. Institute for Informatics, Ludwig-Maximilians-Universität München, Germany, 2008.

[ABK+07] Elke Achtert, Christian Böhm, H.-P. Kriegel, Peer Kröger, and Arthur Zimek. *Robust, complete, and efficient correlation clustering.* In Proceedings of the 7th SIAM International Conference on Data Mining (SDM), Minneapolis, MN. Institute for Informatics, Ludwig-Maximilians-Universität München, Germany, 2007.

[ABM+00] Andreas Abecker, Ansgar Bernardi, Heiko Maus, Michael Sintek, and Claudia Wenzel. *Information supply for business processes coupling workflow with document analysis and information retrieval.* In Knowledge-Based Systems, Special Issue on AI in Knowledge Management, volume 13, pages 271–284, 2000.

[AD99] M.J. Adamson and R.I. Damper. *B-RAAM: A Connectionist Model which Develops Holistic Internal Representations of Symbolic Structures.* 11(1):41–71, 1999.

[ADES02] D. Al-Dabass, D. Evans, and S. Sivayoganathan. *Intelligent System Modelling and Simulation using Hybrid Recurrent Networks.* In Second international workshop on Intelligent systems design and application, pages 23 – 28. Dynamic Publishers, Inc. Atlanta, GA, USA, 2002.

[AIS93] R. Agrawal, T. Imielinski, and A.N. Swami. *Mining Association Rules Between Sets of Items in Large Databases.* In Proceedings of the 1993 ACM SIGMOD International Conference on management of data, Washington, D.C., pages 207–216, 1993.

[Aiz05] Kenneth Aizawa. *The Systematicity Arguments, Studies in Brain and Mind.* In Minds and Machines, volume 17, pages 357–360. Springer Netherlands, 2005.

[AJ96] Honkela T. Alander, J. and M. Jakobsson. *Turing Machines are Recurrent Neural Networks*. In STeP'96—Genes, Nets and Symbols, pages 13–24. Symposium on Artificial Networks (Finnish Artificial Intelligence Conference), Connection Science, 1996.

[AKPS05] Elke Achtert, Hans-Peter Kriegel, Alexey Pryakhin, and Matthias Schubert. *Hierarchical Density-Based Clustering for Multi-Represented Objects*. In Workshop on Mining Complex Data (MCD'05), ICDM, Houston, TX. Institute for Computer Science, University of Munich, 2005.

[ALJ] Dan Ariely and John G. Lynch Jr. *Learning by Collaborative and Individual-Based Recommendation Agents*. Technical report, Sloan School of Management, MIT, Fuqua School of Business, Duke University.

[Amb06] Scott W. Ambler. *The Object Primer: Agile Model-driven Development with UML 2.0*. Cambridge, 2006.

[Amy03] Bernard Amy. *Neuro-Symbolic Hybrid System for Treatment of Gradual Rules*. In Neural Information Processing Letters and Reviews, volume 1, 2003.

[AN00] Ajith Abraham and Baikunth Nath. *Hybrid Intelligent Systems Design - A Review of a Decade of Research*, 2000.

[And97] Carl Andren. *Short PN Sequences for Direct Sequence Spread Spectrum Radios*. Harris Semiconductor Palm Bay, Florida, http://www.sss-mag.com/pdf/shortpn.pdf, 1997.

[AP06] Michael L Anderson and Donald R Perlis. *Symbol Systems*. Encyclopedia of Cognitive Science, John Wiley & Sons, 2006.

[AS94] Rakesh Agrawal and Ramakrishnan Srikant. *Fast Algorithms for Mining Association Rules*. In Proc. of the 20th Int. Conf. Very Large Data Bases, VLDB, Santiago, Chile, 1994.

[AS97] Frederic Alexandre and Ron Sun. *Connectionist-Symbolic Integration: From Unified to Hybrid Approaches*. Lawrence Erlbaum Assoc Inc, 1997.

[BA91] W. Bechtel and A. Abrahamsen. *Connectionism and the mind: An introduction to parallel processing in networks*. Blackwell, 1991.

[BA96] S. Bohner and R Arnold. *Software Change Impact Analysis*. In Los Alamitos, CA, pages 1–28. IEEE Computer Society Press, 1996.

[BBK02] Federico Barber, Vicente J. Botti, and Jana Koehler. *Artificial Intelligence: Technology with a Future*. UPGRADE - The European Online Magazine for the IT Professional, 3(5), 2002. http://www.upgrade-cepis.org.

[BCER05] Marc Barthelemy, Edmond Chowyz, and Tina Eliassi-Ra. *Knowledge Representation Issues in Semantic Graphs for Relationship Detection*. In AAAI Spring Symposium, pages 91–98. AAAI Press, 2005.

[BCR] Victor R. Basili, Gianluigi Caldiera, and H. Dieter Rombach. *THE EXPERIENCE FACTORY*. Technical report, Institute for Advanced Computer Studies, Department of Computer Science, University Of Maryland.

[BD04] Bernd Bruegge and Allen H. Dutoit. *Object-Oriented Software Engineering Using UML, Patterns, and Java*. Prentice Hall, ISBN 0-13-0471100, 2004.

[BDD03] D.P. Berrar, C.S. Downes, and W. Dubitzky. *Multiclass Cancer Classification Using Gene Expression Profiling and Probabilistic Neural Networks*. In Pacific Symposium on Biocomputing, volume 8, pages 5–16, 2003.

[BDW06] B. Bruegge, A. H. Dutoit, and T. Wolf. *Sysiphus: Enabling informal collaboration in global software development*. In In Proceedings of the First International Conference on Global Software Engineering, 2006.

[Bec03] Klaus Becker. *Prognosesystem mit Modellen exponentieller Glättung und Polynomen*. Books on Demand Gmbh, 2003.

[Ber99] Adam Berger. *Error-Correcting Output Coding for Text Classification*. In IJCAI'99: Workshop on machine learning for information filtering, 1999.

[BFH00] Jay Budzik, Xiaobin Fu, and Kristian J. Hammond. *Mining Navigation History for Recommendation*. In Proceedings of the 5th international conference on Intelligent user interfaces, New Orleans, Louisiana, United States, pages 106–112. ACM Press, New York, NY, USA, 2000.

[BFO02] Charles S. Bosa, Philip Hans Fransesb, and Marius Ooms. *Inflation, forecast intervals and long memory regression models*. In International Journal of Forecasting, volume 18, pages 243–264, 2002.

[BGC98]   Rafal Bogacz and Christophe Giraud-Carrier. *BRAINN: A Connectionist Approach to Symbolic Reasoning*. In Proceedings of the First International ICSC/IFAC Symposium on Neural Computation (NC'98), 1998.

[BHK98]   John S. Breese, David Heckerman, and Carl Kadie. *Empirical Analysis of Predictive Algorithms for Collaborative Filtering*. In Proceedings of the Fourteenth Conference on Uncertainty in Artificial Intelligence (UAI-98), pages 43–52, 1998.

[BN00]   Mikael Boden and Lars Niklasson. *Semantic systematicity and context in connectionist networks*. In Connection science, volume 12, pages 111–142, 2000.

[Bö03]   Christian Böhm. *Script 'Knowledge Discovery in Databases'*. Technical report, 2003.

[Boe06]   U.S. Navy Boeing. *Automated Maintenance Environment (AME)*. Outstart Evolution, 2006.

[Bor03]   Alexander Borusan. *Technische Informationssysteme - Domain Engineering*. Technical report, Technische Universität Berlin, Fraunhofer Institut Software- und Systemtechnik, 2003.

[Bor07]   K.M. Borgwardt. *Graph Kernels - PhD thesis*. Technical report, Institute for Mathematics, Ludwig-Maximilians-Universität München, Germany, 2007.

[Bou97]   Andrew Boucher. *Parallel Machines*. In Minds and Machines, volume 7, pages 543–551, 1997.

[BP98]   Sergey Brin and Lawrence Page. *The Anatomy of a Large-Scale Hypertextual Web Search Engine*. In Computer Networks and ISDN Systems, volume 30, pages 107–117, 1998.

[BSK05]   Paul Buitelaar, Michael Sintek, and Malte Kiesel. *Feature Representation for Cross-Lingual, Cross-Media Semantic Web Applications*. In Proceedings of the ISWC 2005 Workshop "SemAnnot", Lecture Notes in Computer Science, 2005.

[Buc07]   Wilfried Buchholz. *Einführung in die Mathematische Logik I*. Technical report, Institute for Mathematics, Ludwig-Maximilians-Universität München, Germany, 2007.

[BVO89]   Barker, E. Virginia, and Dennis E. O'Connor. *Expert Systems for Configuration at Digital: XCON and Beyond*. In Communications of the ACM, volume 32, pages 298–312, 1989.

[BW08] Harald Brandl and Franz Wotawa. *Test Case Generation from QR Models*. In Ngoc Thanh Nguyen, Leszek Borzemski, Adam Grzech, and Moonis Ali, editors, New Frontiers in Applied Artificial Intelligence, volume 5027 of *LNAI*, pages 235–244. Springer, 2008.

[Cal03] Robert Callan. *Neuronale Netze im Klartext*. In Pearson Studium, 2003.

[CBB+01] Robert Cummins, James Blackmon, David Byrd, Pierre Poirier, Martin Roth, and Georg Schwarz. *Systematicity and the Cognition of Structured Domains*. The Journal of Philosophy, 98(4):1–19, 2001.

[CDLD+05] Gennaro Costagliola, Andrea De Lucia, Vincenzo Deufemia, Carmine Gravino, and Michele Risi. *Design Pattern Recovery by Visual Language Parsing*. In Proceedings of the Ninth European Conference on Software Maintenance and Reengineering, CSMR 05, 2005.

[CDLD+06] Gennaro Costagliola, Andrea De Lucia, Vincenzo Deufemia, Carmine Gravino, and Michele Risi. *Case Studies of Visual Language Based Design Patterns Recovery*. In Proceedings of the Conference on Software Maintenance and Reengineering, CSMR 06, pages 165 – 174. IEEE Computer Society, Washington, DC, USA, 2006.

[CF] Richard Cooper and Bradley Franks. *Constraints on Hybrid Symbolic/Connectionist Models of Cognition: A Theoretical Analysis*.

[CF00] Rafael C. Carrasco and Mikel L. Forcada. *Encoding Nondeterministic Finite-State Tree Automata in Sigmoid Recursive Neural Networks*. In Advances in Pattern Recognition: Joint IAPR International Workshops, SSPR 2000 and SPR 2000, Alicante, Spain, volume 1876/2000 of *Lecture Notes in Computer Science*, page 203. Springer Berlin / Heidelberg, 2000.

[Cha90] David J. Chalmers. *Syntactic Transformations on Distributed Representations*. In Connection Science, volume 2, pages 53–62. Center for Research on Concepts and Cognition, 1990.

[CM03] Davor Cubranic and Gail C. Murphy. *Hipikat: Recommending pertinent software development artifacts*. In 25th International Conference on Software Engineering (ICSE'03), page 408 418, 2003.

[CP08] LLC Clark & Parsia. *Pellet: The Open Source OWL DL Reasoner*, 2008.

[CPB97] Robert E. Callan and Dominic Palmer-Brown. *(S)RAAM: An Analytical Technique for Fast and Reliable Derivation of Connectionist Symbol Structure Representations.* volume 9, pages 139–160. Connection Science, 1997.

[CRP06] Coral Calero, Francisco Ruiz, and Mario Piattini. *Ontologies for Software Engineering and Software Technology.* Springer, 2006.

[CSSM89] Axel Cleeremans, David Servan-Schreiber, and James L. McClelland. *Finite State Automata and Simple Recurrent Networks.* In Neural Computation, volume 1, pages 372–381. Addision-Wesley, Bonn, 1989.

[CV08] Francesco Camastra and Alessandro Vinciarelli. *Machine Learning for Audio, Image and Video Analysis.* In Advanced Information and Knowledge Processing, pages 83–89. Springer London, 2008.

[CW99] Jin-Liang Chen and Jung-Hua Wang. *A New Robust Clustering Algorithm - Density-Weighted Fuzzy C-means.* volume 3, pages 90–94, 1999.

[CW05] Todd E. Clarka and Kenneth D. West. *Using out-of-sample mean squared prediction errors to test the martingale difference hypothesis.* In NBER Technical Working Papers from National Bureau of Economic Research, Inc, 2005.

[Dav08a] Joern David. *Navigation Recommendation On Knowledge Artifacts.* In Workshop "Agile Knowledge Sharing for Distributed Software Teams", Lecture Notes in Informatics, Munich. Springer, 2008.

[Dav08b] Joern David. *Noise Robust Classification Based On Spread Spectrum.* In Submitted to the IEEE International Conference on Data Mining (ICDM 08), Pisa, Italy, 2008.

[Dav08c] Joern David. *Recommending Software Artifacts From Repository Transactions.* In The Twenty First International Conference on Industrial, Engineering and Other Applications of Applied Intelligent Systems (IEA/AIE 2008), LNAI 5027, pages 189–198. Springer-Verlag Berlin Heidelberg, 2008.

[DD08] C.W. Dawson and R.J. Dawson. *An artificial intelligence approach to software development management and planning.* In WIT eLibrary. Witpress, 2008.

[DDF+90] Scott Deerwester, Susan T. Dumais, George W. Furnas, Richard Harshman, and Thomas K. Landauer. *Indexing by Latent Semantic Analysis.* volume 41, pages 391–407, 1990.

[Deb00]   John Debenham. *Supporting knowledge-driven processes in a multi-agent process management system*. In Proceedings of the 5th International Conference on the Practical Application of Intelligent Agents and Multi-Agent Technology (PAAM 2000), 2000.

[Dek08]   Deka. *DekaStruktur: 4 ErtragPlus Inhaber-Anteile o.N.*, 2008.

[DF79]   D.A. Dickey and W.A. Fuller. *Distribution of the Estimators for Autoregressive Time Series with a Unit Root*. Journal of the American Statistical Association, 74, pages 427–431, 1979.

[DGL06]   Artur S. D'Avila Garcez and Lus C. Lamb. *A Connectionist Computational Model for Epistemic and Temporal Reasoning*. In Neural Computation, volume 18, pages 1711–1738, 2006.

[Din92]   John Dinsmore. *The symbolic and connectionist paradigms: closing the gap*. Lawrence Erlbaum Associates, 1992.

[DJLLP94]   T. G. Dietterich, A. Jain, R. H. Lathrop, and T. Lozano-Perez. *A comparison of dynamic reposing and tangent distance for drug activity prediction*. In Advances in Neural Information Processing Systems, San Mateo, CA, pages 216–223. Morgan Kaufmann, 1994.

[DK95]   Thomas G. Dietterich and Eun Bae Kong. *Error-Correcting Output Coding Corrects Bias and Variance*. In International Conference on Machine Learning, pages 313–321, 1995.

[DLDGR07]   Andrea De Lucia, Vincenzo Deufemia, Carmine Gravino, and Michele Risi. *A Two Phase Approach to Design Pattern Recovery*. In Proceedings of the 11th European Conference on Software Maintenance and Reengineering, CSMR 07, pages 297–306. IEEE Computer Society, Washington, DC, USA, 2007.

[DMMP06]   Allen H. Dutoit, Raymond McCall, Ivan Mistrik, and Barbara Paech. *Rationale Management in Software Engineering*. In Springer-Verlag, Berlin Heidelberg Wien New York, 2006.

[Dol07]   *Distributed Online Logistics and Location Infrastructure (DOLLI)*, http://www1.in.tum.de/static/dolli/, 2007.

[DOP08]   Wlodzislaw Duch, Richard J. Oentaryo, and Michel Pasquier. *Cognitive Architectures: Where do we go from here?* In The First Conference on Artificial General Intelligence, 2008.

[Dur96]   John Durkin. *Parallel Machines*. In IEEE Expert: Intelligent Systems and Their Applications, volume 11, pages 56–63, 1996.

[EB07] Matthew Easley and Elizabeth Bradley. *Incorporating Engineering Formalisms into Automated Model Builders*. In Computational Discovery of Scientific Knowledge, volume 4660/2007, pages 44–68. Springer Berlin / Heidelberg, 2007.

[EKSX96] Martin Ester, Hans-Peter Kriegel, Jörg Sander, and Xiaowei Xu. *A Density-Based Algorithm for Discovering Clusters in Large Spatial Databases with Noise*. In Proceedings of 2nd International Conference on Knowledge Discovery and Data Mining (KDD-96), 1996.

[EUD02] *EUD-NET Network of Excellence on End-User Development*, 2002. http://giove.cnuce.cnr.it/eud-net.htm.

[Fak96] John Fakatselis. *Processing Gain for Direct Sequence Spread Spectrum Communication Systems and PRISM, http://www.qsl.net/n9zia/pdf/AN9633.pdf*. Technical report, Intersil Corporation, Melbourne, 1996.

[Fal04] David C. Fallside. *XML Schema Part 0: Primer Second Edition*. W3C Recommendation, http://www.w3.org/TR/xmlschema-0/, October 2004.

[FF98] M. Feder and E. Federovski. *Prediction of binary sequences using finite memory*. In IEEE International Symposium on Information Theory, pages 137 –, 1998.

[FGV01] Pasquale Foggia, Roberto Genna, and Mario Vento. *Symbolic vs. Connectionist Learning: An Experimental Comparison in a Structured Domain*. In IEEE Transactions on Knowledge and Data Engineering, volume 13, pages 176 – 195. IEEE Educational Activities Department, 2001.

[FHH03] Jürgen Franke, Wolfgang Härdle, and Christian Hafner. *Einführung in die Statistik der Finanzmärkte*. 2003. http://www.xplore-stat.de/ebooks/ebooks.html.

[FK96] Hichem Frigui and Raghu Krishnapuram. *A Robust Clustering Algorithm Based on Competitive Agglomeration and Soft Rejection of Outliers*. In Proceedings of the 1996 Conference on Computer Vision and Pattern Recognition (CVPR '96), page 550. IEEE Computer Society, Washington, DC, USA, 1996.

[Fle01] Eric S. Fleischman. *A cognitive model of learning from examples*. In Journal of Computing Sciences in Colleges archive, volume 16, pages 302 – 303. Consortium for Computing Sciences in Colleges, USA, 2001.

[FPSS96] Fayyad, Piatetsky-Shapiro, and Smyth. In Lecture Notes in Computer Science, 1996.

[Fre00] Reva Freedman. *What is an Intelligent Tutoring System?* 11(3):15–16, 2000.

[FTL04] John C. Flackett, John Tait, and Guy Littlefair. *Scaling Connectionist Compositional Representations*. In Compositional Connectionism in Cognitive Science, 2004 AAAI Fall Symposium. Center for Research on Concepts and Cognition, 2004.

[Gha00] Rayid Ghani. *Using Error-Correcting Codes For Text Classification*. In Proceedings of ICML-00, 17th International Conference on Machine Learning, 2000.

[GHJ98] Harald Gall, Karin Hajek, and Mehdi Jazayeri. *Detection of logical coupling based on product release history*. In International Conference on Software Maintenance (ICSM 98), 1998.

[GHJV95] Erich Gamma, Richard Helm, Ralph Johnson, and John Vlissides. *Design Patterns. Elements of Reusable Object-Oriented Software*. Addison Wesley, 1995.

[GK96] Christoph Goller and Andreas Küchler. *Learning Task-Dependent Distributed Representations by Backpropagation Through Structure*. In Proceedings of the International Conference on Neural Networks (ICNN-96), volume 1, 1996.

[GK07] Yann-Gael Guhneuc and Foutse Khomh. *Perception and Reality: What are Design Patterns Good For?* In Proceedings of the 11th ECOOP Workshop on Quantitative Approaches in Object-Oriented Software (QAOOSE 2007), pages 20–26. University of Montreal, Canada, 2007.

[GLZ04] Miroslaw Galicki, Lutz Leistritz, and Bernhard Zwick. *Improving Generalization Capabilities of Dynamic Neural Networks*. In Neural Computation, volume 16, pages 1253–1282. MIT Press Journals, 2004.

[GM08] Lars Marius Garshol and Graham Moore. *Topic Maps Data Model*, 2008.

[GNP05] S. Ghita, W. Nejdl, and R. Paiu. *Semantically Rich Recommendations in Social Networks for Sharing, Exchanging and Ranking Semantic Context*. In Proc. of the 4th International Semantic Web Conference, pages 285–295, 2005.

[GR05]   W. Gleißner and Frank Romeike. *Risikomanagement Umsetzung, Werkzeuge, Risikobewertung*. Haufe, 2005.

[Gra08]   Alex Graves. *Supervised Sequence Labelling with Recurrent Neural Networks*. Technical report, 2008.

[Gru08]   Tom Gruber. *Ontology*. In Encyclopedia of Database Systems, Ling Liu and M. Tamer Özsu (Eds.). Springer-Verlag, 2008.

[GSW05]   Faustino J. Gomez, Jürgen Schmidhuber, and Daan Wierstra. *Modeling Systems with Internal State using Evolino*. In Proc. of the 2005 conference on genetic and evolutionary computation (GECCO), Washington, D. C., New York, USA, pages 1795–1802. ACM Press, 2005.

[GWW91]   M. D. Garris, R. A. Wilkinson, and C. L. Wilson. *Analysis of a biologically motivated neural network for character recognition*. In Proceedings of the conference on Analysis of neural network applications, Fairfax, Virginia, United States, pages 160–175, 1991.

[Ham94]   J.D. Hamilton. *Time Series Analysis*. Princeton University Press, 1994.

[Ham97]   James A. Hammerton. *Holistic Computation: Reconstructing a muddled concept*. Technical report, University of Birmingham, 1997.

[Ham01]   Barbara Hammer. *On the Generalization Ability of Recurrent Networks*. In Lecture Notes in Computer Science, Artificial Neural Networks ICANN 2001, volume 2130/2001, pages 731–736. Springer Berlin / Heidelberg, 2001.

[HAM05]   Karen Hovsepian, Peter C. Anselmo, and Subhasish Mazumdar. *Detection and Prediction of Relative Clustered Volatility in Financial Markets*. In Fourth International Conference on Computational Intelligence in Economics and Finance (CIEF 2005), Salt Lake City, 2005.

[Han97]   Jun Han. *Supporting Impact Analysis and Change Propagation in Software Engineering Environments*. In Proceedings of the 8th International Workshop on Software Technology and Engineering Practice (STEP '97). IEEE Computer Society, Washington, DC, USA, 1997.

[Har43]   S. Harnad. *The symbol grounding problem*. 42:335–346, 1943.

[Has03]   Uwe Hassler. *Zeitabhängige Volatilität und instationäre Zeitreihen*. Wirtschaftsdienst, Wissenschaft Für Die Praxis, 2003.

[Hau03]   Gregory T. Haugan. *The Work Breakdown Structure in Government Contracting.* Management Concepts, 2003.

[HBG05]   Pascal Hitzler, Sebastian Bader, and Artur Garcez. *Ontology Learning as a Use-Case for Neural-Symbolic Integration.* 2005.

[Heb49]   D. Hebb. *The Organization of Behavior: a neuropsychological approach.* New York: Wiley, 1949.

[HEK99]   Joachim Hartung, Bärbel Elpelt, and Karl-Heinz Klösener. *Statistik, 12. Auflage.* Oldenbourg, 1999.

[Hel08]   Jonas Helming. *Integrating Software Lifecycle Models into a uniform Software Engineering Model.* In Workshop "Integration von heterogenen Werkzeugen im agilen Zeitalter (IntegrA 08)", Lecture Notes in Informatics. Springer, 2008.

[HFO98]   Bart Hobijn, Philip Hans Franses, and Marius Ooms. *Generalizations of the KPSS-test for Stationarity.* In Econometric Institute Report, number 9802/A, 1998.

[HH97]   Robert F. Hadley and Michael B. Hayward. *Strong Semantic Systematicity from Hebbian Connectionist Learning.* In Minds and Machines, volume 7, pages 1–37. Springer Netherlands, 1997.

[HH04]   Ahmed E. Hassan and Richard C. Holt. *Predicting Change Propagation in Software Systems.* In Proceedings of the 20th IEEE International Conference on Software Maintenance, pages 284 – 293. IEEE, 2004.

[HHS04]   Pascal Hitzler, Steffen Hölldobler, and Anthony K. Seda. *Logic programs and connectionist networks.* Journal of Applied Logic, 3(2):245–272, 2004.

[HLC06]   Sun-Jen Huang, Chieh-Yi Lin, and Nan-Hsing Chiu. *Fuzzy Decision Tree Approach for Embedding Risk Assessment Information into Software Cost Estimation Model.* In Journal of Information Science and Engineering, volume 22, pages 297–313, 2006.

[HM03]   Andreas Henrich and Karlheinz Morgenroth. *Supporting Collaborative Software Development by Context-Aware Information Retrieval Facilities.* In 14th International Workshop on Database and Expert Systems Applications, pages 249 – 253, 2003.

[HMW+05]   Joe Hicklin, Cleve Moler, Peter Webb, Ronald F. Boisvert, Bruce Miller, Roldan Pozo, and Karin Remington. *JAMA: A Java Matrix Package.* In The MathWorks and the National Institute of Standards and Technology (NIST), 2005.

[Hoc91]	S. Hochreiter. *Untersuchungen zu dynamischen neuronalen Netzen.* Technical report, 1991.
[HP01]	Ioannis Hatzilygeroudis and Jim Prentzas. *An Efficient Hybrid Rule Based Inference Engine with Explanation Capability.* In Proceedings of the 14th International FLAIRS Conference, Key West, Florida, 2001.
[htt07]	http://www.scrumalliance.org. *Scrum Alliance.* 2007.
[Huf52]	D.A. Huffman. *A method for the construction of minimum-redundancy codes.* In Proceedings of the I.R.E., pages 1098–1102, 1952.
[HvC93]	G. E. Hinton and D. van Camp. *Keeping neural networks simple by minimizing the description length of the weights.* In Sixth ACM Conference on Computational Learning Theory, Santa Cruz, 1993.
[HZ96]	G.E. Hinton and R.S. Zemel. *Minimizing description length in an unsupervised neural network.* In Sixth ACM Conference on Computational Learning Theory, Santa Cruz, 1996.
[HZC05]	Zan Huang, Daniel D. Zeng, and Hsinchun Chen. *A Unified Recommendation Framework Based on Probabilistic Relational Models.* Social Science Research Network (SSRN), 2005. http://ssrn.com/abstract=906513.
[IAC06]	Mitsuru Ikeda, Kevin Ashlay, and Tak-Wai Chan. *Intelligent Tutoring Systems.* In 8th International Conference, ITS 2006, Jhongli, Taiwan. Lecture Notes in Computer Science, Vol. 4053, 2006.
[Int07]	Avail Intelligence. *Navigation Predictor^{TM}*, 2007. http://www.avail.net/index.php.
[Inv08]	Investolution. *Probabilistic stock market forecasts*, 2008. http://www.investolution.com/DowJones.php.
[J.97]	Fodor J. *Connectionism and the problem of systematicity (continued): why Smolensky's solution still doesn't work.* Cognition, 62(1):109–119, 1997.
[JH92]	Nowlan. S. J. and G. E. Hinton. *Simplifying neural networks by soft weight sharing.* In Neural Computation, volume 4, pages 173–193, 1992.
[JMDO07]	C. Julin Moreno, A. Demetrio, and C. Ovalle. *Computational Hybrid System based on Neural-Fuzzy Techniques & Intelligent Software Agents to Assist Colombian Electricity Free Market.* 3(2):111–122, 2007.

[JPSS99]   Arun Jagota, Tony Plate, Lokendra Shastri, and Ron Sun. *Connectionist Symbol Processing: Dead or Alive?* In Neural Computing Surveys 2, page 140, 1999. http://www.icsi.berkeley.edu/jagota/NCS.

[J.R90]   W. Premerlani F. Eddy W. Lorensen J.Rumbaugh, M. Blaha. *Object-Oriented Modeling and Design*. Prentice Hall, 1990.

[KA01]   Daniel Kustrin and Jim Austin. *Connectionist Propositional Logic, A Simple Correlation Matrix Memory Based Reasoning System*. In Lecture Notes in Computer Science, Emergent Neural Computational Architectures Based on Neuroscience : Towards Neuroscience-Inspired Computing, volume 2036/2001, page 534. Springer Berlin / Heidelberg, 2001.

[KAD01]   Taghi M. Khoshgoftaar, Edward B. Allen, and Jianyu Deng. *Controlling Overfitting in Software Quality Models: Experiments with Regression Trees and Classification*. In Seventh International Software Metrics Symposium (METRICS'01), 2001.

[KFM+02]   Stefan Kaiser, Uwe-Carsten Fiebig, Naoto Matoba, Andy Jeffries, Marc de Courville, and Arne Svensson. *Broadband Multi-Carrier Based Air Interface*. Technical report, WWRF/WG4/Subgroup on New Air Interfaces, 2002.

[Kim02]   Benjamin B. Kimia. *Shape Representation for Image Retrieval*. Image Databases, April 2002. Print ISBN: 9780471321163, Online ISBN: 9780471224631.

[KK01]   Michihiro Kuramochi and George Karypis. *Frequent Subgraph Discovery*. In 1st IEEE Conference on Data Mining, ICDM, pages 313–320, 2001.

[KK02]   Michihiro Kuramochi and George Karypis. *An efficient algorithm for discovering frequent subgraphs*. In Technical report. Department of Computer Science, University of Minnesota, 2002, 2002.

[Koe08]   M. Koegel. *Towards Software Configuration Management for Unified Models*. In ICSE CVSM'08 Workshop Proceedings, pages 19–24, 2008.

[Kra91]   Klaus Peter Kratzer. *Neuronale Netze*. 1991.

[Kri00]   Prof. Dr. Hans-Peter Kriegel. Institute for Informatics, Ludwig-Maximilians-Universität München, Germany, 2000. http://www.dbs.informatik.uni-muenchen.de/Forschung/KDD/Clustering/index.html.

[KSH08]   Jennifer A. Kaminski, Vladimir M. Sloutsky, and Andrew F. Heckler1. *The Advantage of Abstract Examples in Learning Math*. In Science 25, volume 320, pages 454 – 455, 2008.

[Kü04]   Axel Küpper. *Mobile Communications 1, Multiplexing and Modulation, http://www.mobile.ifi.lmu.de/Vorlesungen/ss06 /mk/chapter4.pdf*. Technical report, Mobile and Distributed Systems Group, University of Munich, Germany, 2004.

[Lam61]   Joachim Lambek. *On the calculus of syntactic types - Structure of Language and its mathematical aspects*. In American Mathematical Society, page 166 178, 1961.

[Lam78]   Leslie Lamport. *Time, Clocks, and the Ordering of Events in a Distributed System*. volume 21, pages 558–565. ACM, New York, NY, USA, 1978.

[LH03]   Peter C.R. Lane and James B. Henderson. *Towards Effective Parsing with Neural Networks: Inherent Generalisations and Bounded Resource Effects*. 19(1-2):83–99, 2003.

[Liu06]   Yang Liu. *Using SVM and Error-correcting Codes for Multiclass Dialog Act Classification in Meeting Corpus*. In INTERSPEECH 2006 - ICSLP, 2006.

[LKB06]   Mark Last, Abraham Kandel, and Horst Bunke. *Artificial Intelligence Methods In Software Testing*. 2006.

[LM98]   Huan Liu and Hiroshi Motoda. *Feature Selection for Knowledge Discovery and Data Mining*. In The Springer International Series in Engineering and Computer Science, volume 454, pages 1226–1238, 1998.

[LM06]   K. Lakshmi and S. Mukherjee. *An Improved Feature Selection using Maximized Signal to Noise Ratio Technique for TC*. In Third International Conference on Information Technology: New Generations (ITNG), pages 541 – 546, 2006.

[LSK04]   S. N. Lindstaedt, Koller S., and T. Krämer. *Eine Wissensinfrastruktur für Projektrisikomanagement - Identifikation und Management von Wissensrisiken*. In KnowTech 2004, 6. Konferenz zum Einsatz von Knowledge Management in Wirtschaft und Verwaltung, München, 2004.

[LSY03]   G. Linden, B. Smith, and J. York. *Amazon.com recommendations: Item-to-item collaborative filtering*. In IEEE Internet Computing, volume 4, 1, 2003.

[LZZZ05] Nan Lu, Jing-Zhou Zhou, Wang Zhe, and Chun-Guang Zhou. *Research on Association Rules Mining Algorithm With Item Constraints*. In International Conference on Cyberworlds (CW'05), pages 325–329, 2005.

[Mas05] Bart Massey. *Nickle Repository Transaction Data*, 2005. Computer Science Dept., Portland State University, Portland, OR, USA.

[MB00] L.M. MacKinnon and K.E. Brown. *Context Separation Using Structured Knowledge Models For Reusable Interactive Computer Assisted Learning Resources*. In 6th ERCIM Workshop "User Interfaces for All", 2000.

[McL04] G.J. McLachlan. *Discriminant Analysis and Statistical Pattern Recognition*. Wiley-Interscience, 2004.

[MG05] Xiaoxu Ma and W. Eric L. Grimson. *Edge-based rich representation for vehicle classification*. In ICCV 05, 2005.

[Mic05] Microsoft. *Microsoft Neural Network-Algorithmus (SSAS)*. 2005. http://msdn2.microsoft.com/de-de/library/ms174941.aspx.

[MLP00] O. Melnik, S. Levy, and J. Pollack. *RAAM for infinite context-free languages*. In Proceedings of the International Joint Conference on Neural Networks, IJCNN, volume 5, pages 585–590, 2000.

[MM89] W. Bruce MacDonald and Enid Mumford. *XSEL'S progress: the continuing journey of an expert system*. 1989.

[Moc08] A. Mockus. *Missing Data in Software Engineering*. In Guide to Advanced Empirical Software Engineering, pages 185–200, 2008.

[MP43] W. McCulloch and W. Pitts. *A logical calculus of the ideas immanent in nervous activity*. 5:115–133, 1943.

[Mue06] Erik T. Mueller. *Commonsense Reasoning*. San Francisco: Morgan Kaufmann, 2006.

[MV03] R.C. Mintram and J. Vincent. *A General Framework for the Transformation of Structured Data into Vector Representations*. In Proceeding in Applied Informatics, Innsbruck, Austria, 2003.

[MW99] Gerhard Merziger and Thomas Wirth. *Repetitorium der höheren Mathematik*. In Binomi Verlag, ISBN 3-923 923-33-3, 1999.

[MWH01] Anthony N. Michel, Kaining Wang, and Bo Hu. *Qualitative Theory of Dynamical Systems: The Role of Stability Preserving Mappings*. 2001.

[MWM03] Kenneth McGarry, Stefan Wermter, and John MacIntyre. *Hybrid Neural Systems: From Simple Coupling to Fully Integrated Neural Networks.* 2(3):62–93, 2003.

[Nav97] Pavol Navrat. *A Note On Using Artificial Intelligence Techniques in Software Engineering*, 1997.

[Neu00] Jane Neumann. *Holistic Transformation of Holographic Reduced Representations.* In ECAI'00, 2000.

[Neu01] Jane Neumann. *Holistic Processing of Hierarchical Structures in Connectionist Networks.* Technical report, University of Edinburgh, 2001.

[NN001] *Artificial Neural Networks and their Biological Motivation.* In NNets, 2001.

[NP04] O. Nasraoui and M. Pavuluri. *Complete this Puzzle: A Connectionist Approach to Accurate Web Recommendations based on a Committee of Predictors.* 2004.

[NS72] A Newell and H A. Simon. *Human problem solving.* Englewood Cliffs, NJ: Prentice-Hall, 1972.

[NS76] Allen Newell and Herbert A. Simon. *Computer science as empirical inquiry: symbols and search.* In Communications of the ACM, volume 19, pages 113 – 126. ACM, New York, NY, USA, 1976. http://www.rci.rutgers.edu/ cfs/472_html/AI_SEARCH/PSS/PSSH1.html.

[NS93] Lars Niklasson and Noel E. Sharkey. *Systematicity and Generalisation in Connectionist Compositional Representations.* 1993.

[NvG94] L.F. Niklasson and T. van Gelder. *Can connectionist models exhibit non-classical structure sensitivity?* In Proceedings of the Sixteenth Annual Conference of the Cognitive Society, Atlanta, Hillsdale, NJ, pages 664–669. Lawrence Erlbaum Associates, 1994.

[NZ99] Ralph Neuneier and Hans-Georg Zimmermann. *Neural Network Architectures for the Modeling of Dynamic Systems.* Technical report, Siemens Corporate Technology, 1999.

[Par02] Domenico Parisi. *Increasing the Biological Inspiration of Neural Networks.* In NNets, volume 2486/2002, pages 243–252. Springer Berlin / Heidelberg, 2002.

[Pea97] Annie R. Pearce. *Cost-Based Risk Prediction and Identification of Project Cost Drivers Using Artificial Neural Networks.* Technical report, School of Civil and Environmental Engineering, Georgia Institute of Technology, Atlanta, GA 30332-0355 USA, 1997.

[Per96]   *System compositions and shared dependencies.* In Software Configuration Management, volume 1167, pages 139–153. Springer Berlin / Heidelberg, 1996.

[Phi96]   Steven Phillips. *Connectionism and Systematicity.* 1996.

[Pla03]   Tony A. Plate. *Holographic Reduced Representation: Distributed Representation for Cognitive Structures.* C S L I Publications, 2003.

[PLD05]   H.C. Peng, F. Long, and C. Ding. *Feature selection based on mutual information: criteria of max-dependency, max-relevance, and min-redundancy.* In IEEE Transactions on Pattern Analysis and Machine Intelligence, volume 27, pages 1226–1238, 2005.

[PMG00]   K.A. Papanikolaou, G.D. Magoulas, and M. Grigoriadou. *A Connectionist Approach for Supporting Personalized Learning in a Web-based Learning Environment.* In Lecture Notes in Computer Science, Adaptive Hypermedia and Adaptive Web-based Systems, number 1892, pages 189–201, 2000.

[PN02]   Gabriela Policov1 and Pavol Nvrat. *Semantic Similarity in Content-Based Filtering.* In Lecture Notes in Computer Science, Advances in Databases and Information Systems : 6th East European Conference, ADBIS 2002, Bratislava, Slovakia, volume 2435/2002, pages 143–180. Springer Berlin / Heidelberg, 2002.

[Por80]   M.F. Porter. *An algorithm for suffix stripping.* Technical Report 3, 1980.

[Pow01]   David M. W. Powers. *Symbolism Versus Connectionism: an Introduction.* In Psycoloquy, volume 12, 2001.

[Pre97]   Wolfgang Pree. *Komponentenbasierte Softwareentwicklung mit Frameworks.* dpunkt, 1997.

[Pru05]   Helmut Pruscha. *Statistisches Methodenbuch.* Springer Berlin Heidelberg New York, 2005.

[Qui93]   J. R. Quinlan. *C4.5: Programs for Machine Learning.* Morgan Kaufmann Publishers, 1993.

[RdPWB06]   Peter Rawbone, Paschall de Paor, Andrew Ware, and Jim Barrett. *Interactive Causation: a Neurosymbolic Agent.* In IC-AI, pages 51–55, 2006.

[RHW86]   D. E. Rumelhart, G. E. Hinton, and R. J. Williams. *Learning representations by back-propagating errors.* 323:533–536, 1986.

[Rot97] Daniela Rothenhöfer. *Ein Konzept für ein intelligentes Tutorsystem zum Erlernen des Testens und Debugging paralleler Prozessysteme.* Herbert Utz Verlag Wissenschaft, 1997.

[RS04] Laura Elena Raileanu and Kilian Stoffel. *Theoretical Comparison between the Gini Index and Information Gain Criteria.* In Annals of Mathematics and Artificial Intelligence, volume 41, pages 77 – 93. Kluwer Academic Publishers, Hingham, MA, USA, 2004.

[RSS$^+$07] R. Rifkin, K. Schutte, M. Saad, J. Bouvrie, and J. Glass. *Noise Robust Phonetic Classification with Linear Regularized Least Squares and Second-Order Features.* In IEEE International Conference, ICASSP 2007 Proceedings on Acoustics, Speech and Signal Processing, volume 4, 2007.

[RV97] Paul Resnick and Hal R. Varian. *Recommender systems.* In Communications of the ACM, volume 40, pages 56 – 58. ACM New York, NY, USA, 1997.

[SAD97] Michael St Aubyn and Neil Davey. *Connectionist Rule Processing Using Recursive Auto-Associative Memory.* In ESANN '97 : European symposium on artificial neural networks, Bruges, 16-18 April, 1997.

[SB75] EH Shortliffe and BG Buchanan. *A model of inexact reasoning in medicine.* In Mathematical Biosciences, volume 23, pages 351–379, 1975.

[SCD05] Rosario Sotomayor, Joe Carthy, and John Dunnion. *The Design and Implementation of an Intelligent Online Recommender System.* In Mixed-Initiative Problem-Solving Assistants, Fall Symposium Series, AAAI, Virginia, USA. AAAI Press, 2005.

[Sch36] Hans Schickling. *Sinn und Grenze des aristotelischen Satzes: "Das Ganze ist vor dem Teil".* 1936.

[Sch89] Schöneburg. *Aktienkursprognose mit neuronalen Netzwerken.* Computerwoche 40, 1989.

[Sch95] Uwe Schöning. *Perlen der Theoretischen Informatik.* BI Wissenschaftsverlag, 1995.

[Sch97] Jürgen Schmidhuber. *Discovering Neural Nets With Low Kolmogorov Complexity And High Generalization Capability.* In Neural Networks, volume 10, pages 857 – 873, 1997.

[Sch01] Uwe Schöning. *Theoretische Informatik - kurzgefasst.* Spektrum, akademischer Verlag, 2001.

[SCKM05]   Andreas L. Symeonidis, Kyriakos C. Chatzidimitriou, Dionisis Kehagias, and Pericles A. Mitkas. *An Intelligent Recommendation Framework for ERP Systems.* In Artificial Intelligence and Applications, pages 715–720, 2005.

[SCWM02]   Xiaoming Sun, Zheng Chen, Liu Wenyin, and Wei-Ying Ma. *Intention Modeling for Web Navigation.* In Proceedings of the 11th World Wide Web Conference (WWW), 2002.

[SDD99]   Christian Schittenkopf, Georg Dorffner, and Engelbert J. Dockner. *Forecasting Time-dependent Conditional Densities: A Neural Network Approach.* In Systems and Modelling in Economics and Management Science, 1999.

[Sed06]   Anthony Karel Seda. *On the Integration of Connectionist and Logic-Based Systems.* In Electronic Notes in Theoretical Computer Science, volume 161, pages 109–130, 2006.

[SES05]   Janice Singer, Robert Elves, and Margaret-Anne Storey. *NavTracks: Supporting Navigation in Software Maintenance.* In In Proceedings of the International Conference on Software Maintenance, 2005.

[SH97]   Jürgen Schmidhuber and Sepp Hochreiter. *Long Short-Term Memory.* In Neural Computation, volume 9, pages 1735–1780, 1997.

[Sha48]   C.E. Shannon. *A Mathematical Theory of Communication.* In Bell System Technical Journal, volume 27, pages 379–423, 623–656, 1948.

[She05]   M. Shepperd. *Evaluating software project prediction systems.* In Software Metrics, 11th IEEE International Symposium, page 2 pp., 2005.

[SJ94]   N.E. Sharkey and S.A. Jackson. *Three Horns of the Representational Trilemma.* In V.Honovar and L.Uhr (Eds) Artificial Intelligence and Neural Networks. Cambridge, MA: Academic Press, 1994.

[SJ00]   Alan T. Schroeder Jr. *Data mining with neural networks: Solving business problems from application development to decision support.* In Journal of the American Society for Information Science, volume 48, pages 862 – 863. John Wiley & Sons, Inc., 2000.

[SK05]   Richard Stenzel and Thomas Kamps. *Improving content-based similarity measures by training a collaborative model.* In 6th International Conference on Music Information Retrieval, London, UK, pages 264–271, 2005.

[SKKR01] Badrul Sarwar, George Karypis, Joseph Konstan, and John Riedl. *Item-based Collaborative Filtering Recommendation Algorithms*. In The 10th International World Wide Web Conference (WWW10), Hong Kong, pages 285–295, 2001.

[SLD96] I. Syu, S.D. Lang, and N. Deo. *A neural network model for information retrieval using latent semantic indexing*. In ICNN 96, The 1996 IEEE International Conference on Neural Networks, volume 2, pages 1318–1323, 1996.

[SLW07] Mark Sherriff, Mike Lake, and Laurie Williams. *Empirical Software Change Impact Analysis using Singular Value Decomposition*. IBM, North Carolina State University, 2007. ftp://ftp.ncsu.edu/pub/unity/lockers/ftp/csc_anon/tech/2007/TR-2007-13.pdf.

[Smi07] Darja Smite. *Project Outcome Predictions: Risk Barometer Based on Historical Data*. In International Conference on Global Software Engineering (ICGSE07), Munich, Germany. Riga Information Technology Institute, Latvia, 2007.

[Smu38] Jan Christiaan Smuts. *Die holistische Welt*. 1938.

[SON95] Ashoka Savasere, Edward Omiecinski, and Shamkant B. Navathe. *An Efficient Algorithm for Mining Association Rules in Large Databases*. In Proceedings of the 21th International Conference on Very Large Data Bases, pages 432–444. Morgan Kaufmann Publishers Inc., 1995.

[SP03] Christin Seifert and Jan Parthey. *Simulation Rekursiver Auto-Assoziativer Speicher (RAAM) durch Erweiterung eines klassischen Backpropagation-Simulators*. Technical report, Technische Universität Chemnitz, 2003. http://archiv.tu-chemnitz.de/pub/2003/0053.

[SR87] Terrence J. Sejnowski and Charles R. Rosenberg. *Parallel Networks that Learn to Pronounce English Text*. In Complex Systems, volume 1, pages 145–168, 1987.

[SS92] Hava T. Siegelmann and Eduardo D. Sontag. *On the computational power of neural nets*. In Proceedings of the fifth annual workshop on Computational learning theory, pages 440–449. ACM, New York, USA, 1992.

[SS94] A. Sperduti and A. Starita. *On the access by content capabilities of the LRAAM*. In Proceedings of the International Joint Conference on Neural Networks, IJCNN, IEEE World Congress on Computational Intelligence, volume 2, pages 1143–1148, 1994.

[SS05] Roza Shkundina and Sven Schwarz. *A Similarity Measure for Task Contexts*. In Proceedings of the Workshop Similarities - Processes - Workflows in conjunction with the 6th International Conference on Case-Based Reasoning, Chicago, 2005.

[SSL08] J. Singer, S.E. Sim, and T.C. Lethbridge. *Software Engineering Data Collection for Field Studies*. In Guide to Advanced Empirical Software Engineering, pages 9–34, 2008.

[SSM05] J. Sayyad Shirabad and T.J. Menzies. *The PROMISE Repository of Software Engineering Databases*. School of Information Technology and Engineering, University of Ottawa, Canada, 2005.

[SSS91] Manfred Schmidt-Schauß and Gert Smolka. *Attributive Concept Descriptions with Complements*. Artificial Intelligence, 48:1–26, 1991.

[ST07] Renate A. Schmidt and Dmitry Tishkovsky. *Using Tableau to Decide Expressive Description Logics with Role Negation*. 2007.

[Str94] S. H. Strogatz. *Nonlinear Dynamics and Chaos: With Applications to Physics, Biology, Chemistry and Engineering*. Westview Press, 1994.

[Str03] Thomas Strang. *Service-Interoperabilität in Ubiquitous Computing Umgebungen*. 2003.

[SV97] Peter Stone and Manuela Veloso. *Multiagent Systems: A Survey from a Machine Learning Perspective*. Technical report, School of Computer Science, Carnegie Mellon University, 1997.

[Svi90] John J. Sviokla. *An Examination of the Impact of Expert Systems on the Firm: The Case of XCON*. In MIS Quarterly, volume 32, pages 127–142, 1990.

[SWM04] Michael K. Smith, Chris Welty, and Deborah L. McGuinness. *OWL Web Ontology Language Guide*, 2004.

[SWY75] G. Salton, A. Wong, and C. S. Yang. *A Vector Space Model for Automatic Indexing*. In Communications of the ACM, volume 18, pages 613–620, 1975.

[TCL06] B. Twala, M. Cartwright, and G. Liebchen. *Classifying Incomplete Software Engineering Data using Decision Trees: An Improved Probabilistic Approach*. In Software Engineering Applications, SEA 2006, Dallas, TX, USA. ACTA Press, 2006.

[TCSH06] Nikolaos Tsantalis, Alexander Chatzigeorgiou, George Stephanides, and Spyros T. Halkidis. *Design Pattern Detection Using Similarity Scoring.* In IEEE Transactions on Software Engineering, volume 32, pages 896–909, 2006.

[TEA09] *TEAM - Tightening knowledge sharing in distributed software communities by applying semantic technologies*, 2006-2009. IST PROJECT 35111 - Information Society Technologies (IST).

[Tec05] Technical Publications Specification Maintenance Group TPSMG. *International specification for technical publications utilizing a common source database*, 2005. http://www.s1000d.org.

[TF05] Mariarosaria Taddeo and Luciano Floridi. *Solving the Symbol Grounding Problem: a Critical Review of Fifteen Years of Research.* Journal of Experimental and Theoretical Artificial Intelligence, 17(4):419–445, 2005.

[Tof70] Alvin Toffler. *Future Shock.* Random House, 1970.

[Tre07] *Decision Analysis: Strategies for Decision Making*, 2007. http://www.treeage.com/learnMore/DecisionAnalysis.html.

[UK95] Alfred Ultsch and Dieter Korus. *Integration of Neural Networks with Knowledge-Based Systems.* In Proc. IEEE Int. Conf. Neural Networks, Perth/Australia, 1995.

[UoSCCC08] Dept. of Health Services Policy University of South Carolina, Arnold School of Public Health, Management Courses, and Curricula. *Durbin-Watson critical values*, 2008.

[vdL08] Peter Michael von der Lippe. *Grenzwertsätze, Gesetze der Großen Zahl(en).* Technical report, 2008. Induktive Statistik.

[Ver04] Marno Verbeek. *A Guide to Modern Econometrics, 2. ed.* Chichester, John Wiley & Sons, 2004.

[vGN94] Tim van Gelder and Lars Niklasson. *Classicalism and Cognitive Architecture.* In Proceedings of the Sixteenth Annual Conference of the Cognitive Science Society, Atlanta, Georgia, pages 905–909, 1994.

[VS07] B. Vinayagasundaram and S.K. Srivatsa. *Implementation of hybrid software architecture for Artificial Intelligence System.* IJCSNS International Journal of Computer Science and Network Security, 7(1), 2007.

[Was07] Larry Wasserman. *All of Nonparametric Statistics.* Springer, 2007.

[Wes00] Marcus Wesselowski. *Die koordinative Verbindung in der Kategorialgrammatik*. Technical report, Universität Osnabrück, 2000.

[WI01] Sholom M. Weiss and Nitin Indurkhya. *Lightweight Collaborative Filtering Method for Binary-Encoded Data*. In Principles of Data Mining and Knowledge Discovery, Lecture Notes in Computer Science, volume 2168/2001, pages 484–491. Springer Berlin / Heidelberg, 2001.

[Wil94] R.G. Williams. *Development cost prediction*. In IEE Colloquium on Life Cycle Costing and the Business Plan, pages 4/1 – 4/4, 1994.

[WMO97] Xinyu Wu, Michael Mctear, and Piyush Ojha. *SYMCONA Hybrid Symbolic/Connectionist System for Word Sense Disambiguation*. In Applied Intelligence, pages 5–26. Springer Netherlands, 1997.

[Wol07] T. Wolf. *Rationale-based Unified Software Engineering Model*. In Dissertation, Technische Universität München, 2007.

[WRH97] W. Wilson, L. Rosenberg, and L. Hyatt. *Automated Analysis of Requirement Specifications*. In Proceedings of the 19th International Conference on Software Engineering, pages 161–171, 1997.

[WSP01] Cody Wong, Simon Shiu, and Sankar Pal. *Mining fuzzy association rules for web access case adaptation*. 2001.

[WZ89] R. Williams and D. Zipser. *Experimental analysis of the real-time recurrent learning algorithm*. 1(1):87–111, 1989.

[Xia06] Shi Xiaowei. *An Intelligent Recommendation System Based On Fuzzy Logic*. In Informatics in Control, Automation and Robotics I. Springer Netherlands, 2006.

[XTDL06] Haitian Xu, Zheng-Hua Tan, Paul Dalsgaard, and Brge Lindberg. *Robust Speech Recognition From Noise-Type Based Feature Compensation and Model Interpolation in a Multiple Model Framework*. In IEEE International Conference, ICASSP 2006 Proceedings on Acoustics, Speech and Signal Processing, volume 1, 2006.

[XZZ05] Guandong Xu, Yanchun Zhang, and Xiaofang Zhou. *A Web Recommendation Technique Based on Probabilistic Latent Semantic Analysis*. In School of Computer Science and Mathematics, Victoria University, 2005.

[Yag08] Ronald Yager. *Including Semantics and Probabilistic Uncertainty in Business Rules Using Fuzzy Modeling and Dempster-Shafer Theory*. In AAAI 2008 Spring Symposium, AI Meets Business Rules and Process Management, 2008.

[YH02]   Xifeng Yan and Jiawei Han. *gSpan: Graph-Based Substructure Pattern Mining*. In International Conference on Data Mining (ICDM), 2002.

[YW04]   Miin-Shen Yang and Kuo-Lung Wu. *A Similarity-Based Robust Clustering Method.* volume 26, pages 434–448, 2004.

[YWC02]   Heng-Li Yang, Chen-Shu Wang, and Mu-Yen Chen. *A Personalization Recommendation Framework of IT Certification e-Learning System*. In Lecture Notes in Computer Science, Knowledge-Based Intelligent Information and Engineering Systems, volume 4693/2007, pages 50–57. Springer Berlin / Heidelberg, 2002.

[Zak00]   M.J. Zaki. *Scalable algorithms for association mining.* In IEEE Transactions on Knowledge and Data Engineering, volume 12, pages 372–390, 2000.

[ZJC03]   Z.-H. Zhou, Y. Jiang, and S.-F. Chen. *Extracting Symbolic Rules from Trained Neural Network Ensembles.* 16(1):3–15, 2003.

[ZWDZ04] Thomas Zimmermann, Peter Weißgerber, Stephan Diehl, and Andreas Zeller. *Mining Version Histories to Guide Software Changes.* In International Conference on Software Engineering (ICSE 2004), 2004.

Index

A
Accuracy, 89, 134, 135, 157, 158, 161, 174, 204, 205, 233–235, 263, 270, 271, 277
Action item, 152–156, 160, 161
Activation function, 77, 78, 82, 98, 102–104, 117, 252, 282
Activity
 -oriented, 151, 156
 diagram, 65, 120, 226
Adaptive, 18, 43
Additive winter model, 263
Agile
 development, 147
 life cycle model, 159
 process, 156
Antecedent, 32, 56, 93, 118, 147, 172
Application domain, 31, 49, 61, 62, 64, 82, 175, 207, 222, 275
Apriori algorithm, 211, 214
Asset management, 255
Association rule mining, 17, 31, 46, 69, 152, 167, 171, 172, 175, 205, 208, 211–216, 219, 228, 231, 267, 270, 279
Auto
 associative, 76, 79, 82, 84, 139
 regressive, 237, 245, 247, 254, 258, 262
Autocorrelation, 124, 241, 256, 260, 262
 function, 259

B
Backpropagation, 71, 76, 81, 84, 91, 102–105, 254, 269, 280
Bag-of-words, 174, 210, 219, 220
Banach fixed-point theorem, 282
Barker code, 127, 133
Basic population, 31, 162, 176, 232
Bayesian
 classification, 91
 network, 43, 46
 theorem, 90
Beam search, 190
Behavior
 browsing, 17, 208, 222
 navigation, 45, 46, 222–224, 226, 232, 235
 network, 282
 user, 71, 130, 272, 279
Bias, 126, 148, 203, 240, 241, 256, 271
Blackbox, 211, 216, 268, 273
Bug report, 152
Burn-down chart, 152, 273

C
Canonical labeling, 167, 168
Capability
 Generalization, 49
 Learning, 49
CASE tool, 150, 167, 187, 190, 273
Cauchy-Schwarz inequality, 242
Causality, 151, 152
Change impact analysis, 17, 30, 59, 91, 151, 163, 165, 167–170, 172, 204, 205, 270
Change propagation, 163
Chaos theory, 162
Chi-Square, 285
Classification, 16–18, 27, 31, 34, 39–41,

43, 49, 55, 56, 59, 62, 64, 65, 71, 78, 82, 84, 85, 88–94, 98, 106, 107, 109, 111, 113, 120, 122, 125–135, 147, 148, 150–153, 155, 156, 158–162, 175, 176, 178, 180, 183, 185, 187, 189, 193–195, 197, 199–207, 211, 237, 238, 268, 270–273, 280, 283
accuracy, 84, 88, 93, 109, 126, 134, 158–162
certainty, 129, 130, 197
Clustering, 18, 34, 39–41, 46, 49, 54, 78, 80, 89, 126, 208, 272
Collaborative filtering, 15, 16, 41, 45, 46, 207, 219, 224, 230, 232, 233, 269
Commit set, 173, 205, 270
Compositionality, 26
  concatenative, 26
  semantic, 25
Compression, 78, 82, 84, 86, 88, 89
Constant Error Carousels (CEC), 280
Content-based, 15, 16, 32, 41, 45, 46, 59, 62, 113, 117, 118, 167, 170, 171, 204, 205, 207, 211, 215, 216, 223, 224, 226, 228, 230–234, 250, 269, 270
Contextualization, 225, 232, 233
Contraction, 282
Correlation, 30, 34, 124, 223, 237, 244, 248, 256, 257, 263, 264
Correlation coefficient, 41, 242, 244, 257, 264
Coupling, 165, 192, 275
Covariance, 241–243, 284, 285
Critical
  mass, 279
  value, 259
Cross-correlation, 124, 244, 255, 257

D
Data cube, 255
Decision
  making, 15

problem, 237
support, 15, 204, 210, 255, 256, 261
table, 117, 118
tree, 85, 176, 179–181
Decomposability, 26
Deduction theorem, 22, 23
Deductive, 22–24, 33, 41, 42, 46, 94
Delegation, 145, 175, 268, 275, 276
Demand planning, 249, 255, 256, 261, 262
Dendrogram, 272
Dependent variable, 43, 174, 237, 244, 246, 249, 255, 256, 258
Design adviser, 185
Design pattern, 17, 55, 69, 99, 125, 137, 147, 151, 165, 175–177, 181–189, 193–196, 199, 202–206, 270, 271, 283
  Adapter, 195, 196
  Bridge, 196, 198
  Composite, 195, 197–199
  Facade, 197, 199
  Observer, 72, 192
  Strategy, 194, 195
  Template, 190, 191, 194
Despreading, 126–131, 201, 203
Diagonalization, 220, 285
Dickey-Fuller test, 259
Differentiation, 101, 242, 248, 258, 260, 262, 265
Discriminative, 181
Drift, 258, 260
Durbin-Watson test, 260
Dynamic system, 71, 96, 97, 250

E
Eigenvalue, 158, 284–286
Eigenvector, 284, 285
Entropy, 27, 85–88, 110, 129, 130, 176, 179, 181, 197
Equivalence class, 167
Error
  mean squared, 240, 241, 244, 248, 252, 256

systematic, 126, 240, 241
Estimation, 66, 91, 150, 237, 241, 246, 248, 252, 263, 264
  period, 263, 264
Estimator, 240, 241, 259
Expected value, 90, 241, 242, 247, 258, 260
Explosive process, 258
Exponential smoothing, 65, 66, 237, 244, 248, 252, 253, 255, 263, 269
External shock, 247
Extrapolation, 66, 238, 248, 257

F
F-Measure, 158, 161, 162
Feed-forward network, 71, 76, 110, 137, 254
Filtration, 246
Fixpoint, 282
Forecast, 10, 43, 64, 95, 237, 255, 256, 261, 262
  horizon, 244, 248
Forecasting, 237, 249, 255, 257
Formal
  language, 24, 37, 51, 79
  system, 23, 24
Fuzzy, 15, 18, 22, 27, 32, 36, 43, 61, 62, 66, 77, 82, 92, 125, 126, 147, 148, 150, 153, 158, 195, 196, 204, 270, 271, 278
Fuzzyfication, 115

G
Gaussian, 81, 91, 92
Generalization, 15, 22, 27, 38, 41, 51–54, 65, 66, 85, 86, 91, 114, 117, 118, 120, 126, 143, 145, 146, 148, 159, 173, 194, 200, 202, 207, 220, 228, 232, 284
  capability, 47, 49–53, 64, 66, 88, 100, 109, 134, 146, 173, 181, 193, 201, 219, 231, 236, 262
  hierarchy, 51, 54, 64, 65, 114, 145, 193, 207
Gini Index, 181

Godel, 23
Grammar, 21, 33–35, 51, 70, 97, 113, 116, 118–122, 131–136, 151, 175, 183, 185, 189, 200, 225, 235, 271, 277, 280
  Reber, 118, 278
Graph serialization, 164

H
Heteroscedasticity, 249, 257
Hidden state layer, 94, 97, 203, 250
Holism, 135
Holistic, 114, 136–139, 143, 148, 175, 187, 199, 203, 204, 334
Holographic Reduced Representation, 30, 53
Hopfield, 76
  network, 80
Hybrid, 16, 17, 30, 32, 43, 46, 62, 115, 137, 143, 145–147, 171, 204, 205, 207, 208, 267, 269

I
Incompleteness Theorem, 23
Independent
  domain-, 16, 23, 43, 64, 66, 69, 81, 267
  stochastically, 90, 220, 244
Inductive, 22, 23, 38, 41, 42, 138
Inference, 21–24, 29, 30, 32, 37, 39–42, 44, 46, 47, 53, 57, 61, 94, 114, 232, 271
Information
  filtering, 207
  gain, 31, 85, 176, 179, 181
  overload, 15
  theory, 27, 75, 81–83, 86–88, 110
Inheritance, 33, 42, 54, 70, 122–125, 175, 176, 181, 183, 190, 194, 196–198, 200, 201, 224, 275, 276
Intelligence
  artificial, 15, 18, 21, 23, 28, 29, 44, 46, 82, 115, 136, 150, 268
  computational, 18, 77, 82, 83, 86
  human, 18, 92

Intelligent
  recommendation, 15, 27, 29, 37, 41, 43, 53, 56, 221, 267, 268
  tutoring system, 44, 45
Inter-model link, 166, 167
Interpretation, 25
Isomorphism, 167, 168

K

Keyterm, 70, 279
Knowledge
  base, 33, 37, 58, 114, 120, 133, 174, 207–210, 219–222
  engineering, 17, 33, 34, 40, 113, 267, 271
  model, 16, 49, 58, 59, 136, 150, 164, 165, 218
  representation, 16, 24, 26, 29, 34–37, 44, 57, 59, 61, 66, 69, 70, 76, 82, 89, 92, 121, 135, 164, 195, 205, 219, 227, 228, 276
Knowledge Discovery in Databases, 34
Kohonen, 76
  network, 76, 80
Kolmogorov, 87, 110

L

Latent semantic indexing, 159, 207, 208, 220, 231, 233, 236, 269, 286
Learning by example, 50, 94, 120, 171, 199, 222
Least squares, 99, 252, 259
Linear combination, 244, 246, 247
Log-linear, 240
Logic
  Mathematical, 24
  Predicate, 22, 24, 25, 37

M

Machine learning framework, 16, 41, 49, 75, 81, 90, 207, 255, 268
Memorization, 51, 109, 145
Middleware, 186
Minimax-strategy, 27
Model
  dynamic, 149, 226
  functional, 16, 149, 275
Moving average, 246, 247, 253, 256, 264
Multi-represented object, 59, 61, 70, 108, 165, 209, 223
Multi-variate, 263
Multilayer perceptron, 94

N

Naive Bayes, 90, 91, 93
Navigation
  history, 215, 221, 222, 229, 231, 233–236
  recommendation, 151, 171, 207, 208, 211, 215, 216, 218, 219, 221, 222, 226, 227, 229, 231, 232, 234–236, 250, 269, 271, 278
  space, 207, 217, 219, 235, 279
Neuron, 76–78, 95, 97, 98, 136, 254
Noise, 30, 40, 88, 93, 109, 113, 126, 127, 131–134
  uniform, 134
  white, 134, 239, 243, 246, 247, 253, 254, 256, 258, 259
Null hypothesis, 258–260

O

Objective function, 101, 252
Ontology, 31, 33, 37, 54, 58
Operative application, 65, 96, 228, 250
Optimization, 18, 26, 39, 62, 82, 99, 100, 105, 126, 235, 246, 248, 259
Orthogonal Variable Spreading Factor, 124
Out-of-sample, 232, 249, 263
Outlier, 78, 159, 163

P

Periodogram, 255
Phase-in, 260, 264
Planning history, 255, 265
Polysemy, 219
Postmortem, 150
Power Spectral Density (PSD), 129
Precision, 155, 157, 158, 160, 175, 199, 205, 217, 233, 270, 271

Prediction, 16–18, 27, 30, 39, 40, 43, 46, 49, 55, 57, 62–67, 69, 71, 78, 82, 90, 91, 93–98, 121, 129, 130, 133, 134, 145, 150, 167, 174, 190, 205, 215, 220, 226, 227, 230–242, 244, 246, 248–258, 261–265, 268–271, 273, 277–279, 281, 282
   horizon, 277, 282
Predictive information, 172, 175
Predictor variable, 257, 260, 264
Principal Component Analysis, 67, 220, 284
Process gain, 88, 128, 129, 201, 271
Project graph, 152, 163, 164, 167, 169, 273
Promotion, 166

R

Radial Basis Function, 81
Random
   process, 238, 241, 246, 252, 254, 258, 259
   variable, 85–87, 234, 242, 243, 259
   walk, 258
Random walk process, 248, 260
Rationale, 75, 110, 149, 150, 204
Rationale Unified Process, 151
Real-Time Recurrent Learning (RTRL), 99
Realization, 17, 29, 43, 114, 117, 118, 146, 176, 177, 179, 190, 211, 223, 237–244, 246–249, 252, 254, 255, 258, 260
Reasoning, 18, 19, 31, 33, 37, 41, 46, 47, 50, 93, 94, 115, 118, 150
Recall, 100, 146, 155, 157, 158, 199
Recommendation system, 15, 17, 92, 205, 215, 221, 235
Recursive, 95, 138–141, 144, 148, 217, 255
Recursive Autoassociative Memory, 26, 30, 53, 78, 79, 83, 84, 114, 136–147

Refinement, 220, 256, 257, 261
Regression, 17, 91, 93, 150, 237, 242, 244–246, 248, 256, 258–260, 262, 269
Release, 166, 273
Repository, 126, 167, 170, 171, 173, 210, 272
Representation
   context-sensitive, 29
   distributed, 30, 187, 204
   document, 209
   internal, 26, 37, 79, 136, 138, 139, 146, 188, 189, 199
   rich, 58, 61, 147, 172, 215, 221
   rule-based, 17, 71, 185, 187
   symbolic, 18, 171, 228, 233, 234
   text, 159, 219, 232, 236, 269
   URL-based, 215
Requirement
   functional, 43, 50, 66, 114, 152, 225, 283
   nonfunctional, 43, 93
Residual, 126, 241, 256, 257, 259, 260
Reusability, 175
Robustness, 161, 271

S

Scrum, 152, 155, 156, 160, 273
Search
   heuristic, 26
   informed, 27
   uninformed, 27
Self-Organizing Map, 71, 272
Semantics, 24, 25, 29, 34, 171, 200, 208, 210, 215, 220, 223, 235
Sequence
   node, 59, 70, 97, 100, 187, 228, 277, 281
   processing, 49, 272
Serialization, 190, 331
Sigmoidal, 282
Signal transmission, 88, 124, 126, 127, 129, 270
Signature, 182, 183, 191, 283

Significance
  level, 259
  test, 254
Simulation, 78, 238
Singular Value Decomposition, 172, 220, 221, 284
Software
  development, 17, 40, 54–57, 66, 115, 126, 147, 150, 153, 162, 165, 171, 175, 204, 267–269, 271–273
  engineering, 33, 34, 84, 92, 114, 140, 145, 147, 149, 150, 152–154, 163, 175, 211, 267, 268, 272
  metrics, 150, 162
Split attribute, 179, 181
Spreading code, 109, 124, 127, 128, 131, 133, 135, 182, 203
Standard deviation, 244
Stationarity, 242, 243, 258, 259, 262, 265
Steady state, 282
Stochastic process, 237, 239, 241–243, 245, 249
Stock price, 239, 246, 262
Stopword, 209
Structure
  Symbol, 27, 28
  Symbolic, 30
Subsymbolic, 22
Supply chain, 255
Support vector machine, 92, 93
Symbol
  grounding, 28–30
  manipulation, 18, 30, 54, 146
Symbol system hypothesis, 24, 26, 29, 86
Symbolic, 49
Synonymy, 219
Systematicity, 21–23, 26, 29, 30, 53, 97, 108–110, 113, 146

T
Tacit, 152
Term-document matrix, 174, 219, 220, 232
Terminal symbol, 117, 139, 141, 142, 144, 146, 205
Test statistic, 259, 260
Text mining, 69, 70, 171, 174, 208, 209, 218, 219, 231, 234, 235, 284
Time lag, 242, 250, 257, 259, 280
Time series, 17, 30, 40, 41, 43, 57, 62, 64–66, 69, 71, 90, 91, 95, 237–246, 248–253, 255–265, 269
Time-indexed, 57, 94, 149, 242, 250, 256, 262
Topology, 55, 77–79, 81, 82, 93–95, 97, 100–102, 104, 108, 109, 114, 115, 117, 139, 141, 160, 226, 249, 250, 252, 254, 264, 269, 277, 283
Traceability, 135, 153, 166, 187, 204
  link, 167
Training
  pattern, 62, 156, 173, 182, 184, 222, 250, 277, 281
  set, 17, 62, 151, 158, 160, 173, 174, 183, 194, 201, 211, 223, 225, 226, 228, 231, 232, 254, 273, 281, 283
Transformation
  algebraic, 27
  holistic, 148
  lossy, 159
  rule, 53
Triple, 96, 146, 165, 170
Turing test, 18

U
Underlying, 249
Unit root, 258
Univariate, 262

V
Valence, 137–140, 221
Vector space model, 59, 173, 210, 219, 220, 230, 233
Versioning, 172
Vertical slice, 268

W
Wiener process, 259

X
XML element, 118, 132
XOR-problem, 76, 91, 92

Die VDM Verlagsservicegesellschaft sucht für wissenschaftliche Verlage abgeschlossene und herausragende

Dissertationen, Habilitationen, Diplomarbeiten, Master Theses, Magisterarbeiten usw.

für die kostenlose Publikation als Fachbuch.

Sie verfügen über eine Arbeit, die hohen inhaltlichen und formalen Ansprüchen genügt, und haben Interesse an einer honorarvergüteten Publikation?

Dann senden Sie bitte erste Informationen über sich und Ihre Arbeit per Email an *info@vdm-vsg.de*.

Sie erhalten kurzfristig unser Feedback!

VDM Verlagsservicegesellschaft mbH
Dudweiler Landstr. 99   Telefon +49 681 3720 174
D - 66123 Saarbrücken   Fax   +49 681 3720 1749
www.vdm-vsg.de

Die VDM Verlagsservicegesellschaft mbH vertritt

Printed by Books on Demand GmbH, Norderstedt / Germany